Financial Performance of Conglomerates

Financial Performance of Conglomerates

HARRY H. LYNCH

DIVISION OF RESEARCH

GRADUATE SCHOOL OF BUSINESS ADMINISTRATION

HARVARD UNIVERSITY

Boston · 1971

Library of Congress Catalog Card No. 76–146709

ISBN 0–87584–089–2

*This book won the Richard D. Irwin Prize for the
Best Doctoral Dissertation 1968–1969 at the
Harvard Business School*

Printed in the United States of America

ABSTRACT

Financial Performance of Conglomerates

The subject of corporate mergers and acquisitions has been a matter of scrutiny for three-quarters of a century, and especially during the 1960s when firms called "acquisitive conglomerates" attained prominence. These are defined as corporations growing through continuing programs of aggressive, diversified acquisition.

These firms, their growth, and their relative success have become of interest for a variety of reasons, and better understanding of them is of significance for business executives, investors, economists, and legislators who face the tasks of managing, evaluating, and regulating these firms.

This study by Harry H. Lynch, focusing on the manner in which the shareholder performance of conglomerates has been achieved, won the Richard D. Irwin Prize for the Best Doctoral Dissertation 1968–1969 at the Harvard Business School, where the author was an Assistant Professor prior to joining the investment banking firm of Laird Incorporated in New York City.

This study seeks explanation and understanding of the performance for shareholders achieved by corporations growing through programs of aggressive, diversified acquisition. Attention is focused on those years of the 1960s when the acquisitive conglomerates were in their heyday and were provoking a controversy regarding the sources of their performance which persists today.

The evidence that exists on industrial mergers and acquisitions in general indicates that such combinations have not on the average been very successful. Yet, during the period studied a significant group of aggressive acquirers performed very well for their shareholders. Because of these and other conflicting indications, substantial controversy developed regarding the sources of shareholder performance within these firms. The extreme views polarized around the power of modern professional management to improve diverse acquired operations on the one hand and the prevalence of financial chicanery on the other. Some suggested that the acquisitive conglomerate was to become the corporate form for the twenty-first century; others forecast impending disaster.

The companies of interest in this study have three basic characteristics: (1) rapid expansion through acquisition; (2) diversification; and (3) superior performance for shareholders. Performance for the shareholder is defined as the return over time from the ownership of common stock, as determined by the rate of growth in market price per share plus the dividend yield. Based on these three characteristics, criteria were established and used to identify 28 corporations which, during the 1962–1967 period, substantially exceeded the average firm in acquisition activity, diversification, and shareholder performance. Many of these firms are well known, such as Textron, Litton, Gulf & Western, Ling-Temco-Vought, Walter Kidde & Company, and Teledyne; others, such as Condec, Mid-Continent, and Vernitron, are not.

Collectively, the 28 identified firms had annual revenues in 1967 of $17.7 billion and made 588 reported acquisitions during the 1962–1967 period. This implies that approximately 1% of the roughly 2,400 firms with assets exceeding $10 million in 1967 made about 14% of the 4,128 acquisitions by such firms during 1962–1967. The "average" acquisitive conglomerate acquired 21 firms in diverse fields during this six-year period, or almost one per quarter. On the average it increased its equity investment annually by more than twice as much as it earned, implying substantial, continuing reliance on external equity financing. Shares outstanding increased at the average rate of 18% per year. The results of this growth process over 1962–1967 were an average rate of increase in total earnings of 76% per year and, more importantly, an average rate of increase in earnings per share of 50% per year. Market price per share increased during the period at the average rate of approximately 45% per year. In comparison with the average U.S. corporation, the shareholder performance of the acquisitive conglomerate during this period was clearly quite different, both in form and in degree of achievement.

The analysis of this performance begins in the first chapter by identifying and reviewing the various existing arguments. The framework for discussion, which provides the underlying structure for the remainder of the study, groups the possible sources of performance in two broad categories: those which depend on improvement of operations through acquisition and those which depend on the various financial characteristics of acquisition.

The second and third chapters provide historical perspective for the study of acquisitive conglomerates and examine the evidence of other studies which is related to the sources of their performance.

The fourth chapter examines in detail the 28 acquisitive conglomerates studied. Published financial and descriptive material regarding these companies is used to develop conclusions regarding common characteristics and objectives.

The next three chapters develop a series of generalized models of the process of growth through acquisition. The objective in this section is to provide a better understanding of the manner in which the key financial variables interact in determining shareholder performance in the complex process of corporate expansion through a combination of internal and external growth.

The eighth and ninth chapters examine and compare two selected acquisitive conglomerate firms. In the first of these chapters attention is focused on the financial strategy and mechanics of the growth process. The latter chapter analyzes the influence which these corporations have had on the operating performance of their acquired subsidiaries. Information obtained includes interviews with corporate level and subsidiary managers and internal financial data regarding five acquired subsidiaries within each of the two corporations.

The last chapter summarizes the conclusions and management implications of the study. In particular, there is evidence that within the category of improved operations through acquisition the most likely source of performance is the influence on subsidiary operations without substantial integration. This may occur either through change in the subsidiary management process which may improve internal efficiency and hence profitability, or through change in subsidiary technologies, products, and markets which may improve external demand and hence growth. In either event, the implication is that improved performance is less likely to result from the traditionally discussed economies in the combined use of physical resources than from the more effective use of specialized human resources, specifically managerial and technical expertise.

There is further evidence that of the possible influences on subsidiary operating performance the most important are (1) the improvement of the planning and control process in the acquired subsidiary, and (2) the impact on objectives, aggressiveness, and "professionalization" of managers of acquired firms.

In the category of financial effects of growth through acquisition, there is evidence that the potentially most important source of performance results from the immediate effects on earnings per share, and hence on market price per share, of acquisitions having values relative to earnings lower than the parent. This implies a "feedback relationship" between market value and performance through acquisition. Further, it is demontrated in one case that it has been possible to provide outstanding performance for shareholders over a number of years based only on the immediate impact of new acquistions on earnings per share and without any improvement in operating performance within acquired subsidiaries.

The primary implications are of two kinds. First, within the category of operating economies through merger, only economies in the use of specialized human resources appear of widespread significance for aggressive, diversified acquirers. Second, within the category of financial effects of mergers, the interdependence of market value and shareholder performance appears to have played a major role in the performance achieved by acquisitive conglomerates.

(Published by Division of Research, Harvard Business School, Soldiers Field, Boston, Mass. 02163. LC 76–146709; ISBN 0–87584–089–2. xvii + 297 pp.)
$12.00 1971

Foreword

Students of business have subjected corporate mergers and acquisitions to close scrutiny for three-quarters of a century. The single great trust movement of 1887–1904, which historians have recorded as the era that set the pattern of twentieth-century American business, gave rise to a stream of books and articles constituting a library of impressive size. By the time Congress passed the Clayton Act and the Federal Trade Commission Act in 1914, largely in response to the early merger movement, John Moody's *The Truth about the Trusts* (1904), Richard T. Ely's *Monopolies and Trusts* (1900), and the United States Industrial Commission's *Report on Trusts and Industrial Combinations* (1901), among others, had become standard references on the subject.

The stream of studies continued to swell in the wakes of the subsequent merger waves of the 1920s and the post World War II period, reflecting on the one hand the public's concern with the possible effects of mergers on the structure and competitive performance of the manufacturing economy, and on the other the business incentives underlying the managerial decisions to merge. Two studies merit singling out from the many others of this more recent period because they brought into clearer focus what the merger issues consisted of and the extent to which the then available facts on postwar mergers resolved them. The Federal Trade Commission's *The Merger Movement: A Summary Report,* issued in 1948, sounded the alarm that giant corporations were, through their many acquisitions, about to take over the country. The study by J. Keith Butters, John Lintner, and William L. Cary, *Effects of Taxation on Corporate Mergers,* published three years later by the Harvard Business School's Division of Research, significantly muted, but did not silence, the alarm. The public issue of the effect of business mergers and acquisitions on the structure of industry is still with us, and will remain as long as they continue to occur in large number.

There is another and related issue that, while receiving much less attention, may be taking on commensurate importance; namely, what has been the financial performance of those companies that have been among the leaders in making acquisitions, and what accounts for this performance? This question is being raised with increasing frequency and intensity in connection with the newly created "conglomerates" — those corporations that have been especially active participants in what has been popularly called the current conglomerate merger wave. This is clearly no longer regarded as a question of importance only to the participants, if indeed it ever was. It is frequently asserted that the new conglomerates bring about significant alterations in the competitive environment. To the extent that they do, the financial performance of the new conglomerates has important implications for business management generally. Moreover, the public corporation is far more public than it once was, and this is especially true of the rapidly growing acquisitive conglomerates whose new security issues must be absorbed in the capital market. Their financial performance vitally affects the economic state of the growing number of institutional investors which includes colleges and universities, retirement funds, mutual funds, and similar public and quasi-public organizations.

Mr. Lynch's study is a careful factual analysis of the financial performance of a selected number of the new conglomerates during the years 1962–1967. The three criteria he applied in the selection of companies were that they (1) had recently expanded rapidly through acquisitions; (2) were diversified; and (3) had a record of superior performance for stockholders. The list of 28 corporations that met these three criteria included such well-known conglomerates as ITT, Textron, Litton, Gulf & Western, Ling-Temco-Vought, Teledyne, and Walter Kidde & Company; it also included others that were not so well-known, such as Hydrometals, Condec, and Vernitron. Collectively, the 28 companies were reported to have made 588 acquisitions in the 1962–1967 period, or 14% of all the acquisitions made by firms with assets exceeding $10 million. On the average they increased their equity investment annually by more than twice their earnings, their outstanding shares by 18%, their total earnings by 76%, their average rate of earnings per share by 50%, and their market price per share by 45%. In respect to all these indicia of growth and financial performance the group as a whole is clearly distinguishable from the "average" U.S. corporation.

Lynch then analyzes the various factors that might logically explain the group's superior financial performance. While he concludes that there is no single explanation for the performance of all acquisitive conglomerates, he ascribes most of the relative financial success of such conglomerates to a "feedback" relationship between the market value of stock and performance. Out of this discovery emerges a theory of firm growth and financial performance of extreme interest to corporate managers, financial analysts, public policy administrators, and students of business mergers and acquisitions. Lynch observes that the stock prices of large, diversified growth firms tend to be more volatile than stock prices generally. This means that in a period of high and rising stock prices the price-earnings ratios for acquisitive conglomerates are likely to be higher than those for other corporations. Because acquisitions are usually effected through the exchange of the stock of the acquiring for that of the acquired company, the market stock price ratios are advantageous to the acquiring firm. Successive acquisitions of firms with relatively low price-earnings ratios result in increases in the reported earnings and rates of return for the acquisitive conglomerate, and hence to further bolster its stock price, thereby maintaining the conditions conducive to acquisition. Lynch tests out this feedback effect through a detailed analysis of two acquisitive conglomerates and finds that the results confirmed his general conclusion.

While Lynch's empirical findings contribute greatly to an understanding of the financial performance of acquisitive conglomerates, the theoretical models he develops provide a useful framework for other researchers disposed to carry the analysis further, and on a broader scale. In this connection he offers the provocative hypothesis that financial performance analysis might fruitfully be integrated with the life cycle of firms. Meanwhile, Lynch's study is a welcome addition to the literature on business mergers and acquisitions, and has the distinction of being the first comprehensive inquiry into the principal factors underlying the financial performance of the new conglomerates.

In recognition of the high quality of his doctoral thesis the Harvard Business School awarded Mr. Lynch the Richard D. Irwin Prize for the academic year 1968–1969. The prize, made possible through a grant by Richard D. Irwin in 1968, is awarded annually to the author judged to have written the best dissertation for the year in which it was accepted, provided the dissertation is also of sufficiently high quality to merit the prize. Mr. Lynch's dissertation is the first to be so honored.

JESSE W. MARKHAM
Professor of Business Administration

Soldiers Field
Boston, Massachusetts
February 1971

Acknowledgments

The number of individuals who have contributed to the progress of this study is unusually large. My appreciation extends to many who cannot reasonably be mentioned here.

John Lintner, chairman of the thesis committee, has been a constant source of wise counsel and enthusiasm. His willingness to venture with me into a relatively new and complex area combined with his high standards for analytical rigor have provided a most valuable contribution to the form and quality of the study. Each of the other three members of the thesis committee — Gordon Donaldson, John H. McArthur, and William L. White — has provided a most important contribution in helping me to refine and focus my ideas. John McArthur in addition provided a degree of momentum to the progression of the work which it might otherwise have never achieved.

Individuals in a number of industrial and financial corporations have given generously of their time, knowledge, and efforts. Without such cooperation this study literally could not have been completed. Several executives, and in particular the president, of the corporation discussed under the disguised name of "Contek Incorporated" provided assistance and information that was essential. Invaluable assistance was also provided by Fred R. Sullivan, Franc M. Ricciardi, and other executives of Walter Kidde & Company, Incorporated.

Several other individuals at the Harvard Business School have read and commented upon parts of the study or have otherwise been helpful in its completion. Patrick R. Liles has been an unusually patient and valuable source of feedback and commentary. Others include Norman A. Berg, Malcolm S. Salter, Howard H. Stevenson, Christopher S. Taylor, and Richard F. Tozer.

Financial support by the Ford Foundation during the early part of the study and by the Division of Research of the Harvard Business School during later parts of the study is very gratefully acknowledged. Publication of the study was made possible through its receipt of the recently established Richard D. Irwin Prize, by which I have felt highly honored and pleased.

Transformation of the thesis manuscript has been accomplished by the staff of the Division of Research at the Harvard Business School, where Miss Ruth Norton has been a diligent yet patient editor.

A special note of thanks is due my wife, Patricia, who has constantly been a source of cheerful encouragement. Her ready acceptance of my evenings and weekends of research, writing, and editing has done a great deal to make the project an enjoyable experience.

In general, the study has benefited from a high order of intellectual, moral, and financial support. The responsibility for its shortcomings is mine.

HARRY H. LYNCH

Table of Contents

List of Tables

List of Figures

CHAPTER I

Introduction

The passage of time has brought new forms of industrial combination and organization. The multifirm horizontal consolidation dominated the industrial scene at the turn of the century; large-scale vertical integration, particularly in the basic metals industries, occurred during that same period and again in the 1920s; the multilayered public utility holding company was prevalent in the 1920s and early 1930s. The phenomenon of the 1950s and 1960s has been the "acquisitive conglomerate," the corporation growing through a continuing program of aggressive, diversified acquisition. In 1969 it was still a growing phenomenon, comprising a substantial group of firms. Some have suggested that this is the corporate form for the 21st century;[1] others have forecast impending disaster.[2]

The "acquisitive conglomerate" corporation is of interest for a variety of reasons: historical; economic; social; financial. Our particular interest is rather narrow as it must be in a study of this type. We are interested in the manner in which these firms as a group have provided outstanding performance for their shareholders. It is a question with possibly broad implications. However, attention here is focused on the shareholder and the manager attempting to provide financial performance for the shareholder.

The topic is of interest for several reasons. There have been no careful studies of the manner in which the superior performance of "acquisitive conglomerates" has been achieved. The evidence that exists on industrial mergers and acquisitions in general indicates that such combinations have on the average not been very successful; for the firm engaging in numerous acquisitions we are led to expect inferior performance.[3] In light of this and other evidence a substantial amount of controversy has developed in recent years regarding what is going on within these firms to provide the sources of their performance. A variety of possible and conflicting explanations have been provided with little evidence. The manager seeking to emulate this performance or the shareholder seeking to analyze it must have some difficulty deciding where to focus his attention.

No pretense is made of providing all the answers to this controversy. The

---

[1] Such as the statement of G. William Miller, President of Textron, quoted in *Dun's Review,* May 1968, p. 21.

[2] See, for example, Biggs, "Day of Reckoning? Conglomerates Can't Keep Making Two Plus Two Equal Five Forever."

[3] The most important study in recent years is Reid, Bossons, and Cohen, "Mergers for Whom — Managers or Stockholders?"; presented by Reid in U.S. Senate Hearings, *Economic Concentration,* Part 5. This study will be discussed in some detail in Chapter III.

objective is simply to provide better evidence and understanding for the sources
of acquisitive conglomerate performance that appear to be the most important.
The general approach is one of first bringing together various types of published
evidence and developing conceptual models of the determinants of performance
which allow us to argue that particular sources of performance are potentially
more important for this type of corporation. Then those sources of performance
are examined through the detailed analysis of two corporations.

In this introductory chapter we provide a systematic discussion of the recent
controversy regarding acquisitive conglomerate performance. Also, we provide an
outline of the study covering the nature of the investigation and the conclusions
reached. First, however, we want to provide a better description of the characteristics of this group of firms we refer to as "acquisitive conglomerates."

BASIC CHARACTERISTICS OF ACQUISITIVE CONGLOMERATES

The companies of interest to us have three basic characteristics: (1) rapid
expansion through acquisition; (2) diversification; (3) superior performance for
shareholders. By performance for the shareholder or "per-share" performance we
mean the return over time that an individual achieves from the ownership of
equity securities. This is composed of the rate of growth in market price per
share plus dividends relative to market price. As a "proxy" for this we typically
discuss per-share performance as determined by the rate of growth in earnings
per share and dividend policy. The measures of diversification and rate of expansion through acquisition will become more explicit as we progress.

These three characteristics or criteria provide the definition for "acquisitive
conglomerates" in this study. They are criteria which capture the essence of the
controversy and which seem necessary and sufficient for identification of companies which provide the subject of that controversy. It should be obvious that
they are not criteria which are necessarily co-existent. In particular, there have
been companies that aggressively acquired other firms in widely diverse fields
and did not perform well at all.[4] This, we suggest, is what most of the evidence
and argument on mergers, conglomerate mergers in particular, would lead one to
expect. The interesting thing is that so many firms have performed so well following this type of growth strategy. It is the latter group in which we are interested.

It is also useful to point out that we are only interested in corporations during
the periods when they satisfy the criteria specified in our definition. We are
interested in the achievement of performance for shareholders through the process
of growth through aggressive, diversified acquisition. That is to say, we are *not*
interested in the corporation that at some point in its past was an "acquisitive
conglomerate" *or* in the corporation that might be at some point in its future.

---

[4] See, for example, the discussion of the experience of Olin Mathieson, Blaw Knox, Phillip
Morris, and Borg Warner in Burck, "The Perils of the Multi-Market Corporation." Each of
these firms turned out considerably less than "superior" shareholder performance based on
programs of aggressive, diversified acquisition in the late 1950s and early 1960s.

It would be interesting and meaningful, we suggest, to take a "life cycle" or "stages of development" kind of approach to our topic, treating the "acquisitive conglomerate" as a possible stage through which a company might pass and studying preceding and following stages as well. Viewed in this way, however, our concern is only with the process of corporate growth in the "acquisitive conglomerate stage."[5]

Many of the firms that interest us have become rather well known: Textron; Litton; Gulf & Western; Ling-Temco-Vought; Walter Kidde & Company; Teledyne. Some of the others are not so well known: Hydrometals; Condec; Mid-Continent; Vernitron. In a later chapter we establish our definition in "operational form" and use it to identify 28 corporations which in recent years have substantially exceeded the average firm in acquisition activity, diversification, and shareholder performance. These are listed in Table 1.1. Without going into the details

TABLE 1.1

The "Population" of Acquisitive Conglomerates

"Automatic" Sprinkler	MSL Industries
Automation Industries	Nytronics
Bangor Punta	Occidental
Condec	Ogden
FMC	Royal Industries
W. R. Grace	The Signal Companies
Gulf & Western Industries	Teledyne
Hydrometals	Textron
ITT	TRW
Walter Kidde & Company	Tyco Laboratories
Litton Industries	U.S. Industries
Ling-Temco-Vought	Vernitron
Mid-Continent Manufacturing	White Consolidated Industries
Monogram Industries	Whittaker

of the identification process here, we can briefly describe some of the characteristics of the group and of the "average" member of the group.[6] Collectively these 28 firms had annual revenues in 1967 of $17.7 billion and made 588 reported acquisitions during the 1962–1967 period. This implies that approximately 1% of the roughly 2,400 firms with assets exceeding $10 million in 1967 made about 14% of the 4,128 acquisitions made by such firms during 1962–1967. Collectively it is a significant group. The "average acquisitive conglomerate" acquired 21

---

[5] For several corporations there has been no other "stage." Litton Industries is perhaps the prime example; by our definition it has been an "acquisitive conglomerate" virtually since its founding in 1953. Certainly the acquisitive conglomerate must become "unacquisitive" at some point. Roy Ash, President of Litton, provided a few thoughts about the next stage: "When they [companies like Litton] stop making acquisitions they probably won't be regarded as conglomerates and will merely be considered alongside other already matured multi-industry companies." (Quoted in *The Wall Street Journal,* July 25, 1968.)

[6] This paragraph provides a preview of some of the data presented and discussed in Chapter IV. The sources for all these data items are listed in the later chapter.

firms in diverse fields during the 1962–1967 period, or approximately one per quarter, and reached a size of $633 million in annual sales revenues in 1967. On the average it annually increased its equity investment by more than twice as much as it earned, implying substantial, continuing reliance on external equity financing.[7] Shares outstanding increased at the average rate of 18% per year.[8] The results of this growth process over 1962–1967 were an average rate of increase in total earnings of 76% per year and, more importantly, an average rate of increase in earnings per share of 50% per year. Market price per share increased during the period at the average rate of approximately 45% per year.[9]

Compare this with the "average" U.S. corporation. During 1962–1967 the average of all firms with assets exceeding $10 million made 1.7 acquisitions; the average of all U.S. manufacturing corporations annually increased its equity investment by 50% of its annual earnings; the average firm comprising the Standard and Poor's Industrial Average achieved a rate of increase in earnings per share of 8.3% per year. The "acquisitive conglomerate" is different, and it has performed rather remarkably.

CONTROVERSY ON ACQUISITIVE CONGLOMERATE PERFORMANCE

The acquisitive conglomerate is a complex economic creature. A number of variables influence per-share performance; all of these variables are interrelated. We will later attempt to capture some of this complexity, but for the moment we will lean in the direction of simplification. Specifically, we will attempt to compartmentalize the recent discussion of acquisitive conglomerate performance, looking at various factors independently. Our treatment here is brief because the existing evidence on this argument is the subject of Chapter III.

The framework for our analysis is provided by Figure 1.1. This exhibit bears some scrutiny since we shall refer to it at various times throughout the study. As implied in Figure 1.1, we begin by dividing the discussion into two parts: (1) arguments that superior acquisitive conglomerate performance largely reflects the ability to achieve superior *operating* performance in companies acquired; (2) arguments that superior acquisitive conglomerate performance has resulted largely from the immediate *financial* effects of acquisition. We begin with the latter.

It is one of these immediate "financial effects" that initially aroused our interest in "acquisitive conglomerates." Specifically, some have suggested[10] that there

---

[7] Much of this financing was based on the issuance of securities in acquisition transactions.

[8] Adjusted for all stock splits and dividends.

[9] Based on 22 of the 28 firms for which "sufficient" market price data were available; see Chapter IV.

[10] The earliest published discussion we were able to find suggesting the importance of this effect was in Burck, "Perils of the Multi-Market Corporation," where an executive is quoted as saying that Roy Ash, President of Litton, "has a chain letter operation going for him." For progressively more detailed statements see Biggs, "Day of Reckoning"; Wall, "Want to Get Rich Quick?"; "Time of Testing for Conglomerates," *Business Week*, March 2, 1968; Stabler, "The Conglomerates, Antitrusters and Investors Eye Combines Warily, but Firms Still Grow"; May, "The Chain Letter Revisited."

Summary

FIGURE 1.1

Sources of Earnings-per-Share Growth in Corporate Growth Through Aggressive, Diversified Acquisition

Objective	General Nature of Acquisition Effects	Potentially Possible Because of	Source of Advantage
earnings per share growth through diversified acquisition	longer term "operating" effects of acquisitions ("real" economic effects)	operating integration	horizontal integration — for scale economies
			vertical integration — for functional elimination economies
			integration for "balance"
			integration for "power"
		operating influence without operating integration	influence on technologies, products, markets
			influence on the "management process"
	immediate "financial" effects of acquisitions (no "real" economic effects)	market system of valuation of equity securities; corporate reporting practices	interdependence of market value and performance through acquisition
		altering structure of risk and return; market imperfections	capital structure
			diversification
			size
		accounting flexibility	accounting treatment
		structure of tax laws	tax reduction

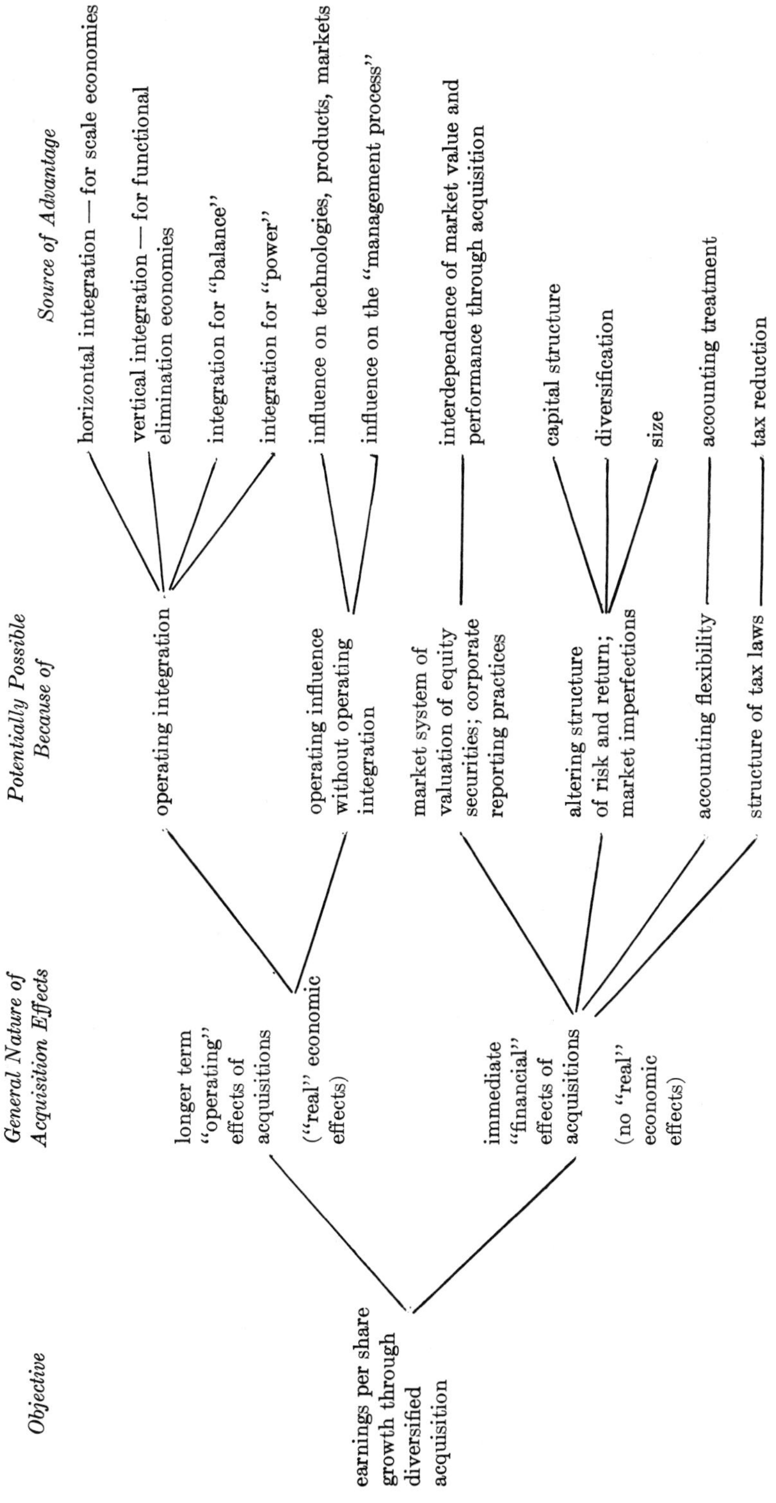

may be what we will call a "feedback effect" operating on the market prices of firms actively engaged in using their common stock for the acquisition of other firms with lower price-earnings ratios. Each time such an acquisition is made it provides an immediate increase in the earnings per share of the acquiring firm.[11] The continuation of this process over time creates a pattern of growth in earnings per share which may cause the market to place a high price-earnings ratio on the common stock of the acquiring corporation. This price-earnings ratio is, in turn, the vehicle which enables the process to continue. (It would appear that this feedback effect from earnings-per-share growth through acquisition to price-earnings ratio, if indeed it exists, increases the market value of the acquired firm without any change in its "economic value" as an operating unit.[12] To the extent that this type of "financial synergy" occurs, it has many of the characteristics of the old-fashioned "chain letter." That is, to the extent there is *no* change in the operating performance that would have been achieved in the absence of acquisition, there is no creation of wealth, only a redistribution of wealth.[13]

This relationship between valuation and performance through acquisition will receive quite a bit of attention before we are through. Primarily, this is because we conclude that it is an important element in the performance acquisitive conglomerates have achieved.[14] In part, however, this is because the "feedback relationship" coexists with anything else that affects per-share financial position as a result of acquisition, so we find it necessary to discuss it in several contexts.

---

[11] Consider the following example. A, with $1 million in earnings after tax, 1 million shares outstanding, and therefore $1 in earnings per share, has a price-earnings ratio of 20. B has exactly the same current earnings, shares, and earnings per share but has a price-earnings ratio of only 10. A has a total market value of $20 million; B a total market value of $10 million. A acquires B in a stock-for-stock transaction based on market values of the securities of the two companies. After the acquisition, A has 50% more shares outstanding and total earnings have doubled. Earnings per share have therefore increased to ($2,000,000/1,500,000 shares) = $1.33.

[12] If, for example, the hypothetical acquisition discussed in the footnote above was one of a continuing series, and the acquiring company was able to maintain its price-earnings ratio of 20, the value placed by the market on the earnings of the acquired company would appear to double from $10 million to $20 million as a result of the acquisition.

[13] The most detailed discussion of this has been provided by May, "The Chain Letter Revisited." If the high price-earnings ratio is based only on earnings growth from use of the high price-earnings ratio in acquisitions, every investor buying the stock or accepting it in an acquisition transaction is banking on the assumption that others will continue to do so in the future. If the market price falls or the acquisition process stops, so that in either case the "chain letter" is broken, prices revert to levels "justified" by internal growth. The total value, so the argument goes, becomes what it would have been for all the individual parts without the acquisition process. Just like in a "chain letter" people gain or lose depending on how early in the process they entered.

[14] In addition, it is an important relationship not only for growth through acquisition but for any corporate growth process involving continuing reliance on significant amounts of new equity financing. The central principle involved, as we shall later discuss, is that with significant new equity financing over time, market price becomes more than a measure of shareholder wealth; it becomes a major determinant of performance. This leads us to look at some of the traditional concepts of financial management in a slightly different manner.

In fact, given some preliminary understanding of the "feedback relationship," particularly "one side of it" — the dependence of performance through acquisition on market value — we can discuss Figure 1.1 in a slightly different manner. For a continuing series of acquisitions to add to the performance which acquiring and previously acquired firms can achieve internally, acquisitions must on the average provide some immediate addition to the per-share position of the acquiring firm. This is only possible if the parent maintains a market value advantage over those acquired, which in turn demands that the market value of acquired firms increase with their acquisition. Hence the sources of superior performance for acquisitive conglomerates are the sources of increased market value for firms that are acquired. Increased market value for acquired firms might occur simply because of the "other side of the feedback relationship" — the dependence of market value on per-share performance — as discussed above. Or it may occur because of any of the other "sources of advantage" listed in Figure 1.1, as we shall proceed to discuss.

The next potentially important immediate financial effect of the acquisition process which does not depend on operating change is that the structure of risk and return is altered for the shareholder. Combined with market imperfections which prevent the shareholder from easily structuring his risk and return to best meet his own preferences, this may provide a source of increased market value and hence performance through acquisition. The alteration of risk and return in acquisitions may result from increase in diversification, increase in size, change in capital structure.

Increased diversification, some argue, makes the corporation more valuable for the shareholder because variations of returns in different fields of activity cancel to some extent, reducing the overall level of variability.[15] The opposite argument is that there is no increase in value from diversification because, given the degree of mobility in today's financial markets, the shareholder would prefer to structure his own "diversification packages." Acquisition inevitably creates a firm of greater size. The larger corporation may have greater resistance to failure, more marketable securities, more accessible and cheaper sources of financing. There is a fair amount of evidence that, "other things being the same," the shares of the large corporation will be valued more highly than those of the small corporation.[16] Finally, there has been a significant amount of conceptual argument and evidence that share values increase with increasing amounts of debt in the capital structure, at least over some range of possible capital structures. And while there

---

[15] In "Royal Little Looks at Conglomerates" (p. 26) Mr. Little, in explaining the decision in the 1950s to diversify Textron, stated: "Textron [then a textile company] and many other companies had the problem of cycles. Earnings and security prices fluctuated widely and return on equity was inadequate. We felt that by unrelated diversification we would completely eliminate the one-industry cycle and achieve stability of earnings, a good growth rate, and a reasonable price-earnings ratio."

[16] See, for example, Gordon, *The Investment, Financing, and Valuation of the Corporation,* evidence from which will be discussed in Chapter III. The implication, however, is that differences in per-share values are relatively small unless there is a very substantial difference in sizes.

is also evidence to the contrary, some observers have suggested that this is a significant element in the success of acquisitive conglomerates.[17]

Other types of immediate advantages of acquisitions that do not require any change in operations may result from (1) accounting flexibility, and (2) the structure of taxation. There has been a considerable amount of discussion that would imply that the performance conglomerates have achieved through their acquisitions is attributable in part either to the ability to change accounting treatment for various items in acquired firms or from the mechanics of poolings of interest transactions.[18] And while a small amount of evidence will be presented which suggests the contrary, this is an area where convincing conclusions are difficult to achieve. In this study at least, the general significance of accounting flexibility for performance unfortunately shall remain largely unknown.

There has also been some discussion that tax provisions have provided advantages through merger for the acquisitive conglomerates. The ability to take advantage of tax loss carry-forwards[19] and the ability to balance development costs in one division against the profits of another[20] are both possible sources of advantage.[21] These kinds of cash flow advantages generally demand, however, that somewhere in the picture will be the acquisition of a company operating at a loss. And as we shall later discuss, the "acquisitive conglomerate" typically does not look favorably upon the immediate effect on per-share earnings of acquisitions operating at a loss.

Those are the immediate financial effects on which we shall focus attention. Our analysis will lead us to conclude that most important for the performance of acquisitive conglomerates is the "feedback relationship" between market value and earnings-per-share growth through acquisition. The complication that will continually hinder us is that any of the other immediate financial effects may initiate or reinforce this "feedback effect." It is therefore difficult to differentiate among the various sources.

---

[17] Equity Research Associates, an investment research organization which has made a reputation for itself in recent years writing about the "free-form" corporation (which largely corresponds to our definition for an "acquisitive conglomerate"), in discussing the strengths of these companies suggests that their managements have "a high degree of financial sophistication and a willingness to apply financial leverage in expanding facilities and making acquisitions," and elsewhere suggests that for these corporations "there exists in most cases a capital structure which will permit management's efforts to reflect significantly and quickly to the benefit of common shareholders." Quoted from "Investing in Modern Management: The 'Free-Form' Corporation," September 20, 1966, pp. 4 and 2 respectively.

[18] For suggestions of the former variety see "What *Are* Earnings? The Growing Credibility Gap"; and Stabler, "The Conglomerates: Even Accountants Find Some Financial Reports of Combines Baffling." For suggestions of the latter variety see Siedman, "Pooling Must Go," and Briloff, "Dirty Pooling."

[19] At various points in their histories the ability to take advantage of tax loss carry-forwards has been of some importance to Textron, Bangor Punta, and Indian Head, to name three.

[20] This, for example, is the theme of a pamphlet prepared by The Boston Consulting Group on "Conglomerates and the Future" (1968), one of their *Strategy Series on Perspectives.*

[21] Often mentioned in connection with mergers are estate taxation and the availability of tax-free exchanges. We suggest that both of these factors provide motivation for the seller to participate in a merger but cannot be considered significant influences on the performance of the buying corporation.

The other side of the discussion is that superior acquisitive conglomerate performance is solely or largely attributable to the ability to achieve superior operating performance in acquired subsidiaries. Several possible explanations have been offered. First, there is evidence and argument that most conglomerate acquisitions do not involve completely unrelated firms; usually there are similarities in technologies, products, or markets, some "common thread"; usually economies and efficiencies from assimilation and integration are at least possible.[22] To the extent that this is true, all the traditionally discussed advantages from integrating the operations of combining corporations become relevant. Horizontal integration may provide economies from larger scale operations in purchasing, production, marketing, and other functions, including those typically considered "staff" functions. Vertical integration may provide economies through elimination of functions at a market interface such as advertising, selling, and transportation. Integration of so-called "complementary" operations may provide for each company needed specialized factors, the absence of which may have been inhibiting profitability and growth; such integration may provide the "balance" of resources needed for future progress. Finally, integration, particularly in the marketing and purchasing areas, may provide increased market power, which is a private if not a social advantage.

The difficulty in achieving these kinds of advantages or sources of performance which depend on operating integration of acquired subsidiaries is that, outside of staff functions, operating integration seems to occur only in exceptional situations for acquisitive conglomerates.[23] The rapid pace of acquisition, the diversity of operations, the need to retain previous operating management are all factors working against the integration of acquired operations.

There are, however, various kinds of possible influences on the operating performance of the acquired subsidiary which may occur without any significant integration of its operations with other parts of the parent corporation. Knowledge, expertise, funds, personnel, and other resources may be transferred across the organizational boundaries within the acquisitive conglomerate in such a way as to benefit the acquired subsidiary. We divide such influences into two categories: those which affect the basic "product-service stream" or *what* the subsidiary is providing to *what* customers, and those which affect the "management process" or *how* the subsidiary conducts its operations. The distinction is "fuzzy" in some cases; however, it proves useful for several reasons. In particular, we will eventually conclude that influences in the latter area are somewhat more important than those in the former. At the moment, however, it suffices to say that both types of influences have been discussed as important.

Executives of several acquisitive conglomerates have emphasized technological influence. The general idea is that the technical expertise of one corporation may

---

[22] In the next chapter we will discuss some evidence and opinions to this effect. In particular, the statement in the text approximately paraphrases a statement by Donald F. Turner, former head of the Antitrust Division of the Department of Justice, in "Conglomerate Mergers and Section 7 of the Clayton Act," p. 1322.

[23] This is one of the primary arguments pursued in Chapter IV.

be used for the development of new or improved products in another.[24] Or the technologies of two or more subsidiaries may be combined by one of them in an endeavor that none could have carried out independently.[25] While such "technological cross-fertilization," as it is frequently called, may occur without operating integration of subsidiaries, it does require close cooperation in the interchange of knowledge and expertise. The question which we will later touch upon is whether it is possible to achieve enough technological similarity and subsidiary cooperation in the acquisitive conglomerate growth process for such "technical synergy" to occur frequently rather than rarely.

There may also be influence without operating integration on the marketing programs of acquired subsidiaries. The marketing expertise of one subsidiary or of the parent corporation may be used to the advantage of another subsidiary in developing a more aggressive and effective approach to the market for their products. Subsidiaries that have products that are quite different but that have some similarity in customer group may find it advantageous to market them through the same distributors or representatives. The information on potential customers, particularly for technical products, is often far from perfect; the acquisitive conglomerate may provide a useful network of market information. The reputation or "goodwill" of the parent corporation may provide an effective marketing tool for the smaller acquired subsidiary.[26] These effects become intermingled with and difficult to separate from the possible market power advantages of reciprocal, exclusive, tying, and other types of marketing agreements.[27] At the same time, the acquisitive conglomerates are known for highly decentralized operations and the considerable dependence of psychological and real rewards for subsidiary managers on the performance of their respective subsidiaries. It is questionable whether there is sufficient incentive for those potential marketing advantages that require intersubsidiary cooperation.[28] In addition, significant

---

[24] William Duke, President of Whittaker Corporation, has been particularly vocal on this subject. For example: "We have had a plethora of research end-products. The question has been: What to do with this plenitude? We have found that acquisition is a useful method for rapidly and effectively dealing with this assignment." ("Report to Shareholders on 1967 Annual Meeting.") And elsewhere: Acquisitions "provide rivers of marketing into which we can feed the higher technology materials and products" (quoted in *Business Week*, "The Thread that Ties Diversity Together," December 2, 1967). Tyco Laboratories has also told an interesting story of this kind. In its 1967 *Annual Report* it suggests: "Our strength rests on the horizontal and vertical exchange of knowledge. Horizontal, in that we transfer technology from one field to another. . . . Vertical, in that we continuously try to channel the ideas developed in our Laboratory into our manufacturing operations" (all of which have been acquired).

[25] For example, this apparently has been the case for Teledyne's successful Integrated Helicopter Avionics System, for Litton's original inertial navigation systems, and for Litton's planned Great Lakes ore transportation system.

[26] All of these effects have been discussed by the management of Walter Kidde & Company, as will be covered in Chapter IX.

[27] Corwin D. Edwards has been the outstanding critic of these and other "power" advantages of conglomerate companies. See, for example, "Conglomerate Bigness as a Source of Power."

[28] In some acquisitive conglomerates competition between acquired subsidiaries is permitted or encouraged. Textron, Teledyne, and Walter Kidde are examples.

influence on either the technology or the marketing of a given acquired subsidiary demands considerable expertise elsewhere in the organization, substantially specialized to the type of operation conducted by that subsidiary. The extent to which such specialization exists within the widely diversified acquisitive conglomerate is also questionable.

The acquisitive conglomerate may also influence the expansion of the acquired subsidiary into new technologies, products, and markets through the provision of funds[29] and through the injection of a more "entrepreneurial spirit."[30] As was discussed earlier, funds are more accessible and cheaper for the acquisitive conglomerate than for its smaller acquired subsidiary. If an acquired company previously had an urgent need of funds for expansion and had found them inaccessible, making such funds available obviously can provide a very significant advantage. Encouragement to behave "entrepreneurially" in taking advantage of available funds may also be of importance. However, we shall later argue that the acquisitive conglomerate has a strong preference for successful, profitable companies. For such companies needed funds are infrequently completely unavailable. Also, the manager of the acquired subsidiary often was the entrepreneur who built his own company. There is some question regarding the advisability of encouraging such a man to be more entrepreneurial.

The types of operating influence without operating integration discussed thus far are, we suggest, most likely to be reflected in the rate of *growth* of the acquired subsidiary. Those we will discuss immediately below are more likely to be reflected in the *profitability*, relative to sales or investment, of the acquired subsidiary. These are influences less on *what* the subsidiary is doing in a technology-product-market sense, but more on *how* it manages its operations.

We are speaking of influences on the "management process," areas of activity common to any business enterprise. Any business corporation needs to plan, make rational decisions, budget, collect adequate information, control. It needs to have clear objectives for its future activities, rapid feedback and adequate information regarding progress toward those objectives, time to react to departures from previous plans. It needs to have clear and timely indicators of which areas are more profitable, which areas less, where the problems are, what needs to be done about them. It needs to structure its system of measurements and rewards and to structure its organization so that people are properly motivated to perform. It needs to use the best available techniques for planning and scheduling its manufacturing, its inventories, its distribution. Individuals in the acquired subsidiary must be encouraged to incorporate these ingredients of intelligent, efficient, "professional" management in the conduct of their operations.

Some of these ingredients seem to be required elements of the acquisitive con-

---

[29] One writer has concluded that the provision of needed funds has been the most important positive influence in recent mergers. See Kitching, "Why Do Mergers Miscarry?"

[30] Equity Research Associates in "Investing in Modern Management: The 'Free-Form' Corporation" suggests the "essential characteristic is an ability to motivate the management of companies which have not developed or attracted scientific, professional, entrepreneurial leadership," and lists the "entrepreneurial spirit" as an essential ingredient for the "free-form" corporation.

glomerate management process. Corporate level management in the acquisitive conglomerate must have a highly developed planning and control system in order to maintain "visibility," in order to provide the subsidiary independence involved in a highly decentralized operation, in order to be effective in general. This demands the development of adequate planning and control in all its subsidiaries. For the acquired company that had not previously developed such a system, this can be a major advantage.

Managements of some acquisitive conglomerates have suggested that the acquired subsidiary can frequently benefit from assistance in achieving management that is "more professional" or more effective and efficient, through improved planning, decision making, budgeting, control, and other common management functions.[31] We will ultimately conclude that this is the most important "category" of influence on the operating performance of the subsidiary within the acquisitive conglomerate environment.

We have "compartmentalized" the controversy on acquisitive conglomerate performance based on the framework shown in Figure 1.1. We dichotomized the achievement of per-share performance through acquisition into the categories of longer term "operating" effects and immediate "financial" effects. These are potentially possible because of several categories of influence and characteristics of the environment. To these are related the more specific sources of advantage we have discussed. Having presented this framework, we may restate in a different way the approach taken in this study.

Through the examination of existing evidence, the examination of financial and operating characteristics of acquisitive conglomerates, and the development of models of the process of growth through acquisition, some preliminary conclusions are reached regarding the relative importance of the various sources of performance. As suggested above, the more important categories appear to be (1) the "feedback relationship" and (2) operating influence without significant integration. We then pursue in more detail the nature and significance of these potentially important influences through the detailed analysis of two corporations. The chapter outline follows. A few comments are first in order, however, on the

---

[31] For example, Robert E. Grant, a Group Vice President of Textron who has been particularly articulate on this subject, suggested in its 1967 *Annual Report*: "We carry on a continuing effort toward upgrading within the divisions in the areas of specific management techniques, such as systems and controls, data processing, and manufacturing and marketing methods. We have an advantage in a business structure such as ours in being able to circulate ideas and experience freely from division to division. . . . This exposure to the ideas of other divisions is also provided on a more formal basis by a continuing program of company-wide meetings on mutual problems, such as electronic data processing, financial controls, and performance improvement." Elsewhere he has stated: "I sincerely feel that at least half of the companies in the U.S. are poorly managed and that their operations could be improved considerably by the addition of the resources, management skills, and incentives a company like ours can offer. . . . The real thing that we are contributing is a generalized business knowledge, and not expert knowledge about specific products and marketing. The division people will always know more about their own business than we will here at the corporate level. Our contribution stems from being more expert in more generalized business procedures and knowledge." (Quoted in "Textron, Inc. (B)," Harvard Business School case, BP 912, 1968.)

general nature of existing information about acquisitive conglomerate performance. This influences somewhat the character of the later investigation.

We have mentioned before that there have been no careful studies of acquisitive conglomerate performance and how it has been achieved. More specifically, there has been nothing but speculation about the significance of that "immediate financial effect" that appears on the surface to be most important: the "feedback relationship" between performance and market value through acquisition. Also, there have been no careful studies of the operating impact of the conglomerate on its acquired subsidiary.[32] Discussions of this impact have appeared largely in the financial press, annual reports, speeches by executives, investment analysts' reports, and other "informal" media. These discussions have too often been framed in very general terms about "better management," "technological cross-fertilization," and so forth with little detail to indicate how, if at all, these things are achieved. The positive arguments about operating influence have almost without exception been made by individuals with a vested interest in telling a positive story: executives of acquisitive conglomerate companies and investment analysts promoting their securities. In general, there has been a lack of evidence. In particular, one obvious source of information appears not to have been tapped. This is the management of the acquired company who presumably are in the best positions to observe the operating impact of acquisition and the new environment. Our objective is to present somewhat better and more detailed evidence based on more reliable sources of information.

OUTLINE OF THE STUDY

In Chapter II we develop historical perspective for our study of acquisitive conglomerates. As suggested at the outset, the character of merger activity has changed dramatically over time from the large horizontal, multifirm consolidations of the turn of the century to the acquisitive conglomerates of today. We suggest that greater understanding of acquisitive conglomerates is provided by tracing the changes in merger environment and changes in merger motivation which have brought the character of merger activity to its current form. At the same time, we trace the record of merger success and failure which highlights the exceptional character of conglomerate performance.

Chapter III examines the evidence of other studies which is related, either directly or indirectly, to the sources of performance discussed above. Most of this evidence is of an indirect variety in that it has not been provided by the literature on acquisitive conglomerates or even by the literature regarding ac-

---

[32] In the late 1960s more attention was given to the management process in the acquisitive conglomerate type company. For example, Richard Hanna in his Harvard Business School doctoral dissertation (1968, unpublished), "The Concept of Corporate Strategy in Multi-Industry Companies," provides detailed descriptions of the management process at Litton Industries, Bangor Punta, and Indian Head. However, neither in this study nor in others has an analysis been provided of the nature of subsidiary operations and performance before and after acquisition.

quisitions and mergers. Rather, it primarily concerns the relationships between various operating and financial variables and either operating performance or market values. Through cross-sectional studies of the relationships between variables, we can gain insight regarding the impact of change in such variables within a given combination.

In Chapter IV our definition for acquisitive conglomerates is converted into operational form and used to identify 28 companies out of a substantially larger group of firms which have been discussed as diversified, acquisitive firms in the financial press and elsewhere. We use the data on these firms to argue first that they are a "significant" element in the U.S. corporate world; that they are quite different from the "average" U.S. corporation; that they have achieved exceptional performance in quite a different manner from firms achieving superior performance through "internal growth." We then employ published descriptive information about the identified group of corporations to argue that they have some other common financial and operating characteristics. The financial characteristics indicate that these firms are behaving in such a way as to take advantage of the interdependence of valuation and performance if in fact it is possible to do so. The operating characteristics imply that if performance improvement is to be achieved within the acquired subsidiary in the "typical" situation, it will result from "operating improvement without operating integration." Then we examine via regression analysis the importance in determining price-earnings multiples for these companies of (1) past per-share performance and (2) other characteristics of the growth process. The greater investor attention is to per-share performance and the smaller their attention is to how it is achieved, the more important the valuation-performance relationship becomes for "low return, high expansion" growth strategies. We find, as has been found in other studies, a positive relationship between past per-share performance and price-earnings multiple, indicating that at least to some extent the discussed "feedback effect" exists. The analysis also indicates that investors are exhibiting some preference for (1) internal growth and (2) growth strategies that provide per-share performance based on higher rates of return on investment.

In Chapter V we suggest that one of the sources of confusion about corporate performance through aggressive acquisition is a lack of understanding of the manner in which various financial variables interact to determine per-share performance in this growth process. If a given corporation is growing internally, expanding rapidly through acquisition, changing such things as the leverage, profitability, and growth of companies acquired, how can we say which things are contributing what to per-share performance? Needed, we suggest, is a model which represents the growth process as a three-part "system," based on characteristics of (1) the acquiring firm, (2) the acquired firms, and (3) the market system of valuation. In this chapter we take the first step by developing a model for valuation of the rapidly growing firm. In any growth process involving substantial amounts of new equity financing over time, market price per share becomes more than a measure of shareholder wealth; it is a major determinant of performance. Aggressive, acquisitive growth is probably the prime example of a growth strategy that is heavily market-price-dependent. Any attempt to model this growth process must include a model of the market system of valuation. The problem is that existing models for valuation of the firm growing rapidly in per-share terms are not very satisfactory for our purposes. A model is proposed and developed in detail which treats the growth of rapidly growing companies as composed of a "normal" and an "excess" component. The investing public, it is argued, must expect the "excess" component to decay at some rate toward zero. Otherwise, the company in question would occupy an ever-increasing proportion of the economy. The primary reason for this chapter and the model developed therein is the conceptual development in the two succeeding chapters. As a possible "by-product" the chapter offers another way to look at valuation for "high performance" companies.

In Chapter VI we represent abstractly the process of rapid internal growth with continuing reliance on external equity financing. Within this setting we examine the determinants of per-share performance and the manner in which they are related. In particular we demonstrate that a given level of per-share performance (rate of growth in earnings per share for a given dividend policy) can be achieved through various combinations of rate of return on invested equity and rate of expansion of invested equity; there are "high return, low expansion" and "low return, high expansion" strategies which may provide a given level of per-share performance. This is done in order to be able to discuss market-price-dependent growth initially in a setting that is more familiar and less complex. In addition the chapter serves to demonstrate that the characteristics of corporate performance where market value is a determinant are not particular to growth through acquisition, that these characteristics are in fact quite general. In terms of the central argument, however, this chapter is strictly preparatory for the succeeding one.

In Chapter VII we examine abstractly the determinants of per-share performance in rapid growth through acquisition. In doing so we discuss several cases of change or lack of change by the parent corporation in the financial characteristics of companies acquired: (1) no change in financial characteristics or performance of acquired firms; the possible role of the relationship between price-earnings ratio and earnings-per-share growth through acquisition in this setting; (2) change in the leverage or other financial characteristics of acquired firms that might increase perceived value without change in performance; (3) change in the profitability of acquired firms; (4) change in the rate of growth of acquired firms. We then make use of a hypothetical numerical example to discuss the properties of a more complex "combined case." This chapter completes the abstract, symbolic representation of the process of growth through acquisition. It provides a way of looking at various strategies for providing per-share performance and it is hoped provides a means for a better understanding of the mechanics of corporate growth through acquisition. Of prime importance for the central argument of the study, it suggests two things: (1) the "feedback relationship" between the price-earnings ratio and earnings-per-share growth is potentially very important for per-share performance, either without change in acquired companies or in combination with changes in operating performance or in other financial characteristics; (2) significant though perhaps relatively small changes in the profitability or growth of companies acquired at a rapid pace will result in attractive per-share performance.

In Chapter VIII we analyze in detail the financial strategy and performance of one acquisitive conglomerate with particular attention to the relationship between valuation and performance. We find that for this corporation the interdependence of the price-earnings ratio and earnings-per-share growth through acquisition has been the major source of an exceptional level of per-share performance. The earnings of the average subsidiary of this corporation have declined since acquisition; changes in market value can in no way be explained by performance improvement. This provides implications regarding the structure of the environment. Because of (1) the attention given per-share performance in our market system of equity security valuation and (2) the lack of attention given to the manner in which per-share performance is achieved or the inability to determine from publicly available information the manner in which it is achieved, the valuation-performance interdependence is potentially a very important factor for all companies using large amounts of new equity in their growth process, as are the acquisitive conglomerates.

In Chapter IX we provide a comparative analysis of the influence on subsidiary operating performance within two acquisitive conglomerates. This analysis is based on opinions at the corporate and subsidiary level, internal corporate documents, and financial data on subsidiaries. Since there had been little integration of subsidiaries in these companies, it is an analysis of operating improvement without significant operating integration. We conclude that the most important operating influences are those which affect *how* the subsidiary manages its operations, rather than *what* technologies, products, and services are offered in *what* markets. These are influences on the "management process," primarily the planning, budgeting, reporting, and control process, influences that more likely result in greater profitability for the subsidiary but not faster rates of growth.

In Chapter X the conclusions of the study are summarized and some of their possible management implications are discussed.

CHAPTER II

Historical Perspective of Acquisitive Conglomerates

In this chapter we employ the evidence and argument of previous studies to develop historical perspective for our study of acquisitive conglomerates. The chief distinguishing characteristics of these companies are their aggressive acquisition activity and the success they have achieved through this strategy of corporate growth. We consider it helpful in understanding acquisitive conglomerates to be able to relate their merger activity to previous corporate merger activity and to be able to relate the success they have achieved to the evidence on merger success provided in previous studies.

Several lines of thought are woven together in this development of historical perspective. To begin with, there is a factual record regarding the changing nature of merger activity over time. During the past 70 years there has been a transition from a predominance of large, horizontal, multifirm consolidations to a predominance of conglomerate acquisitions of relatively smaller firms. This transition has been caused and permitted by the changing nature of institutional and other elements in the merger environment, including antitrust law, securities regulation, promotional activities, and management capabilities. Accompanying the change in environment there has been a change in apparent motivations from monopoly, economies of scale, and promotional profit toward shareholder performance based on other types of operating and financial advantages. The one constant in past merger activity appears to have been the level of demonstrated success. The evidence is indicative of poor results and causes the performance of acquisitive conglomerates to appear particularly exceptional.

This chapter is divided into four parts. We begin with a very brief discussion of the statistical record of aggregate merger activity and its importance within U.S. industry. We then proceed through each of the three major periods of aggregate merger activity, discussing the nature of mergers, the environment, the motivations, and the record of success. In the end, we reach the point of the controversy on acquisitive conglomerate performance discussed in the first chapter. The relevant evidence on that controversy which has been provided by other studies is examined in the following chapter.

THE STATISTICAL RECORD OF AGGREGATE MERGER ACTIVITY

The most complete historical series on aggregate corporate merger activity measures the annual number of disappearances of manufacturing and mining firms in the United States during the period from 1895 to the present. This is

portrayed in Figure 2.1. The immediately striking feature of this record is the
existence of three peaks of activity; one occurring around the turn of the century,
a second in the late 1920s, and the third beginning after World War II and reaching particularly large proportions beginning in 1955.

FIGURE 2.1

ANNUAL DISAPPEARANCES THROUGH MERGER OF MANUFACTURING
AND MINING FIRMS: 1895–1967

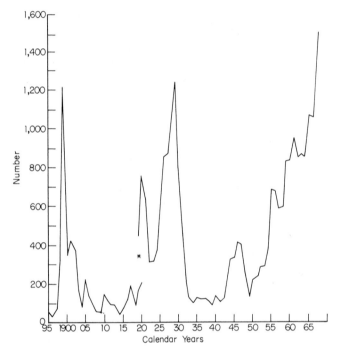

* The two series are not directly comparable.
SOURCES: Data for 1895-1920: Ralph L. Nelson, *Merger Movements in American Industry, 1895–*
1956; data for 1919–1967: Federal Trade Commission.

The historical record is composed of two series which are not directly comparable. The data for the period 1895–1920 were compiled by Ralph L. Nelson[1]
using the weekly *Commercial and Financial Chronicle* as a primary source of
information. A more comprehensive series of merger activity was compiled by
Willard L. Thorp[2] for the years 1919–1939 and continued by the Federal Trade
Commission after 1939. For the Thorp series the primary source was the *Standard
Daily Trade Service*, first published in 1914.

The Nelson series is less complete than the Thorp-FTC series, but even for
the latter there is no claim of complete coverage. For some types of corporate

[1] *Merger Movements in American Industry, 1895–1956.*
[2] "Persistence of the Merger Movement" and "The Merger Movement."

combinations no form of reporting is legally required and, particularly for some smaller acquisitions, it may be assumed that none is provided. Thus, even the later series provides an understatement of total annual merger activity.

The other striking feature of the record of aggregate merger activity is the intensity that has been reached in recent years. If we could ignore the gap between the Nelson and Thorp series,[3] the occurrence of 1,496 mergers in 1967 would provide a record exceeding all previous periods.

Another measure of aggregate merger activity has been provided in a study by J. Frederick Weston.[4] The primary objective of this study was determination of the importance of growth through merger relative to internal growth for American corporations. Weston sought firms for which data were available on a continuing basis from around 1900 to the time of his study in 1948.

Data were collected on 74 corporations. For each firm Weston recorded the growth in assets due to mergers and due to internal growth since the first year for which data were available. For all 74 firms combined, the total growth in assets was $28.0 billion. Of this amount $6.2 billion or 22.3% was achieved through merger and $21.8 billion or 77.7% was achieved through internal growth. For the firms in Weston's sample the percentage asset growth through merger and acquisition ranged from a negative amount (divestiture) to 75.8%.

Weston recognized some shortcomings in his method of measurement. For each firm the growth in assets was measured as total assets in 1948 less total assets in the initial or base year. Growth in assets through merger was defined as the sum of the total assets of all acquired firms measured at the times of the respective acquisitions. Thus, if a firm with $1 million of assets at the start of the base year acquired another of the same size during that year, and without further acquisitions grew to have total assets of $100 million in 1948, the growth would be recorded as 1% external and 99% internal. One could argue that the proportion of asset growth caused by merger was more likely to be on the order of 50%.

Conclusions such as the latter would require estimates of the growth of the respective parts after the merger, and such estimates could not be made on an objective basis. However, the example serves to indicate that Weston's measure undoubtedly understated by a wide margin the proportion of the total asset growth of large American firms which was caused by merger.

Another criticism was provided by Stigler in a discussion of Weston's study.[5] He pointed out that no adjustment was made for price-level changes and that over the 1900–1948 period this would lead to serious errors. Using one of the firms in Weston's study, the Socony-Vacuum Oil Co., as an example, Stigler demon-

---

[3] Probably we cannot ignore this gap in the data. For the two years of overlap, 1919 and 1920, the Thorp series contains 3.2 times as many disappearances as does the Nelson series. In a crude adjustment, the data for 1895–1920 would be revised upward accordingly. Nelson recorded 2,653 disappearances for the five peak years of turn-of-the-century merger activity. With the upward adjustment this number would exceed 8,400. By comparison the number of mergers recorded in the Thorp-FTC series for the five peak years of the twenties, 1926–1930, was 4,838. For the five years, 1963–1967, the number was 5,214.

[4] *The Role of Mergers in the Growth of Large Firms.*

[5] "The Statistics of Monopoly and Merger."

strated that for this company price-level adjustments would increase the proportion of growth in assets through merger from 46.2% to 76.0%. So on another count Weston's findings must be viewed as conservative.

Measured either in terms of their numbers or in terms of their proportional role in the growth of large corporations, mergers have had a major impact on the structure of U.S. industry. The nature of that impact has, however, changed considerably over the years. It is this changing character of merger activity over previous periods and the changing conditions which have led to the "acquisitive conglomerate movement" of recent years which will next occupy our attention.

THE FIRST MERGER PERIOD — THE TURN OF THE CENTURY

By almost any measure the first merger movement had a dramatic impact on American industry. This would certainly be the conclusion if one were to measure the impact by the amount of literature it generated. A spate of books devoted to this early merger movement appeared before it had run its course.[6] Then, after a period of less intensive documentation, a number of studies viewing the subject with somewhat more perspective began to appear in the late 1920s and early 1930s.[7] The most recent major work devoted to the early combination movement is also the one providing the most comprehensive statistical data; this is the previously discussed study by Nelson[8] which was published in 1959. Still there is much regarding the causes and impact of this period of merger activity that is unknown and will remain so.

Business combinations were not unknown before the latter part of the 19th century.[9] However, the first major period of merger activity is generally considered to have begun in 1879 with the organization of the Standard Oil Trust. In this trust the combined facilities represented over 90% of the oil refining capacity in the United States and an almost equal proportion of the pipelines for transportation of oil.[10] There followed a series of combinations of some magnitude which were trusts in the literal sense. That is, the ownership of a group of companies was transferred from the shareholders to a group of trustees who managed

---

[6] See, for example: von Halle, *Trusts, or Industrial Combinations and Coalitions in the United States,* 1895; Ely, *Monopolies and Trusts,* 1900; Jenks, *The Trust Problem,* 1900; Collier, *The Trusts,* 1900; Le Rossignol, *Monopolies Past and Present,* 1901; Moody, *The Truth about the Trusts,* 1904; Nolan, *Combinations, Trusts and Monopolies,* 1904.

[7] For example: Watkins, *Industrial Combinations and Public Policy,* 1927; Seager and Gulick, *Trust and Corporation Problems,* 1929; Jones, *The Trust Problem in the United States,* 1929; Basset, *Operating Aspects of Industrial Mergers,* 1930; Curtis, *The Trusts and Economic Control,* 1931; Tippetts and Livermore, *Business Organization and Public Control,* 1932.

[8] *Merger Movements in American Industry.*

[9] Stigler speculates: "Sporadic mergers, often founded on marriage, are no doubt as ancient as man; probably for long they were occasional and relatively small in scale, and they were offset by the divestitures necessary to endow sons in a more fertile age." Quoted from "Monopoly and Oligopoly by Merger," p. 23.

[10] Seager and Gulick, *op. cit.,* p. 49.

the combination. The stockholders were issued trust certificates and became in effect trust beneficiaries. The more important groups following the Standard Oil form of combination were the Cottonseed Oil Trust, the Linseed Oil Trust, the National Lead Trust, the Distillers and Cattle Feeders Trust, and the Sugar Trust, all formed during the 1884–1887 period. Other combinations, organized as single corporations or holding companies, occurred in the period around 1890. The more important of these were the Diamond Match Company (1889), the American Tobacco Company (1890), the United States Rubber Company (1892), and the General Electric Company (1892).[11]

This early surge of combination activity was brought to a near halt in the early 1890s; business activity entered a cyclical downturn in 1893, and the trust form of organization was declared illegal in a series of common law cases. While the subsequent combinations were often referred to as "trusts," in a strict sense they were not. Rather, they represented the transformation, by one of several means, of two or more legal entities into one.

Merger activity began to take on major proportions in the period after 1895, and the years of intensive merger activity were the five years 1898–1902. During the 1895–1904 decade, Nelson recorded 3,012 disappearances of firms through merger and the total authorized capitalizations for the resulting corporations was $6.91 billion. Over one-third of this activity was recorded in the peak year of 1899; in this year 1,208 disappearances were recorded having merger capitalizations amounting to $2.26 billion.[12]

In a number of industries horizontal combinations provided one large corporation with a dominant position. During the 1895–1904 period, 170 firms disappeared into the newly formed U.S. Steel Corporation with a market share estimated at 65%; 162 firms were absorbed by American Tobacco resulting in a market share of 90%; 65 firms disappeared into E. I. du Pont de Nemours resulting in an 85% market share; 64 firms disappeared into American Can resulting in an estimated market share of 65% to 75%; and so on for a long list of companies.[13] It appears beyond question that this early merger movement was one of the major determinants of the present structure of American industry.

Part of the explanation for this period of intensive combinations seems to be that certain institutional developments provided an environment in which it was possible for such combinations to occur. During the latter part of the 19th century the state incorporation laws and the American capital market changed significantly.

Incorporation laws in the early part of the 19th century were quite restrictive. Corporations could not hold the stock of another corporation; mergers were not permitted; limits were placed on corporate capitalizations; and the exchange of stock for assets required unanimous stockholder approval.[14] The changes in incorporation laws are largely attributed to "the discovery by some smaller states

---

[11] These early trusts and consolidations are discussed in Seager and Gulick, pp. 50–52.

[12] Nelson, *Merger Movements in American Industry*, p. 37.

[13] Firm disappearances from Nelson, *op. cit.*, pp. 161–162; estimated market shares from Moody, *op. cit.*, various pages.

[14] Stigler, "Monopoly and Oligopoly by Merger," p. 28.

that by modifying corporation laws to suit the views of corporate promoters, substantial revenues might be derived from incorporation fees and franchise taxes." [15] New Jersey initiated this development in 1889 with the removal of restrictions on holding companies and in the competition among states which followed, many of the former restrictions, including those on mergers, vanished within a short number of years.

New Jersey remained a leader in this new field of state enterprise for some time and during the 1895–1920 period accounted for 54% of all merger capitalizations and 47% of all firm disappearances through merger. [16]

Stigler has argued that an organized large-scale capital market was a prerequisite for the large securities issues which accompanied many of the early consolidations. [17] Conversely, it has been argued that the consolidation movement provided the basis for the development of securities markets during this period. [18] As with many economic phenomena it is difficult to differentiate between cause and effect. However, that this was a period of substantial development of the market for corporate securities seems beyond question. The number of issues listed on the New York Stock Exchange increased from about 150 to 400 between 1875 and 1900, and the number of shares traded annually increased from about 50 million in 1895 to a peak of over 250 million in 1901. The trading activity of 1901 was exceeded in only one year before 1919. [19]

While an established securities market was important in making it technically feasible for the large consolidations to be carried out, it was important in another respect; it provided an arena for the operations of the professional promoter.

Numerous authors have commented on the significance of promotion in explaining the magnitude of this merger movement. To cite an example:

> [The] favorable attitude of businessmen [toward consolidation] would have resulted in the launching of numerous trusts after 1897, but to explain the veritable furore for combination that developed we must give due credit to the professional promoter. Businessmen who have been active competitors do not easily put aside the dislike and suspicion to which competition too often gives rise to join their properties and abilities in friendly cooperation. . . . The sensational progress of [this] trust movement was possible only because a group of shrewd, plausible, and aggressive promoters was at hand to make fullest use of the favorable business situation. [20]

While comprehensive data on the form and magnitude of such promotional activities are lacking, information on specific cases provides some indications. The typical trust promotion is described along the following lines. [21] First, the promoter obtained options on the companies or their securities which he sought to com-

---

[15] Seager and Gulick, *op. cit.,* p. 36.

[16] Nelson, *Merger Movements in American Industry,* p. 66.

[17] "Monopoly and Oligopoly by Merger."

[18] Navin and Sears, "The Rise of a Market for Industrial Securities, 1887–1902."

[19] See Nelson, *op. cit.,* pp. 90–91.

[20] Seager and Gulick, *op. cit.,* p. 64; quoted in part in Butters, Lintner, and Cary, *Effects of Taxation: Corporate Mergers,* p. 310.

[21] See, for example, Jones, *The Trust Problem in the United States,* pp. 283–285.

bine. Without options the constituent companies would in all likelihood have increased the price at which they would agree to sell upon realization that a trust was being formed. Second, a corporation was formed which would acquire the companies involved. The securities of this corporation would be offered to the participating firms in sufficiently attractive amounts to persuade as many as possible to accept securities in lieu of cash. Third, the promoter arranged, usually through an underwriting syndicate, for the raising of necessary funds. Since it was the physical property of companies which was typically acquired and not the working capital, funds would be needed for working capital of the new corporation. Also, some owners would undoubtedly be unwilling to accept securities for their properties, demanding cash instead and imposing upon the promoter another requirement for funds. To satisfy both of these requirements for cash, securities would be issued to the public. In order to make the new securities more attractive, both to the selling companies and to the public, earnings significantly exceeding the total of the independent companies were usually projected, based on the alleged more efficient and effective operations of the firms operating in combination. Finally, the promoter arranged for the transfer of the individual companies to the new corporation. For his services the promoter usually received a portion of the securities of the consolidated firm. The promoter's share was increased the more attractive the earnings of the consolidation could be made to appear and, hence, the smaller the percentage of the new securities required to purchase the participating companies and raise necessary funds.

For some of the larger consolidations information has been collected on the returns to the promoting group.[22] For example, in the formation of the United States Steel Corporation it was reported that approximately $150 million of the stock of the Corporation, nearly one-seventh of the total, was issued, directly or indirectly, to promoters or underwriters. The American Can Company was formed with an authorized capitalization of $82 million, and of this amount it is estimated that promoters and underwriters received $17 million or approximately one-fifth. Examples such as these cannot be relied upon, however, for a measure of the overall importance of promotion to the movement, and other indicators must be examined.

It appears that the efforts of an outside promoter were more likely to be involved when a number of individual firms were consolidated, and data on the proportion of consolidations involving several firms may provide an indication of the extent of promotional activities. Nelson found that 75% of firm disappearances during the 1895–1904 period were accounted for by consolidations of five or more firms. Moreover, this prevalence of large consolidations was peculiar to the period of intensive merger activity. Consolidations of five or more firms accounted for 37.7% of firm disappearances in the 1905–1914 period and only 13.9% in the 1915–1920 period. The mean number of firm disappearances into consolidations was 9.0 in the 1895–1904 period and declined to 3.5 by the 1915–1920 period. The proportion of consolidations involving the simultaneous com-

---

[22] *Ibid.* In Chapter XII Jones provides a detailed account of promoters' profits for several consolidations including the two examples cited in the text.

bination of 10 or more firms was 26.3% in 1895–1904 and only 1.4% in 1915–1920.[23]

Another type of evidence cited as indicative of promotional activities is the high incidence of failure among early mergers.[24] Dewing made the classic statement that "the trusts turned out ill," [25] and he appears to have been the first to collect data on the record of success achieved by the early consolidations. In his study[26] of 35 major consolidations formed during the turn-of-the-century period, aggregate earnings for each group of firms in the year prior to their consolidation were compared with promoters' estimates of subsequent earnings, actual earnings for the first year of consolidated operations, and earnings for the ten-year period following consolidation.

Dewing found that on the average promoters' estimates of earnings subsequent to consolidation exceeded by approximately 45% the aggregate of the participating companies in the year prior to consolidation. Actually, average earnings in the first year subsequent to consolidation were exceeded by prior earnings by 19% and exceeded by promoters' estimates by 86%. Average earnings for the ten years following consolidation were very nearly the same as those in the first year, and in the tenth year 8% less. In only 5 out of the 35 cases did average earnings for the ten-year period following consolidation equal or exceed promoters' estimates.

A study by Shaw Livermore[27] provides evidence on a larger sample. Information was collected on 328 industrial mergers and consolidations occurring within the 1888–1905 period.[28] The sample was divided into primary and secondary groups where 156 consolidations in the primary group "had power enough to influence markedly the conditions of their industry." Those in the secondary group did not meet this criterion of market power.

Performance was observed over the period beginning with the date of consolidation and ending in 1932. Each merger was classified according to one of five classifications. The results of this classification are as shown in Table 2.1.

---

[23] Nelson, *op. cit.*, pp. 53–54.

[24] See, for example, Markham, "Survey of the Evidence and Findings on Mergers," p. 163. Markham explains his basis for this argument as follows: "This hypothesis finds its origin in a very simple line of logic. The mergers that actually turned out to be profitable operating firms were *expected* to be more profitable than those that did not. Where expectations of operating profitability were high, however, less professional promotional services were needed. While readily available data on this point include a very small proportion of the total number of mergers, they seem generally to support the hypothesis." Markham briefly discusses the promotion and profitability of 25 mergers to support his point.

[25] *Financial Policy of Corporations,* p. 734.

[26] "A Statistical Test of the Success of Consolidation."

[27] "The Success of Industrial Mergers."

[28] Livermore's sample appears to account for a large proportion of the mergers included in the series later compiled by Nelson. While Nelson recorded 3,012 firm disappearances during 1895–1904, these were accounted for by 313 consolidations of parent firms. Livermore's data are derived from a period eight years longer but these eight years appear to have provided considerably less merger activity than 1895–1904.

TABLE 2.1

DEGREE OF SUCCESS ACHIEVED BY INDUSTRIAL MERGERS
DURING THE 1888–1905 PERIOD

	Primary Group		Secondary Group	
	Number	*% of Total*	*Number*	*% of Total*
Successes	66	42.3%	80	46.5%
Limping Successes	17	10.9	11	6.4
Rejuvenations	10	6.4	3	1.8
Failures				
Early	53	32.6		
Later	10	6.1		
Subtotal	63	40.4	78	45.3
Total	156	100.0%	172	100.0%

SOURCE: Shaw Livermore, "The Success of Industrial Mergers," *Quarterly Journal of Economics*, November 1935.

Livermore is somewhat vague in his definitions of these categories and admits subjectivity in the classification process. Definitions of the five categories are roughly as follows: (1) early failures — firms which were liquidated or which suffered a major reorganization with losses in both shareholder and creditor interests within a decade after the consolidation; (2) later failures — firms which survived for at least a decade before failure as defined above; (3) rejuvenations — firms which suffered reorganizations involving replacement of management and loss for shareholders but not resulting in losses for creditors; (4) limping successes — firms which operated at losses for significant periods but which apparently survived without major change until the end of the observation period, a total of 25 to 35 years; (5) successes — firms which survived without change and without significant periods of unprofitable operations. For the firms in the success category the average rate of return on capital was approximately the same as the average for all industrial firms.[29]

While Livermore suggested that his findings (that over 40% of the consolidations met his definition of success) required a reappraisal of prevalent unfavorable views on the first merger movement, this appears questionable. From the stockholder's point of view, the rejuvenations would have to be added to the list of failures. This brings the total number of failures to 154 or 47% of the 328 mergers. As others have suggested,[30] the high proportion of failures and the modest

---

[29] Livermore compared the average rate of return achieved by his successful group with the return achieved by a sample of over 3,000 firms which were able to maintain continuous existence over the 1919–1928 period. Data on this latter sample were taken from Epstein, *Source Book for Industrial Profits*.

[30] Markham states: "When it is considered that mergers represent not entirely new and untried ventures but fusions of firms that have already survived their uncertain years of infancy, such a high incidence of failure suggests that promotional rather than operational gains motivated formation of a large number of them." *Op. cit.*, p. 165.

definition of success imply that promotional gains rather than operating economies motivated many early mergers.

While the profits of promotion emerge as one of the more important causes of the early merger movement, this was, in most cases, a motivation for individuals and groups outside the companies participating in the consolidations. The desire, or at least willingness, of such producing units to combine must be explained in terms of advantages, real or apparent, to the participants in the consolidation.

Several authors have suggested that foremost among the objectives of merging firms was the avoidance of competition and the achievement of a monopoly position.[31] And for many, the major trusts and consolidations of the early period were synonymous with monopoly. Thus, Jones' treatise is "not a study of all combinations, but merely of those combinations that have (or had) monopolistic power, and that are properly designated as trusts." [32] Livermore, in selecting his sample of 328 combinations, omitted a number of others for which data were available because they were not properly described by "the term 'merger' in its economic sense — gaining more power by the elimination of active competitors." [33]

The importance of monopoly power as a cause or motivation may perhaps be inferred from the extent to which market control was achieved. Moody investigated "trusts" in 92 industries which were established during this period. He found that 78 controlled 50% or more of the output in their respective fields; 57 controlled 60% or more; and 26 controlled 80% or more.[34]

Nelson examined the 92 trusts discussed by Moody. He listed 86 of these as controlling an amount of their respective fields which either exceeded 42.5% or was "large," although not accurately known. These 86 consolidations or parent corporations accounted for 1,465 or 48.6% of the 3,012 firm disappearances recorded for the 1895–1904 period and accounted for 70.4% of all authorized merger capitalization.[35] The evidence, Nelson argued,[36] was indicative of a fairly strong desire to avoid competition. Also, if promotion was an important motivation, the promise of "monopoly" benefits may have induced managements and owners to combine.

Another indication of the importance of monopoly as a motivation is the success of those consolidations which achieved monopoly positions in comparison with those which did not. Returning to the findings of Livermore as presented

---

[31] Tippetts and Livermore may be cited as an example: "If we were asked to state the *chief* reason for the organization of trusts, we should emphasize the desire to secure monopoly profits through control of the market. Competition had become severe and the rise of large-scale industries and mass production with a high level of fixed charges necessitated the presence of an orderly market. Unrestrained and energetic price cutting had worked havoc in many lines of business and had driven many individual producers to the wall. If the supply placed on the market could be limited, the price could be controlled, and even if not raised to a high level it could be prevented from falling to an unprofitable one." *Business Organization and Public Control*, p. 373.

[32] *The Trust Problem in the United States*, p. vii.

[33] "The Success of Industrial Mergers," p. 71.

[34] *The Truth About the Trusts*, p. 487.

[35] *Merger Movements in American Industry*, p. 102.

[36] *Ibid.*, p. 103.

in Table 2.1, it may be observed that the record of success was no better for mergers in the primary group, those which achieved significant market control, than for those in the secondary group which achieved only minor increases in market control. The record indicates that those consolidations achieving market control were unable to achieve their alleged profit objectives.

In determining motivation, however, results are less important than expectations. That a large number of the consolidations became the dominant producers in their respective fields seems beyond question; and if one is to be guided by the majority of the students of this era, it was the expectation of monopoly profits which provided a major, if not *the* major, motivation for such combinations.

Another factor claimed to be of major importance in providing motivation for prospective participants in consolidations was the expectation of increased profits resulting from economies of scale. Some have viewed the consolidation movement at the turn of the century as the natural conclusion of a number of developments leading toward more economical large-scale production.[37] The changing nature of industry undoubtedly created a more favorable environment for larger-scale operations, and expectations of increased profits from economies of scale must have influenced formation of many of the early consolidations. However, for several reasons it is questionable whether scale economies provided a dominant motivation for the intensive merger activity of the late 1890s and early 1900s.

First, the observed merger activity occurred in a wide variety of fields. It will be recalled that Moody investigated trusts in 92 different industries. As Nelson suggests, it is difficult to believe that technological developments creating the potential for production economies could have suddenly developed in all these varied industries within a few years of the end of the nineteenth century.[38]

Second, while it undoubtedly is true that significant potential for decreased production and distribution costs through scale economies exists for the smallest of firms, the potential for firms of medium or large size is questionable. For the 1895–1904 period the average consolidation combined nine firms and had an authorized capitalization of $19.2 million, or more than $2 million for the average participating company.[39] Many of the consolidations involved the largest firms in their respective industries. As will be discussed, the ability of established,

---

[37] Bain, for example, suggests that ". . . the rise of 'monopolies' or 'trusts' was in no sense an aberration from the orderly development of a free enterprise economy. It was rather one of several phases of the adaptation of economic life to the primary stimuli of technological innovation that had influenced the industrial development of the preceding century. Improvements in methods of textile making, a revolution in the technique of iron and steel manufacture, the development of steam power, and the building of railroad systems had provided the technological basis for the shift of production to factories, for the movement of population to the cities, and for the organization of the production of more and more goods under the direction of private enterprise. As this reorganization of the economy was proceeding, a further implication of the technical revolution became evident, namely, that industrial firms would find it both more economical and more profitable to expand, to integrate, and to combine." Quoted from "Industrial Concentration and Government Antitrust Policy," p. 354.

[38] Nelson, *Merger Movements in American History*, p. 103.

[39] *Ibid.*, p. 54.

viable firms of significant size to achieve scale economies has not been clearly established.

Third, production economies are typically discussed in terms of increased size of plant. However, the typical consolidation resulted in multiplant operations. A larger scale of production may result from such a combination only with the later replacement of existing facilities. If the achievement of scale economies was important, such economies must have been expected to occur only after integration of production operations, or they must have been expected in areas other than production.

Since scale economies and other possible merger economies are of particular importance to the shareholder's position, we defer a more detailed discussion of the topic to the next chapter. The brief discussion above suggests, however, that while scale economies probably provided one important source of motivation, it was not a dominant motivation.

The motives discussed thus far have been based on the potential achievement of some economic result of interest to one or more groups affected by mergers. The final source of motivation to be discussed for this period is based on non-economic results. A variety of psychological needs of both management and external promoting groups could be satisfied by the early consolidations. The surviving management reaped the prestige, the recognition, and the power of directing a large industrial enterprise. The promoting group or individual derived the satisfaction of founding a giant corporation, of participating in an exciting and hazardous game, and of finishing with a sense of accomplishment. If the promoting group was also the surviving management, it was doubly rewarded. The overall significance of the motivation provided by potential psychological gain is unknown and will remain so. Some students of the era ignored this source of influence; others placed substantial stress upon it.[40] Wealthy individuals often appear to be pursuing psychological rather than economic objectives; and it appears likely that the financiers, professional promoters, and prominent businessmen active in the early consolidation period were strongly affected by psychological drives. However, given the magnitude of the potential economic impact of these consolidations, it is once again doubtful that this source of motivation was a dominant one.

Indeed, none of the possible sources of motivation or the favorable environmental factors may be considered individually sufficient to explain this period of merger activity. The intention has been to portray them as integral pieces of a puzzle which must be viewed in combination before one is able to approach a

---

[40] Tippetts and Livermore suggest that ". . . perhaps in many instances, the driving force on the part of those who were to head up the combination was a desire for recognition, for prestige, for dominance and power in American industrial life. . . . If they could bring a group of previously independent companies together into one large organization, they would secure recognition as 'big' men, men who must be respected and whose influence was very great. . . . Many promoters did not choose to remain with the new company in an executive capacity, . . . [but] they could be pointed out as the 'father' of this or that combination, and in this manner gain prestige." *Business Organization and Public Control,* pp. 362 and 379.

meaningful picture of the underlying forces at work. Some attempt to summarize and to expand slightly this array of forces may be worthwhile.

By the latter part of the 19th century the factory system of production had become widely understood, accepted, and employed. The settlement of the West and the expansion of the railroad system had expanded markets, making larger-scale production feasible. Technological improvements had expanded industry's capability to produce on a large scale through automation, specialization, and standardization. State incorporation laws were made more permissive in the 1880s and 1890s, permitting mergers to occur. The trust form of organization was ruled illegal in a series of common law cases forcing combining firms to consolidate as a single legal entity. The Sherman Act, declaring illegal "[e]very contract, combination . . . or conspiracy in restraint of trade or commerce . . . ,"[41] had been passed in 1890. But in the first test of the law, the E. C. Knight case,[42] it was held to apply only to commerce, not to manufacturing or mining, thus opening the door for the coming wave of mergers. Meanwhile, the New York Stock Exchange had developed significantly as an effective national market for corporate securities, providing the basis for the large security issues accompanying many consolidations. Stock prices rose by 83% from the low of 1897 to the high of 1901. Further, it was a period of rapid business expansion with accompanying favorable expectations; industrial production increased 57% from the low in 1896 to the high in 1901. The stage was set and previous consolidations had shown the way. The direct motivation for participants was provided by expectations of promoters' profits, increased power and prestige, monopoly profits, and economies of scale. What followed must have been to some extent a psychological chain reaction with consolidation in one industry encouraged by the apparent success of those in other fields. Mergers proceeded at a rapid pace, and within a few years much of the existing potential for consolidation in American industry had been exhausted.

The decline of merger activity was equally rapid. Some of the consolidations began to show signs of early failure, and in 1901 the stock market began to fall. Stock prices declined gradually at first, then much more rapidly leading to the "Rich Man's Panic" of 1903–1904. From the high in 1901 to the low of 1903 market prices dropped 40%. At the same time a contraction of general business activity occurred in 1903–1904. Also considered of importance in bringing an end to this merger era was a change in attitude on the part of the Federal Government. In the Addyston Pipe case[43] of 1899 a combination of manufacturers, although in the form of a pool, was ruled by the Supreme Court to be acting in restraint of trade. In 1903 the Bureau of Corporations, later to become the Federal Trade Commission, was formed under the initiative of President Theodore Roosevelt and began investigations of the Standard Oil, American Tobacco, and other consolidations. Finally, in the Northern Securities decision[44] of 1904 a

---

[41] 26 Stat: 209; 15 U.S.C. 1-7; Public Law No. 190, 51st Cong. (1890), Section 1.

[42] U.S. *v.* E. C. Knight Company, 156 U.S. 1 (1895).

[43] Addyston Pipe and Steel Co., et al., *v.* U.S., 175 U.S. 211 (1899).

[44] Northern Securities Company *v.* U.S., 193 U.S. 332 (1904).

combination in the form of a single corporation was found to be acting in violation of the Sherman Act. While the companies involved were railroads, and some question remained regarding the applicability of the Sherman Act to the consolidation of manufacturing and mining firms into a single corporation, it was widely inferred that the merger route to monopoly had been closed. The first merger era had come to an end.

THE SECOND MERGER PERIOD — THE LATE 1920s

From the decline of merger activity in the early 1900s until the early 1920s, mergers proceeded at a relatively slow pace. The number of annual disappearances of manufacturing and mining firms fluctuated in the range of 50 to 200 during this period.[45] Immediately following World War I there was a period of business expansion accompanied by a rise in stock prices, and merger activity reached a minor peak. However, mergers declined with the recession of business and the stock market in 1921. In the prosperous and speculative period which followed, merger activity increased rather steadily until 1929, reaching a peak of 1,245 annual disappearances. After 1929 merger activity dropped precipitously, completing a pattern which closely followed the pattern of stock market prices during the late 1920s and early 1930s.

In comparison with the first merger era this second period of intensive merger activity evoked a relatively small amount of literature. The wave of mergers at the turn of the century had provided a new and unique phenomenon which dominated the economic scene and begged explanation. Consolidations of large firms monopolized industry after industry, dramatically altering the structure of American business and creating great controversy. The merger activity of the 1920s played a subordinate role to the rise of speculative activity in the stock market and the rapid expansion of business activity generally. Also, as will be discussed, this merger period had a less pervasive effect on the competitive structure of industry and hence brought forth less controversy. As a result the period is less well documented than the early merger era, and explanation of mergers in the 1920s must be based less on data and more on the opinions of students of the period.

The character of mergers during the 1920s appears to have been strongly influenced by the changing structure of antitrust law. The initial change of government position resulting from the first consolidation period has been noted. In the period which followed, at least until the start of World War I, prevailing opinion opposed any trend toward further consolidation.[46] The investigations of the Standard Oil and American Tobacco consolidations led to their dissolution

---

[45] According to Nelson's data, *op. cit.* There were in this period of low merger activity a few consolidations of major importance. For example, between 1908 and 1910 William C. Durant brought together the Buick, Olds (now Oldsmobile), Oakland (now Pontiac), and Cadillac companies to form the General Motors Corporation. See Sloan, *My Years With General Motors*, p. 5.

[46] This is at least the opinion of Thorp, "The Persistence of the Merger Movement," p. 88.

in two Supreme Court decisions in 1911.[47] And in 1914 Congress, with the intent of strengthening antitrust law, passed the Clayton Act holding:

> That no corporation engaged in commerce shall acquire, directly or indirectly, the whole or any part of the stock or other share capital of another corporation engaged also in commerce, where the effect of such acquisition may be to substantially lessen competition between the corporation whose stock is so acquired and the corporation making the acquisition, or to restrain such commerce in any section or community, or to tend to create a monopoly of any line of commerce.[48]

After World War I the legal atmosphere appears to have become somewhat more permissive toward mergers. In the Standard Oil and American Tobacco dissolution cases of 1911, the "rule of reason" had been established. In effect, it was held that the dissolved consolidations were illegal because they had abused their power. But it was the opinion of the Court that a monopoly could provide social advantages through increased efficiency, and if there was no attempt to drive competitors from the field, monopoly *per se* would not be considered illegal. For example, in two cases in 1918 and 1920,[49] the Supreme Court allowed United Shoe Machinery Co. and United States Steel Corporation to maintain their existence based on this judicial precedent. It was shown that both controlled in excess of 80% of the production in their respective fields, but the Court found them to be efficient producers which had not abused their market power.

The judicial precedent of the "rule of reason" apparently would have been nullified for new combinations by the Clayton Act had it not been for the asset acquisition "loophole." [50] This loophole was widened by the Supreme Court in 1926. In the Thatcher case[51] it held that a corporation which acquired stock and used its voting position to bring about a sale of assets before the Federal Trade Commission could institute proceedings was beyond the reach of the law.

From the dissolution of some of the major trusts it was obvious that consolidations to achieve monopoly profits through restrictive trade practices would not be tolerated. However, the "rule of reason" implied that market power *per se* was not illegal, and the working of the Clayton Act combined with its interpretation in the courts rendered it ineffectual. Thus, in the 1920s a considerable degree of flexibility for mergers remained, but the environment clearly was less permissive than it had been at the turn of the century. The merger activity which took place within this atmosphere of legal and public opinion was of a different character from that of the previous period.

In comparing the first and second merger movements, Stigler suggests that

---

[47] Standard Oil Co. *v.* U.S., 221 U.S. 1 (1911); U.S. *v.* American Tobacco Company, 221 U.S. 106 (1911).

[48] Public Law No. 212, Section 7, first paragraph.

[49] U.S. *v.* United States Steel Corporation, 251 U.S. 417 (1920); U.S. *v.* United Shoe Machinery Co., 247 U.S. 32 (1918).

[50] As may be noted in the section of the Clayton Act quoted above, reference was made only to acquisition of stock; there was no reference to purchase of assets. Presumably this was done because previous large consolidations had typically been effected through stock acquisition.

[51] Thatcher Manufacturing Co. *v.* FTC, 272 U.S. 554 (1926).

whereas the motivation in the former was monopoly the goal in the latter was oligopoly.[52] He suggests that mergers in the 1920s were not undertaken by firms which were dominant in their industries but by "firms of the second class." He illustrates this with the steel industry where acquisitions by Bethlehem and Republic transformed two relatively small firms into major competitors of the United States Steel Corporation. "In the early period," Stigler suggests, "the leading firms seldom merged less than 50% of the industry's output; in the later period the percentage has hardly ever risen that high." [53]

Stocking and Watkins also provide a comparison of the first two merger periods which indicates the decline of monopoly power as a motivation. They cite two distinguishing features: one, a change from the large multifirm combination toward "piecemeal absorption" of firms of more moderate size; two, a change away from combinations which primarily involved competing firms toward more combinations of noncompeting firms.[54] But in spite of their emphasis on noncompeting firms, Stocking and Watkins do not appear in complete disagreement with the "merger for oligopoly" idea. They later state that "in many fields mergers reduced to a mere handful the number of sellers whose policies really mattered in shaping the market." [55] A similar point of view is expressed by Thorp, who suggests that one important motivation for the period was provided by the creation of "local or partial monopolies" in "certain branches of industry." [56]

Thus, the desire to limit and control competition was clearly evident in this merger period, but because of the prevailing legal climate it appears to have been expressed in the achievement of much smaller gains in market power than was the case in the earlier period. Further, it was not just the smaller variety of horizontal and vertical mergers which caused the character of merger activity in the 1920s to differ from that in the 1890s. As noted above by Stocking and Watkins, many firms merging during this period dealt either in noncompeting geographical markets or noncompeting products. Several authors have emphasized one or the other of these latter forms and have suggested different motivations.

Galbraith[57] emphasizes geographical diversification. He suggests that while a few of the mergers in the 1920s were motivated by a desire to "reduce, eliminate, or regularize competition," most "brought together firms doing the same thing in different communities." The motivation, he claims, was the elimination of "the incompetence, somnambulance, naivete, or even the unwarranted integrity of local managements." Such combinations reportedly occurred in a variety of

---

[52] "Monopoly and Oligopoly by Merger," p. 31. In discussing this paper Bain suggests that "Stigler has set out to rework the economic history of the American merger movement" by emphasizing the market power motivations and ignoring others. ("Industrial Concentration and Government Antitrust Policy," p. 64.) While Stigler's emphasis on monopoly and oligopoly cannot be taken literally, it appears to provide a meaningful characterization of the difference between the two periods.

[53] *Ibid.,* p. 31.

[54] *Cartels or Competition?,* pp. 40–41.

[55] *Ibid.,* p. 41.

[56] "Persistence of the Merger Movement," p. 86.

[57] *The Great Crash.*

different fields. Galbraith cites the corporate chains which were established through merger in food retailing, variety stores, department stores, and motion picture theaters.

Dewing emphasizes the combination of firms with noncompeting products which could be distributed through the same outlets providing "economies of merchandising."

> In the period immediately before 1929, all forms of industrial consolidations were brought into existence with the avowed hope of dealing better with merchandising problems. Rubber factories and stationery factories were brought together because both rubber goods and stationery could be sold in drug stores; the manufacture of washing powder and breakfast foods was consolidated under a single management because both articles were found on the shelves at grocery stores.[58]

The heavy emphasis on a particular type of merger by the above authors does not appear justified. Tippetts and Livermore[59] discuss mergers of the period under four headings: horizontal, vertical, chain, and complementary. The latter two types, they suggest, were products of the period following passage of the Clayton Act in 1914. As examples of important vertical combinations of the period they discuss three acquiring firms in the copper industry: Anaconda, Kennecott, and Phelps-Dodge. Chain mergers are exemplified by National Dairy, Allied Stores, and McKesson and Robbins; and complementary acquiring firms by International Business Machines, Allied Chemical and Dye, General Foods, and Borg-Warner.

In Markham's survey of the merger literature[60] he characterizes the types of mergers in those industries where merger activity was most prevalent. He notes that five-eighths of the firms disappearing through merger between 1919 and 1930 were in the food, steel, and chemical industries. With a number of examples he attempts to illustrate that in the food industry mergers were "largely of the chain- and conglomerate-firm variety." In metals, particularly the copper industry, "mergers extended vertical integration." And in chemicals mergers were "mostly of the conglomerate firm type."

These different opinions are relevant because no attempt has been made to classify mergers comprehensively by type for the second merger period. In the first period the findings of Nelson allowed us to state that the vast majority of firms disappeared into large multifirm, horizontal consolidations. In the most recent period, as we shall discuss, the FTC has attempted a comprehensive classification which indicates a dominance of conglomerate mergers. The 1920s may be viewed as a period of transition. While horizontal combinations leading to oligopolistic market conditions apparently remained an important feature, it appears that a significant, but undetermined, proportion of the mergers during this period would today be classified as conglomerate of the geographic market extension or product extension variety. Thus, the achievement of market power

---

[58] *The Financial Policy of Corporations,* p. 877.
[59] *Organization and Public Control,* pp. 481–490.
[60] "Survey of the Evidence and Findings on Mergers," pp. 168–171.

and economies of large-scale production must be considered motivations of reduced importance in comparison with the turn-of-the-century period.

An innovation of the period which probably influenced the shift toward conglomerate mergers was the development of decentralized management techniques. Chandler describes in detail the shift from the centralized, functionally specialized form of organization to the decentralized, multidivisional form which was first carried out by such large firms as General Motors, Du Pont, Standard Oil of New Jersey, and Sears Roebuck during the decade of the 1920s. He suggests that the expansion of large firms through product and market diversification:

> . . . enlarged the range, number and complexity of the entrepreneurial activities required of the senior executives. The long-term allocation of resources now involved deciding between the expansion, maintenance, and contraction of personnel, plant, and equipment in several different, large-scale, widespread businesses. The appraisal of existing performance as well as the planning of future uses of resources called for a general office in which the executives were given the time, the information, and the encouragement to develop a broad view, all so necessary for the handling of the new and more complex problems. The multidivisional structure met both the short-term and long-term requirements for the profitable application of resources to the changing markets.[61]

This type of structure was developed first within the General Motors Corporation by Alfred Sloan who has provided a comprehensive description of the process.[62] Mr. Sloan's "Organization Study" for General Motors was written in 1918 in response to operating difficulties which their existing form of organization had presented during a previous period of expansion, and was adopted when Pierre S. du Pont became President in 1920. In his study Mr. Sloan advocated the decentralized, multidivisional structure for reasons which are widely accepted today but were unfamiliar at the time. In particular he suggested that this form of organization (1) increases managerial motivation through decentralized authority and responsibility and through the increased visibility of divisonal performance; (2) increases the ability of top management to measure and control performance because of the ability to evaluate divisional earnings relative to invested capital; (3) improves the opportunities for overall performance through the ability to apply additional capital to those divisions where it will earn the highest returns.[63]

The improved organizational structure and management practices adopted by General Motors and others during the 1920s greatly enhanced the ability to manage large diversified businesses effectively. The strategy and techniques of diversification followed by Du Pont were imitated by other chemical companies during the 1920s, and this may be related to the trend toward conglomerate mergers in that industry. However, it is questionable that improvements in the management of large-scale diversification had a pervasive impact on the trend toward mergers of the conglomerate form in the 1920s because the new type of structure did not

---

[61] *Strategy and Structure*, p. 489.

[62] *My Years With General Motors.*

[63] *Ibid.*, p. 50, paraphrased from his "Organization Study" of 1918.

become widely known and accepted until the 1930s.[64] These developments are nonetheless worthy of attention, for their importance for conglomerate mergers in the current period appears beyond question.

Finally, it appears that the role of the external promoter continued to be of considerable importance in the second merger period. There are some indications, however, that this role was not so important as in the early period. As noted, the large multifirm consolidation had become the exception rather than the rule. Also, several authors have argued that the history of failures of consolidations formed in the 1895–1905 period caused businessmen to have a more critical attitude toward mergers and hence to be more careful in concluding that a merger would be economically justified.[65] Both factors may have diminished the importance of the role of external promotion. Still, it was a period of great optimism and speculation; new security issues were eagerly absorbed; and an ideal environment was provided for the promoter. Willard Thorp suggests that "the same basic forces were present in the twenties as in the earlier period of merger activity. Promoters were extremely active, new issues were frequently floated where the sum exceeded the parts." [66] Elsewhere, Thorp elaborates this emphasis on promotion:

> Many mergers and some acquisitions involve the flotation of new securities. In periods like 1928 and early 1929, when there is almost an insatiable demand for securities, the merger movement will be certain to flourish. Its most active sponsor is the investment banker. Reputable business houses merely carrying on their business under their existing organization bring a very slight volume of new securities for the banker to handle. But if they can be brought together into a new organization it may mean a large flotation of stock. . . . A group of businessmen and financiers in discussing this matter in the summer of 1928 agreed that nine out of ten mergers had the investment banker at the core. The fact that the public will take the securities makes possible a sharing of the increased capitalization between the banker and the original owners and makes the owners willing to join the merger even when they can see little technical advantage to be gained from the new organization.[67]

In summary, the influence provided by the profits of external promotion appears to have diminished somewhat from the previous period but continued to be of major importance. Psychological drives of managers and promoters are not discussed in the literature but presumably remained a contributory factor. The economic environment was ideal for mergers; it was a period of unprecedented prosperity and optimism, and major expansions in motor transportation and radio communication enlarged markets and influenced changes in industry structure. However, adverse public reaction to the anticompetitive effects of earlier horizontal consolidations had led to an enlarged structure of antitrust law. This canalized the forces leading to combination in the direction of smaller horizontal combina-

---

[64] Chandler, *op. cit.*, p. 490.
[65] See, for example, Tippetts and Livermore, *op. cit.*, pp. 480–481.
[66] "The Merger Movement," p. 234.
[67] "The Persistence of the Merger Movement," pp. 85–86.

tions and conglomerate mergers of the product and market extension variety. This diminishes our ability to explain the motivation for mergers of the period in terms of monopoly profits and economies of scale.

THE CURRENT MERGER PERIOD — BEGINNING AFTER WORLD WAR II

From the 1929 peak annual rate of 1,245 disappearances of manufacturing and mining firms, merger activity declined rapidly with the decline in the stock market and in business activity generally. Between 1932 and 1943 the annual rate remained below 200 disappearances, then increased to exceed 400 annual disappearances in both 1946 and 1947 before declining again in 1948 and 1949.[68] While merger activity during the 1940s never approached the intensity of the two earlier merger periods nor the intensity of recent years, two important studies[69] published around 1950 treated it as a third major period of merger activity. We shall consider this the initial part of the merger movement still in progress. The increase of merger activity beginning from the low of 126 annual disappearances in 1949 continued in irregular fashion, reaching an annual rate of 1,496 in 1967. The more gradual increase and the greater duration of this period distinguish it from the periods around 1900 and in the 1920s.

The duration of intensive merger activity in recent years appears to have created an atmosphere in which frequent corporate combinations are considered a normal business phenomenon. This is perhaps illustrated by the magnitude of recent literature discussing procedures for dealing with the management, legal, tax, and accounting problems of merging businesses. While one such study made its ill-timed appearance in 1930,[70] we find no other volumes devoted specifically to these problems until recent years when a number of such studies have appeared.[71]

The increasing merger activity since the 1940s has taken place within an increasingly restrictive environment of antitrust law. A significant change occurred in 1945 when the Supreme Court held the "rule of reason" no longer applied; it was decided that the Aluminum Company of America[72] had violated the Sherman Act by monopolizing 90% of the manufacture of newly refined aluminum. The most important aspect of the case, for this discussion, was that monopoly power no longer need be abused to be unlawful.

In 1950 the Celler-Kefauver Act amended Section 7 of the Clayton Act, closing the asset acquisition "loophole." The new Section 7 stated in part:

---

[68] Disappearances through merger based on the Federal Trade Commission series.

[69] U.S. Federal Trade Commission, *Report of the Federal Trade Commission on the Merger Movement*, 1948; and Butters, Lintner, and Cary, *Effects of Taxation: Corporate Mergers*.

[70] Basset, *Operating Aspects of Industrial Mergers*.

[71] Drayton, ed., *Mergers and Acquisitions: Planning and Action*, 1963. Scharf, *Techniques for Buying, Selling and Merging Business*, 1964. Hennessy, *Acquiring and Merging Business*, 1966. Wyatt, *A Critical Study of Accounting for Business Combinations*, 1963. Mace and Montgomery, *Management Problems of Corporate Acquisitions*, 1962. Alberts and Segall, eds., *The Corporate Merger*, 1966. McCarthy, *Acquisitions and Mergers*, 1963.

[72] U.S. *v.* Aluminum Company of America, 148F 2d 416 (1945).

That no corporation engaged in commerce shall acquire, directly or indirectly, the whole or any part of the stock or other share capital and no corporation subject to the jurisdiction of the Federal Trade Commission shall acquire the whole or any part of the assets of another corporation engaged also in commerce, where in any line of commerce in any section of the country, the effect of such acquisition may be substantially to lessen competition, or to tend to create a monopoly.[73]

This section has become the basis for the majority of antitrust proceedings. In recent cases the Supreme Court seems to have pursued the Congressional intent with regard to Section 7 "to limit future increases in the level of economic concentration resulting from corporate mergers and acquisitions." [74] Mergers have been blocked which would have provided a moderate share of a regional market[75] and which would have provided only a minor share of a national market.[76] Section 7 has also been applied to vertical mergers which would foreclose a substantial part of a particular market, thus concentrating the remainder.[77]

The applicability of Section 7 to conglomerate mergers is less clear. In the House Report on the 1950 amendment, Section 7 was held to apply to "all types of mergers and acquisitions, vertical and conglomerate as well as horizontal, which have the specified effects." [78] As one economist has pointed out,[79] in the case of the "pure" conglomerate merger where one firm acquired another "producing an altogether unrelated product, one which is neither competing, nor a raw material for its own product, nor a commodity into which it is to be embodied" it is difficult to see how the "specified effects" can be present. He suggests that "perhaps Congress intended to stop conglomerate mergers, but their act does not. . . ." The problem with this point of view is that the "pure" conglomerate merger is relatively rare. Most current conglomerate mergers, as will be presently discussed, involve some product or market relationships. The recent Supreme Court decision in favor of the divestiture by Procter & Gamble of the previously acquired Clorox Chemical Company[80] has illustrated how little relationship there need be for a merger to be illegal under Section 7. The principal basis for the Court's decision appears to have been that bleach was sufficiently related to the Procter & Gamble

---

[73] Public Law 889, Section 7, paragraph 1.

[74] U.S. Senate, 81st Cong., 2d Sess. (1950), S. R. 1775, p. 3.

[75] In U.S. *v.* The Philadelphia National Bank, 374 U.S. 312 (1963), a bank merger was blocked which would have resulted in control of 30% of the commercial banking business in the four-county Philadelphia metropolitan area.

[76] In Brown Shoe Co. *v.* U.S., 370 U.S. 294 (1962), the Court blocked the acquisition by Brown of Kinney which would have "placed under Brown's control . . . about 7.2% of the nation's total retail shoe outlets" (p. 346). This merger, however, had vertical aspects as well.

[77] In U.S. *v.* E. I. du Pont de Nemours & Company, 353 U.S. 586 (1957), the Court held that Du Pont's acquisition of 23% of the stock of General Motors had foreclosed one-third of the total market for automotive finishes and one-fourth of the total market for automotive fabrics.

[78] U.S. House of Representatives, 81st Cong., 1st Sess. (1949), HR 1191, p. 11.

[79] Andelman, "Acquire the Whole or Any Part of the Stock or Assets of Another Corporation," pp. 120–121.

[80] U.S. *v.* Procter & Gamble Co., 386 U.S. 568 (1967).

product line in function and in market that P&G would have expanded internally to become a major competitor in the bleach market had it not acquired Clorox, the major producer of bleach at the time.[81]

The future applicability of antitrust law to conglomerate mergers is unclear and is the subject of considerable controversy. In general, however, it seems clear that the less related the products and markets of merging firms are and the smaller their positions in markets they serve, the less subject they will be to our antitrust laws. This has had a significant impact on the changing character of mergers since passage of the Celler-Kefauver amendment to the Clayton Act.

The Federal Trade Commission has classified mergers according to whether they were horizontal, vertical, or conglomerate for the period from 1940 to the present. Within the conglomerate classification it has categorized mergers since 1948 according to product extensions, market extensions, and unrelated firms. The results of this classification through 1964 are shown in Table 2.2.

TABLE 2.2

CLASSIFICATION OF MINING AND MANUFACTURING MERGERS
BY TYPE AND BY PERIOD: 1940–1964

Type of Merger	1940–47*	1948–53	1954–59	1960–64
Conglomerate				
Market extension		6.9%	6.4%	6.9%
Product extension		46.6	46.2	52.9
Unrelated		5.2	8.9	11.2
Subtotal	21%	58.7%	61.5%	71.0%
Vertical	17	10.3	13.7	17.0
Horizontal	62	31.0	24.8	12.0
	100%	100.0%	100.0%	100.0%

* Period 1940–1947 not directly comparable with later periods; see text.
SOURCE: Federal Trade Commission.

For the 1940–1947 period, 62% of all mergers were classified as horizontal and only 21% as conglomerate. This is based on the classification of all mergers recorded by the FTC for this period, a total exceeding 2,000.[82] The classifications for the later three periods shown in Table 2.2 are not directly comparable with 1940–1947 for two reasons. First, the latter periods are classifications on only those acquired firms having assets exceeding $10 million; a total of 720 such

---

[81] This, of course, is a drastic oversimplification of the issues involved as any one-sentence summary must be. A major part of the decision was based on the "huge assets and advertising advantages" of P&G which "would dissuade new entrants" into the bleach business "and discourage active competition from the companies already in the industry due to fear of retaliation by Procter." (Quoted from the Supreme Court's Opinion in Kahlmeier, "High Court Extends Antitrust Law, Voids Procter & Gamble — Clorox Tie.")

[82] This classification was presented in the *Report of the Federal Trade Commission on the Merger Movement*, 1948, pp. 24–30.

acquisitions were recorded for 1948–1964. Second, the FTC's definition of the horizontal category appears to have become more narrow in the later classifications.[83] Thus the indicated decrease of horizontal mergers from 62.0% to 31.0% and the increase of conglomerate mergers from 21.0% to 58.7% between the 1940–1947 and 1948–1953 periods, while dramatic in appearance, may not be entirely meaningful.

Data for the three periods spanning 1948–1964 were reported in a single study,[84] and presumably these classifications were made on a consistent basis. It is of particular interest that the proportion of horizontal mergers declined from 31.0% to 12.0% while that of conglomerate mergers increased from 58.7% to 71.0% between 1948–1953 and 1960–1964. Also of interest is the increase of conglomerate mergers of unrelated firms from 5.2% to 11.2% over the three periods.

Although only a very small percentage of mergers since 1950 have been challenged under our antitrust laws,[85] the tightening of these laws has had a very significant effect on the type of mergers if not their number. Enforcement of antitrust law has been compared with enforcement of our local traffic ordinances;[86] the vast majority are kept from exceeding legal limits by the apprehension of a small proportion of those that do. The monopoly power merger motivation, dominant in the first merger era, appears to have become effectively curtailed. Also substantially reduced, it would seem, are the potential operating advantages from horizontal and vertical integration.

Changes in the legal structure also seem to have been the major influence for the decline in another type of motivation, the profits which might be achieved by the external promoter. The speculative and promotional excesses of the 1920s led to the Securities Act of 1933 and the Securities and Exchange Act of 1934. The early promoters had achieved their handsome profits in connection with new security issues floated for merging firms. Under the Securities Act of 1933 any new issue accompanying a merger requires disclosure of extensive information regarding the participating companies and, in particular, disclosure of information regarding any payments made or to be made to underwriters or promoters and the consideration for such payments.[87] Under the Securities and Exchange Act of 1934 similar information must be provided in proxy solicitations in connection with proposed mergers.[88] The required disclosure of detailed information regarding the re-

---

[83] In the FTC report horizontal mergers were considered to encompass three subclasses: direct, substitute products, and chain. Chain mergers would appear to fall under the conglomerate market extension group in the later classification.

[84] Testimony of Willard F. Mueller in U.S. Senate Hearings, *Economic Concentration,* Part 2, pp. 501–520.

[85] Kottke observes that 619 of the 1,000 largest industrial companies in 1950 made one or more acquisitions over the 1951–1959 period; only 33 of these companies were challenged in any of their merger proceedings; in "Mergers of Large Manufacturing Companies 1951 to 1959," pp. 430–433.

[86] This analogy is developed in Caves, *American Industry: Structure, Conduct, Performance,* pp. 65–67.

[87] See Schedule A of the Securities Act of 1933, Public, No. 22, 73d Cong.

[88] See Schedule 14A of *General Rules and Regulations Under the Securities and Exchange Act of 1934* (as in effect April 1, 1967), GPO, 1967.

muneration and activities of promoters has almost certainly diminished their role. Also, combinations which involve outside financing have become the exception rather than the rule. Butters, Lintner, and Cary found that in the 26 largest mergers during 1940–1947 only six involved outside financing and only one outside equity financing. In the sample of more than 100 mergers which they examined in detail, the services of a "broker" were involved in about one-fifth of the cases. But such brokers generally receive only a modest commission, and their role, primarily as a finder, is "quite different from that of the financial promoters who were so active in the earlier merger movements." [89] McCarthy states that the commissions to brokers or finders generally range from 1% to 5% and have an inverse relation to the size of the transaction.[90] Thus, for a large merger transaction today a commission of approximately 1% might be compared with the 15% to 20% received by the professional promoter in consolidations such as United States Steel and American Can, as discussed for the turn-of-the-century merger period. In current merger transactions negotiations are generally conducted directly between management or ownership groups of the buying and selling firms, with the activities of external promoters explaining only a small part of the motivation.

In smaller merger transactions the management and ownership interests are frequently represented by one individual or one group of individuals. In the larger corporation the management group frequently represents only a small ownership interest, but it is typically management which provides the initiative for merger. The importance of this stems from the existence of a management interest which may be viewed as separate and distinct from the shareholder interest. It is reasonable to ask whether management, in pursuing merger transactions, is seeking to further its own interests or is acting primarily for the benefit of the shareholder. An important study of mergers during a recent period by Reid, Bossons, and Cohen[91] addresses this question. They proceed to the development of their hypothesis along the following lines:

(1) There has been an increasing separation of ownership and managerial control in the large industrial corporation.
(2) The interest of the management group is served by increased power, prestige, and remuneration; management may pursue these goals while retaining a secure position so long as they satisfy some minimum profitability constraint which will keep shareholders passive.
(3) Corporate acquisitions unquestionably meet two of these goals by providing power over more employees and more productive capacity and by providing the prestige of such a position.
(4) There is evidence that management compensation is more closely correlated with sales and assets than with profits;[92] thus mergers should serve the remuneration goal as long as the profitability constraint is not violated.

---

[89] *Effects of Taxation: Corporate Mergers*, p. 311.
[90] *Acquisitions and Mergers*, p. 256.
[91] "Mergers for Whom — Managers or Stockholders?"
[92] Evidence is cited from McGuire, Chin, and Elbing, "Executive Incomes, Sales and Profits"; Patton, "Deterioration in Top Executive Pay"; Roberts, *Executive Compensation*.

(5) It is specifically hypothesized that "large publicly held firms which merge are firms which tend to be oriented more to managers' than to stockholders' interests." [93]

To test this hypothesis, variables indicative of the extent to which management and shareholder interests have been served are examined in relation to the extent of merger activity in which a firm has been engaged. The 500 largest industrial firms as of 1960 are divided into four groups according to the number of acquisitions made in the 1951–1961 period: (1) firms with no reported acquisitions; (2) firms with 1 to 5 acquisitions; (3) firms with 6 to 10 acquisitions; (4) firms with 11 or more acquisitions. Variables proposed to measure benefits to management are:

Y_1 Proportional change in sales over the 1951–1961 period;
Y_2 Proportional change in assets;
Y_3 Proportional change in employees.

Those proposed to measure benefits to shareholders are:

Y_4 Proportional change in market price per share over 1951–1961, adjusted for stock splits, etc.;
Y_5 Increase in profits attributable to shareholders at the beginning of the period, measured as a proportion of assets at the beginning of the period;
Y_6 The same as Y_5 but measured as a proportion of sales at the beginning of the period.

Variables Y_5 and Y_6 are used in lieu of the proportional change in earnings per share because, for a number of companies, either the beginning or ending profit figure was negative. The values of each variable were examined for each of the four groups of firms representing varying degrees of merger activity. The results are as shown in Table 2.3.

As would be expected, the rate of increase in sales, assets, and employees is positively related to the rate of merger activity. The noteworthy finding is that the rate of per-share market price and earnings growth is negatively related to the rate of merger activity. For each variable the observed differences in group means are significant to the 0.005 level or lower.

Reid et al. suggest that the reasons for the observed negative relationship between shareholder benefits and mergers may be that (1) large increments of sudden expansion through acquisition may generally be less profitable than internal "step-by-step expansion that is subject to repetitive re-examination of costs and benefits for each additional increment of growth," (2) sales and asset maximization will not generally coincide with profit maximization, (3) substantial premiums are often paid for acquired companies.[94]

It may be observed from Table 2.3 that as merger activity increased beyond the pure internal growth firm, per-share market price growth was positively re-

---

[93] Reid et al., *op. cit.*, p. 1915.

[94] Evidence is cited from a study by W. T. Grimm & Co., a merger consulting firm, that during 1964 an average of 113% of the pre-merger market price was paid for acquired companies in those cases where merger transaction data were available (from the *Wall Street Journal,* February 5, 1965, p. 12).

lated to the merger rate; and there was an increase in the second shareholder earnings variable as merger activity increased from the third to the last group. Reid et al. suggest that active acquirers in some cases have developed an expertise and an organization which permit them to pursue this line of growth more profitably than others who have been less active.[95]

TABLE 2.3

MEANS OF THE VARIABLES FOR ALL FIRMS IN THE STUDY AND BY MERGER GROUPS

Variable	All Firms (478 Firms)	Group 1 No Mergers (48 Firms)	Group 2 1–5 Mergers (214 Firms)	Group 3 6–10 Mergers (142 Firms)	Group 4 11+ Mergers (74 Firms)	F-ratio*
Managers' interests:						
Y_1 Growth in sales	1.8229	1.5976	1.2061	2.0047	3.4047	7.03**
Y_2 Growth in assets	2.0349	1.6395	1.3444	2.2267	3.9204	8.80**
Y_3 Growth in employment	.9429	.4275	.5518	1.1199	2.0686	7.64**
Stockholders' interests: (per share)						
Y_4 Growth in market price	2.9164	6.8035	2.3042	2.4471	3.0659	4.84†
Y_5 Growth in earnings‡	.0366	.1212	.0320	.0228	.0215	5.11†
Y_6 Growth in earnings‡	.0280	.1089	.0245	.0134	.0139	6.01†

* The F-ratio shown for each variable is based on a one-way analysis of variance tests of the significance of the observed differences in group means for that variable.

** The probability is less than 0.001 that the observed differences in group means could be the result of chance.

† The probability is less than 0.005 that the observed differences in group means could be the result of chance.

‡ See text for definitions of these two variables.

To determine whether their results could have been caused by systematic variations among different industries (i.e., those that were least profitable might have shown the greatest tendency to merge) the total sample was divided into 14 industry categories and the tests rerun. The findings were less consistent, but they considered them sufficiently convincing to conclude that, in general, their hypothesis "that those firms which merge tend to be more oriented to managers' interests than to stockholders' interests, appears to be true for large American industrial firms during 1951–1961."

Three criticisms may be made of this general conclusion. First, the important overlooked variable may be the performance of those *individual* firms most likely to make acquisitions. It is possible that the majority of acquirers are less profitable firms seeking new areas for increased profitability and growth. Indeed, it could reasonably be argued that in the study of Reid et al. lower profitability

---

[95] This provides an interesting initial indication of the performance we have observed for acquisitive conglomerates during 1962–1967, the years immediately following their study.

and growth provide the cause, mergers the effect.[96] Second, it seems inevitable that those variables associated by the authors with management interests will be positively related to merger activity. That the expected relationship is found is not necessarily conclusive evidence that it is being pursued.

Third, management treatment of per-share performance as no more than a constraint in the pursuit of corporate size is difficult to accept. In the large corporation, management need own only a very small share of the total before ownership gains may exceed management remuneration. Prevalent use of stock-option compensation provides most executives with a meaningful ownership position.[97] The prestige of corporate management is dependent in large part on the acclaim or criticism provided by the investment community, where per-share performance is pre-eminent. Overall, sufficient forces seem to be present to lead managements to strive for improved per-share performance.

In general, we find the conclusions which Reid et al. draw from their findings subject to question. However, the evidence which they provide does clearly indicate a negative relationship between merger activity and shareholder performance. Other recent merger studies provide somewhat less pessimistic conclusions.[98] However, we find none which provide the sample size or the adequacy of financial data required to question the Reid findings on the negative correlation between performance and merger activity.

One interesting aspect of this negative correlation between merger activity and performance is that it was observed during a period when conglomerate mergers

---

[96] This points to a more meaningful question regarding merger performance: What would have been the performance of merging firms had they not merged? This question obviously is an extremely difficult one to answer, a problem we shall not avoid.

[97] Lewellen in his research on executive compensation for the National Bureau of Economic Research found that for the last decade studied, 1954–1963, stock options provided compensation approximately equal that provided by salary and bonus. Over-all he found that "one-third to one-half of the typical senior executive's annual earnings arises from what are essentially ownership oriented arrangements. . . . The alleged separation of present-day ownership and management objectives seems, in short, to be vastly overstated." See his summary article, "Executives Lose Out, Even With Options," p. 134.

[98] Bjorksten recorded the number of manufacturing acquisitions and the number of "failures" of previous acquisitions reported during 1955–1965 in the *Wall Street Journal*. Previous acquisitions were considered failures if he found indications that (1) the acquired company did not make a profit within three years, (2) the acquired company was later sold or liquidated, (3) acquired products or processes had to be radically changed in materials or engineering. Using these questionable criteria, he found that one of every six mergers "failed." See "Merger Lemons." Kelley paired 21 companies formed through mergers of significant size with 21 companies in the same respective industries which were not involved in significant mergers. He observed performance for each pair for periods of four years before and four years after each respective combination. He concluded that "the form of investment, external versus internal, does not have a significant impact on profitability, whether judged in terms of market valuation or rate of return." See *The Profitability of Growth Through Merger*. In a study by Kitching the measure of failure or success was whether executives in the buying corporations felt the acquired company had achieved performance equal to the executives' prior expectations. Of 69 mergers 21 were admitted failures by the executives in buying firms. See "Why Do Mergers Miscarry?"

were the dominant type of combination. The findings are at least consistent with the frequent criticism that, on the average, conglomerate mergers offer little potential for economic advantage. However, based on the discussed evidence from other periods, the lack of performance hardly differentiates conglomerate mergers from other types.

But while the record of average performance has remained poor, the apparent motivations for merger activity have changed substantially. Motivations emphasized for early merger activity were promotion, monopoly power, operating economies from vertical and horizontal integration, and psychological influences. Through the "transition period" of the 1920s to the current period of merger activity, we have seen a reduction in each of these motivations except possibly the psychological ones.

With the evolution of antitrust law the early predominance of the large, horizontal, multifirm consolidation has gradually been replaced by the predominance of conglomerate mergers in which a larger firm typically acquires a relatively small one. This transition has to a large extent been possible because of the development of techniques for the management of decentralized, multidivisional corporations. As the character of merger activity has changed, the pursuit of monopoly power has diminished from primary importance to a position of little apparent significance. Also, the "traditional" merger economies argument, regarding large-scale operation and vertical integration, has lost much of its strength. The case for merger economies has been less persuasive where companies with disparate operations are combined. In general those shareholder-oriented motivations given primary attention in previous periods appear to have substantially diminished.

The early consolidations were frequently accompanied by large public securities issues; this is the exception in acquisitions today. The opportunities of the external promoter have thus become limited. At the same time the evolution of securities law has forced exposure of the promoter's activities. With promotional opportunities limited and the activities exposed, the influence of external promotion appears to have greatly diminished. The professional promoter who played a major initiating role in the early consolidations has practically become extinct. The investment banker and the business broker undoubtedly exert an influence on current merger activity, but the primary initiating force in current mergers is provided by corporate managements.

Determination of managerial motivation in pursuing merger activity is difficult. From the evidence on the rather dismal performance provided for the shareholder in the early consolidations, some have inferred that external promoters were seeking personal psychological and financial gain without attention to the economic logic of combinations. Similarly, the below-average performance of merging firms in recent years has led some writers to argue that corporate managements promoting mergers are pursuing psychological and financial gains while the shareholder interest plays a subordinate role. We have argued that the evidence is not necessarily indicative of self-serving management action and that sufficient forces exist to align management interests with those of shareholders to a substantial degree.

As we will later discuss, this seems particularly true for the successful "acquisitive conglomerates." Here the managers are major owners in most cases, and there is no lack of shareholder performance causing us to look elsewhere for motivation. The importance of the psychological drive to build an industrial empire is not to be slighted. However, our decision to study shareholder performance reflects in part our belief that this is the major driving force for acquisitive conglomerates. Moreover, the shareholder performance of acquisitive conglomerates may explain a large amount of merger activity by those who have less successfully attempted to emulate this strategy.

Greater understanding of this motivation demands greater understanding of how the shareholder performance of acquisitive conglomerates has been achieved, which is what the remainder of this study is all about. In terms of the historical development this brings us back to the current argument on sources of performance discussed in the introductory chapter. In the next chapter we will discuss the nature and quality of existing evidence which, either directly or indirectly, is relevant to that argument; that is, evidence regarding relationships between those operating and financial variables affected by acquisitions and resulting performance.

CHAPTER III

Existing Evidence on the Sources
of Acquisitive Conglomerate Performance

In this chapter we discuss evidence provided by previous studies which is relevant to those sources of performance through acquisition identified in the introduction. Structurally, the chapter proceeds sequentially through these various potential sources of performance. At the outset, however, we need to discuss briefly the kinds of evidence we consider relevant and what we may hope to learn from them.

As indicated in the introduction, market values and performance are interrelated for acquisitive conglomerates. If the parent corporation is continually valued more highly than those acquired, each acquisition adds to the earnings per share of the parent and a series of such acquisitions provides a level of per-share performance exceeding that which would be provided by internal growth alone. It is clear that the parent corporation can only maintain its market value advantage if acquired companies increase in market value after the acquisition. The critical question concerns the reasons why this may occur. Our discussion of potential reasons has been divided into two categories: (1) the ability of the parent corporation to improve operating performance in companies acquired, and (2) the immediate financial effects of the combinations.

In the "operating category" we discussed horizontal and vertical scale, better "balance," market power, improvements in the "management process," influence on technologies, products, and markets. The principal questions regarding this category concern the extent to which potential operating changes may lead to improved operating performance for acquired firms. And it is on the relationships between these operating variables and operating performance that we focus attention. We give only minor attention to the remaining question — whether improved operating performance for acquired firms may be expected to increase their market value — where the conceptual argument and empirical evidence is reasonably affirmative and clear.

In the category of "immediate financial effects" we discussed the potential for parent company market value and performance to be mutually supporting in growth through acquisition and the potential for increased market value of acquired firms from increased leverage, increased size, increased diversification, altered accounting treatments, and reduced taxation. Here, where there is no change in operating performance involved, the principal questions concern the relationships between these financial variables and market value.

In general, then, our attention is directed toward evidence regarding the re-

lationships between operating variables and operating performance and the relationships between financial variables and market valuation.

Very little of this evidence is of a "direct" nature. That is, we find few studies
which relate particular types or characteristics of acquisitions or acquisition programs to resulting levels of success. Most of the relevant information takes the
form of "indirect" evidence. We refer to studies which have looked more generally at one or more of those principal operating and financial variables which
may be affected by acquisitions and their relationship to value or performance.
Examples are studies of the relationship between horizontal scale and operating
performance or studies of the relationship between leverage and valuation. From
cross-sectional studies of variables within different firms, insight may be gained
regarding the effects of change in those variables within a given combination.

While this kind of information is clearly relevant, it can answer only half of
what is necessarily a two-part question. We must know (1) how important are
changes in the operating and financial variables for changes in operating performance or market values and (2) to what extent are successful acquisitive
conglomerates causing changes in these variables. The kinds of evidence discussed
immediately above clearly are relevant only to the former question. Any significant insight regarding the second question must wait until characteristics of
the subject companies are examined in later chapters.

At the same time, a negative or "near-negative" answer to the first question,
regarding the importance of changes in particular variables, may suggest areas
less worthy of further attention. It is in this way that the information in the
present chapter is perhaps most useful.

INTERDEPENDENCE OF MARKET VALUE AND PERFORMANCE

As in the introduction, we begin with the "feedback effect" between market
value and per-share performance through acquisition. We find no direct evidence
regarding the importance of this effect for the performance through acquisition
of any company or companies. Indirect evidence, however, suggests the importance of this effect for aggressive acquisition programs.

The question of relevance, as shall be discussed later in more detail, concerns
the strength of the relationship between demonstrated per-share performance and
price-earnings ratios. To the extent that investor expectations and hence price-
earnings ratios are based on demonstrated performance, with little regard for
the manner in which it is achieved, the potential importance of the "feedback
effect" is substantial.

In several regression studies[1] demonstrated per-share performance has been

---

[1] For example, Benishay, "Variability in Earnings-Price Ratios of Corporate Equities";
Gordon, *The Investment, Financing, and Valuation of the Corporation*; Whippern, "Financial
Structure and the Value of the Firm"; Miller and Modigliani, "Cost of Capital to the Electric
Utility Industry."

included as an independent variable to explain either market price or price-earnings ratio. The relationship has consistently been positive and significant. In fact, one of the few relationships involving market price which appears to have gained "general acceptance" is that more rapid rates of demonstrated growth in earnings per share, for a given dividend policy and "all other things the same," will be given higher price-earnings ratios. The regression studies have typically been conducted, however, for fairly settled and uncomplicated industries. To our knowledge such a study has not been conducted for acquisition-minded companies where, as suggested previously, there is some confusion regarding the manner in which demonstrated performance has been achieved. In addition, there have not to our knowledge been studies of the effect on valuation of the type of growth process through which particular levels of performance have been achieved. Nonetheless, the existing evidence would suggest that the "feedback relationship" should be effective in the pursuit of performance through acquisition.

For the effect to be important, acquiring corporations must be pursuing it. That is, acquisitions must be sought which provide immediate increases in per-share earnings. While we shall postpone discussion of this aspect of acquisitive conglomerate behavior until the next chapter, there is some evidence that this is a motivation of more general importance in acquisition activity. This is provided by studies of the timing of aggregate merger activity, typically measured in terms of numbers of corporate disappearances per period.[2] While we have discussed aggregate activity in three major periods or "movements," there appear to be superimposed on these "wide swings" cycles of shorter duration. The studies to which we refer have attempted to correlate the cycles in merger activity with other economic indicators. Consistently, the most positive correlation has been found with measures of the general level of stock market prices. At the same time, the explanations which have been offered for this are less than convincing. Part of the suggested explanation is psychological, which seems plausible. When stock prices are high, expectations are high in general; and people are more likely to take an optimistic outlook toward any proposed transaction. But both Weston and Nelson imply that the issuance of stock for mergers will be financially more advantageous when stock prices are higher. Carried no further, this explanation seems weak. As Nelson recognized in his later study, the cost of funds for merger may not actually be lower in times of relatively high securities prices because expectations and values may increase for buyer and seller alike. If all corporate values moved up and down together in such a way as to maintain their respective proportional relationships, there clearly would be no cost advantage to merger in times of high securities prices. The existence of a cost advantage will depend on disparities in these movements.

There is one type of disparity which seems important. As the "conventional wisdom" of the financial press and some small amount of evidence[3] suggest,

---

[2] See Weston, *The Role of Mergers in the Growth of Large Firms*; Nelson, *Merger Movements in American Industry 1895–1956*; Nelson, "Business Cycle Factors in the Choice Between Internal and External Growth."

[3] Malkiel, "Equity Yields, Growth and the Structure of Share Prices."

"growth stocks" are more volatile than the stocks of companies growing at more "normal" rates; the ratio of price-earnings multiples for "growth stocks" to those for "average" companies is positively related to the general level of stock market prices. Since this kind of disparity occurs with some consistency and since market prices are the primary determinant of share exchange ratios or purchase prices in merger transactions,[4] it will be more desirable for high price-earnings ratio companies to acquire lower price-earnings ratio companies when security prices are at a relatively high level. Thus, the increased merger activity at times of high security prices provides some support for an argument that the majority of acquiring companies are higher growth, higher price-earnings ratio firms, firms which can achieve immediate positive effects on their per-share position through acquisition.

Another possible explanation which links aggregate merger activity to price-earnings ratio differentials concerns the relative sizes of buying and selling companies. It is likely that owners' estimates of value for a smaller company whose securities are not publicly traded do not fluctuate as widely as do the stock prices of a larger, publicly traded corporation. Because of this, the larger company may be able to issue stock, either directly to the smaller company or for cash to be paid to the smaller company, on a more favorable basis when stock prices are relatively high.

While data are not available on the percentage of acquired corporations which do not have publicly traded securities, data on the size of acquiring and acquired corporations are. Butters, Lintner, and Cary[5] found that of 1,990 corporations acquired during the 1940–1947 period, 1,455 or 73% had assets of less than $1 million. During the same period 94% of the acquiring companies had assets exceeding $5 million. The smaller company is of course less likely to have publicly traded securities.

We are suggesting that when the data on aggregate merger activity and its correlation with stock prices are combined with the greater volatility of "growth stocks" and the greater size of acquiring firms, there is some support for the argument that acquiring firms are seeking transactions which will immediately improve their per-share financial position. These, of course, are the kinds of transactions which are required for a mutually supporting relationship between high market values and performance through acquisition. In general, then, there is some indirect evidence that the "feedback relationship" should "work" and a minor amount of evidence that corporations, knowingly or unknowingly, are pursuing it.

---

[4] See Dellenbarger, "A Study of Relative Common Equity Values in Fifty Mergers of Industrial Corporations, 1950–1957." Dellenbarger found a simple correlation coefficient of .95 between the share exchange ratios and the ratios of pre-merger-announcement common stock prices for 50 stock-for-stock merger transactions. The addition of earnings, book values, and dividends as independent variables provided a multiple correlation coefficient of .98.

[5] *Effects of Taxation: Corporate Mergers,* p. 246.

LEVERAGE

The acquisitive conglomerate alters the structure of risk and return for the shareholder. Some have argued that advantages are gained through increased leverage, diversification, and size. The principal question, as we indicated earlier and shall later discuss in more detail, is the extent to which changes in leverage, diversification, and size through acquisition cause changes in the market value of acquired firms.

As in part of the discussion above, the principal sources of information are regression studies of the relationships between market value and other financial variables. Probably more attention has been given to the relationship between market value and leverage than any other question in the area of financial management. The question of general interest is whether there is an optimal capital structure for each particular firm which provides significantly greater market value than other, non-optimal capital structures. Phrased in a different way, it is the same question which is of interest here: To what extent can we expect changes in the leverage of acquired firms, toward more nearly optimal capital structures, to provide increases in market values?

Empirical studies of the relationship between market value and leverage have been hindered by measurement limitations and biases. Such studies have typically been regression analyses on cross-sectional samples within particular industries. Firms in a given industry which choose to employ greater leverage are likely to be those which have lower business risk, higher rates of return, and therefore greater growth, lower capital costs, and higher market prices. It is difficult to "hold everything else the same" in evaluating the effect of leverage on market value. In addition, firms within a given industry typically do not provide a very wide range of leverage. Without extreme values, substantial effects on market prices are not likely to be found. The biases and limitations do not stop with these.[6] The point, however, is that the evidence regarding this relationship is only suggestive.

In addition the evidence is mixed. The "traditional" position, that there are optimal capital structures, was attacked by Modigliani and Miller in their original paper on the subject.[7] They argued that in a taxless and otherwise idealized world, market value is independent of leverage. Further, they provided cross-sectional evidence on the utility and petroleum industries supporting the position that leverage does not affect market values for actual corporations. Given the tax advantages of debt, which Modigliani and Miller later recognized,[8] this evidence

---

[6] For a summary discussion of the theory and the problems of testing it, see Van Horne, *Financial Management and Policy,* Chapter 7, "Capital Structure," pp. 144–177.

[7] "The Cost of Capital, Corporation Finance and the Theory of Investment."

[8] "Corporate Income Taxes and the Cost of Capital: A Correction." This corrected formulation implies that the value of the levered firm should exceed that of the unlevered firm by the tax rate times the value of debt (other things being the same, of course). This would imply, for example, that an unlevered corporation selling at book value with a tax rate of 50%

is surprising. More recent studies have provided evidence supporting arguments for either optimal capital structures or decreasing capital costs over the range of observed values of leverage.

Barges,[9] employing a different measure for leverage than that used by Modigliani and Miller,[10] found evidence of optimal capital structures based on cross-sectional studies of the railroad, department store, and cement industries. Weston,[11] by adding a measure of growth to the independent variables, found decreasing capital costs with leverage for the utility industry. Whippern,[12] using a leverage measure based on the probability of default,[13] found evidence from a multi-industry sample of advantages of debt beyond those provided by the tax deductibility of interest.

Evidence provided by the more recent studies suggests some market value advantage as leverage is increased from zero through some undefined range. We find the evidence sufficiently inconclusive, however, to be unwilling to believe a substantial proportional increase in market value resulting from changes in leverage.[14] The extent to which acquisitive conglomerates have actually changed the capital structures within acquired firms is an open question at this point and, unfortunately, to a large extent shall remain so within this study.

DIVERSIFICATION

Diversification through acquisition may lead to a reduction in the variability of operating earnings if the returns of combining firms are negatively correlated. If investors are risk averse and hindered by market imperfections in structuring combinations of risk and return to meet their particular preferences, we might

---

could increase its total market value 20% by increasing debt to 40% of total capital at book value. The difficulty is that the formulation ignores several factors such as the risk and possible costs of default or foreclosure.

[9] *The Effect of Capital Structure on the Cost of Capital.*

[10] Barges uses a book value measure of leverage because the market value measure employed by Modigliani and Miller implies lower leverage for greater equity valuations. The latter may be caused by lower business risk or greater rates of return on capital, as suggested earlier in the text, providing a source of bias.

[11] "A Test of the Cost of Capital Propositions."

[12] "Financial Structure and the Value of the Firm."

[13] Whippern's measure of leverage is the ratio of interest to mean operating earnings diminished by two standard deviations. This provides a measure of leverage relative to "debt capacity" as determined by rate of return on capital and variability.

[14] Gordon provides some estimates of this using his theoretically derived equation for market price and empirically determined parameter values. His formulation implies the relationship between leverage and market value depends on the rate of return on invested capital, which is reasonable. For rates of return "typical" for his sample of companies, he suggests increases in market value per share of 17% to 33% for increases in leverage from 0% to 50% of total capital at book value (see *The Investment, Financing, and Valuation of the Corporation,* pp. 189–193). We are skeptical, however, regarding Gordon's avoidance of those measurement biases discussed in the text. Also, we are afraid he is extrapolating beyond the range of data values which were of principal importance in determining the parameter values for his equation.

expect such reduced variability to be accorded higher market values. At the same time, some have argued that the achievement of such gains is illusory.[15]

Given the mobility of the investor in the modern capital market, diversification may be achieved by portfolio adjustments and need not require corporate combinations. Since any desired combination of ownership may be achieved by the individual, there will be no reduction in shareholder risk, no reduction in capitalization rate, and hence no increase in value due to the diversifying aspect of a merger. Indeed, it is argued that there may be a reduction in value due to corporate diversification through merger. Before a combination, firms may be owned in proportions meeting various individual preferences; afterwards they must be owned in a fixed proportion. This may reduce demand for the securities and hence their value.

The evidence again is mixed. Regression studies of the determinants of market value consistently indicate a significant negative relationship with the variability of either operating returns or the returns to equity.[16] This of course suggests that, to the extent that diversification through acquisition reduces such variability, market value enhancement will result. On the other hand, there is the inescapable fact that closed-end investment companies rather consistently sell below net asset values (market values of portfolio securities).[17] Further, companies such as Ling-Temco-Vought convinced quite a few conglomerate watchers that significant market value advantages resulted from creating separate public ownership for major operating divisions.[18] The mixed evidence causes us to be skeptical that any substantial increase in market value may be expected, based only on the diversification aspects of acquisitions. This negative conclusion is perhaps a fortunate one in terms of our understanding of important sources of performance, for we do not know and will not know the extent to which the diversification of acquisitive conglomerates has reduced the variability of operating returns for combining companies. In fact, since many acquisitions were previously privately held firms, we are unable to think of a meaningful way in which this could be determined.

---

[15] See, for example, Alberts, "Profitability of Growth by Merger." For a carefully developed theoretical argument supporting this position, see Myers, "A Time-State-Preference Model of Security Valuation."

[16] See, in particular, Arditti, "Risk and the Required Return on Equity." This provides impressive evidence on the relationship between required returns on equity (inversely related to market prices) and measures of variability. Using the mean return on equity over 1946–1963 for all corporations comprising the Standard and Poors' Composite Index as the dependent variable, Arditti finds significant relationships with variance (positive relationship) and positive skewness (negative relationship). Both of these relationships are of course as predicted by the mathematical expression for investor risk aversion which decreases with wealth. Other studies which have suggested a significant relationship between market values and variability include Benishay, "Variability in Earnings-Price Ratios of Corporate Entities," and Gordon, *The Investment, Financing, and Valuation of the Corporation.*

[17] For example, on June 30, 1966, nine of the ten largest diversified, closed-end investment companies were selling at a discount. The average discount was 14.5%. See U.S. House, *Report of the Securities and Exchange Commission on the Public Policy Implications of Investment Company Growth,* p. 44.

[18] See, for example, Cossaboom, "Segmental Financing of Corporate Conglomerates."

Size

Acquisition creates a firm of larger size. Increased size may provide greater resistance to failure, greater marketability of securities, more accessible and cheaper sources of financing.[19] Here, the evidence is more consistent than it is for leverage or diversification. Statistical studies of market value which have attempted to determine the effect of size, other things being the same, have found a significant, positive relationship.[20] Furthermore, studies of borrowing and new issue costs have found significant reductions as size is increased beyond the smallest of firms.[21] Finally, there is evidence that in the typical merger in recent years, the acquired firm is substantially smaller than the acquirer and therefore becomes part of a firm several times its pre-acquisition size.[22]

The extent to which such increases in size provide greater market values for acquired firms is a more difficult question. Gordon's model implies that a fivefold increase in size should provide an increase in market value of approximately 15%; a thirtyfold increase in size, an increase in market value of 25%.[23] On the other hand, Miller and Modigliani found a significant but "virtually negligible contribution of size to value." The largest firm in their sample had assets on the order of 100 times the smallest. Yet, they found "the difference in valuation, other things being equal, between a firm of indefinitely large size and that of mean size in our sample turns out to be on the order of 1% or 2% of total market value." [24] This may simply indicate that size is of less importance in a regulated industry such as the electric utilities studied by Miller and Modigliani than in industries such as food and machinery studied by Gordon. We consider the

---

[19] The possible operating advantages of greater size are discussed later in this chapter.

[20] See the studies of Benishay, Gordon, Whippern, Miller and Modigliani ("Cost of Capital to the Electric Utility Industry") ; all cited earlier.

[21] A comprehensive discussion is provided in U.S. Board of Governors of the Federal Reserve System, *Financing Small Business, Parts 1 and 2.* For example, in 1957 the average interest rate charged by Federal Reserve System member banks on business loans for borrowers with less than $50,000 in total assets was 6.5%. This average rate decreased steadily for firms of increasing size to 4.1% for borrowers having greater than $100 million in assets (p. 389). For public issues of securities the difference is more striking. Flotation costs on debt issues registered with the SEC for the years 1951–1955 decreased from 12% on issues of approximately $500,000 to approximately 1% for issues of $50 million and over. Flotation costs for common stock during the same period decreased from 27% for issues of approximately $250,000 to approximately 5% for issues of $15 million and over (p. 195).

[22] In addition to the evidence discussed earlier from Butters, Lintner, and Cary, more recent evidence is provided by the FTC for their large merger series covering acquisitions with assets exceeding $10 million. In 1967, 74% of these acquired firms had assets of $10–$50 million. On the other hand, 80% of the acquiring firms had assets exceeding $50 million. Data from "Merger Activity Set New Record Last Year, FTC Reports," News Release from the Federal Trade Commission, March 18, 1968.

[23] *The Investment, Financing, and Valuation of the Corporation,* p. 195. Gordon's measure of size is the logarithm of noncurrent assets plus working capital.

[24] "Cost of Capital to the Electric Utility Industry," p. 373.

Miller-Modigliani study to have been a careful one, however, and its findings influence us toward the belief that the market value effects of increased size, while significant, are smaller in percentage terms than Gordon's study would indicate.

TAXATION

Differences in position with respect to taxation of two firms or their owners provide another source of possible increase in value without operating change.[25] Estate taxation appears to be the most frequent object of discussion. When one individual has a major position in a corporation which has no market for its securities, when no buyer for his ownership can be found, and when the owner's other assets are small in comparison with the value of this equity position, death of the individual might require a forced sale or liquidation of the firm in order to pay estate taxes. The value of such an individual's equity is reduced from his point of view because of his position. The value of such a firm as a going concern to a larger corporation may be sufficiently greater that an acquisition can be arranged on favorable terms to both parties.

Other reasons for merger may be provided by the differential between income and capital gains taxation and by the accumulated earnings tax.[26] An individual who has built a corporation of some size and wishes to enjoy the benefits of his wealth may find it preferable to sell and be taxed at capital gains rates rather than receive dividends to be taxed at income tax rates. A public issue may provide a solution to this situation, and to the estate tax problem as well, but as we have discussed, the cost of such an issue will be great unless the firm is large. The accumulated earnings tax applies to profits retained beyond the reasonable needs of the business; the income tax on dividends cannot be avoided simply by holding funds within the corporation. A company having a need for investible funds may be able to acquire on a mutually advantageous basis a firm which faces the possibility of the accumulated earnings tax.

Finally, provided that certain requirements are met,[27] the tax loss carryover of one firm may be offset against the future profits of another firm with which it merges. If the carryover is large, this may significantly enhance the desirability of a merger.

Butters, Lintner, and Cary conducted field interviews concerning more than 100 merger transactions occurring between 1940 and 1947. Mergers were classified in two groups: (1) those in which taxes provided one of the major sources of

[25] See Butters, Lintner and Cary; Sommers, "Estate Taxes and Business Mergers: The Effects of Estate Taxes on Business Structure and Practice in the United States"; Butters, "Taxation, Incentives and Financial Capacity."

[26] The accumulated earnings tax is perhaps better known as the "section 102 surtax," having originally been described in that section in the *Internal Revenue Code of 1939*. In the *Internal Revenue Code of 1954* it is covered in sections 531 through 536.

[27] The primary ones are that the transaction be a tax-free exchange and that the merger is not carried out for the purpose of taking advantage of this tax provision. Sections 269, 381, and 382 of the *Internal Revenue Code of 1954* are relevant.

motivation; (2) those in which taxes were of little or no importance. Their detailed findings led them to estimate "that taxes were of major importance for something less than one-tenth of the total number of mergers of manufacturing and mining companies reported in the financial manuals for the years 1940 through 1947." They concluded that "the number of businesses actually sold for tax reasons appears to be considerably smaller than is frequently asserted." [28]

In those situations where taxation does provide an important reason for merger it does not necessarily follow that substantial advantage is gained by the buyer. In the "sellers' market" of recent years it is unlikely that the owner with longer term estate plans in mind is going to sell at a "bargain price." On the other hand, the tax advantage to be derived from loss situations would appear more substantial. The question here is whether acquisitive conglomerates seek such transactions. The information to be examined in the next chapter indicates that they usually do not.

FINANCIAL ACCOUNTING

Most difficult to deal with are potential advantages which result from the flexibility permitted in financial accounting. There is no lack of examples of recent situations where, either because of the accounting treatment selected for the combination or because of changes in post-acquisition accounting for certain revenue or expense items, reported earnings appear more favorable than would otherwise have been the case. [29] The important question, however, is whether the investing public is "fooled," whether they attach greater value to combining firms because of such changes in financial accounting practices. Our guess is that to some extent they do. However, we know of no evidence that they do or of any studies which have even attempted to provide any. A small amount of information regarding the practices of two companies will be given later. But the general importance of financial accounting practices for acquisitive conglomerate performance unfortunately will remain an important unknown. We choose not to pursue it further than we do because of (1) our *opinion* that other factors are of greater importance and (2) our reluctance to believe that convincing evidence can be developed on the relationship between accounting practices and market values.

At this point we have covered each of the "immediate financial effects" discussed in the introduction. Sorting out the more important ones is a difficult and hazardous process given the sparseness and inclusiveness of the relevant evidence. Nonetheless, it is our judgment that the potentially most important and least well understood of these effects is the "feedback relationship" between market value and performance through acquisition. Accordingly, it is this relationship that will be given greatest attention in coming chapters. Of the others, the evidence is perhaps most consistent regarding the market value (and hence perform-

---

[28] *Effects of Taxation: Corporate Mergers,* quotes from pp. 17 and 9 respectively.

[29] See those references cited in this connection in the introduction.

ance through acquisition) advantages of increased size. Tax reduction could be important if pursued, but we will later argue that it is not. The potentially important area on which there is the least meaningful evidence is the area of financial accounting practices; unfortunately, we cannot significantly improve that situation.

OPERATING IMPROVEMENT THROUGH ACQUISITION

If the existing evidence is sparse and inclusive regarding the relative importance of the different "financial effects" in performance through acquisition, it is even more so regarding the relative importance of the different sources of improved operating performance. Generally indicative and therefore of some relevance are the data already discussed regarding the success which has, on the average, been achieved in growth through acquisition. If those possible sources of improved operating performance had collectively worked to provide substantially improved operations within the average acquisition, we would not have the dismal record of performance that has in general resulted. If the exceptional performance of acquisitive conglomerates has resulted from better operating performance within acquired companies, some of the possible sources of improved operations have been used to much greater advantage than has generally been the case. Discussion of the existing evidence, however meager, on these potential sources of advantage provides some insight regarding where to "look" in our more detailed examination of acquisitive conglomerates.

The acquisitions of those companies in which we are interested are predominantly of the conglomerate variety; they lead to new products and new markets. There has been much criticism that there is little opportunity for economic advantage in such combinations.[30] Evidence of any generalized variety seems to be lacking. However, there is a small amount of indirect evidence which argues against this criticism. The firm that grows through conglomerate merger becomes a large, diversified firm. If this is less economically advantageous than becoming a large company with greater horizontal or vertical scale, we would expect large diversified firms to perform significantly less well than large firms operating in one or a few product-market areas. The available evidence indicates that there

---

[30] Blair has suggested that: "Of all types of merger activity conglomerate acquisitions have the least claim to promoting efficiency in the economic sense. The lower costs that might result in a horizontal acquisition from the pooling of skills and know-how gained in the production of the same product from different facilities are absent. Likewise the conglomerate acquisition affords little opportunity for the closing down of the less efficient facilities and the centralization of production in the more efficient. Similarly, the gains in a vertical acquisition which might result from the more logical and orderly arrangement of facilities employed in the successive stages of a continuous production process are not present. Because what is involved is the production of unrelated products the conglomerate acquisition provides few opportunities for the securing of economic efficiency. . . ." Quoted from "The Conglomerate Merger in Economics and Law," in U.S. Senate Hearings, *Economic Concentration*, Part 3, *Concentration, Invention, and Innovation*, pp. 1405–6.

is no significant difference between the average performance of large firms with varying degrees of diversification.[31]

At the same time, there have been arguments which counter the criticism of conglomerate mergers on another front. Even in the conglomerate merger, it is suggested, significant opportunities typically exist for improved efficiency through operating integration.[32] That is, in the "typical" conglomerate merger we may find some horizontal, vertical, or complementary aspects.

HORIZONTAL SCALE

Frequently discussed economies of large-scale production include: (1) reduced raw material purchase costs and inventory costs due to the ability to order larger quantities on a more frequent basis; (2) reduced production costs due to the ability to utilize more automated processes and more specialized functions; (3) reduced distribution and selling costs due to increased volume and increased geographical concentration. Such economies imply declining long-run average costs as a result of the increasing output of a homogeneous product. Within some range this is unquestionably representative of most production costs, and in some highly automated industries the declining curve may persist over a large range of possible output. However, what happens after a level of output is reached which allows a company to attain a viable position is less certain. It is frequently assumed that long-run average costs continue to decline over some range of output and then begin to rise as a result of diseconomies of scale caused primarily by administrative inefficiencies in the large organization. Thus there is thought to be an optimum size of plant or firm for each homogeneous product where average unit costs will be at a minimum.[33]

A substantial amount of work has been done over the years in the attempt to determine the extent of horizontal scale advantages.[34] Despite substantial meas-

---

[31] See Gort, *Diversification and Integration in American Industry*; Gort, "Diversification, Mergers and Profits"; O'Hanlon, "The Odd News about Conglomerates."

[32] Donald F. Turner, during his tenure as head of the Antitrust Division of the Department of Justice, wrote: "Conglomerate acquisitions involving no significant economic relationships have been relatively infrequent as compared to those that 'fit' the operations of the acquirer in some tangible respect. Companies looking for new lines of business tend to buy into those fields with which they have at least some degree of familiarity, and where economies and efficiencies from assimilation are at least possible." From "Conglomerate Mergers and Section 7 of the Clayton Act," p. 1322. Also, it may be noted from Table 2.2 that of the 71% of mergers in the "conglomerate" category during the 1960–1964 period, only 11.2% are in the "unrelated" category. By the FTC definition these are the mergers involving "companies that do not have any buyer-seller relationships nor are they functionally related in manufacturing or distribution."

[33] For a discussion of the development of the theory of scale economies see, for example, Blair, "Does Large Scale Enterprise Result in Lower Costs?"

[34] See: U.S. Temporary National Economic Committee, *Relative Efficiency of Large, Medium-Sized, and Small Business*; Blair, "The Relation Between Size and Efficiency of Business"; Chenery, "Engineering Production Functions"; Smith, "Survey of the Empirical Evidence on Economies of Scale"; Stigler, "The Economies of Scale"; Moore, "Economies of Scale: Some Statistical Evidence."

urement problems[35] and a variety of approaches to such measurement,[36] the conclusions of various studies are, at a high level of generality, quite similar. There are significant improvements in operating efficiency as size of plant or size of firm increases from "very small" to some "intermediate" level, beyond which there are not further significant improvements. Decreases in efficiency have been observed for firms of very large size in some industries and not in others.[37]

Granted, however, that at least to some extent economies of large-scale production exist, it is questionable whether they can be fully realized through merger. In the conglomerate combination with substantial horizontal aspects the immediate result is more plants rather than larger plants. Increased market position may permit subsequent expansion in one location on a larger scale. But the immediate advantages of horizontal combinations must be sought in the purchasing, distribution, and administration functions. There has been substantial argument and a small amount of evidence that there are significant scale advantages to be achieved in such areas.[38] Some of these advantages, however, appear to result from greater corporate size rather than greater product scale.

In particular, the advantage of scale in administration, or in corporate level management and staff functions, seems to be the one "horizontal aspect" common to any merger, conglomerate or otherwise. Product diversification should not prevent the large corporation from being able to effectively employ more competent and more highly specialized management and staff personnel. To the extent that this is an important advantage, we would expect corporations of large size generally to be more profitable than small corporations. There is some evidence to that effect.[39] It is difficult to say, however, whether this is primarily the result of management and staff advantages or a combination of reasons.[40]

---

[35] See Smith, *op. cit.*, regarding difficulties caused by (1) the nonhomogeneous output of plants and firms; (2) the inevitable operation of different plants and firms at different levels of capacity; (3) differences in technology caused by factors other than size.

[36] In the references cited above we find scale measured by physical output, revenues, and capital employed; efficiency measured by actual unit costs, engineering estimates of unit costs, return on investment, and rate of growth or "survival."

[37] Stigler in "The Economies of Scale," for example, found evidence of decreased efficiency for very large sized firms in 29 of 48 industries studied.

[38] In Blair, "Does Large-Scale Enterprise Result in Lower Costs?", costs for different size classes are broken down into various expense categories for four industries: bread; rubber tires; mixed fertilizer; superphosphate. Blair found some evidence that raw material costs and general and administrative expenses, both expressed in terms of units of output, declined from the smallest to the largest size class of firms.

[39] The classic study is Crum's *Corporate Size and Earning Power*. Crum examined 10 size classifications within 12 manufacturing industries for a six-year period. For all industries the combined rate of return on equity rose consistently with increasing size. The bulk of the increase in return occurred with increase in size up to $1 million in equity, a size-range where production-scale economies are likely to be most important. However, for the larger size classifications, which include multiplant and somewhat diversified firms, there may be evidence of administrative economies.

[40] Such as market power and cheaper sources of financing.

VERTICAL INTEGRATION

The alleged advantages of vertical integration result from the elimination of functions at a market interface. When the transfer of materials from one stage of production to the next is changed through vertical combination, from an external market transaction to an internal transaction, certain functions are no longer required. The competitive selling and buying process entails costs of advertising, sales promotion, packaging, bidding, salesmen, and purchasing agents. Credit investigations must be conducted and bad debt losses incurred. Vertical combination eliminates these costs at the interface where integration is achieved. Further, transportation and inventory costs may be reduced because of more efficient scheduling of production and transfer. Stability and security can be achieved in that the second stage of production has an assured source of supply, the first an assured market.

As with horizontal combination, vertical combination cannot achieve all the advantages of vertical internal expansion. Proximate geographical location of successive steps in the production process may eliminate entirely certain transportation costs, and in some industries certain types of reprocessing may be avoided.[41] Still, it would appear that the more important advantages may be achieved through merger.

The unfortunate and surprising thing is that, to our knowledge, there is no meaningful evidence regarding the extent of efficiencies to be attained through vertical integration. And indeed it seems to us that such efficiencies would be difficult to demonstrate empirically.[42] The conceptual argument is sufficiently convincing to conclude that some advantage exists; the magnitude of such advantages appear unknown.

BALANCE

Perhaps more likely than the existence of substantial horizontal or vertical relationships in acquisitions of the acquisitive conglomerate is the existence of resources that are in some way "complementary." In particular, there may be

---

[41] An example of the latter which has been frequently cited is the saving in reheating derived from integration of steel ingot production and rolling mills. See, for example, Estes, "Vertical Integration in the Steel Industry."

[42] Part of a vertically integrated firm could not reasonably be compared with a producer at one level because of the arbitrary nature of fixed cost allocation and, possibly, of transfer price determination within the integrated firm. Thus, unit costs of the vertically integrated producer would have to be compared with those of a series of nonintegrated firms covering the same stages of production. Since this requirement is in addition to problems of the same sort that exist in measuring horizontal scale economies, the task approaches impossibility.

specialized resources within one firm which provide an important ingredient for the future progress of the other.[43]

The additional resources required by an expanding firm are determined to a large extent by the resources it presently employs. A particular mix of intellectual and physical resources working in combination over time results in a specialized complex of productive capabilities. Internal developments or changes in the external environment may reveal paths for expansion where the firm's resources provide special competitive advantages. Yet it is likely that some additional specialized resource or resources are needed to move in the chosen direction of expansion; that is, the firm is not in a balanced position for this expansion. Another firm may hold needed resources which are either unique or which would take a substantial amount of time to develop. In either case, the existing competitive advantage of the first firm creates an opportunity cost of waiting to develop the needed specialized resources or of ignoring this favored direction of expansion because of unique resources held by others. Because of this opportunity cost, such specialized or unique resources may be of greater value to the expanding firm than to the firm which now holds them, and an acquisition may be economically justified.

The process of unbalanced expansion and the opportunity cost of allowing it to remain unbalanced seem to underlie many of the reasons frequently suggested for acquisitions. Penrose gives a long list of examples of resources which may block the expansion path of one firm when they are under the control of another and thus may lead to acquisition: "patent protection of products, equipment, or productive processes; trade names, brands, and other protected methods of differentiating otherwise similar products and thus of holding consumers' loyalty; private control of nonreproducible factors of production such as particular sites of land and certain mineral deposits; knowledge of processes which can be kept secret; occasionally even possession of the services of especially gifted, trained, or experienced individuals." [44] Another study provides examples of firms which have bought a sales organization or distribution system.[45] Butters, Lintner, and Cary found that the "most frequently mentioned [reasons for acquisition] were the desire to acquire a new product, new plant capacity, or a new production organization. One or the other of these reasons was important in well over half the acquisitions." [46]

Also, it is the problem of unbalanced resources which appears to justify the frequently suggested motive in acquisitions of "buying time." [47] However, the

---

[43] This argument is taken largely from Penrose, *The Theory of the Growth of the Firm,* in particular, Chapter V, "Inherited Resources and the Direction of Expansion," and Chapter VIII, "Expansion Through Acquisition and Merger."

[44] *Ibid.,* p. 169.

[45] Scharf, *Techniques for Buying, Selling and Merging Businesses,* p. 7.

[46] *Op. cit.,* p. 225.

[47] Thus Butters, Lintner, and Cary suggest: "Another advantage of expanding by means of a merger is that the same results can be accomplished with much greater speed and certainty by mergers than by direct action. It takes time to build a new plant and even more time to develop and merchandise a new product, but a merger can be negotiated very quickly. Frequently, time is of the essence, or is considered to be so." *Op. cit.,* p. 21.

simple statement that a firm is "buying time" does not seem sufficient as an economic justification for a merger. Unless the resources of a company complement those of a potential acquirer in such a way as to enhance their combined future returns, it is difficult to understand the justification for "buying time." If in fact an acquisition balances the resource position of the acquirer, allowing it to move ahead and enhancing the value of existing resources, this enhanced value justifies "buying time" through acquisition.

Where complementary resources provide needed "balance" we would expect the advantages to be substantial. In most of the situations described above such balance would be achieved through combining major parts of the operations of merging firms (e.g., a marketing organization with a production facility). However, where specialized resources take the form of managerial or technical expertise, advantages would be realized without significant operating integration. Viewed in this way, the influences without operating integration, to be discussed later, are simply a subset within the process of providing the needed balance of specialized resources.

MARKET POWER

The company which joins the acquisitive conglomerate may enter an environment which provides increased market power. It has been suggested that the large conglomerate corporation (1) is capable of cutting prices in particular markets or on particular products for periods of substantial duration to enhance its market position, (2) can afford to pay more for specialized factors, (3) may receive favorable discriminatory treatment from suppliers, (4) may create tie-in selling and exclusive dealing arrangements, (5) may cooperate with its equals to avoid retaliation while aggressively competing with smaller firms, and (6) may engage in reciprocal exchanges of favors with other large firms providing mutual advantages.[48]

Particular attention has been given the first factor listed above. John M. Blair has suggested that "particularly suited to the conglomerate and particularly destructive to competition is the practice of, in effect, subsidizing the sale of some products at abnormally low prices by monopoly profits made on others."[49] It is difficult to understand, however, why a firm would want to subsidize any of its products or markets indefinitely. If lower pricing is intended to drive competitors from the market so that monopoly profits can subsequently be realized, then such action can be understood, but this clearly constitutes a case of illegal predatory pricing. Donald F. Turner has indicated that predatory pricing is not, in fact, frequently encountered.

> It appears to many to be obvious that the large firm, cushioned by substantial profits from its other lines, will be strongly if not irresistibly tempted to absorb the temporary losses of predatory pricing in order to reap the supposedly greater rewards

---

[48] This is the argument of Edwards in "Conglomerate Bigness as a Source of Power."
[49] "The Conglomerate Merger in Economics and Law," p. 1412.

of monopoly profits when its hapless rivals have been driven out of all or a good share of the market. Nevertheless, the belief that predatory pricing is a likely consequence of conglomerate size, and hence of conglomerate merger, is wholly unverified by any careful studies; research and analysis suggest that in all likelihood this belief is just wrong. . . . The infrequency of predatory pricing is suggested, though of course not proved, by the paucity of antitrust cases in which the offense has even arguably been proved. The leading cases are old, and of the few recent decisions, most have been relatively small firms.[50]

The issue of possible advantage from differential pricing is not, however, so easily resolved as this particular statement by Turner may imply. A large firm may be able to achieve an overall profit goal while adjusting margins on different products and in different markets to best meet each competitive situation. Such a firm might achieve an advantage in this way while selling above costs in all markets. The small firm frequently must rely on a particular product or a particular market for its profitability and survival.

In testimony before the Subcommittee on Antitrust and Monopoly, Donald F. Turner[51] defended the right of the large firm to engage in differential pricing. Differential pricing only becomes predatory and thus illegal when it meets the definition employed by the Department of Justice; the seller must be pricing below cost with the intent of driving competitors from the market. The question of when this definition applies, or when differential pricing may be considered predatory, is a complex one. It is difficult to distinguish predatory pricing from aggressive but healthy competition, which presumably is what we are striving to protect. The Department of Justice apparently feels it is necessary to preserve a considerable amount of pricing flexibility; an overly zealous attack on low prices, Turner suggests, would clearly have anticompetitive effects.

Whether the flexibility of the large firm to adjust prices differentially provides a substantial advantage for acquisitive conglomerates, or whether any of the alleged elements of conglomerate market power provide substantial advantage, are questions for which there is unfortunately no convincing evidence. One argument against such advantages is that their achievement generally requires a coordinated effort by the parent corporation. That is, they cannot be achieved effectively under a philosophy of decentralized management responsibility and authority. Since this is the prevailing type of management system within acquisitive conglomerates,[52] we suggest that market power advantages are not likely to be of substantial importance.

IMPROVEMENT IN OPERATING PERFORMANCE WITHOUT INTEGRATION

To a greater or lesser degree the potential operating advantages of merger discussed above require the integration of operations of combining firms. We would

---

[50] "Conglomerate Mergers and Section 7 of the Clayton Act," p. 1339.

[51] U.S. Senate Hearings, *Dual Distribution,* Part 2, pp. 271–292.

[52] Information to support this statement is discussed in the next chapter.

expect this to be generally feasible in the case of some common management and staff functions. However, it will be argued later that more substantial integration of combining firms is, for acquisitive conglomerates at least, more the exception than the rule. An important question, therefore, concerns what we may learn from other studies regarding the potential for one company to influence the operations of another while allowing it to remain a largely separate operating entity.

In the introduction we discussed the kinds of resources which may be easily transferred across the organizational boundaries of an acquired corporation: knowledge, expertise, personnel, funds. These may influence the technology, products, and markets of the acquired firm. They may influence the nature of the "management process" within the acquired firm.

The provision of needed funds is a relatively straightforward and readily understood process. It is easy to see that it may play an important role in some mergers, and one study of recent mergers concludes that it is the most important advantage.[53] On the other hand, it will be concluded that for the acquisitive conglomerates it is the knowledge, the expertise, the personnel, or in general the specialized human resources which play the more important role. Regarding the nature and significance of these influences, sometimes discussed under the rubric of "better management," we learn surprising little from existing studies.

All too often, it seems, studies of merger activity have ignored the power and importance of the human element, the quality of managerial and technical expertise. Emphasis has been placed on other factors of production. These factors are viewed as inflexible quantities whose possible interactions are both known and predetermined. Thus, a merger may affect efficiency if it changes the conditions which govern these interactions.

This approach is readily understandable; it may be considered a natural outgrowth of the economic theory of the firm. While there is no general agreement on precisely what this theory is, certain elements are commonly included.[54] The firm is assumed to have the objective of maximizing net revenue, given externally determined price-quantity relations for inputs and outputs and a technologically determined production function. The production function expresses a relation between inputs and their corresponding outputs and is determined by physical conditions within the firm. At equilibrium the firm will be maximizing net revenue by combining a mix of inputs to provide a mix of outputs, both of which are optimal, given the price-quantity and production relations.

In the analysis of operating economies created through merger the discussion has often explored those physical characteristics of the combination which will alter the production function so that unit costs of outputs may be reduced. Management and technical personnel are inherently assumed to be operating within their constraints in an optimal manner before and after the merger. In effect, the variety and quality of specialized individual effort are omitted from the resource picture, and other resources or inputs have values which are predetermined by their prices and technologically determined interrelationships.

---

[53] Kitching, "Why Do Mergers Miscarry?"

[54] See the discussion of Cyert and March, *A Behavioral Theory of the Firm,* Chapter 2, "Antecedents to the Behavioral Theory of the Firm."

Some of the more recent theoretical discussions of the firm recognize, however, the degree of flexibility which exists within the corporate environment and the degree of influence which may be provided by the managerial element.[55] A given demand schedule may be influenced internally, and through various combinations of resources, possibilities may exist for producing to meet a variety of different demand schedules. The knowledge, judgment, and aggressiveness of management personnel, and the creativeness of technical personnel, as expressed through their effect on the manner in which resources are combined, may have a dramatic impact on the cost of and demand for the firm's output and hence on its profitability and growth.

While the possible effect of changing the quality of management on value in mergers has too often been ignored, it has occasionally been stressed. For example, in Livermore's attempted defense of combinations in the first merger period he states:

> An extraordinary number of successes among these companies were the result of astute business leadership, not of monopoly power or "unfair" tactics toward competitors. This striking change in the leadership of a large proportion of the mergers, bringing with it substantial and relatively stable points, has received almost no attention.[56]

A theory of mergers based on different qualities of management is provided by Manne.[57] His fundamental premise is that the firm with inefficient management will exhibit lower profitability and growth than others in its industry and that this will be reflected in a relatively lower market price for the firm's shares. In this way market price per share reflects not only the extent of managerial inefficiency but the potential capital gain which might be achieved with improved management. If this is important, we should expect less profitable firms to be more frequently acquired. To a small extent this appears to have been true.[58]

Hale and Hale,[59] in a questionnaire survey on merger motivations, found that 35% of the responding acquirers had based their decision, in part, on the belief that better management of the acquired company would increase profits. Kilmer[60]

---

[55] See in particular Penrose, *op. cit.;* Marris, *The Economic Theory of Managerial Capitalism;* and Cyert and March, *op. cit.*

[56] "The Success of Industrial Mergers," p. 70.

[57] "Mergers and the Market for Corporate Control."

[58] The Federal Trade Commission has collected data regarding the rate of return on equity in the year prior to acquisition for 165 large corporations acquired during the 1951–1963 period. From their data the average rate of return for these firms was calculated to be 8.2%. The average rate of return for all manufacturing firms during this same period was 10.0%. FTC data from testimony of Willard F. Mueller, U.S. Senate Hearings, *Economic Concentration,* Part 2, p. 129. Data on average rates of return calculated from issues of *Quarterly Financial Report for Manufacturing Corporations.*

[59] "More on Mergers." Questionnaires were sent to acquirers in all mergers listed in the *Wall Street Journal* between January 1960 and September 1961. Responses were received from approximately one-third (136) of the firms addressed. "Better management," however, was only one of a large number of possible motivations about which acquiring companies were queried in this study so that its overall significance is unclear.

[60] "Growth by Acquisition, Some Guidelines for Success."

studied the experience of ten multi-industry companies that relied on acquisition for a major part of their growth over a ten-year period. He concluded that those which had achieved success in shareholder terms "do far more than just invest in attractive businesses; they move in and manage them with vigor and imagination." Some examples are discussed but with little detail.

Somewhat more detail is provided in the study of recent merger activity by Kitching.[61] Information was obtained on 69 acquisitions made by an apparently "random" sample of 20 acquirers. For those where information on integration was obtained, 74% either remained "autonomous" or reported to a group executive; that is, they were not "merged" in an operating sense. Executives in the acquiring firms rated a specified list of possible merger advantages in terms of both financial results and ease of achievement. Rated first on both counts was the provision of funds for the acquired firm. Rated only on ease of achievement, the next most important advantages were improvement in managerial motivation and improvement in operational efficiency through centralized staff functions. Then in decreasing order were marketing, technology (including R&D), and production. For the 31 of the 69 acquisitions classified as "conglomerate," the ranking was the same except that "technology" moved to last place. The curious thing is that Kitching fails to consider that potential advantage we find most important: change in the management process within acquired firms.

SUMMARY ON THE EVIDENCE ON SOURCES OF PERFORMANCE

We have examined evidence relevant to performance through acquisition in an attempt to gain insight regarding those sources which seem potentially more important for acquisitive conglomerates and therefore more worthy of detailed attention.

In the area of "immediate financial effects" the evidence seems to imply that potentially most important is the interdependence of market value and performance through acquisition. Of the others, the evidence is most consistent regarding the market value advantages of size. Advantages resulting from the flexibility of financial accounting are, and to a large extent shall remain in this study, an important unknown.

In the area of sources of operating improvement, there appear to be some potential advantages from the vertical, horizontal, and "balancing" aspects of conglomerate acquisitions, to the extent that there is the integration required to achieve them. To the extent that there is little integration, we may expect only the advantages of scale in management and staff functions. The possibilities for influence without operating integration appear more important. Unfortunately, there is little detailed evidence regarding their nature or significance.

---

[61] "Why Do Mergers Miscarry?"

CHAPTER IV

Characteristics of the Population
of Acquisitive Conglomerates

In the preliminary analysis of the two preceding chapters we have developed historical background and examined existing evidence regarding the activities and performance of acquisitive conglomerates. We now begin to deal more directly with this group of companies.

The general objective in this chapter is to look at the characteristics of these companies in an effort to extend our preliminary conclusions about their performance and to suggest a framework for more detailed investigation. In more specific terms there are three objectives. First, aside from the brief discussion in the opening chapter, not much information has been provided about the companies that we are trying to understand. Is there really a significant segment of the corporate world that has achieved impressive performance through aggressive diversified acquisition? How is a company identified that is an "acquisitive conglomerate" from one that is not? What are the characteristics, financial and otherwise, that distinguish such a company from the "average" corporation or from the corporation oriented toward performance through "internal growth"?

Second, we will argue that members of the "acquisitive conglomerate population" have some important similarities. If a company meets the established criteria for aggressive acquisition, diversification, and performance, it is very likely to have other characteristics meaningful for what we may and may not expect it to accomplish.

Third, we attempt to learn something of the way these firms are valued. As will be discussed in detail, the more the investor focuses on per-share performance and the less attention he pays to the manner in which it is achieved, the more important becomes the interdependence of value and performance in high-expansion-rate strategies of corporate growth, such as growth through aggressive acquisition. The nature of market price determination is therefore of prime importance for acquisitive conglomerates.

An Operational Definition

At the outset we defined the successful acquisitive conglomerate as a corporation having three characteristics: (1) aggressive acquisition, (2) diversification, and (3) performance. At this level of generality it is impossible to say which corporations meet these criteria and which do not. In order to identify a group of companies to be studied, the definition had to be made "operational." We had to be able to examine characteristics of a corporation's growth over a specified period, compare these characteristics with some well-specified criteria, and include the corporation as a member of the "population" if the criteria were met.

First, we chose the period 1962–1967, which provided five items of data on annual rates of change and six items of data on balance sheet and income figures. Second, we established some "significance" criteria: (1) a minimum of $10 million in annual sales in 1967; (2) a minimum of three full years under the management group pursuing the "acquisitive conglomerate" growth strategy.

To reach a decision regarding criteria for acquisition, performance, and diversification we began by looking at the characteristics of the "average" corporation. An appropriate measure for the scale of expansion through acquisition would be the average annual increase in sales or assets resulting from acquisition. Unfortunately, this is impossible to determine from published data.[1] As a compromise we examined separately measures of acquisition activity and of expansion. The average U.S. manufacturing corporation with assets exceeding $10 million made 1.7 acquisitions during the 1962–1967 period.[2] We decided to look for companies that had made at least five acquisitions in this period. The average U.S. manufacturing corporation annually reinvested 50.0% of its earnings during the 1962–1967 period.[3] We decided to look for companies that necessarily had some continuing reliance on external equity financing for their acquisition activities, those for which annual additions to invested equity exceeded earnings after tax.

For performance we examined the annual increase in earnings per share for those corporations making up the Standard and Poor's Industrial Average. This averaged 8.3% per year during 1962–1967. We set 10% per year as a cutoff point for acquisitive conglomerates that had achieved "superior performance."

We found it impossible to get a very precise measure of diversification, either for the "average" corporation or for the firms we would call acquisitive conglomerates. We decided that a corporation met the diversification criterion if it had made acquisitions in at least three different product areas. While it was quite clear in most cases whether a corporation met this criterion for diversification, borderline cases obviously were decided subjectively.

To summarize the operational definition used for identifying "acquisitive conglomerates" we required for the 1962–1967 period at least five acquisitions in at least three different product areas causing a ratio of equity increase to earnings which exceeded unity and resulting in earnings per share growth exceeding 10% per year. These minimum criteria and the similar figures for the "average" U.S.

---

[1] Because of frequent acquisitions involving previously private corporations, for which data regarding size are unavailable.

[2] From data provided in the March 18, 1968, Federal Trade Commission news release, "Merger Activity Set New Record Last Year," it is possible to determine that the approximately 2,400 U.S. manufacturing corporations with assets exceeding $10 million made 4,128 acquisitions during 1962–1967, or approximately 1.7 per corporation.

[3] U.S. Federal Trade Commission–Securities and Exchange Commission, *Quarterly Financial Report for Manufacturing Corporations,* various editions.

TABLE 4.1

CHARACTERISTICS OF THE POPULATION OF ACQUISITIVE CONGLOMERATES

(shown in comparison with: (1) "average" U.S. Corporation; (2) selected
sample of high performance internal growth corporations)

	Population of Acquisitive Conglomerates			*"Average" United States Corporation*[3]	*Average 5 Selected "Internal Growth" Corporations*[4]
For the Period 1962–1967	*Specified Minimum*[1]	*Population Range*[2]	*Population Average*[2]		
Average annual rate of growth in earnings per share (%)	10	10–134	50	8.3	25
Number of acquisitions	5	5– 72	21	1.7	1
Average annual change in net worth/annual earnings (%)	100	102–534	205	50.0	56
Return on book value of equity (%)	*	1– 25	14	11.6	27
Average annual rate of growth in total earnings (%)	*	13–188	76	10.8	25
Average annual increase in number of shares outstanding (%)	*	2– 88	18	na	0

[1] As specified in "operational definition"; see text.

[2] Data taken from Table 4.4.

[3] Average annual rate of growth in earnings per share based on 425 firms comprising Standard and Poor's Industrial Average; number of acquisitions based on Federal Trade Commission data covering firms with assets exceeding $10 million in 1967 (see text for source and nature of calculation); average annual change in net worth/annual earnings, return on book value of equity, and average annual rate of growth in total earnings are figures for all U.S. manufacturing corporations as calculated from data provided in U.S. Federal Trade Commission–Securities and Exchange Commission, *Quarterly Financial Report of Manufacturing Corporations*, various editions.

[4] The five selected "internal growth" companies are Avon Products, Magnavox, Merck and Co., Polaroid, and G. D. Searle. Xerox, which would perhaps seem an obvious choice, was not included because its growth rate demanded significant reliance on new equity financing during this period, it was not a "low expansion rate company" during the 1962–1967 period in terms of the ratio of new equity to earnings after tax.

* Quantity not specified.

corporation are listed in columns one and four of Table 4.1 (the other columns we shall discuss presently).

SEARCHING FOR ACQUISITIVE CONGLOMERATES

The characteristics of growth during 1962–1967 were analyzed for various corporations in relation to the established operational definition. The initial screen was less than foolproof. For 18 months we followed the financial press, read analysts' reports, and queried people in the investment community. Any company mentioned as an acquisitive, diversified company, frequently referred to simply as a "conglomerate," became a candidate for investigation.[4]

Standard and Poor's *Corporation Records* provided the principal source of information on acquisitions; financial data were taken principally from annual reports. The criteria for numbers of acquisitions and diversification eliminated some "candidates" without requiring any analysis. In order to check other criteria and, more importantly, to provide more detailed information on financial characteristics, a computer program was written to perform an analysis of the relevant data.

In Table 4.2 the analysis of Teledyne is presented as an example. Inputs include: annual data for 1962–1967 on corporate sales, earnings, debt, equity; annual per-share data on earnings, dividends, high and low market prices; numbers of acquisitions. The outputs from the analysis are essentially the principal variables used in the conceptual analysis of the following three chapters. These are calculated for each annual period, and the averages shown are simple averages of the annual figures. The variable C is a measure of the rate of expansion of invested equity and of the reliance on external equity financing; it equals the annual increase in book value of equity divided by annual earnings after tax. The variable G is our principal measure of corporate performance; it equals the annual increase in earnings per share as a fraction of earnings per share in the earlier period. The variable GT is the annual rate of increase of total corporate earnings and will be larger than the rate of growth in earnings per share if the number of shares outstanding is continually increasing. The variable Z is a measure of the rate of increase in outstanding shares of common stock. The number of shares outstanding is approximated by the quotient of annual earnings divided by earnings per share. This is exact except in those cases where there are cash dividends on preferred stock.[5] The variable R is the measure of profitability and equals annual earnings after tax as a fraction of ending book value of equity. The variable M is a measure of "average" price-earnings multiples for each period and equals the average of the high and low market prices divided by annual earnings per share. The variable H is the "reinvestment ratio" and equals one minus the proportion of reported

---

[4] It would obviously have been more desirable to have followed an entirely systematic procedure for collecting from the total corporate population the initial sample of companies to be examined. However, because of the wide range of sizes considered (anything exceeding $10 million in sales for 1967) there was no "bank of data" which could be systematically screened. In addition, we saw no necessity to be exhaustive in the search for companies meeting the specified criteria (although we suspect we found most of them). We consider the collected sample sufficiently significant in terms of numbers, sales revenues, and acquisitions to more than justify our interest.

[5] This approximation was necessary because in a few cases we were unable to develop a complete picture of the number of common shares outstanding for all years in the period, adjusted for all stock splits and dividends. However, it was possible in all cases to obtain information on earnings and earnings per share, since most annual reports provide such information for several preceding years. Where the information was available and the approximation caused any material error, the necessary adjustments were made for dividends on preferred.

TABLE 4.2

TELEDYNE, INCORPORATED: ANALYSIS OF PUBLISHED FINANCIAL DATA
FOR FISCAL YEARS ENDED OCTOBER 31

	1967	1966	1965	1964	1963	1962	Average
SALES[1]	451,060	256,751	86,504	38,187	31,925	10,438	
EARNS	21,745	12,035	3,402	1,441	731	157	
DEBT	116,383	40,824	16,101	10,972	5,866	1,842	
EQUIT	153,092	90,205	34,765	13,672	8,629	3,527	
EPS	2.66	1.77	0.96	0.65	0.37	0.12	
DPS	0.00	0.00	0.00	0.00	0.00	0.00	
MKTLO	38.63	24.25	13.50	10.75	10.38	9.13	
KNTHI	143.00	64.25	36.25	24.13	15.50	16.50	
NOACQ	21.00	22.00	7.00	8.00	11.00	3.00	
C^2	2.892	4.607	6.200	3.500	6.979		4.836
G	0.503	0.844	0.477	0.757	2.083		0.933
GT	0.807	2.538	1.361	0.971	3.656		1.867
Z	0.202	0.919	0.598	0.122	0.510		1.470
R	0.142	0.133	0.098	0.105	0.085	0.045	0.101
M	34.140	25.000	25.911	26.827	34.966	106.771	42.269
H	1.000	1.000	1.000	1.000	1.000	1.000	1.000
XB	0.568	0.688	0.683	0.555	0.595	0.657	0.625

[1] The items of financial data are defined as follows:

SALES — net annual sales in thousands of dollars as reported each fiscal year; neither this item nor any of the others has been restated for subsequent acquisitions treated as poolings of interest.

EARNS — annual earnings in thousands of dollars after tax and before extraordinary items.

DEBT — book value of outstanding debt in thousands of dollars at end of fiscal period, including convertible debt securities.

EQUIT — book value of equity at end of fiscal period in thousands of dollars.

EPS   — annual earnings per share as reported.

DPS   — annual dividends per share.

MKTLO — high and low market prices per share respectively for calendar year.

MKTHI — most closely corresponding to fiscal year.

NOACQ — number of acquisitions completed during the indicated fiscal year.

[2] The calculated variables describing various aspects of the growth process are defined as follows:

C — annual increase in book equity divided by annual earnings after tax.

G — annual increase in earnings per share as a fraction of earnings per share in earlier period.

GT — annual increase in earnings after tax as a fraction of earnings in earlier period.

Z — proxy for annual rate of increase in number of shares outstanding; shares outstanding are approximated by earnings after tax divided by earnings per share (which ignores dividends, if any, on preferred stock).

R — annual earnings after tax as a fraction of ending book equity.

M — average of high and low market prices divided by earnings per share.

H — one minus the proportion of reported earnings paid in dividends, the "reinvestment ratio."

XB — book equity as a proportion of total capital.

See text for more interpretation.

earnings paid in dividends. The variable XB is a measure of the amount of leverage in the capital structure, or more precisely, a measure of the lack of leverage. It equals the book value of equity divided by the book value of equity plus long-term debt.

Teledyne is an outstanding example of an acquisitive conglomerate; as may be observed it far exceeds all of our minimum criteria. During the period 1962–1967 Teledyne made 72 acquisitions compared with our criterion of 5. The average annual increase in book equity divided by annual earnings after tax was 4.836 compared with our criterion of 1.00. The average rate of increase in earnings per share that Teledyne achieved through this growth process of 93.3% per year far exceeds our criterion of 10% per year.

In addition, the calculated value for C = 4.836 is almost certainly an understatement. In poolings of interests acquisition transactions new equity comes in at the book value for the old corporation rather than at the market value of the acquisition transaction. In order to get a more realistic measure of the increase in invested equity at *market value,* it may be recalled that new equity financing as a multiple of earnings, Q, equals the rate of increase of outstanding common shares, Z, times the price earning multiple, M. This of course is strictly true only where the growth process proceeds uniformly over time and all proportional relationships between variables remain constant, which of course they do not here. Nonetheless, as a rough measure we have for Teledyne, $Q = ZM = (.47)(42.3) = 19.88 = C - H$. Since H equals one for Teledyne, C on a market value basis is closer to 20 than to 5 as the book value calculation would indicate. This means that the measure of return on equity, calculated on a book value basis here as $R = 10.0\%$, is a substantial overstatement.

Approximately 80 corporations were investigated on a preliminary basis, and the analysis program was run for about 45 of these. Only 28 corporations met all the established criteria. In Table 4.3 we provide a partial list of corporations which were examined but which did *not* satisfy the established criteria. Some of the corporations which we thought would satisfy the criteria failed to do so on one or more counts. Avnet, Indian Head, and Lear Siegler did not meet the criteria for expansion rate: City Investing and Fuqua had too short a history under present management; Dresser Industries and Singer had neither expanded rapidly enough nor performed well enough; and so forth.

The 28 corporations that did meet the established criteria are listed in Table 4.4 along with their 1967 sales volume, the number of acquisitions during 1962–1967, and average figures for each of the calculated financial variables. Averages of the characteristics listed for each company, shown at the bottom of Table 4.4, provide a profile of the "average acquisitive conglomerate." This hypothetical company had annual sales in 1967 of $633 million and during 1962–1967 made 21 acquisitions, or almost one a quarter. On a book value basis, which for reasons discussed earlier provides an understatement, the annual increase in equity was 2.05 times annual earnings. The number of outstanding shares increased at the average rate of 18% per year and these shares were issued at an average market value of 18.8 times earnings. The return on the book value of equity was 14%, undoubtedly an overstatement of what the return would be for new equity brought in at market value. Of reported earnings, only 13% on the average was paid out in dividends, or the "reinvestment ratio" was 87%. The ratio of book value of equity to book value of total capital was 66% on the average. The result of this pattern of growth for the "average acquisitive conglomerate" over the 1962–1967 period was total earnings growth at the annual average rate of 76% per year and, more importantly, earnings-per-share growth at the average annual rate of 50%. It is this kind of performance that makes the previously discussed evidence on the general lack of success in industrial mergers so interesting.

TABLE 4.3

A PARTIAL LIST OF CORPORATIONS EXAMINED FOR "ACQUISITIVE CONGLOMERATE" CRITERIA AND REJECTED

Athlone Industries	Lear Siegler
AMK	Minnesota Mining and Manufacturing
Avnet	Norris Industries
Burgess Manning	Novo Industrial
City Investing	Oak Electro/Netics
Colt Industries	Olin Mathieson
Dresser Industries	Republic Corporation
EG&G	Singer
Esquire	Soss Manufacturing
Fuqua Industries	Standard International
General Dynamics	Tenneco
General Interiors	Transcontinental Investing
General Precision	Trinity Industries
Houdaille Industries	Ventron
Indian Head	Zurn Industries
Iroquois Industries	

In an effort to correct for the understatement of C caused by poolings accounting, we provide in Table 4.5 rough estimates of equity expansion at market value relative to earnings after tax. The calculation is performed as previously discussed for Teledyne. While in several cases the market value estimate for C is only slightly greater than the previous calculation and in three cases is actually less (for Condec, MSL, and Signal), it is in most cases substantially higher. For the "average" acquisitive conglomerate the market value estimate for C is 4.43 compared with the book value measure of 2.05.

Finally, the population of acquisitive conglomerates is of significant size and importance. Collectively the 28 identified firms had $17.7 billion in annual revenues in 1967 and made 588 acquisitions during the 1962–1967 period. This implies that 1.2% of the approximately 2,400 firms with assets exceeding $10 million in 1967 made 14.2% of the 4,128 acquisitions made by such firms during 1962–1967.[6]

---

[6] Source cited in footnote 2.

TABLE 4.4

FINANCIAL CHARACTERISTICS[1] OF ACQUISITIVE CONGLOMERATES

Company[2]	S[3]	N[4]	C[5]	G	GT	Z	R	M	H	XB
"Automatic" Sprinkler (4)	242	18	2.46	0.55	0.98	0.32	0.25	25.89	0.94	0.56
Automation Industries (6)	55	8	1.99	0.65	0.77	0.08	0.15	17.32	1.00	0.66
Bangor Punta (6)	161	18	1.85	0.19	0.33	0.13	0.22	7.90	0.97	0.56
Condec (6)	75	5	1.52	0.43	0.48	0.03	0.12	15.93	1.00	0.50
FMC (6)	1,313	7	1.02	0.17	0.19	0.03	0.14	19.42	0.64	0.68
Grace (W. R.) (6)	1,576	38	1.12	0.10	0.21	0.10	0.10	16.45	0.60	0.57
Gulf & Western Ind. (6)	645	58	2.39	0.72	1.07	0.23	0.15	17.75	0.95	0.61
Hydrometals (6)	40	13	1.32	1.25	1.36	0.03	0.01	17.96	1.00	0.63
ITT (6)	2,761	45	1.56	0.14	0.24	0.09	0.10	18.25	0.64	0.65
Kidde (Walter) (5)	424	29	4.07	0.73	1.88	0.69	0.08	22.19	1.00	0.74
Litton Industries (6)	1,562	40	1.42	0.29	0.34	0.04	0.17	35.00	1.00	0.54
LTV (6)	1,833	8	1.60	0.33	0.50	0.11	0.21	10.42	0.87	0.43
Mid-Continent Mfg. (4)	27	11	3.01	0.28	1.32	0.88	0.22	9.09	0.90	0.59
Monogram Ind. (6)	27	9	2.12	0.91	0.90	0.07	0.13	32.16	1.00	0.83
MSL Industries (6)	108	14	1.08	0.11	0.13	0.02	0.13	11.72	0.55	0.69
Nytronics (6)	14	11	2.48	0.39	0.64	0.15	0.11	15.00	1.00	0.65
Occidental (6)	826	22	2.91	0.23	0.53	0.24	0.20	21.56	0.69	0.63
Ogden (6)	815	10	1.61	0.38	0.60	0.21	0.10	10.72	0.80	0.64
Royal Industries (6)	60	17	1.08	0.54	0.58	0.03	0.15	13.06	1.00	0.78
Signal Companies (6)	1,505	13	1.71	0.13	0.23	0.09	0.09	11.84	0.59	0.78
Teledyne (6)	451	72	4.84	0.93	1.87	0.47	0.10	42.27	1.00	0.63
Textron (6)	1,446	28	1.21	0.23	0.34	0.08	0.15	12.35	0.63	0.77
TRW (6)	1,041	13	1.04	0.20	0.29	0.07	0.12	14.43	0.62	0.70
Tyco Laboratories (5)	10	7	5.34	0.90	1.35	0.20	0.19	51.00	1.00	0.86
U.S. Industries (4)	283	27	1.93	0.81	0.87	0.15	0.13	10.42	0.87	0.67
Vernitron (6)	22	5	1.81	0.51	0.85	0.20	0.18	19.38	1.00	0.72
White Consolidated (6)	173	21	1.35	1.34	1.49	0.20	0.12	13.91	1.00	0.57
Whittaker (5)	225	31	1.45	0.63	0.86	0.08	0.14	12.58	1.00	0.87
Average[6]	633	21	2.05	0.50	0.76	0.18	0.14	18.78	0.87	0.66

[1] Financial characteristics summarized from analyses of each corporation such as that shown for Teledyne in Table 4.2.

[2] The number in parentheses after each company name indicates the number of fiscal years of financial data relevant for the company's program of growth through diversified acquisition. For example Harry Figgie joined "Automatic" as President in December 1963. The four years in this case are a base year under the old management and three full years under the direction of Mr. Figgie.

[3] Annual sales in thousands of dollars for the 1967 fiscal year.

[4] Number of acquisitions during the 1962–1967 period.

[5] This variable and those in the remaining columns are as defined in Table 4.2.

[6] Simple averages of data listed for each company.

TABLE 4.5

COMPARISON OF MEASURES OF EXPANSION RATE

(1) As calculated from financial data at book value
(2) As estimated from data on rate of new share issuance and market values

	Estimated from New Share Issuance and Market Value Data[1]		*Calculated from Book Value Data*[2]
	$Q = ZM$	$C = Q + H$	C
"Automatic" Sprinkler	8.28	9.22	2.46
Automation Industries	1.39	2.39	1.99
Bangor Punta	1.03	2.00	1.85
Condec	0.48	1.48	1.52
FMC	0.58	1.22	1.02
Grace (W. R.)	1.65	2.25	1.12
Gulf & Western Ind.	4.08	5.03	2.39
Hydrometals	0.54	1.54	1.32
ITT	1.64	2.28	1.56
Kidde (Walter)	15.31	16.31	4.07
Litton Industries	1.40	2.40	1.42
LTV	1.15	2.02	1.60
Mid-Continent Mfg.	8.00	8.90	3.01
Monogram Ind.	2.25	3.25	2.48
MSL Industries	0.23	0.78	1.12
Nytronics	2.25	3.25	2.48
Occidental	5.17	5.86	2.91
Ogden	2.25	3.05	1.61
Royal Industries	0.39	1.39	1.08
Signal Companies	1.07	1.66	1.71
Teledyne	19.87	20.87	4.84
Textron	0.99	1.62	1.21
TRW	1.01	1.63	1.04
Tyco Laboratories	9.69	10.69	5.34
U.S. Industries	1.56	2.43	1.93
Vernitron	3.88	4.88	1.81
White Consolidated	2.78	3.78	1.35
Whittaker	1.01	2.01	1.45
Average	3.27	4.43	2.05

[1] Values for Z, M, and H from Table 4.4.
[2] Repeated from Table 4.4 for convenience in comparison.

THE ACQUISITIVE CONGLOMERATE IS DIFFERENT

It should be evident at this point that the "average acquisitive conglomerate" is not like the "average" U.S. corporation. On the dimensions of acquisition activity, expansion rate, and performance the acquisitive conglomerate on the average displays characteristics far exceeding specified minimum criteria which, in turn, significantly exceed those displayed by "average" corporations.

We also want to demonstrate that the acquisitive conglomerate is quite different from other corporations that achieve superior performance in different ways. In succeeding chapters we will pursue a detailed conceptual argument that it is possible to achieve a given level of per-share performance with various combinations of rate of return on equity and rate of expansion of invested equity.[7] We may provide some motivation for this conceptual development, while demonstrating the above mentioned difference, though comparison of the "population" of acquisitive conglomerates with a group of U.S. corporations that have achieved superior performance with a high rate of return on equity and no significant reliance on acquisition or external equity financing. We attempted to select the "cream of the crop" of "internal growth" corporations. For example, consider the growth pattern of Avon Products Corporation. The results of running the financial data for this company through our analysis program are shown in Table 4.6. Avon achieved an

TABLE 4.6

AVON PRODUCTS, INCORPORATED: ANALYSIS OF PUBLISHED
FINANCIAL DATA FOR FISCAL YEARS ENDED DECEMBER 31

	1967	1966	1965	1964	1963	1962	Average
SALES[1]	474,814	408,178	351,990	299,449	248,594	210,818	
EARNS	65,383	55,328	47,569	39,839	29,443	25,364	
DEBT	16,872	17,841	2,503	4,676	3,660	3,640	
EQUIT	175,123	149,334	126,833	104,962	85,827	74,409	
EPS	2.27	1.92	1.65	1.38	1.02	0.88	
DPS	1.40	1.15	0.90	0.73	0.63	0.46	
MKTLO	76.00	66.00	52.00	51.25	29.00	19.25	
MKTHI	142.50	89.50	76.38	56.50	46.00	35.63	
NOACQ	0.00	0.00	0.00	0.00	0.00	0.00	
C	0.394	0.407	0.460	0.480	0.388		0.426
G	0.182	0.164	0.196	0.353	0.159		0.211
GT	0.182	0.163	0.194	0.353	0.161		0.211
Z	0.000	0.000	−0.001	0.000	0.001		0.000
R	0.373	0.370	0.375	0.380	0.343	0.341	0.364
M	48.128	40.495	38.902	39.040	36.765	31.179	39.085
H	0.383	0.401	0.455	0.471	0.382	0.477	0.428
XB	0.912	0.893	0.981	0.957	0.959	0.953	0.943

[1] See notes to Table 4.2.

average annual increase in earnings per share and in total earnings of 21% per year during 1962–1967. The return on equity averaged 36% and remained in the range of 34% to 38% throughout this period. There were no acquisitions and no significant increases in the number of outstanding shares. Data for five similar companies are summarized in Table 4.7. Averages of the characteristics are compared with those for the population of acquisitive conglomerates. The acquisitive conglomerates achieved even better per-share performance than the "internal

---

[7] Other factors such as dividend policy and how the market reacts to the process as reflected in price-earnings ratio are also important, of course.

TABLE 4.7

FINANCIAL CHARACTERISTICS OF SELECTED HIGH PERFORMANCE
"INTERNAL GROWTH" CORPORATIONS[1]

Company	S	N	C	G	GT	Z	R	M	H	XB
Avon Products	475	0	0.42	0.21	0.21	0.00	0.36	39.09	0.43	0.94
Magnavox	464	2	0.65	0.22	0.23	0.01	0.26	21.48	0.60	0.83
Merck & Co.	540	2	0.42	0.23	0.23	0.00	0.23	30.65	0.38	0.97
Polaroid	374	0	0.92	0.44	0.44	0.00	0.21	51.51	1.00	1.00
Searle (GD)	133	1	0.38	0.15	0.14	(0.01)	0.30	37.00	0.35	0.97
Average	397	1	0.56	0.25	0.25	0.00	0.27	35.95	0.55	0.94
Average for acquisitive conglomerates	633	21	2.05	0.50	0.76	0.18	0.14	18.78	0.87	0.66

[1] See notes to Table 4.4.

growth" firms (G equal to 0.50 versus 0.25) based on much more rapid expansion of invested equity relative to earnings (C equal to 0.25 versus 0.56) and a much lower rate of return on equity (R equal to 0.14 versus 0.27). The comparison of return and expansion for these two groups of companies obviously would be more dramatic if the additions to equity for the acquisitive conglomerates were based on the market value estimates of Table 4.5.

Finally, we display graphically in Figure 4.1 the rate of return and rate of expansion for the five selected "internal growth" firms and for five selected acquisitive conglomerates. The numbers in parentheses following each company name are average rates of growth in earnings per share over 1962–1967. These acquisitive conglomerates with lower rates of return than the "internal growth" firms generally have higher rates of performance.

Regarding the forthcoming conceptual development, the pattern of points in Figure 4.1 is similar to trade-off relationships between rates of return and rates of expansion for given rates of earnings-per-share growth[8] that will be derived and explained in later chapters. We selected the five members of the "population" in Figure 4.1 to dramatize the difference between combinations of return on equity and expansion of equity employed by the "internal growth" corporations and by the acquisitive conglomerates. The point of significance, however, is that it was possible to do so, that corporations have found it possible to achieve exceptional performance relying on very different combinations of rates of return and expansion. It is toward a better understanding of this that much of the analysis in the next three chapters is directed.

OTHER COMMON CHARACTERISTICS OF ACQUISITIVE CONGLOMERATES

We have identified a group of firms that meet specified criteria on three dimensions: (1) aggressive acquisition; (2) diversification; and (3) performance. We

---

[8] Of course the rates of growth in earnings per share for these ten companies are not all the same; they are similar only in that they are all far above "average."

suggest that those firms meeting these criteria are likely to have some other characteristics in common. Further, knowledge of these characteristics will be useful
in (1) providing some insight regarding which potential sources of performance
are likely to be most important; (2) suggesting approaches for more detailed in-

FIGURE 4.1

COMPARISON OF RETURN AND EXPANSION CHARACTERISTICS OF SELECTED
ACQUISITIVE CONGLOMERATES AND HIGH-PERFORMANCE, "INTERNAL
GROWTH" CORPORATIONS

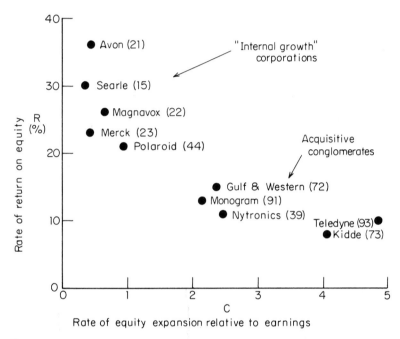

NOTE: The numbers in parentheses following each company show average annual increase
in earnings per share over 1962–1967.

vestigation of particular corporations; (3) and providing better understanding
generally of the nature of the acquisitive conglomerate corporation. Our primary
sources of information here are materials published by the companies and material
published regarding these companies by the investment community and the financial press. Second, we rely on information gained in a small number of preliminary interviews with individuals in these companies and in the investment
community. The first three of these "common characteristics" are primarily "financial" in nature; the last five are primarily "operating" characteristics.

1. The Objective Is Growth in Earnings per Share

It is perhaps not surprising that a group of firms that have performed so well in
terms of growth in earnings per share would express their corporate objectives in
these terms. Still, the tendency for these firms to do so is strikingly uniform. Some

of the 28 companies have not discussed their objectives in published material. But many have, and almost without exception growth in earnings per share is given special emphasis.

Examples abound. Harry Figgie at "Automatic" Sprinkler has said, "A growth company worries about one thing; increasing its earnings per share between 20% and 40% a year." [9] At LTV Clyde Skeen, President, stated, "We desire to grow but as we grow we will always keep our eye on that precious commodity — the shares of our company. Our objective is to grow in terms of sales and earnings per equity share. . . ." [10] Harold Geneen, President of ITT, talked of "aiming at and achieving a sustained 10–12% compound annual per-share growth. . . ." [11] Ralph Ablon, President of Ogden, said, "We are committed to an average growth in per-share earnings of 20% per year." [12] J. R. Johnson, President of Royal Industries, put it more emphatically: "Earnings per share. That's what we're here for. All of our decisions are based on it." [13] One writer in a recent interview study concluded: "The outstanding specific common objective (in acquisition programs) is growth in earnings per share of common stock." [14]

Textron is almost an exception. It traditionally has expressed its objectives in terms of a 20% after-tax return on equity, but in recent years has made a transition toward more emphasis on earnings-per-share growth. In the fall of 1967 the Executive Vice President–Finance and Administration, Mr. Collinson, stated:

> We have to be concerned with increasing our earnings per share, just like everyone else, because that seems to be the way the game is scored in the stock market. The market seems to value increasing earnings per share more than a high return on corporate net worth.[15]

In the 1967 Annual Report Chairman Rupert Thompson discussed return on equity but stated, "We have an objective of averaging a 15% increase in earnings per share annually. . . ." [16]

We have argued earlier that growth in earnings per share is a logical operating objective where the underlying objective is growth over time in the market price per share of common stock. It seems reasonable to expect that the long-term trend in market price per share will closely follow the long-term trend in earnings per share.[17] Given the appropriateness of the earnings-per-share objective for the shareholder interest, we suspected that the executives of acquisitive conglomerates had substantial ownership interests. In Table 4.8 we examine the importance of

---

[9] Quoted in *Business Week,* August 12, 1967.

[10] James J. Ling and Clyde Skeen, "Comments to the Los Angeles Society of Security Analysts," January 31, 1967.

[11] Harold Geneen, "An Address Before the New York Society of Security Analysts," November 16, 1966.

[12] Ralph E. Ablon, "Speech Before the Los Angeles Society of Security Analysts," January 18, 1968.

[13] "Johnson Shoots for Fortune's 500," *California Business,* July 16, 1967, p. 9.

[14] Holmes, "Corporate Acquisition Patterns," p. 3.

[15] Quoted in "Textron, Inc. (A)", Harvard Business School case, BP 912, 1968.

[16] Textron, Inc., *Annual Report for 1967,* p. 3.

[17] Later in this chapter we provide some evidence on this relationship.

TABLE 4.8

ACQUISITIVE CONGLOMERATES: IMPORTANCE OF EXECUTIVE STOCK OWNERSHIP RELATIVE TO SALARY

(as Listed in Corporation Proxy Statements)

Company	Chief Executive(s)	Date of Proxy	Ownership of Outstanding Shares[1]		Mkt Value Chief Exec(s) Shares[2] ($000)	Chief Exec(s) Salary[3] ($000)	Salary as % Mkt Value of Shares	Average Annual Increase in Earnings per Share[4]
			Directors	Chief Exec				
"Automatic"	H. E. Figgie[5]	6/7/67	13%	6%	$ 9,875	$ 75	0.8%	55%
Automation Ind	C. D. Denny	4/25/68	28	24	19,404	60	0.3	65
Bangor Punta	N. M. Salgo, Chm	1/17/67	29	13	8,203	65	0.8	19
	W. G. Robertson, Pres			1	316	79	25.0	
Condec	N. I. Shafler	11/15/67	24	22	8,958	76	0.8	43
FMC	J. M. Hait, Chm	5/11/67	1	*	762	186	24.4	17
	J. M. Pope, Pres			*	519	120	23.1	
Grace (W. R.)	J. P. Grace	5/10/67	3	1	11,895	335	2.8	10
G & W Industries	C. G. Bluhdorn	12/11/67	5	3	13,650	113	0.8	72
Hydrometals	F. M. Zeder II	7/31/67	8	5	1,007	53	5.3	125
ITT	H. S. Geneen	3/22/68	1	*	5,207	250	4.8	14
Kidde (Walter)	F. R. Sullivan, Chm	7/1/68	4	1	3,883	104	2.7	73
	F. M. Ricciardi, Pres			1	3,883	93	2.4	
Litton Industries	C. B. Thornton	12/2/67	8	4	101,137	150	0.1	29
	R. L. Ash			1	30,781	145	0.5	
LTV	J. J. Ling	5/25/68	12	9	45,718	234	0.5	33
Mid-Continent	E. L. Smith, Chm	8/24/67	15	2	241	39	16.2	28
	M. J. O'Freil, Pres[6]			*	16	69	429.6	
Monogram Ind	M. Stone	10/26/67	9	4	2,073	50	2.4	91
MSL	J. T. Zoline	3/8/68	7	1	628	90	14.3	11
Occidental	A. Hammer	6/17/68	7	4	135,349	94	0.1	23
Ogden	R. E. Ablon	5/17/67	32	1	2,271	144	6.3	38
Royal Industries	J. R. Johnson	3/29/68	9	2	660	65	9.8	54
Signal Companies	S. B. Mosher	7/10/67	5	3	14,665	151	1.0	13
Teledyne	H. E. Singleton	1/31/68	7	4	30,059	113	0.4	93
Textron	R. C. Thompson, Chm	3/15/67	2	1	3,522	120	3.4	23
	G. W. Miller, Pres			*	1,066	90	8.4	
TRW	J. D. Wright	3/28/68	3	*	3,867	240	6.2	20
Tyco	A. J. Rosenberg	8/23/67	10	6	2,070	37	1.8	90
U.S. Industries	I. J. Billera	3/11/68	2	1	693	130	18.8	81
Vernitron	Bernard Levine	4/12/68	19	5	1,914	55	2.9	51
White Consolidated	V. W. Fries, Chm	2/23/68	14	3	6,420	105	1.6	134
	E. S. Reddig, Pres			3	6,585	115	1.7	
Whittaker	W. R. Whittaker, Chm	12/29/67	20	15	38,600	93	0.2	63
	W. M. Duke, Pres			1	2,919	110	3.8	
Average[7]			11%	4%	$ 14,823	$116	5.7%	50%

[1] Percentage ownership of all classes of common stock. Does not include ownership of convertible debt on equity securities. Also, excludes shares held by family and indirectly for which executive disclaims beneficial ownership.

[2] Based on number of common shares owned at proxy statement date shown multiplied by average market price per share for 1967.

[3] Excludes bonus except where not shown separately in Proxy Statement.

[4] Taken from Table 4.4.

[5] As an example of the understatement of ownership provided by this table, at the time of this proxy statement, there were 136,101 shares owned beneficially by members of Mr. Figgie's immediate family (as to which Mr. Figgie disclaimed beneficial ownership) and 75,000 common shares owned by Clark Reliance Corp. of which Mr. Figgie was Chairman and principal shareholder. Mr. Figgie also owned a warrant to purchase 153,125 shares at $.60 per share. Figures in table based on direct ownership of 1,980,000 shares.

[6] Mr. O'Friel, at the time of this proxy statement, held options for the purchase of 11,250 shares of common stock. An increase in market value of 38% would provide an increase in the market value of this option equal to Mr. O'Friel's annual salary.

[7] Simple averages of figures listed above in every case. Average figure for Salary as % of Market Value of Shares in last column excludes the large entry for the president of Mid-Continent Manufacturing; see note 3 above. Average figure for earnings-per-share growth includes Nytronics for which proxy statement was not obtained and which therefore is not included in other averages.

* Less than 0.5%.

common stock performance for the chief executives of these firms. The information for the table comes from company proxy statements issued during 1967 and early 1968. Market prices are averages for 1967. Where one individual was not clearly designated as the chief executive we listed ownership interests of both chairman and president.

Of principal interest here are the last two columns. The next to last shows chief executive salary as a percentage of market value of his equity ownership. This is the percentage annual increase in market value per share required for capital appreciation of his equity interest to exceed his annual salary. For the average chief executive in the acquisitive conglomerate firm, market value of equity was $14.8 million in 1967 and annual salary $116,000. The average of the figures measuring required percentage increase for capital appreciation to equal salary was 5.7%. This percentage is almost certainly an overstatement. We have listed only common stock interests, excluding in some cases significant amounts of convertible debt or equity securities. Also, we have used ownership figures as stated in company proxies which often exclude what appear to be substantial beneficial interests for which the executive disclaims beneficial ownership.[18] Finally, we are looking at values for the executive before payment of personal income taxes; this again underestimates the value to the individual of capital appreciation.

As a proxy for rate of increase in market price per share we list the average annual increase in earnings per share over 1962–1967. This rate of increase was greater than required for capital appreciation to exceed salary for the chief executives in 23 of 27 companies. The average rate of earnings-per-share growth was 50% per year, as discussed earlier, as compared with the "required" figure of 5.6%. This means that for the average acquisitive conglomerate chief executive, capital appreciation was roughly ten times more important than salary as a source of personal wealth.[19] This is in spite of the fact that these executives typically owned only a relatively small *proportion* of the total equity in their respective corporations. In no case did an executive own as much as 30% and the average figure was 4%. The average figure for all directors as a group was 11%. Such small ownership proportions are certainly to be expected in the corporation that is continually issuing additional shares in acquisitions. Still, we would argue that it is the market value of ownership relative to annual salary rather than percentage ownership of total equity that is most important in determining how the executive is motivated.[20] The evidence serves, we suggest, both to explain in part

---

[18] For an example of this see note 5 to Table 4.8.

[19] This appears much larger than has been the case for the "average" large corporation. Lewellen ("Executives Lose Out, Even with Options") found that for the average of the five top executives in 50 large firms the returns from stock options approximately equaled salary plus bonus during 1955–1963. In an earlier period (1940–1949) he found that the returns from stock options played a negligible role. In comparing this to the above, it should be noted, however, that the returns from stock options are not necessarily the same as returns from stock ownership.

[20] This line of thinking, we suggest, would be very useful to some who have attempted to relate management ownership and performance beneficial to stockholders. For example, in a study by Kamerschen, "Ownership and Control and Profit Rates," the author measured the

the observed tendency toward the objective of earnings per share growth and to confirm its importance. Again, we make no attempt to exclude other objectives. Both profitability and expansion are required to provide per-share performance. However, as Martin Stone, President of Monogram Industries, put it, "Remember, constantly increasing earnings per share is the name of the game." [21]

2. Acquisitions Are Expected to Make an Immediate Contribution to Earnings per Share

With a strategy of aggressive acquisition and an objective of increasing earnings per share, the natural tendency is to seek acquisitions that, among other things, will increase earnings per share immediately and to avoid those that will not. While strong arguments could be made in some cases, it would seem, for short-term dilution of earnings per share in exchange for expected longer term increases, that this appears to be done only rarely by the acquisitive conglomerates. Harry E. Figgie at "Automatic" in discussing acquisition policy has said, "There must be an increase in earnings per common share; we will never dilute the earnings on common shares." [22] William M. Duke, President of Whittaker, similarly stated, "We will not dilute the earnings per common share in any acquisition or merger." [23] George T. Sharffenberger, President of City Investing, in discussing acquisition criteria said, "It (an acquisition) must add, when joined to City, at least 20¢ a share in earnings." [24] At TRW Charles R. Allen, Vice President–Chief Financial Officer, recently listed acquisition criteria with both short-term and longer-term implications: "The price of the acquisition must be such that it will not dilute earnings per share on a fully converted basis now or in the future." [25] This objective of immediately increasing earnings per share through merger appears well appreciated even by the regulatory authorities. Dr. Willard F. Mueller, Chief Economist at the Federal Trade Commission, conceded that "so far we haven't stopped mergers, large or small . . . merger makers have discovered that the simplest way from management's standpoint to increase earnings per share is to merge — and that's management's job." [26]

When the contrary to this policy is discussed, and that does not appear very often, it seems to be directed toward the exceptional acquisition. Ralph E. Ablon, President of Ogden, for example, said:

---

importance of ownership to management by percentage of total equity owned and assumed that "if managers act in the best interest of owners they will try to maximize the rate of return after tax on year end equity" (p. 433). His measures of both importance of ownership to management and performance for owners are misconceived.

[21] "Acquisition Technique as a Growth Product," An Address Before the Bond Club of Los Angeles, October 16, 1967, p. 8.

[22] "An Address to the New York Society of Security Analysts," August 22, 1966, p. 11.

[23] Quoted in "Whittaker Corporation 1967 Annual Meeting, Report to Shareholders."

[24] Quoted in *Business Week*, March 23, 1968, p. 152. City Investing was not included in our "population" of 28 companies only because its history under present management was too short by a small margin.

[25] Quoted in Georgeson & Co., "Trends in Management-Stockholder Relations," No. 177, November 1967.

[26] Quoted in *Business Week*, March 23, 1968, p. 69.

. . . blind application of this (immediate increase in eps through acquisition) criterion could very well result in substantial amounts of lost profits in the long run. . . . Just as a chess player sometimes knowingly plans to lose a piece in order to gain a position, a corporation may very well plan to face a temporary setback in its per-share earnings in order to improve its long-run position.[27]

The principal reason why such acquisitions must be the exception is that a significant number would damage not only the per-share earnings trend but the price-earnings ratio as well and therefore would impair the ability to make acquisitions on attractive terms in the future. This brings us to the next common characteristic.

3. *The High Price-Earnings Ratio Is Viewed as an Important Resource for Growth*

The immediate impact of acquisitions on earnings per share of the buying corporation depends on the respective price-earnings ratios of buyer and seller.[28] For this reason the price-earnings ratio of the acquisition-minded company is viewed as an important resource. In particular, the ability to buy companies which appear attractive over the longer term and which will at the same time provide some immediate contribution to per-share earnings depends on a high price-earnings ratio.

We will argue in detail in the conceptual argument of succeeding chapters that the more rapid the corporate rate of expansion the more important becomes the price-earnings ratio as a determinant of corporate performance. And for our rapidly expanding acquisitive companies there is some evidence of its importance. On the one hand, because of the interdependencies in this type of growth process, the importance of maintaining a high price-earnings ratio is reflected in statements such as "constantly increasing earnings per share is the name of the game," or more generally, in the earnings-per-share growth objective. On the other hand the importance of the price-earnings ratio is reflected in the kinds of published material which the acquisitive conglomerate uses to communicate to the investing public. Most of the discussion of the latter seems to come from companies that have low price-earnings ratios and wish very badly that they did not. One financial executive, lamenting his own situation and comparing it with Litton Industries, offered the following:

> I don't know how in the world we can increase our p/e ratio. . . . we have a very conservative board; they don't want to do anything that anyone can interpret as a promotion. . . . I think many of these companies like Litton have done a terrific job in promoting the heck out of their company. . . . Every time they get an order you pick up the paper and Litton did so and so, Litton hired a new vice president for this company, and Litton did so and so, Litton, Litton, Litton. . . . I'm sure that

---

[27] "The Man in Management — Dispensable or Not?" Talk presented to the Association for Corporate Growth, February 15, 1967.

[28] It may be argued that this is irrelevant when acquisitions are made for cash. However, use of cash at one point in time will require issue of stock at another, so that the principle stated is in fact quite general.

has a great deal to do with getting that p/e ratio up there higher which puts them in a wonderful position to make these acquisitions and keep that ball rolling.[29]

While there is not any significant public discussion by acquisitive conglomerates of the objective of obtaining and maintaining a high multiple (for such discussion would almost certainly not work in favor of the objective) many of the annual reports, speeches, and press releases appear to be designed with this clearly in mind. In fact the investment community appears to have become increasingly aware that high multiples are very important for and therefore are eagerly sought by acquisitive conglomerates, a type of "investor public relations" not always viewed with complete approval. Typically conservative *Barron's* published a satirical jab at acquisitive conglomerate promotion in the form of a long letter to a hypothetical foundry owner attempting to become a conglomerate builder. In advising on the need and means for obtaining a high price-earnings ratio the author suggests:

> Get hold of the speeches and annual reports of the real savvy swingers, who know the lingo and can make it sing. Guys like Duke of Whittaker, Singleton of Teledyne, Stone of Monogram. . . . You have to project the right image to the analysts so they realize you're the new breed of entrepreneur. Talk about the synergy of the free-form company and its interface with change and technology. Tell them you have a windowless room full of researchers . . . scrutinizing the future so your corporation will be opportunity-technology oriented. . . . Analysts and investors want conceptually oriented (as opposed to opportunistic) conglomerates, preferably in high-technology areas. That's what they pay the high price-earnings ratios for, and life is a lot less sweaty with a high multiple.[30]

4. Successful, Profitable Companies Are Acquired

Thus far the "other common characteristics" we have discussed have been primarily of a "financial" nature. These lead into and to a significant degree cause some common operating characteristics. If acquisitions must make some favorable immediate impact on earnings per share, the companies purchased must have earnings to contribute. Also, if companies are to be purchased at a rapid pace, it is virtually impossible to deal with firms that are having major difficulties and are therefore operating unsuccessfully. Needed are acquisitions that can continue to be successful without drastic changes requiring major inputs from the parent corporation. One acquisition per quarter can hardly be handled any other way.

The preference for profitable companies with demonstrated records of success is fairly uniform among acquisitive conglomerate companies. LTV listed as a major criterion the acquisition of companies that are "demonstrably profitable and therefore able to improve LTV's earnings per common share." [31] Collinson, an executive vice president of Textron, discussing acquisition standards stated:

---

[29] Interview June 8, 1967; executive chose not to be identified.

[30] Wall, "Want to Get Rich Quick? An Expert Gives Some Friendly Advice on Conglomerates."

[31] *1967 Annual Report,* Letter to Shareholders from James J. Ling, Chairman, and Clyde Skeen, President.

"We want profitable companies with good management; we don't have the corporate resources to provide management to poorly managed companies." [32]

We found only a few isolated exceptions to this philosophy in acquisitive conglomerate type companies. Indian Head [33] began with the philosophy of buying textile companies that were ailing and attempting to rehabilitate them. In recent years, however, this strategy has changed. In the *1965 Annual Report*, James E. Robison, then President and now Chairman, stated that in addition to pursuing internal growth the company "will also seek to acquire strong, sizable businesses with good records, good management, and good prospects for future growth." The one exception in our identified population to the "buy successful, profitable companies" strategy appears to be White Consolidated Industries, which has developed a reputation for buying unprofitable or marginally profitable companies with the objective of "turning them around." [34]

5. *Companies Are Acquired with Capable Management That Can Be Retained*

This is an extension of the preceding "common characteristic" but one given so much attention as to be worthy of special mention. The development of a new management team for an acquired company seems to be viewed by the typical acquisitive conglomerate as the requirement that is most time-consuming and least desirable. G. William Miller, President of Textron, in discussing the success of their acquisition program said that: "Most important, Textron desired companies whose personnel had been responsible for its success, whose management was highly competent and intended to continue operating the business as a part of Textron";[35] and later, "We always retain management of an acquired company. . . ." [36] Jim Hait, Chairman of FMC, stated: "We prefer a company with good management because we're growing so fast we're thin in people who can step into important jobs." [37] David N. Judelson, President of Gulf & Western, put it this way: "Good acquisition oriented companies make the presence of sound management a prerequisite to almost any merger. The few exceptions to this rule occur in cases where potential is extremely great — and even then there must be a supply of good lower-level managers to offset any weaknesses at the top." [38]

This is not to say that management changes are never made. As we shall discuss in a later chapter, the previous management of an acquired company in some significant proportion of cases seems to have difficulty in making the transition to the management of a division of subsidiary. Where for this reason or

---

[32] Quoted in Textron, Inc. (A), Harvard Business School case, BP 912, 1968, p. 18.

[33] Which made 21 acquisitions in diverse areas during 1962–1967 but did not quite meet the expansion rate criteria we had established.

[34] Within two years it bought the Hupp Corporation, the Davidson Division of Fairchild Camera and Instrument, and the Kelvinator Division of American Motors, all three of which were either unprofitable or only marginally so. Recently, White purchased a major interest in and appeared headed toward a merger with Allis-Chalmers, which had a net loss of $55 million in 1968.

[35] "Organizing the Conglomerate Company."

[36] Textron, Inc., *1967 Annual Report*, p. 12.

[37] Quoted in Burck, "The Perils of the Multi-Market Corporation."

[38] "The Role of the Conglomerate Corporation in Today's Economy," p. 21.

any other the previous management fails to perform, the typical acquisitive conglomerate seems quick to make needed management changes. The objective,
however, is typically to retain the management and to help it develop and do
a "better job" in the new environment. Again the only admitted exception appears to be White Consolidated Industries, which has become known for making
sweeping management changes.[39]

6. Management Responsibility and Authority Are Decentralized

The decentralization of management responsibility and authority follows naturally from the preceding characteristics. If an acquisition has a capable management team that has demonstrated success in operating an independent company, it can hardly be expected to continue successfully without some freedom
to operate independently. Equally important, this is seen as the primary strength
in many acquisitions. The former company president may have an entrepreneurial
and aggressive spirit that the ordinary division manager could not be expected
to have. Taking advantage of this capability demands a decentralized management philosophy. Finally, with acquisitions being made at a rapid pace in widely
diversified areas there is little choice.

While the philosophy of decentralized management is discussed and undoubtedly
practiced in different ways in different acquisitive conglomerates, there is no
discussion of centralized authority for any of these 28 firms. Roy Ash, President
of Litton, has said:

> We are decentralized, period. We grew up decentralized. We leave acquired companies
> alone because it is ridiculous to make everything conform to one pattern. You destroy
> everything that was there.[40]

During 1968 Signal Companies was running an advertisement series in *The Wall
Street Journal* which began: "We told our companies to mind their own business
. . . our corporate philosophy is like a declaration of independence for every
one of The Signal Companies." G. William Miller, President of Textron, suggested
that their operating philosophy "is very simple: have the decision made as close
to the point of impact as possible, provided the knowledge, information and
experience are there to make it." [41] H. E. Singleton, Chairman of Teledyne, put
it more bluntly: "We don't try to manage our companies. We can't be looking
over the shoulders of our managers. We can only tell a man to do his best, and
then have to trust and really believe he'll do it." [42]

7. "Visibility" Is Achieved Through the Planning and Control Process

With frequent acquisitions in diversified areas and a decentralized management philosophy, the common feature of management technique is summed up

---

[39] See "Growing Big by Playing It Tough," *Business Week,* August 3, 1968.

[40] Quoted in *Business Week,* "What Puts the Whiz in Litton's Fast Growth?" April 16,
1966.

[41] "Organizing the Conglomerate Company."

[42] Quoted in *Business Week,* "Making Big Waves with Small Fish," December 30, 1967, p. 39.

in the word "visibility." There appears to be a strong and uniform awareness of the need for "visibility" of division and subsidiary operations through rapid feedback of information regarding performance relative to previously established financial and operating plans. The philosophy seems to be that the ability to provide operating freedom to the subsidiary manager is directly related to the degree of "visibility" that is maintained regarding his performance relative to previous projections. The subsidiary manager can be given wide latitude while he performs so long as it is quickly apparent when he is not. Then some corrective action can be taken.

A number of the acquisitive conglomerates have described for the public the mechanics of their planning and control systems.[43] These systems, in terms of mechanics at least, seem quite similar to one another and indeed quite similar to what would be expected of any large, well-managed, divisionalized company.

Annual financial and operating plans or budgets covering all categories of revenues, expenses, capital appropriations, and personnel are reviewed against performance each quarter and a new annual plan prepared. This process is typically accompanied by a review and planning meeting between divisional (or subsidiary) management and corporate level management. Monthly financial and operating reports are prepared by each division and provided to the corporate management shortly after the end of the month. Weekly reports are provided on cash and working capital and in some cases on such other sensitive items as orders, sales, shipments, and backlog by major product lines. In most corporations it appears that the subsidiary manager can be confident that all of this information regarding past performance will meet only a passive review so long as it matches or exceeds projections. In the planning process and in the allocation of capital to major projects or "opportunities," different corporations appear to get involved to varying degrees.

8. *There Is Little Operating Integration of Acquired Subsidiaries*

The lack of significant integration of the operations of acquired companies follows from the previously discussed "common characteristics." It is caused by aggressive acquisition of firms that typically (1) are in widely diversified fields; (2) have demonstrated success through profitable performance; (3) have capable management; and (4) are approached with the objective of retaining previous management to operate in what is hoped will be a highly motivated, relatively independent manner. The lack of operating integration is possible because of (1) the decentralized philosophy of management and (2) the "visibility" provided by the planning and control process.

The avoidance of operating integration is of course not universal. In some cases where the management of an acquired company has demonstrated incom-

---

[43] For examples, see: Automation Industries, *1965 Annual Report*, p. 21; "Gulf & Western Industries, Inc.," Donaldson, Lufkin and Jenrette, Inc., Basic Research Service, March, 1967; "Litton Industries, Inc. (BR)" Harvard Business School case, AM-P 263, 1968; "Textron, Inc. (B)"; Harvard Business School case, BP 913, 1968; Tyco Laboratories, *1967 Annual Report*.

petence, that operation is placed under the management of a more successful subsidiary in a similar product area.[44] In some cases, usually where a smaller acquisition is made in an area of existing operations, operating integration is intended.[45] However, these situations appear to be the exceptions. The common objective, which seems fairly uniform across the 28 acquisitive conglomerate companies, is the acquisition of companies with management teams that can continue with their own operations as a subsidiary of the parent corporation. Hopefully, through provision by the parent corporation of expertise and needed resources, such management teams can perform better than they did on their own.

Implications of the "Common Characteristics"

We have argued in this section that those firms which exceed our specified criteria for acquisition activity, diversification, and performance have some other "common characteristics." We like to think of this "population" of companies as a heterogeneous group with certain uniformities. First we have discussed three common "financial" characteristics: (1) the objective is growth in earnings per share; (2) acquisitions are expected to make an immediate contribution to earnings per share; (3) the high price-earnings ratio is viewed as an important resource. Then we discussed five common "operating" characteristics: (1) successful, profitable companies are acquired; (2) companies are acquired with capable management that can be retained; (3) management responsibility and authority are decentralized; (4) "visibility" is achieved through the planning and control process; (5) there is little operating integration of acquired subsidiaries.

The three financial characteristics collectively imply that these companies are seeking to contribute to their earnings-per-share objective through the use of a relatively high price-earnings ratio in acquisition transactions that will provide an immediate increase in earnings per share. The argument and evidence discussed in preceding and later chapters indicate that the interdependence of price-earnings ratio and earnings-per-share growth through the acquisition process is potentially very important for per-share performance. The analysis of acquisitive conglomerate characteristics in this section indicates that they are behaving in such a way as to take advantage of this relationship. In general, this serves to emphasize the importance of investigating in more detail this potential source of performance.

The five operating characteristics are significant principally because the first

---

[44] This has been the case, for example, in one of the poorly performing subsidiaries of Contek (disguised name), a company we shall examine in detail in a later chapter.

[45] This is an element of what Mr. Figgie at "Automatic" Sprinkler has called the "nucleus theory of growth," which seems to be a fairly prevalent kind of philosophy. Acquisitions in a completely unfamiliar field are expected to be large and self-supporting. Very small acquisitions (relatively speaking) are avoided unless they "fit" very well with some existing subsidiary and can be integrated with (or monitored by) that subsidiary without providing a drain on corporate management time.

four argue logically and convincingly for the fifth, that there is little integration of the operations of acquired companies. The implication is that those potential operating economies involving substantial integration (horizontal scale, vertical integration, "balance," market power) are not likely to be of substantial importance for acquisitive conglomerates. The topic for more detailed investigation is the potential for subsidiary performance improvement in the acquisitive conglomerate environment without operating integration. This provides the starting point for the analysis of operating influence in Chapter IX.

Two of the first four operating characteristics are also of importance for other reasons. As previously discussed, (the most significant opportunities for tax reduction through merger involve loss carry forwards and the offsetting of necessary development losses against other profitable operations.) Either requires that operations be acquired which are currently unprofitable or which very recently have been so. The strong preference of acquisitive conglomerates for successful, profitable acquisitions implies that this will occur only in exceptional cases. For this reason we conclude that tax reduction cannot be of substantial general importance for acquisitive conglomerates and, therefore, give this potential source of performance little further attention.

The other operating characteristic of importance concerns the achievement of "visibility" at the corporate level through the planning and control process. Such "visibility" at the corporate level demands the development of effective planning and control systems within all the divisions and subsidiaries. As we shall later discuss in some detail (Chapter IX), the development of such a system for an acquired company that has not previously had one can be a contribution of major value.

MARKET VALUE FOR ACQUISITIVE CONGLOMERATES

The market system of valuation for the shares of acquisitive conglomerates is of importance for our discussion of performance for two reasons. First, we continually rely on the assumption that over the "long term" the trend for market price per share will have a slope which approximates that for the trend of earnings per share. Based on this relationship, we argue that a given rate of increase in earnings per share (accompanied by a given dividend policy and a given degree of uncertainty) is an appropriate measure of performance over time for shareholders. Second, it will be demonstrated in detail in the next three chapters that the importance of the "feedback relationship" between price-earnings ratio and earnings-per-share growth is dependent on the extent to which investors focus attention on earnings-per-share growth and not on the manner in which that growth is achieved. More specifically, the attractiveness of "low return, high expansion" growth strategies is directly related to the degree to which the investor values earnings-per-share growth achieved in this way as highly as that achieved through "high return, low expansion" growth strategies. We will use the data we have gathered on the acquisitive conglomerate population to examine these two questions briefly.

THE TREND IN EARNINGS PER SHARE AS A MEASURE
OF SHAREHOLDER PERFORMANCE

That the trend of market price per share approximately follows the trend of earnings per share we suggest is self-evident and inevitable if a sufficiently long time period is considered. One way to think about it is that the change in price-earnings ratio over the time period in question is a measure of the degree to which the two trends diverge. But a given change in the price-earnings ratio becomes less important as a longer time period is considered.

Nonetheless, in order to examine the relationship we calculated a measure of the rate of increase in market price per share for the identified acquisitive companies.[46] We used a measure similar to that we have used for per-share earnings growth: the average annual increase in the average of the high and low market prices in each year. We calculated this measure over the same periods that we used to calculate the average annual increase in earnings per share.[47] We analyzed the data only where there were usable market price and earnings figures for either five or six of the years 1962–1967 for which data were gathered.[48] This resulted in data on 22 of the 28 companies. The rates of increase in market price per share and earnings per share are listed in Table 4.9 and are displayed graphically in Figure 4.2. If the relationship was exact, the points in Figure 4.2 would of course all lie on the 45-degree diagonal. The extent to which they do not is an indication of the degree to which price-earnings ratios for these companies changed over the six-year period. For the statistically minded we ran a least squares linear regression as shown in Figure 4.2; rather than the expected constant term of 0% and a coefficient for earnings-per-share growth rate of unity, the figures were 13.6% and 0.702 respectively. However, the regression is reasonably significant as indicated by the multiple correlation coefficient, R, equal to 0.799 and the large F statistic equal to 38.1.

While the trends of earnings per share and market price per share over this six-year period are perhaps not as similar as might be expected, we suggest that the data provide some support for our use of the rate of growth in earnings per share plus the dividend yield as a "proxy" for the return to shareholders.

---

[46] Obviously this relationship has nothing in particular to do with acquisitive companies; we suggest that it is quite general.

[47] Earnings per share had to be positive throughout the period during which this measure was calculated; otherwise the percentage increase becomes meaningless.

[48] "Usable" here means available market price data (in some cases the first public issue of the corporation occurred during the six-year period 1962–1967) and positive earnings per share data (see note 47).

TABLE 4.9

AVERAGE ANNUAL RATES OF INCREASE IN MARKET PRICE
PER SHARE AND EARNINGS PER SHARE

	Average Annual Change in Average Market Price per Share[1]	*Average Annual Change in Earnings per Share*[2]
Automation Industries	63%	65%
Bangor Punta	39	19
Condec	47	43
FMC	15	17
Grace (W. R.)	7	10
Gulf & Western	46	72
ITT	17	14
Kidde (Walter)	55	73
Litton Industries	29	29
LTV	67	33
Monogram Industries	123	91
MSL Industries	9	11
Nytronics	59	39
Occidental	37	23
Ogden	45	38
Royal Industries	47	54
Signal Companies	7	13
Teledyne	52	93
Textron	38	23
TRW	23	20
Vernitron	55	51
White Consolidated	96	134
Average	44%	44%

[1] Simple average of annual percentage increase. Each annual figure is the increase in the average of the high and low prices per share in successive years taken as a percentage of the average price per share for the earlier period.

[2] Taken from Table 4.4.

THE DEPENDENCE OF THE PRICE-EARNINGS RATIO ON THE "TYPE" OF GROWTH STRATEGY

Consider for a moment the idea, which has been frequently discussed, that the market price of a share of stock should logically equal the sum of expected future returns for the person who owns it, discounted at some rate which takes into consideration their futurity and their uncertainty. That is, if we knew the future trend of earnings per share, the anticipated, uncertain variability about that trend, and the proportions of earnings in future periods that would be paid in dividends, we should be able to form reasonable judgments about the "appropriate" present market price per share. The implication is that *given* the earnings-per-share trend, its uncertainty, and the dividend policy, the further information

FIGURE 4.2

RATE OF GROWTH IN EARNINGS PER SHARE AS A MEASURE OF PERFORMANCE FOR SHAREHOLDERS

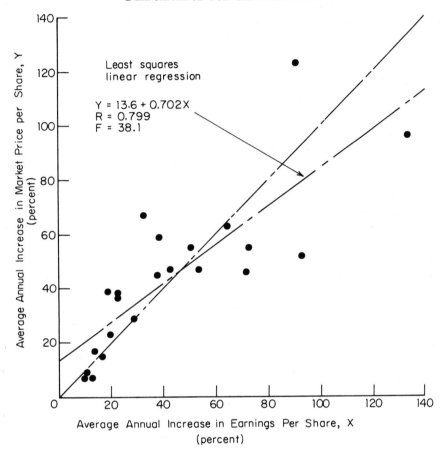

that it would be achieved through a high return, "internal growth" strategy or a low return, high expansion, acquisition strategy should not make any difference. To this point we suggest, the argument has a persuasive logical appeal.

However, if the "feedback relationship" between price-earnings ratio and earnings-per-share growth is to be important, expectations regarding *future* earnings and dividends per share must be based, at least in part, on the per-share performance that has been demonstrated in the *past*. What we would like to know is the extent to which future expectations and hence price-earnings ratios are based on past per-share performance and the extent to which they are based on other factors concerning the manner in which past per-share performance was achieved.[49] In particular, the more the investing public adjusts downward future

---

[49] Given a broad interpretation of the latter category, this divides all possible influences on price-earnings ratios into (1) some fairly well-defined measures of demonstrated per-share performance and (2) everything else.

expectations and hence price-earnings ratios when performance is achieved through "low-return, high-expansion" strategies, the less attractive such strategies become.[50]

In order to get some initial ideas on this we discussed the determinants of acquisitive conglomerate price-earnings ratios with a dozen investment analysts specializing in these companies. We attempt to summarize their collective thinking in a series of statements as follows: (1) a demonstrated record of constantly increasing earnings per share *is* the most important element, "the name of the game," even for acquisitive conglomerates; (2) higher earnings-per-share growth rates warrant higher price-earnings multiples, but there are some important qualifications; (3) in particular, earnings-per-share growth generated through the acquisition process is considered less likely to continue, or more risky to project into the future, than earnings-per-share growth based on internal strength in technology, proprietary products, market positions — that is, demonstrated "internal growth" is considered "more valuable" in terms of what it indicates for the future than growth through acquisition;[51] (4) since the proportions of earnings-per-share growth resulting from internal growth and from acquisition are difficult, usually impossible, to determine based on available information; the industries in which an acquisitive conglomerate participates and the future prospects for those industries become important in making judgments about past and future internal growth; (5) a high rate of return on equity was considered important by some analysts, but because of numerous acquisitions, some pooled, some purchased, a meaningful measure of rate of return is difficult to achieve; (6) finally, there is of course the discussion of the "quality of management," an image that seems to be conveyed to the investment community in a variety of ways.

All of this suggests that while past performance *is* an important determinant of price-earnings ratio and hence of future performance through acquisition, other things are also important. It is important to be in or to appear to be in "exciting" industries with good potential for the future. And some of the acquisitive conglomerate companies have become known for attempting to portray this image by applying fancy titles to lackluster industries. It is important to have or to appear to have substantial internal growth in companies that are purchased. And much verbiage in some annual reports and speeches is directed toward conveying this image. More appropriately, in a few cases corporations have begun to supply data regarding the internal growth that has been achieved.[52]

---

[50] As we will demonstrate in a later chapter, for a given level of per-share performance achieved through a strategy involving continuing additions to invested equity, a lower earnings multiple demands either a higher return on equity or a greater rate of expansion of invested equity (or some combination of the two).

[51] One analyst suggested that while the acquisitive conglomerate deserves something (in terms of projecting earnings-per-share growth) for its demonstrated competence in growth through acquisition, this takes the form of a "fudge factor" that is added on after the analysis of internal growth potential.

[52] See the 1966 and 1967 annual reports of Gulf & Western Industries and the 1967 annual report for Walter Kidde & Company. The data on internal growth presented in the Kidde annual report are discussed in Chapter IX. It is worth noting that none of the data of this type that have been presented is either audited or calculated in a way that is fully explained.

We have attempted to use the data on acquisitive conglomerates to see if we can sort out some of these influences. This attempt consisted of a series of linear regressions for M, the price-earnings multiple. Specifically we have attempted to determine the extent to which M is explained by (1) past per-share performance; (2) rate of expansion, given per-share performance; (3) rate of return, given per-share performance; (4) industries in which the corporation participates and the estimated future potential of those industries; (5) direct estimates by the investment community of future internal growth. The regression results, which we will proceed to interpret, are shown in Table 4.10.

The first five regressions are based on the data of Table 4.4 regarding the population of acquisitive conglomerates. We begin with measures of demonstrated performance in earnings and dividends per share. In the first regression the three independent variables are (1) G—average annual increase in earnings per share over 1962–1967, a measure of earnings-per-share growth rate; (2) GSD—the standard deviation of the figures for annual increase in earnings per share for each year, a measure of variability about earnings-per-share trend; (3) B—the proportion of reported earnings not paid out in dividends or the "reinvestment ratio," a measure of dividend policy. We indicate in the table only the signs of the regression coefficients and their significance. As discussed in the notes to the table we indicate significance all the way to the 20% level. Also shown are the multiple correlation coefficient and the F statistic. As shown, the first regression was not very significant. The signs for earnings-per-share growth and variability are as expected. The sign of the coefficient on the "reinvestment ratio" would indicate that investors prefer to see earnings retained rather than paid out in dividends.[53]

We then attempted to determine whether data regarding the type of growth process that achieved the per-share performance would improve the explanatory power of the regression. In regressions (2) through (5) we add, one at a time, three measures of rate of expansion and a measure of rate of return. The significance of the regression does not improve enough to be noteworthy in any case. The signs of the coefficients are as expected with one exception. For a given level of per-share performance a high expansion rate has a negative impact except as measured by C, the ratio of book equity increase to annual earnings. We have no explanation for the exception. The high rate of return on equity is viewed positively. To repeat, however, none of these coefficients may be considered of significance. The coefficient for earnings-per-share growth becomes significant at the 20% level in the regressions including C, rate of equity expansion relative to earnings, and R, rate of return on book equity. But that is hardly impressive.

Two possible problems (among many) are (1) that these firms are somewhat similar in type of growth process, perhaps making them a poor source of information regarding the impact of different types of growth, and (2) the accounting treatments for acquisitions cause some of these measures, particularly C and R, to be of very low quality. To provide an element of difference in growth strategy and to improve the quality of measures for C and R, we added the five "internal growth" firms to the population of acquisitive conglomerates. We then ran the

---

[53] Given the demonstrated performance of acquisitive conglomerates this may be considered a reasonable investor preference.

TABLE 4.10

DETERMINANTS OF ACQUISITIVE CONGLOMERATE PRICE-EARNINGS RATIOS: MULTIPLE REGRESSION ANALYSIS[1]

Linear Regressions for M [2]	Independent Variables									Multiple Correlation Coefficient	F Statistic
	GA [3]	GI [4]	G [5]	GSD [5]	B [5]	GT [6]	C	Z	R		
(1)			+	−	+					.259	1.62
(2)			+	−	+	−				.158	1.17
(3)			+*	−	+		+			.384	2.12
(4)			+	−	+			−		.241	1.40
(5)			+*	−	+				+	.305	1.67
(6)			+*	−*	−					.086	.92
(7)			+*	−*	−	−				.175	.77
(8)			+*	−*	−		+			.211	.67
(9)			+*	−*	+			−		.165	1.21
(10)			+**	−**	+				+****	.535	4.11***
(11)	+				−					.187	.56
(12)		+***			−					.408	3.50***

[1] Each line represents a linear regression on M of the general form $M = b_0 + b_1 X_1 + \ldots + b_n X_n + e$.

[2] For each regression there is either a positive or a negative sign shown for each independent variable included. The signs indicate a positive or a negative regression coefficient. Asterisks indicate the significance of the respective coefficients. The test used is based on the t distribution and indicates the probability that the regression values for each of the b_i could have resulted if the b_i was actually equal to zero. The following notation is used for these probabilities or "levels of significance": **** indicates 1%; *** indicates 5%; ** indicates 10%; * indicates 20%. For each regression equation we also show the multiple correlation coefficient and the F statistic. The value of F is an indicator of the probability that variance explained by the regression could have resulted if in fact the values of the regression coefficients were $b_0 = b_1 = \ldots = b_n = 0$. The notation for these probabilities or levels of significance is the same as for the t tests on individual coefficients.

[3] Estimates of future growth based on corporate industry participation and estimated growth rates for the respective industries as provided in Almon, *The American Economy to 1975*. See text and Tables 4.11 and 4.12 for more detail.

[4] Estimates of internal growth potential provided by investment research and management organizations. See text and Table 4.12 for more detail.

[5] Definitions as provided in the text.

[6] Definitions for this and the remaining variables are as provided for Table 4.4.

first five regressions again, which are listed as (6) through (10). In the first three the explanatory power of the regression was worse than before, even though the coefficients for earnings-per-share growth and for variability about earnings-per-share trend were significant at the 20% level. For the regression including Z, the rate of increase in outstanding shares, the explanatory power of the regression improved slightly. And for the regression with R, the rate of return on book equity, the explanatory power of the regression improved substantially. Here, the F statistic implies that the variation in M explained by the regression could have occurred "by accident" with only a 5% chance. The coefficient for R is significant at the 1% level and the coefficients for earnings-per-share growth and variability are significant at the 10% level. In general, the results suggest that while the rate and variability of earnings-per-share growth are consistently important, investors are distinguishing to some degree between types of growth processes and seem to prefer strategies that result in high rates of return on equity to those that do not.

None of this says very much about "internal growth," and the investment community seems quite interested in internal growth. The value of R, the rate of return on equity, is perhaps a vague sort of indicator of the company's ability to grow internally. However, it is not a very good indicator for at least two reasons. First, as we have discussed before, the ratio of after-tax earnings to book equity is not a very meaningful figure for these companies. Second, performance for shareholders, either "internally" or through acquisition, requires expansion as well as return. In fact, when a particular industry is considered to have "good potential for the future," this usually implies that the markets for its products are expected to grow rapidly rather than that it is an industry providing a high return on investment. Better measures of "internal growth potential" are obviously needed.

We took two approaches in an attempt to determine whether the ability to grow internally is a significant influence on price-earnings ratios. People in the investment community had told us that the industries in which the acquisitive conglomerate participated were important. And certainly it seemed that some of the "high technology" conglomerates had the higher multiples.[54] We attempted to get a measure of internal growth potential for each acquisitive conglomerate based on the industries in which it had operations and an "objective" estimate of the potential growth of each industry. Examples of the calculations performed are shown in Table 4.11. Data on the percentage of company sales[55] for 1967 in each industry category were taken from prospectuses and from Standard and Poor's *Corporation Records*. For an "objective" estimate of future industry growth we relied on Almon.[56] The resulting weighted averaged growth rates for

---

[54] For example, Litton had an average multiple of 35.0 over 1962–1967; Teledyne, 42.3; Tyco Laboratories, 51.0. See Table 7.4.

[55] Data on earnings by product group or industry were available only in isolated cases.

[56] *The American Economy to 1975*. Almon provides a systematic forecast of the economy in 1975 taking advantage of knowledge regarding the supply connections between industries (input-output coefficients). The results include projected annual growth rates for 90 industries.

TABLE 4.11

AN ESTIMATE OF "INTERNAL GROWTH POTENTIAL"
SOME SELECTED EXAMPLES

(Company Sales Distribution Based on 1967 Fiscal Years)

Company		Industries	
Product Group	*% of Sales*	*Growth Rate in % per Year*	*Industry Category*
GULF & WESTERN INDUSTRIES			
Television productions	.14%	4.0%	Radio, TV broadcasting
Motion picture revenues	.20	3.0	Amusements & recreation
Manufacturing (auto parts)	.35	3.7	Automobile repair services
Distribution (auto parts)	.16	3.7	Automobile repair services
Metals & chemicals	.13	2.5	Nonferrous ore mining
Agriculture (sugar, citrus, cattle)	.02	2.7	Crops & livestock
Weighted Average		3.43%	
ITT			
Telecommunication equipment	.29%	1.8%	Communication equipment
Technical industrial products	.20	4.1	Miscellaneous manufactured products
Components (electrical, electronic) & consumer products (TV, HiFi)	.11	2.7	Household appliances
Defense & space programs	.08	0.3	Research & development
Consumer & business services (car rental, hotels, data processing)	.26	3.9	Business services
Telephone utility operations	.06	4.5	Communication
Weighted Average		2.95%	
WHITE CONSOLIDATED INDUSTRIES			
Industrial machinery	.32%	4.0%	General industrial machinery
Valves & fluid controls	.11	4.1	Miscellaneous manufactured products
Sewing & knitting machinery	.08	4.2	Special industrial machinery
Household appliances	.21	2.7	Household appliances
Cooling & heating products	.15	4.2	Special industrial machinery
Other industrial & commercial	.13	4.1	Miscellaneous manufactured products
Weighted Average		3.80%	

SOURCE: Industry growth based on Almon, *The American Economy to 1975.*

each company are listed in the first column of Table 4.12. Using this as the measure of expected future growth, identified as GA, and the previous measure of variability as a measure of associated uncertainty, we ran a linear regression for M as shown in Table 4.10, equation (11). The results were very disappointing. Two problems stand out. As may be seen in Table 4.11, the process of matching industry categories as listed by the companies and as listed by Almon was frequently less than satisfactory. Second, it is very likely that Almon and the in-

TABLE 4.12

ESTIMATES OF FUTURE GROWTH FOR ACQUISITIVE CONGLOMERATES[1]

	Almon	Investment Research and Management Companies				Average Annual Increase in eps 1962–67
		A	*B*	*C*	*Average*	
"Automatic" Sprinkler	2.9%	15%	0%	7%	7.3%	55%
Automation Industries	1.4	*	15	11	13.0	65
Bangor Punta	3.5	10	10	6	8.7	19
Condec	3.7	12	5	9	8.7	43
FMC	3.7	9	8	7	8.0	17
Grace (W.R.)	4.8	8	6	6	6.7	10
Gulf & Western	3.4	18	10	5	11.0	72
ITT	3.0	10	11	11	10.7	14
Kidde (Walter)	4.0	15	15	7	12.3	73
Litton Industries	3.8	12	10	11	11.0	29
LTV	1.9	10	10	8	9.3	33
Mid-Continent Mfg.	0.6	9	*	15	12.0	28
Monogram Ind.	3.7	10	15	13	12.7	91
MSL Industries	3.2	12	*	5	8.5	11
Nytronics	3.0	12	*	11	11.5	39
Occidental	3.1	*	15	11	13.0	23
Ogden	3.0	8	5	7	6.7	38
Royal Industries	2.3	*	15	9	12.0	54
Signal Companies	2.5	*	5	6	5.5	13
Teledyne	2.7	15	15	20	16.7	93
Textron	1.7	9	8	9	8.7	23
TRW	2.1	12	10	15	12.3	20
Tyco Laboratories	4.1	20	20	18	19.3	90
U.S. Industries	4.0	12	10	7	9.7	81
Vernitron	4.1	*	20	18	19.0	51
White Consolidated	3.8	10	0	6	5.3	134
Whittaker	3.3	15	15	9	13.0	63

[1] For explanations of each column see text.

* Estimate unavailable because of lack of familiarity with company.

vestment community do not think in the same way about potential growth of various industries.[57]

We then decided to seek direct estimates by members of the investment community of future internal growth potential for each of the acquisitive conglomerates. This approach was based directly on the previously discussed statements that there was substantial reluctance to project future performance based on

---

[57] In particular the investment community frequently seems enamored with anything that sounds like "advanced technology." Almon's approach obviously takes into consideration the fact that sales growth requires more than advanced technology; it requires market demand as well. On the other hand, it could well be that the market's collective wisdom is greater than that of Almon. Our evidence only indicates that they are different.

acquisitions. In asking for estimates of "internal growth potential" we provided the following definition:

> The INTERNAL GROWTH POTENTIAL of an acquisitive conglomerate is defined as the expected average annual rate of growth of earnings per share over the next three to five years, assuming that (1) the company made no acquisitions or (2) they were restricted to industries in which it participates at present.

We began by soliciting estimates from individual analysts. This proved generally unsatisfactory because each individual typically could provide estimates on no more than half a dozen companies, and we found that we were getting a number of estimates for some companies and none for others. Finally, three investment research and management organizations cooperated in providing estimates which, in each case, were based on the collective knowledge of their members. Each of these organizations had some orientation toward acquisitive conglomerate companies. The estimates they provided are listed under columns A, B, and C in Table 4.12. We obtained at least two estimates for each company except one (Hydrometals), which we dropped from this part of the analysis. The next to the last column in Table 4.12 provides averages of the estimated growth rates. The last column is simply a repetition of the past earnings-per-share growth rates, provided for comparison.

Using the investment community estimates as a measure of expected earnings-per-share growth rate, identified as GI, and the measure of past variablity as a measure of uncertainty, we ran the regression for M shown as equation (12) in Table 4.10. The regression was significant at the 5% level (F statistic), and the coefficient for the estimate of future earnings-per-share growth was significant at the 20% level. The results imply that the investment community is attempting to make estimates of internal growth for acquisitive conglomerates and that these estimates do have some influence on price-earnings ratios. That is not to say that the estimates of internal growth are accurate. For example, we also obtained estimates of internal growth for Contek (disguised name), a company not listed in this chapter but one which we will examine in detail in Chapter VIII. While there has in fact been *no* internal growth on the average in the past for the profits of acquired companies at Contek, the investment community estimates consistently indicated *substantial* internal growth. Internal growth is important for acquisitive conglomerates, but, in the short run at least, the image may be sufficient.

Summary

Building on the historical perspective and evidence from other studies provided in Chapters II and III, we have progressed in this chapter to a study of the characteristics of specific companies. We have begun by identifying a group of firms that exceed specified criteria for (1) rate of expansion through acquisition, (2) diversification, and (3) per-share performance. The identification process consisted of screening against the specified criteria firms discussed in the financial community as acquisition-oriented, diversified companies. From the examination of approximately 80 firms, 28 were found that met the specifications. While there may well be others that would meet these criteria, we suggest that the number is small. We demonstrated that the 28 firms form a significant segment of the U.S. corporate world and that they are quite "different" with respect to both the "average" U.S. corporation and the corporation achieving superior performance through "high return, low expansion" strategies.

We then argued that those firms meeting the criteria for acquisition activity, diversification, and performance have some other "common characteristics." In particular, three "financial" characteristics were discussed: (1) the objective is growth in earnings per share; (2) acquisitions are expected to make an immediate contribution to earnings per share; (3) the high price-earnings ratio is viewed as an important resource. These characteristics imply that the acquisitive conglomerate is at least behaving in such a manner as to take advantage of the feedback relationship between price-earnings ratio and earnings-per-share growth through acquisition, if in fact this relationship exists. This strengthens the argument for examining in more detail the importance of this source of performance.

Five "operating" characteristics were discussed: (1) successful, profitable companies are acquired; (2) companies are acquired with capable management that can be retained; (3) management responsibility and authority are decentralized; (4) "visibility" is achieved through the planning and control process; (5) there is little operating integration of acquired subsidiaries. These characteristics imply that if performance improvement is to result in companies acquired at a rapid pace by the acquisitive conglomerate, it must result from "operating improvement without operating integration." This helps provide a framework for our later study of the operating influence of the acquisitive conglomerate on its subsidiaries.

We then used the data on the "population of acquisitive conglomerates" to examine two questions regarding market values. First, we continually suggest that earnings-per-share growth rate (for a given dividend policy) is an appropriate measure of performance for shareholders. Over 1962–1967 the average annual increase in earnings per share and market price per share were reasonably similar. We argued that the evidence helps to support our assumption.

Second, we attempted to determine the influence on price-earnings ratios of "type of growth strategy," given the level of per-share performance. Conclusions were based on both discussions with individuals in investment research organizations and on regression analysis. In particular, we were interested in the extent to which acquisitive conglomerate price-earnings ratios are determined by (1) past per-share performance, (2) type of growth strategy, "high return, low expansion" versus "low return, high expansion," given per-share performance, (3) the degree to which per-share performance could be expected to be achieved based on "internal growth" rather than growth through acquisition. We concluded that demonstrated earnings-per-share growth and variability are consistently of some significance in determining price-earnings ratios. Since past per-share performance to some extent determines price-earnings ratios, and price-earnings ratios clearly influence future per-share performance through acquisition, the "feedback relationship" between price-earnings ratio and earnings-per-share growth through acquisition exists and is of some potential significance. At the same time, investors do seem to prefer "high return, low expansion" strategies and "internal growth." This causes strategies for achieving performance through aggressive acquisition to be less attractive than would otherwise be the case. It also provides evidence of investor concern for the post-acquisition performance of companies that are acquired. We have argued, however, that sufficient information is not publicly available in most cases to distinguish internal growth from external growth. Price-earnings ratios are influenced by the image of what is going on internally, and that may not always correspond to reality.

With this as background, we proceed in the next three chapters to discuss the need for and the development of models of performance achievement in growth through acquisition.

CHAPTER V

Development of a Model of Performance
Through Acquisition and the First Model Element:
Valuation of Rapid Growth

In the preceding chapter we have observed that acquisitive conglomerates have some rather unusual characteristics. In achieving outstanding performance through a rapid pace of acquisition they have employed substantial amounts of new equity capital. Because of the relatively rapid rate of increase of outstanding shares, market price assumes a role it does not play for most corporations. For acquisitive conglomerates market price would appear to be a major determinant of per-share performance. At the same time, we have demonstrated that observed per-share performance is an important determinant of market prices. In short, market price and per-share performance through acquisition are interdependent. The significance of that interdependence, however, and the nature of its interaction with other variables in the growth process we have not yet been able to describe adequately.

We observed that acquisitive conglomerates have expanded their outstanding shares and invested equity much more rapidly than corporations achieving superior performance through "internal growth." Also, they have demonstrated much lower rates of return on invested equity than the "internal growth" corporations. Thus both in terms of their operating characteristics *and* in terms of some readily observable financial characteristics, acquisitive conglomerates are pursuing a different kind of strategy from the "internal growth" firms. There are, it would seem, achievable strategies for exceptional performance based on (1) low rates of return on equity and high rates of expansion of invested equity and (2) high return on equity and low expansion of equity. We have suggested that in the "low return, high expansion" strategies of growth through acquisition a variety of activities may be occurring to provide the observed performance. A given corporation may be growing internally, expanding rapidly through acquisition, and changing the leverage, profitability, and growth of companies acquired. All of these things affect market price, and market price affects the performance which they provide. It is a complex, interactive system. To capture it adequately with the written word or the unaided mind is a difficult task.

The ability to perceive clearly the mechanics of acquisitive conglomerate performance is hindered by the variety of elements and the nature of their interaction. A partial solution is provided by the mathematical model. Based on our knowledge of relationships between individual financial variables within the firm, we can build, through deductive logic, a model which abstractly represents the system: the acquiring and acquired firms in their market environment. One of the powers of the mathematical model lies in the ability to manipulate it. Having built, from the knowledge of parts of the system, a model of the system as a whole, we can manipulate it to observe the nature of relationships existing within that system. Hopefully, this will lead to greater understanding of the nature and significance of the relationships between financial variables in performance through acquisition. It is to the development of a model which will make this possible that this and the two following chapters are devoted.

As may be apparent by this point, we are proposing an abstract representation of the world which necessarily incorporates numerous simplifying assumptions. As in all theoretical discussions a compromise is sought. The objective here has been to keep the analysis as simple as possible while capturing enough of the essential characteristics of the system to provide an approximation to reality. That is, the objective has been to provide an analysis which is both readily understandable and meaningful.

OBJECTIVES

In general, our objective is to examine within an analytical framework the characteristics of corporate growth through a combination of internal and external investment and, based on this analysis, to discuss a normative framework for formulation of growth strategy and to provide a conceptual framework for studying the activities of acquisitive conglomerates. This objective may be broken into more specific parts:

1. To examine the role of market price in growth through acquisition or, more generally, in any type of growth process which involves substantial amounts of new equity capital and is thus dependent on market valuation; in particular, to examine the issues raised by the interdependence of market value and growth in these situations.
2. To examine the manner in which implementation of change in the characteristics of acquired companies is reflected in the per-share performance of the parent corporation.
3. To examine the conditions under which and the extent to which the various "immediate financial effects" of acquisitions may contribute to the performance of the acquiring firm.
4. To examine the manner in which different *types* of growth may be employed to achieve a given per-share *rate* of growth.
5. To discuss from a normative point of view the managerial problem of strategy formulation at the highest level, specifically, the problem of selection of a type of growth process which will use managerial capabilities in such a manner as to be most beneficial for shareholders.
6. To provide a conceptual framework for description and analysis of the activities of companies pursuing conglomerate growth through acquisition.

An Underlying Proposition

Acquisitive conglomerates exhibit a tendency to acquire other, typically smaller corporations on a continuing basis over time; acquisition appears to play an integral role in the overall strategy for growth. A basic proposition underlying our model development is that it will be useful for this type of corporation to view acquisition as a continuing process rather than as an isolated event.

This "process" of growth through acquisition, or "external" investment, obviously takes place in discrete steps, and it might be argued that it is only the discrete steps which must be examined. A comparison with the analysis of investment in new capacity, or "internal" investment, is useful. Internal investment takes place in more or less discrete steps as well, and a great deal of attention has been devoted to "project analysis" for capital budgeting. Yet models of corporate growth viewing investment as a continuous *process* have also received considerable attention and have, in our opinion, provided substantial insight regarding the characteristics of corporate growth. Our suggestion is not that the analysis of acquisition as a discrete step or an isolated event is without value; indeed, this type of analysis to which much attention has been devoted is very useful. The contention is simply that for acquisition, as has been the case for internal investment, a continuing *process* type of analysis may provide additional insight.

Nature of the Development

Our development of models is primarily a deductive process. We begin with familiar propositions in the literature on financial theory and attempt to build on these through deductive logic. We use descriptive data only in an indirect manner, in the choice of parameter values for illustration of the characteristics of the system under discussion.

The analysis takes the form of what may be called "comparative dynamics." That is, we shall not, as in the case in "classical dynamics," begin with differential equations describing relationships between variables and proceed to analyze the transient response of the system to various changes and the stability of the system under various conditions. Rather, we shall proceed directly to argue in terms of relationships between variables and their meanings for equilibrium states of growth.

The analysis does not provide a comprehensive treatment of the elements of uncertainty in the system. Inherent in the analysis is the assumption that we may discuss corporations within one "class" of risk for operating flows and that one market discount rate is appropriate for dealing with the expected values of these flows. The impact of varying levels of financial risk or leverage will be discussed where appropriate.

The "system" to be discussed consists of three basic elements: (1) the parent of the subject corporation; (2) the selling corporations; (3) the market system of valuation. Development and discussion of this "system" take place in the sequence described below.

VALUATION

We develop a model for the market valuation of the rapidly growing firm because of our dissatisfaction with the form of existing models. Valuation of rapid growth begins to raise problems when the growth rate exceeds what may be considered a "reasonable" estimate of the rate at which the market discounts future returns. Valuation models incorporating assumptions of constant growth and a single market discount rate for all firms imply prices which approach infinity as the rate of growth approaches the market discount rate.[1] One useful approach has been to assume that the investing public expects constant growth, but that the uncertainty of future returns increases with the rate of expected growth. Then utility theory may be employed to provide present values which are reasonable approximations of actual market prices.[2] The approach taken here avoids an explicit reliance on utility theory in the interest of simplicity. While it is accepted that constant, high rates of growth may be achieved over considerable periods of time, it is proposed that the market valuation system *may be represented* by a model based on expected monetary value where the investor *behaves as though* he expects the rate of growth to decline. Other valuation models have been proposed based on the idea of a declining growth rate.[3] However, because they make unreasonable assumptions regarding the pattern of expected growth or contain a sufficient number of parameters to complicate the intended analytical development excessively, they are considered less suitable for the present analysis.

The proposed model characterizes corporate growth as being composed of a "normal" component, a growth rate which investors might reasonably expect to be achieved by a large, mature firm over an indefinite period of time, and an "excess" component. The investing public, we suggest, must expect the "excess" component to decay at some rate toward zero. Otherwise, the company in question would occupy an ever-increasing proportion of the economy.

INTERNAL GROWTH WITH NEW EQUITY

We first employ the valuation model in the examination of the process of "internal" growth with continuing new equity financing. This is done in order

---

[1] See, for example, "Growth Stocks and the Petersburg Paradox."

[2] In particular see Lintner, "Optimal Dividends and Corporate Growth under Uncertainty"; also, this is the type of reasoning underlying the work of Gordon in *The Investment, Financing, and Valuation of the Corporation.*

[3] Examples include Malkiel, "Equity Yields, Growth and the Structure of Share Prices"; and Williams, *The Theory of Investment Value.*

to begin with a familiar case which has been treated by others[4] and one not complicated by the acquisition process. This analysis will provide a basis for first raising two issues not rigorously examined by others and of interest for the following discussion of growth through acquisition: (1) the interdependence of market value and growth; (2) the possibility of achieving a given rate of per-share growth in earnings and dividends with differing rate-of-return — rate-of-expansion combinations.

The model of internal corporate growth simply expresses in symbolic form the accounting relationships between the financial variables which determine per-share performance: rate of return; scale of investment; dividend policy; market price. Market price, in turn, is represented by the model described above.

The models of corporate growth used in the discussion of "internal" growth and in the subsequent discussion of growth through acquisition assume constant proportional relationships between financial variables. That is, the models represent constant rates of geometric growth.

Our proposition is that the corporation may achieve what approximates constant and rapid geometric growth over periods of considerable duration. But we suggest that, at any point in time, investors will determine market prices behaving as though they expect the rapid rate of growth to decline. Both our use of constant growth models and our combination of such models with a declining growth-rate valuation model warrant some discussion, which will be provided following the next section.

CORPORATE GROWTH THROUGH ACQUISITION

The development of the valuation model and the analysis of internal growth with continuing additions to equity are preparatory to the analysis of growth through acquisition. Here, we proceed through four cases that relate to different possible sources of performance portrayed in Figure 1.1 of the introduction. In each case the acquiring corporation is assumed to undertake internal and external investments each period which bear a constant proportional relationship to its current operations and to make uniform changes (or lack thereof) in all companies acquired. That is to say, just as we and others have examined the *process* of internal growth, it is the *process* of growth through acquisition which we examine here.

First, the acquiring corporation is assumed to make no financial or operating changes in companies acquired. The primary question concerns the possible impact of the interdependence between market value and performance and the conditions under which the shareholder may benefit from this process of acquisition without change.

Second, the parent corporation is assumed to change the leverage or accounting

---

[4] Lintner, "The Cost of Capital and Optimal Financing of Corporate Growth"; Gordon, *op. cit.,* Chapter 9, "Outside Equity Financing"; Miller and Modigliani, "Dividend Policy, Growth, and the Valuation of Shares," in particular, Section III, Earnings, Dividends, and Growth Rates.

treatments for acquired firms or to achieve market value advantages from increased diversification or size.[5] Attention is focused on the question of leverage and the analysis is then generalized to include the other immediate financial effects. The development here includes the demonstration that what is required in each case, in order for there to be a contribution to per-share performance, is an increase in the market value of the acquired firm. Further, we examine the required proportional change in market value and the scale of acquisition required for these immediate financial effects to contribute substantially to performance. We discuss the latter both with and without the assumed interdependence of market value and performance.

We then move to the sources of operating improvement, concentrating, at least in concept, on those not requiring operating integration. Here we incorporate the association, discussed in the introduction, of effects on the management process with altered rates of profitability and of effects on technologies, products, and markets with altered rates of growth.[6]

In the third case, we assume that through change in the management process of the acquired firm and hence the operating efficiency of the acquired firm, there may be an increase in the rate of return on equity. The impact on performance of varying levels of profitability improvement is examined and interaction with the "feedback effect" is discussed.

In the final case, we assume that through influence on the technologies, products, or markets of acquired companies there may be an increase in the rate of expansion of profitably employed capital, or more generally, in the rate of growth. Again, the relationship between the magnitude of change in growth rate and parent per-share performance is examined, and the interaction with the feedback effect is discussed.

This completes the outline of the coming theoretical discussion. We now return to our promised discussion of constant growth models and valuation based on expectations of declining growth.

MODELS OF CONSTANT CORPORATE GROWTH

The most important feature of models of constant corporate growth is the following assumption: for any specified scale of investment which remains a constant proportion of multiple of earnings from period to period, there will be achieved some average rate of return on investment which will remain constant from period to period. The implication is that investment opportunities in successive time periods are interdependent; further, that the nature of the interdependency is rigidly defined. More specifically, it is inherently assumed that the scale of investment which may be undertaken to provide any given average

---

[5] Tax reduction is omitted from the analysis because of our conclusion in the preceding chapter that it is not likely to be important for acquisitive conglomerates.

[6] Whether or not these particular associations are accepted does not alter the validity of the analysis.

rate of return will be, in any period, proportional to the scale of existing operations.

In terms of the possible assumptions which may be made regarding the relationship of corporate investment opportunities over time, this is at one end of the spectrum. At the other is the assumption that opportunities in successive periods are entirely independent.[7] While the strict interdependence assumption is not one which may be considered entirely realistic, it appears much more so than the idea of complete independence.

Two arguments support this contention. First, to some degree investment opportunities over time are inherently dependent. The magnitude of attractive investment opportunities which may be planned and implemented within a given period of time is dependent to a large extent on the magnitude of managerial resources within the firm. New investments require additional managerial capacity for their implementation and operation, but because investment implementation demands an increase in managerial resources, it also may provide an increase in the capacity to seek out, plan, and undertake future investment on

FIGURE 5.1

INTERRELATED GROWTH IN THE SCALE OF INVESTMENT OPPORTUNITIES
AND IN THE SUPPLY OF MANAGERIAL RESOURCES

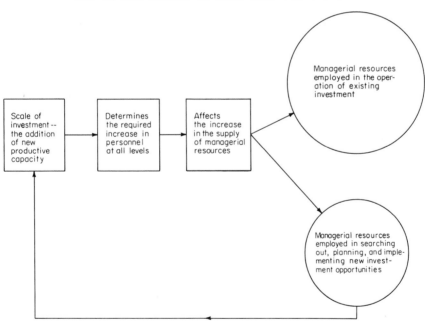

an expanded scale. As implied in Figure 5.1, while managerial resources constrain investment in a given period, the amount of investment undertaken tends to

---

[7] This, for example, is the assumption of Modigliani and Miller in "Dividend Policy, Growth, and the Valuation of Shares."

bring an increase in managerial resources and thus to expand the capacity for future planning and implementation of investment.

Second, there may be, and indeed "should be," a *planned* interdependence of investment opportunities. The investment in research and development, in advertising, in public relations, in training and developing capabilities of personnel all expand the future opportunities of the organization for profitable investment.

Thus, in all cases because of the *nature* of corporate growth and in some cases because of the *planning* for corporate growth, there is some dependence of successive investment opportunities. The idea of the independent investment project is more often than not an illusion. Rather than a collection of independent projects, the firm more closely resembles an economic continuum in which each investment influences the opportunities for future investment.

Some measure of evidence of the dependence of investment opportunities over time is provided by the achievement by a number of firms of patterns of growth which very nearly approximate constant geometric growth over substantial periods.[8] If the availability of attractive investments was truly independent of the scale of existing operations, so that investments became available in some random manner over time, the occurrence of a near geometric growth rate would be a rare coincidence.

To some extent, then, we would argue that current profitable investment enlarges the possibilities for future profitable investment, and a model which portrays this dependence is preferable to one which does not.

Finally, if we are to discuss present investment activities in terms of their effect on value, and if value is to be based on long-term expectations, some framework which relates present scale of investment to future growth must be employed. Either the analysis must be abandoned or a framework employed in which investment opportunities are interdependent over time.

The particular choice of the constant growth model is in part one of convenience. Presumably some retention of randomness in the development of investment opportunities would be desirable. Also, as has been discussed earlier, it would presumably be desirable to portray a rate of growth which gradually declined over time. However, for limited periods of time it does appear reasonable for *management to plan* in terms of a constant per-share growth rate; for geometric growth is, at least in some cases, fairly representative of reality.

The characteristic of the constant growth model which must be clearly kept in mind is that the explicit or direct rate of return on the investment in a given year is only part of the story. As has been discussed elsewhere,[9] there is an *implicit* or

---

[8] We have done no formal analysis to support this contention. However, one need only examine any one of several security analysis services which plot the logarithm of earnings per share versus time for a large sample of securities to find a number of examples (e.g., Litton, IBM, Xerox, Bristol Myers, Avon) where for periods of five years or more this relationship approximates a straight line. This does not of course imply that near constant growth in any one period assures more of the same in another as Raynor and Little (*Higgledy Piggedly Growth Again*) and Lintner and Glauber have demonstrated rather convincingly ("Higgledy Piggledy Growth in America?").

[9] Lintner, "Optimal Dividends and Corporate Growth Under Uncertainty," p. 37.

induced return on any period's investment because of the implied expansion of investment opportunities in future periods. For this reason models of constant growth imply, as we will later discuss in more detail, that the optimal "cutoff" rate of return is the earnings-price ratio. If instead current investment was assumed to be completely independent of future investment opportunities, the optimal cutoff rate under the specified conditions would be the market discount rate as is perhaps more commonly assumed.

CONSTANT GROWTH AND EXPECTATIONS OF DECLINE

A model portraying a constant rate of per-share growth will be combined in the same system with a model incorporating the assumption that investors behave as though they expect growth exceeding the "normal" rate to decay over time. While this implies an inconsistency of sorts, we claim that this inconsistency is fairly representative of reality for the rapidly growing firm.

As has been mentioned, some corporations have achieved near geometric rates over substantial periods of time. Also, corporate objectives are frequently expressed in terms of geometric rates of per-share growth (i.e., increase earnings per share by at least X percent per year).[10] Or, in general, it appears that some corporate managements set objectives and plan in terms of a specified rate or range of rates of per-share geometric growth, and that, based on the patterns of growth which have in some cases been achieved, it appears reasonable to do so. At the same time, for the rapidly growing firm the investing public does behave as though it expects the rate of growth to slow down.[11]

Inherent in the declining-growth-rate valuation model is the assumption that market price implies some rate at which any above "normal" rate of growth will decline. If the rate of growth does in fact decline in line with this implied expectation, the investing public will earn a return equal to the market discount rate. If, on the contrary, the management of a given corporation is able to maintain an above-average rate of growth over some substantial period of time, investors will earn a return exceeding the market discount rate (and vice versa). However, even as this above-average growth proceeds, the market will continue to value the firm's securities as though a decline is expected. This means that for any management which plans to achieve a rapid and fairly constant rate of per-share growth, the

---

[10] See Robichek and McDonald, "Financial Management in Transition." A questionnaire survey showed earnings per share (either the rate of growth or the future level at some specified time) to be substantially more important than five other listed objectives. Responses were from 163 large manufacturing companies in the Fortune 500.

[11] Three types of arguments favoring this contention are brought forward later in this chapter: (1) a rate of growth for a particular firm which is both constant over all future periods and in excess of the rate of growth of the economic environment is impossible; (2) a constant growth valuation model requires discount rates which are entirely "unreasonable" in order to maintain finite representations of price for rapid rates of growth; (3) a minor amount of evidence is provided, based on the model of expected decline and actual market prices.

managerial expectation and the investor expectation (as implied in the market price) will necessarily disagree. It also means that the frequently discussed idea that management should seek to maximize the *discounted present market value* of future returns may be naive for the rapidly growing corporation. The objective may more appropriately be thought of as maximizing the return to the shareholder *over time*. If a rapid rate of growth is maintained, the implied expectation of decline will continually be shifted into the future and valuation as a multiple of earnings will remain approximately the same over time. Thus, market value per share may be expected to grow at a rate which closely approximates the rate of growth of per-share earnings and dividends. In this manner, the potential for constant growth over limited but substantial periods, combined with continuing implied expectations of decline, is claimed to provide a meaningful representation of the behavior of performance, market price, and return to the investor over time for rapid-growth corporations.

The objective then of the management which strives to maintain a maximum rate of per-share growth over time is one which maximizes the return to the share-holder over time and does so by *continually contradicting the expectations for decline in the growth rate* which are implied by market price at any given point in time. The rapid rate of growth must of course eventually decline. However, if the rate of decline does not exceed the market-price-implied expectation, the return to the investor will not fall below the market discount rate.

Valuation with Expectations of Decline

In order to provide a model of market valuation for the rapidly growing corporation we must be more specific regarding the form investor expectations may take. In the remainder of this chapter we provide an argument regarding what we consider a reasonable representation for those expectations. This leads us to a model which implies investor expectations of a constant rate of "decay" of "excess" growth toward zero.

While the model provides considerable flexibility, it does of course take a specific mathematical form as it must. We would like to stress at the outset that this model is not *uniquely* suited to the later analysis. It does satisfy several objectives which we consider important:

1. Market price is an increasing function of the rate of growth in earnings per share for a given dividend policy.
2. Market prices do not, as "real" prices do not, approach infinite prices as the growth rate approaches and exceeds the assumed rate of market discount.
3. The implied pattern of expectations may be considered reasonable in that there are not implied discontinuities in the pattern of future growth or in derivatives of that growth.
4. The model is simple and compact enough to be comprehensible and to be employed in the later analysis without undue complication.

Any model which satisfied these objectives would be appropriate for our purposes here.

CRITICISM OF EXISTING MODELS

There is some agreement that the value of the corporate share may be logically represented by the discounted value of expected future dividends. This may be expressed

$$p_0 = \int_0 v_t e - kt_{dt} \tag{5-1}$$

where p_0 is the current share price, v_t is the expected dividend in period t, and k is the market discount rate.[12]

Several authors have begun with this basic expression and elaborated upon it to provide valuation models expressed in various terms. Among the better known and more extensive pieces of work is that of Myron Gordon.[13] Provided below is a brief criticism of what Gordon does with the above expression in order to develop motivation for doing with it something quite different.

Gordon begins with several assumptions the most important of which, for the present discussion, are that the investing public expects earnings per share to grow at their current rate indefinitely and that a constant proportion of these earnings will be paid out in dividends each year. This leads Gordon to the expression

$$p_0 = \frac{v_0}{k - g}$$

where g is the present and expected future rate of growth in earnings and dividends per share. In order to escape the dilemma in which he finds himself for the firm where the growth rate approaches or exceeds k, Gordon proposes the following form for the dividend yield

$$\frac{v_0}{p_0} = k - g = \lambda_0(1 + g)^{-\lambda}1$$

where λ_0 and λ_1 are constants. This in turn implies that the market discount rate is an increasing function of, and is always greater than, the expected rate of growth.

Gordon provides a rather tenuous effort to justify the increase in the market discount rate with the rate of corporate growth. First he makes the reasonable proposition that the variance of the market's subjective probability distribution for future dividends increases with their futurity. Then he attempts to convince the reader that, because of this, the discount rates appropriate for successive periods will be an increasing function of time. As Gordon demonstrates,[14] this

---

[12] A glossary of symbols used in this and following chapters is provided at the end of this chapter.

[13] See "The Savings, Investment, and Valuation of a Corporation" and *The Investment, Financing, and Valuation of the Corporation.*

[14] *The Investment, Financing, and Valuation of the Corporation*, p. 64.

latter proposition, when considered in comparison with a certainty equivalent approach, implies

$$\frac{u_t}{u_{t+1}} > \frac{1 + k_t}{1 + i}$$

where u_t is the conversion factor for period t which converts the expected dividend to its certainty equivalent, k_t is the discount rate appropriate for returns in period t, and i is the riskless interest rate. Or, for the discount rates to increase in successive periods the certainty equivalent factors must decrease each period at a rate exceeding the ratio of one plus the market discount rate divided by one plus the riskless interest rate.

Alternatively it may be shown[15] that for the discount rate to *remain constant* over time at some value, k, we must have

$$u_t = \frac{(1 + i)^t}{(1 + k)^t} = \left(1 - \frac{k - i}{1 + k}\right)^t.$$

This implies that the certainty equivalent factor decreases exponentially over time at the uniform rate $(k - i)/(1 + k)$; or since u_{t+1} becomes v_t with the passage of a time period, it may be said that uncertainty is resolved at a uniform rate over time. While there is no reason for accepting such a pattern of uncertainty resolution as generally applicable, there also appears to be no reason for accepting any other.

Gordon admits that "we cannot deductively prove anything with respect to the relation between k_{t+1} and k_t." But he suggests, "it is most unlikely that they should turn out to be equal, and the proposition $k_{t+1} < k_t$ is more suspect than its opposite." [16]

Continuing Gordon's argument, if the discount rate in each successive period increases, the equivalent average discount rate will be higher for the rapidly growing firm. The dividends at any future date will be larger the more rapidly the firm is growing, and in the calculation of an appropriate average discount rate, these larger dividends will weight more heavily the larger discount rates of later periods.

The weak link lies in the argument regarding the increase of discount rates with futurity. It appears intuitively plausible that they do. But to jump from the conjecture that they do to the proposition that the appropriate average discount rate will always exceed the rate of growth of the firm requires a considerable amount of imagination.

The implications of Gordon's development for the rapidly growing firm are curious. If we consider a firm which is and has been growing at a high rate, say 30% per year, the obvious implication is that the market discount rate exceeds 30%. Since it is generally suggested that investments should not be undertaken which provide an expected return[17] less than the cost of capital to the firm and

---

[15] See Robichek and Meyers, *Optimal Financing Decisions*, pp. 84–86.

[16] Gordon, *op. cit.*, p. 65.

[17] For the point of view adopted in this study, the "expected return" refers to the combination of the explicit return and the "induced return" as discussed earlier.

that the cost of capital equals the market discount rate, the unacceptable conclusion reached is that the firm in question should reject any investment proposal promising less than a 30% expected return.

The problems with Gordon's model discussed above may be traced to one assumption, that the investor expects the current rate of growth of a corporation to continue indefinitely. This results in such suspicious propositions as the expectation that a firm with $100 million in annual sales, currently growing at the rate of 30% per year, will reach $2 trillion in sales 40 years hence. To assume that the investor expects such growth is to bestow upon him a rather low level of intelligence.

Presumably, the assumption is made because it is analytically simple and results in a tractable model. As noted earlier, several authors have proposed valuation models which include the expectation of declining rates of growth, but unfortunately these have either been too complicated for the analytical development intended here or have incorporated unrealistic assumptions regarding the expected pattern of growth which detract from their credibility. As an example of the former, Williams[18] proposed models composed of elements describing growth in each of several stages. Because of the large number of parameters describing the expected growth pattern, such models would unnecessarily complicate the analytical development. As an example which must be considered unrealistic in terms of investor expectations, a valuation model discussed by Malkiel[19] represents a period of rapid growth which changes abruptly to normal growth at some future time.

The objective here is the development of a valuation model which is both reasonably simple and credible in terms of investor expectations regarding growth.

Moreover, based on the reasonable approximation to a "perfect market" of the market for shares of the larger, publicly held corporations, we consider it desirable to formulate a model in which the market discount rate is assumed constant for all firms in a given risk class regardless of growth rate.

CONCEPTUAL FRAMEWORK FOR THE MODEL

The corporation grows within and is dependent upon its external economic environment. And the external environment ultimately limits corporate growth, provided that other factors do not constrain growth before such environmental limits become effective. The limits on growth provided by the economic environment are not, however, time invariant. The "size" of the economy, in this country at least, has grown rather steadily over time and presumably will continue to do so in the future.

It is proposed that it would be reasonable for investors to expect a corporation to achieve into the indefinite future a "normal" rate of growth corresponding to the expected growth of the economic environment, but that growth in "excess" of

---

[18] See *The Theory of Investment Value.*
[19] See "Equity Yields, Growth and the Structure of Share Prices."

this normal rate cannot reasonably be expected to continue indefinitely. This provides the basic idea for the proposed valuation model. The rapidly growing corporation is assumed to have a "normal" and an "excess" component of growth such that the investing public expects the normal component to continue indefinitely and the excess component to decay gradually over time toward zero.

It may be argued that an assumed declining growth rate is not appropriate. It has frequently been observed that the growth of a firm may follow or logically should follow an "S" shaped pattern. Indeed, any number of patterns of growth might reasonably be expected by individual investors. And for the small firm or a firm which has recently entered a new area considered to have excellent growth potential, it would be reasonable to expect the rate of growth to increase over some limited period of time. However, the proposed pattern of gradual decline in growth rate does appear reasonable for expectations regarding most larger firms. And, if one pattern of growth is to be chosen, the assumption that gradual decline of excess growth is expected seems to be better than any alternative.

The corporation, viewed as a socio-economic system growing within a constrained economic environment, might be expected to have similarities to other types of systems growing within constrained environments. An idea for the expected pattern of growth is drawn from an analogy between the *excess* growth of the corporation and growth within physical or biological systems where the environment supporting growth has definite limits. Such growth frequently has the characteristic that the rate of decay in growth rate is proportional to the growth rate at any given point in time. Applied to the corporation, this would imply that the more the current growth of a firm exceeds some normal rate the more rapidly investors expect that excess rate of growth to decline.

Analogies may be made to systems where the underlying growth process is either geometric or arithmetic. Typically, for a small rate of decay, growth approaches an arithmetic rate in a physical process and a geometric rate in a biological process. Examples of the former are provided by the transient response of density in diffusion processes, of temperature in heat transfer processes, of electrical charge in capacitive-resistive circuits. The growth of a culture of bacteria provides an example of the latter. Both types of growth processes eventually will be examined in the attempt to derive a satisfactory model.

Corporate growth may be better characterized as a geometric process. If the corporation earns a constant rate of return on its equity, reinvests each period an amount bearing a fixed proportional relationship to its earnings, and maintains the same capital structure, the corporation will grow at a geometric rate.

Underlying the proposition that a constant or near constant rate of return may be earned on a geometrically expanding investment base is the assumption, discussed earlier, that the *internal* limits on profitable investment recede as the firm grows and have a tendency to be proportional to the size of the firm. The argument here is that while internal limits recede, another set of limits, *external* limiting factors provided by the economic environment, might be expected to make this process of rapid geometric growth more and more difficult to achieve as the particular corporation becomes a larger part of the economic environment. For the acquisitive conglomerate the Federal Trade Commission, the Antitrust

Division of the Department of Justice, and the supply of large, attractive candidates for acquisition are notable examples.

A biological growth analogy provides the structure for the approach in the initial development. Consider the above-mentioned culture of bacteria multiplying or growing geometrically in an environment containing a limited amount of the elements required for the support of life. When the quantity of living matter present is very small, there is a large surplus of the material which supports it, and the organisms grow rapidly. As the biological process expands, the surplus life-supporting material diminishes, and the rate of biological growth declines and ultimately equals zero when a state of equilibrium is reached between the organisms and their environment.

The *excess* growth of the corporation will initially be viewed as analogous to the above. The excess growth process is isolated by assuming that it takes place in a static economic environment. This environment is assumed to have a limited potential for the "support" of any individual corporation. This potential may be thought of as dependent on the initial characteristics of the firm which determine its capability for profitable expansion. As the corporation grows, less of this potential remains for the support of future growth. As a result, the rate of growth diminishes until the corporation reaches an equilibrium position with respect to its environment.

The analogy is far from perfect. It is considered of value because it provides a useful analytical approach to the problem of a reasonable expectation for the pattern of excess growth.

This analogy supplies conditions which will imply that the rate of decay in excess *geometric* growth is proportional to the corresponding *geometric* growth rate. It will be shown that this, unfortunately, does not lead to an analytically tractable valuation model. It will then be argued that a satisfactory approximation may be developed by reverting to the assumption that the rate of decay in excess *arithmetic* growth is proportional to the corresponding *arithmetic* growth rate. If investors determine market prices *behaving as though* they expect *excess* growth to proceed at *no greater than* an arithmetic rate, then the approximation provides an acceptable model. It is preferable to proceed with the analytical development, deferring a discussion of the results of this approximation until later.

ANALYTICAL DEVELOPMENT OF THE DECLINING-GROWTH-RATE MODEL

It is assumed that valuation is based on the expected stream of future dividends and earnings per share and that the firm follows the frequently observed practice of paying out a constant or near constant proportion of earnings in dividends.[20] Then dividend growth will follow the growth pattern of earnings per share. For analytical simplicity attention is initially focused on the internally financed firm where no new shares are issued. This permits the assumption of an expected

---

[20] Lintner, "Distribution of Incomes of Corporations among Dividends, Retained Earnings and Taxes."

constant relationship between revenue, earnings, and dividends. Effects on investor expectations of relaxation of this assumption will be discussed later.

At the outset attention is focused on the excess growth rate and the static economic environment. Let it be assumed that investors expect a firm in this static environment to have an ultimate revenue potential, R, and that any level of corporate operations supporting a dividend per share, $v'(t)$, requires some given amount of revenue, $r(t)$; further that the dividend rate is proportional to the supporting revenue,

$$v'(t) = \beta r(t) .$$

The dividend at any time t may be viewed as the dividend at time equal zero, v_0, times the multiple created through the excess growth of the corporation, $G_x(t)$:

$$v'(t) = v_0 G_x(t) . \tag{5-2}$$

Since the analysis first focuses upon an underlying geometric growth process, the quantity of interest is the change in the dividend per unit period of time as a proportion of the current dividend; or the rate of geometric growth:

$$\frac{d(v'(t))/dt}{v'(t)} = \frac{d(v_0 G_x(t))/dt}{v_0 G_x(t)} = \frac{d(\ln G_x(t))}{dt} .$$

The decline or rate of decay in geometric growth is then

$$\frac{d^2(\ln G_x(t))}{dt^2} .$$

As the firm grows geometrically, revenue potential declines geometrically. And the more rapidly this potential is disappearing, the more rapidly must the rate of growth slow down. It is assumed that the decay in the rate of geometric growth will be proportional to the decline in remaining revenue potential. The quantity of interest is the rate of decline in revenue potential as a proportion of the currently required revenue:

$$\frac{d(R - r(t))/dt}{r(t)} = \frac{d\left(R - \frac{1}{\beta} v_0 G_x(t)\right)/dt}{\frac{1}{\beta} v_0 G_x(t)} = -\frac{d(\ln G_x(t))}{dt} .$$

Then the assumed proportional relationship between the decline in geometric growth rate and the decline in revenue potential may be expressed:

$$\frac{d^2(\ln G_x(t))}{dt^2} = -w \frac{d(\ln G_x(t))}{dt} ,$$

or, as stated earlier, the rate of change in geometric growth is proportional to the corresponding geometric growth rate.

This differential equation has a solution of the form

$$\ln G_x(t) = c_1 e^{-wt} + c_2 .$$

If $v'(t)$ in equation (5-2) is expressed in the form

$$\ln v'(t) = \ln v_0 + \ln G_x(t) , \tag{5-3}$$

it is readily seen that as an initial condition it is necessary to satisfy

$$\ln G_x(t) = 0, \quad \text{for } t = 0,$$

so that

$$c_1 = -c_2.$$

Also, $\ln G_x(t)$ must be greater than zero for t is greater than zero, implying c_2 must be greater than zero. Letting $c_2 = \lambda$, $\ln G_x(t)$ may be written

$$\ln G_x(t) = \lambda(1 - e^{-wt}).$$

Then the initial rate of excess growth is

$$\frac{d(\ln G_x(t))}{dt} = \lambda w, \quad \text{for } t - 0,$$

or the product λw is determined by the current growth of the corporation, a relationship which will be of importance below.

Substituting the derived expression for $\ln G_x(t)$ into equation (5-3), the dividend in the assumed static economic environment may be expressed:

$$\ln v'(t) = \ln v_0 + \lambda(1 - e^{-wt}),$$

or

$$v'(t) = v_0 \exp (\lambda - \lambda e^{-wt}),$$

and it may be observed that the multiple of the initial dividend ultimately to be provided by the component of excess growth is equal to e^λ.

The "normal" growth component is brought into the above expression by assuming that normal growth is superimposed on the excess growth process. More specifically, it is assumed that the expected future dividend in the actual, expanding economic environment, $v(t)$, is achieved by increasing at the normal rate of growth the dividend due to excess growth in the hypothetical static economic environment, $v'(t)$. The dividend at any time t may now be expressed

$$v(t) = v_0 G_x(t) G_n(t),$$

or

$$\ln v(t) = \ln v_0 + \ln G_x(t) + \ln G_n(t), \tag{5-4}$$

where the assumption that the normal rate of growth may be expected to continue indefinitely can be written

$$\frac{d(\ln G_n(t))}{dt} = n.$$

The differential equation for $\ln G_n(t)$ has a solution of the form

$$\ln G_n(t) = nt + c_3.$$

Then, since it is necessary to satisfy

$$\ln G_n(t) = 0, \quad \text{for } t = 0,$$

the constant $c_3 = 0$, and

$$\ln G_n(t) = nt.$$

Now substituting into equation (5-4) for $\ln G_n(t)$ and $\ln G_x(t)$ the dividend at any time t may be written

$$\ln v(t) = \ln v_0 + \lambda(1 - e^{-wt}) + nt , \qquad (5\text{-}5)$$

or

$$v(t) = v_0 \exp\left(nt + \lambda(1 - e^{-wt})\right) . \qquad (5\text{-}6)$$

From equation (5-5) it may be shown that the rate of geometric growth, $g(t)$, is

$$g(t) = \frac{d(\ln v(t))}{dt} = n + \lambda w e^{-wt}.$$

The initial observed rate of geometric growth is thus

$$g_0 = n + \lambda w , \qquad \text{for } t = 0 ,$$

where, it will be recalled, the *product* λw is determined by the current excess growth of the corporation. Also, it may be readily observed that the rate of geometric growth approaches n as t increases toward infinity.

The parameter w may be considered the determinant of the rate of decay in the geometric growth rate. As w approaches zero, growth approaches a constant geometric rate, $(n + \lambda w)$; and as w increases, the rate at which geometric growth changes from $(n + \lambda w)$ to n increases. Since λw is determined by corporate performance, λ increases as w decreases, and the multiple of the initial dividend ultimately provided by excess growth, e^{λ}, is larger for smaller rates of growth decay, w.

A digression may be worthwhile at this point regarding the assumption that growth is internally financed or that the number of shares of common stock remains constant. The use of new equity capital over time generally implies that revenue growth exceeds growth in earnings per share and dividends per share. In the present analogy to biological growth the firm is viewed as having a given revenue potential. With the use of new equity financing this revenue potential will be exhausted at a more rapid rate than the rate at which dividends per share grow. In the proportional relationship between growth rate decay and disappearance of revenue potential, this would imply a larger value for the constant of proportionality, w. This, in turn, implies that for a given current growth rate, the expected rate of decay would be greater, the multiple of the initial dividend ultimately to be provided by excess growth would be smaller, and for a given discount rate the present value of a share would be smaller. Generally, the implication is that for a given current dividend and a given current rate of growth of earnings and dividends per share, a share will be less highly valued the greater is the rate of employment of new equity capital. Hence, the conceptual approach of the model suggests, as the data in the previous chapter suggest, that the valuation of a share might be expected to be dependent upon the *type of growth process*. A given rate of growth in earnings and dividends per share may be achieved by a particular rate of return on equity with no new equity financing or a lower rate of return with growing additions to equity through new issues. The analytical development here implies that the latter would be less highly valued because per-share growth would be expected to decay more rapidly.

AN APPROXIMATION TO THE MODEL

The model of the growth process developed above is considered to have desirable analytical characteristics, and it is unfortunate that it must come to an untimely end. But substitution of equation (5-6) for $v(t)$ into the basic valuation equation (5-1) yields

$$p_0 = \int_0^\infty v_0 \exp\left((n - k)t + \lambda(1 - e^{-wt})\right) dt , \qquad (5\text{-}7)$$

and equation (5-7) is a "nonelementary" or "nonanalytic" integral. That is, it may not be expressed in terms of the usual array of exponential, trigonometric, or logarithmic functions to which one is accustomed. Since an analytical model is needed, this result is unacceptable.

An approximation to this model of the growth process may be developed by assuming that excess growth *is not expected* to proceed at more than an *arithmetic* rate. The preceding development for excess growth will be reproduced in part based now on an assumed underlying arithmetic process. Here it is assumed that the rate of decay in

$$\frac{dv'(t)}{dt} = \frac{v_0 \, dG_x(t)}{dt}$$

is proportional to the rate at which revenue potential declines. The rate of decay in excess growth is now expressed

$$\frac{d^2v'(t)}{dt^2} = \frac{v_0 \, d^2G_x(t)}{dt^2} .$$

Since growth proceeds arithmetically, revenue potential is exhausted arithmetically and growth decay will be related to

$$\frac{d(R - r(t))}{dt} = -\frac{1}{\beta} v_0 \frac{dG_x(t)}{dt} .$$

Then the proportional relationship between rate of change in growth and decline in revenue potential may be expressed

$$\frac{d^2G_x(t)}{dt^2} = -w \frac{dG_x(t)}{dt} ,$$

where the constant of proportionality, w, is changed from the previous case in that it has here absorbed $1/\beta$, where β is the constant of proportionality between revenue and dividend per share.

The solution of the differential equation for $G_x(t)$ is of the general form

$$G_x(t) = c_1 e^{-wt} + c_2$$

and the requirement that

$$\ln G_x(t) = 0 , \qquad \text{for } t = 0 ,$$

means that in this case we must have

$$c_1 + c_2 = 1 .$$

Letting $c_2 = \lambda + 1$, $G_x(t)$ may be expressed

$$G_x(t) = 1 + \lambda(1 - e^{-wt}),$$ (5-8)

or

$$\ln G_x(t) = \ln (1 + \lambda(1 - e^{-wt})).$$ (5-9)

From equation (5-8) for $G_x(t)$ it is easily seen that the multiple of the dividend ultimately to be provided by the component of excess growth will be $(\lambda + 1)$ rather than e^λ as before. Thus, both λ and w have taken on somewhat different meanings in this second model.

Also from equation (5-8) it may be seen that the arithmetic rate of increase in the excess growth component,

$$\frac{dG_x(t)}{dt} = \lambda w e^{-wt},$$

approaches a linear, arithmetic pregression as w approaches zero for a given value of λw.

Retaining the same form for the normal component of growth and substituting the new equation (5-9) for $\ln G_x(t)$ into equation (5-4),

$$\ln v(t) = \ln v_0 + nt + \ln (1 + \lambda(1 - e^{-wt})),$$

or

$$v(t) = v_0 e^{nt}(1 + \lambda(1 - e^{-wt})).$$ (5-10)

The expression for the *geometric* rate of growth $g(t)$ is then

$$g(t) = \frac{d(\ln v(t))}{dt} = n + \frac{\lambda w e^{-wt}}{1 + \lambda(1 - e^{-wt})},$$ (5-11)

and as before the growth rate for t equal to zero is

$$g_0 = n + \lambda w.$$

It may also be seen from equation (5-11) that the rate of geometric growth declines toward n as t increases, and that the rate of change from the initial growth rate to the normal growth rate increases as w increases for a given λw.

The major difference from the earlier model is that the component of excess growth, the second term in equation (5-11), does not approach a linear logarithmic trend but simply a linear trend as shown from equation (5-8). It is of interest to examine the time before the rate of *excess* geometric growth, $g_e(t)$, falls to half the original value. Specifically, we wish to find t^* for which

$$\frac{\lambda w e^{-wt^*}}{1 + \lambda(1 - e^{-wt^*})} = \frac{\lambda w}{2}.$$

This may be simplified to

$$e^{-wt^*} = \frac{\lambda + 1}{\lambda + 2},$$

or

$$wt^* = \ln \left(\frac{\lambda + 2}{\lambda + 1}\right).$$

Recalling that $g_e(0) = \lambda w$, and substituting in the last expression for w,

$$t^* = \frac{1}{g_e(0)} \lambda \ln \left(1 + \frac{1}{\lambda + 1} \right).$$

Since λw is fixed by the present performance of the corporation, λ increases toward infinity as w decreases toward zero. It may be shown that for λ large the following approximation holds:

$$\lambda \ln \left(1 + \frac{1}{\lambda + 1} \right) \doteq 1 \, ,$$

or

$$\lim_{w \to 0} t^* \doteq \frac{1}{g_e(0)} = \frac{1}{\lambda w} \, .$$

As an example, consider a rapidly growing corporation where the current growth rate in earnings and dividends per share is 26% per year. Further, assume that the expected normal rate of growth (inflation included) is 6%. Then $g_e(0) = 20\%$, and for w very small, t^* is approximately five years. This implies that the expectation must be an excess growth rate *no greater than* 10% five years hence. Or investors must determine market price *behaving as though* they expect that the overall growth rate will have *at least declined* from 26% to 16% by the end of a five-year period. Otherwise, the "approximate" model cannot adequately represent market price.

The patterns of dividend growth provided by the original and the "approximate" model are compared in Figure 5.2 for an assumed initial growth rate of $(n + \lambda w) = 26\%$ and an assumed normal growth rate of $n = 6\%$. For *every* curve in both families of curves the initial geometric rate of growth is thus 26% per year. And for every curve the slope ultimately reaches 6% per year. The values of w determine how rapidly the slope declines from 26% to 6% per year. It should be recalled that the parameter w has taken on a somewhat different meaning in the second model, but in both cases it is the one parameter which varies the rate of expected decay in the initial growth rate.

FIGURE 5.2

COMPARISON OF DIVIDEND GROWTH MODELS

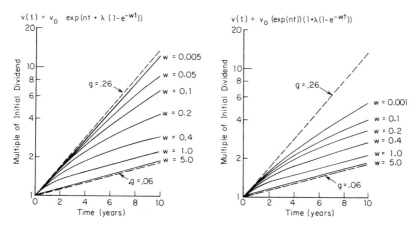

Of particular interest is the maximum pattern of growth which the second model is capable of portraying. If the "approximate" model provides, for small values of w, prices which are greater than those associated in the market with common stocks of corporations growing at various rates, then the model will be satisfactory for the intended purposes here. To determine this, the resulting valuation model must be examined.

Substituting equation (5-10) into the basic valuation equation (5-1) the resulting expression is

$$p_0 = \int_0^\infty v_0 e^{(n-k)t}(1 + \lambda(1 - e^{-wt}))\, dt ,$$

$$p_0 = \int_0^\infty v_0((\lambda + 1)e^{(n-k)t} - \lambda e^{(n-k+w)t})\, dt ,$$

$$p_0 = v_0 \left(\frac{1}{k - n} + \frac{\lambda w}{(k - n)(k - n + s)} \right). \tag{5-12}$$

Recalling that $g_0 = n + \lambda w$, and substituting for λw in the above

$$p_0 = v_0 \left(\frac{1}{k - n} + \frac{g_0 - n}{(k - n)(k - n + w)} \right). \tag{5-13}$$

Recognizing that the price-earnings multiple, m, equals p_0/v_0 times the proportion of earnings paid in dividends, $a = (1 - h)$ where h is the retention ratio, we may write

$$m = a \left[\frac{1}{k - n} + \frac{g_0 - n}{(k - n)(k - n + w)} \right]. \tag{5-14}$$

Typically, we will employ the model within a context which permits most of the variables in the model to be treated as constants. We look at various ways to achieve a given level of growth in earnings per share for a given dividend policy. This implies that the proportion, $a = (1 - h)$, of earnings paid in dividends remains constant. We present the model initially within the context of one "risk class" and assume the "decay constant" is not changed by different levels of performance. That is, we may consider k and w to be constants. In addition, it appears reasonable to consider the "normal" growth rate to remain unaffected by different levels of corporate performance.

For much of our discussion, then, the model simplifies to the form

$$m = a[\alpha_1 + \alpha_2(g - n)] , \tag{5-15}$$

where

$$\alpha_1 = 1/(k - n) ,$$

$$\alpha_2 = 1/(k - n)(k - n + w) ,$$

and a, α_1, α_2, and n are assumed to remain constant.

EVALUATING THE "APPROXIMATE" MODEL

The initial question is whether this model, incorporating the assumption that excess growth is not expected to proceed at greater than an arithmetic rate, has the flexibility to represent the observed market prices for rapidly growing firms while maintaining positive values of w. Or alternatively, as w approaches zero does the model represent price-earnings ratios which exceed those actually observed for rapidly growing firms?

Of critical importance in answering this question are the values to be assumed for the market discount rate, k, and the expected normal rate of growth, n. Both will be stated in *include* price inflation since interest rates and corporate growth rates are rarely expressed in deflated terms. The choice of $n = 6\%$ in the above discussion was based on the growth in GNP and corporate profits during the post-World-War-II era. GNP has grown at a rate very close to 6% and corporate profits have grown at a rate between 6% and 7%. It is assumed here that 6% is a growth rate which corporations might be expected to achieve into the indefinite future.

The market discount rate of course causes problems. The point of view taken here is that investors expect a return from holding common stocks in the future approximately the same as that which has been achieved "over the long run" in the past. Just what "the long run" means and what points in time should be used for such a measurement is pretty much an open question. In one extensive study of returns from common stock ownership[21] the longest period examined was 1926 to 1960. This time span appears reasonably appropriate since price-earnings ratios in 1926, 1960, and those observed at the time of this study were similar. The rate of return to the stockholder over the 1926–1960 period from investment of an equal sum in every company on the New York Stock Exchange in 1926 was 9.01%. This rate of return is based on dividends plus capital appreciation and includes round lot commissions but is before stockholder taxes. Based on this finding a market discount rate, k, of 9% is adopted for the present discussion.

First, the model may be examined for the "average" company. It is assumed that investors expect such a company to grow at the normal rate indefinitely. For this case $g_0 = n = g(t)$ for all t, and equation (5-13) "collapses" to the constant growth model

$$p_0 = v_0 \frac{1}{k - n}.$$

Substituting the assumed values for k and n,

$$\frac{v_0}{p_0} = 0.03 = 3\%.$$

It is encouraging to note that the dividend yield on Standard and Poor's 500 stocks has averaged 3.2% for the five years 1962–1966.

Attention is now focused on prices implied by the model for the rapidly growing firm. Use of the same market discount rate ($k = 9\%$) for such firms in the present argument may cause some concern; and in an attempt to justify doing so, the point of view adopted here for valuation of the company achieving rapid growth will be briefly reviewed.

Two quite different approaches to developing a model for market prices in rapid growth situations have been discussed. The approach taken by Gordon implies

---

[21] Fisher and Lorie, "Rates of Return on Investment in Common Stock."

that investors expect constant growth but the uncertainty which they attach to future returns is directly related to the rate of growth. The approach taken here implies that investors expect rapid growth rates to decline and that the rates at which future returns are discounted are independent of the growth rate *per se*. The "truth" about investor expectations most likely lies somewhere in between. Only a foolish investor will expect rapid growth to continue indefinitely; the economic environment must ultimately constrain such growth if other factors do not do so in the interim. At the same time, it does appear reasonable that the uncertainty of future returns is directly related to the current rate of growth; or more specifically, that if we are to work with expected future returns and market discount rates (rather than subjective distributions, utility functions, certainty equivalents, and riskless interest rates), the appropriate market discount rates should be directly related to current growth rates.

The model developed here implies that the effect of this relationship between uncertainty and growth may be incorporated in the expectation of decline in the growth rate, or that "actual" investor expectations of growth rate decay accompanied by discount rates which are an increasing function of the current growth rate *may be represented by* the expectation of more rapid growth rate decay and discount rates which are independent of the current rate of growth. One possible interpretation of this approach is that subjective distributions of future returns are converted to hypothetical "average risk equivalents" for which the average discount rate k is then appropriate for determining present values.

Table 5.1 has been prepared to investigate the acceptability of the valuation model. The question which this table attempts to answer may be stated: given what might be considered reasonable values for the average market discount rate ($k = 9\%$), and for the expected normal growth rate ($n = 6\%$), can the model represent with positive values of w the high price-earnings ratios observed for some rapidly growing corporations? The positive value of w implies that the excess growth component is expected to follow a pattern which everywhere falls below an arithmetic progression; for negative values of w the model is meaningless. As shown in Table 5.1, the price-earnings ratio, m, equals the ratio of dividends to earnings, a, times the price-dividend ratio taken from equation (5-13).

The ten companies shown in Table 5.1 were selected on the basis of stable growth patterns in earnings per share and unusually high price-earnings ratios. It is assumed that the stability in growth of earnings per share allows investors to develop reasonably uniform estimates of the current growth of the firm. It is also assumed that earnings-per-share growth is considered by investors to be a better measure of dividend growth than is the actual growth in dividends per share, or that the current dividend payout ratio is expected by investors to remain the "target" payout ratio in the future. The estimate of current growth in earnings per share used in Table 5.1 is the slope of the logarithmic trend for the five years 1962–1966.

For eight of the ten companies the valuation model is capable of representing the observed price-earnings ratios with positive values of w. The assumption that dividend growth is inferred from earnings growth is part of the difficulty in

TABLE 5.1

FLEXIBILITY OF THE DECLINING-GROWTH-RATE VALUATION MODEL

$$m = a \left[\frac{1}{k-n} + \frac{g_0 - n}{(k-n)(k-n+s)} \right]$$

based on assumed values: $k = 9\%$, $n = 6\%$

Company	Price-Earnings Ratio[1] m	Dividend Payout Ratio[2] a	Price-Dividend Ratio m/a	Five-Year Average Growth Rate[3] (%)	Growth Decay Parameter w	Price-Earnings Ratio for $w = 0$[4]
Avon	44	.58	76	23	.102	129
Bristol-Myers	39	.48	81	20	.067	93
Eastman Kodak	39	.51	77	22	.091	108
Emery Air Freight	50	.70	71	28	.154	194
Fairchild Camera	47	.23	204	40	.037	95
Hewlett-Packard	43	.15	286	25	*	37
IBM	43	.43	100	13	.005	47
Polaroid	66	.09	734	51	*	48
Texas Instruments	32	.17	188	39	.040	68
Xerox	63	.21	300	52	.027	125

[1] Price per share at year-end 1966 divided by earnings for 1966, where earnings have been normalized based on 5-year logarithmic trend.

[2] Actual dividends paid during 1966 divided by normalized earnings for 1966.

[3] Slope of logarithmic trend fitted by least squares method for earnings in 5 years 1962–1966 represents current growth rate, g_0.

[4] Price-earnings ratio if excess growth component were expected to increase in arithmetic progression.

* Current price indicates that expected growth pattern for excess growth component is greater than arithmetic progression.

the two cases where the model is inadequate. The dividend payout ratio for these two firms was extremely low (see column 2 of Table 5.1), and it would be reasonable for investors to expect future dividend growth greater than growth in earnings per share due to an increasing payout ratio. However, the alternative of using actual dividend growth does not seem to provide a solution for valuation of these firms. Hewlett-Packard did not initiate dividend payments until 1964 so that actual dividend growth over the five-year period used in preparation of the table is infinite. Polaroid paid only a "token" dividend until 1965 and 1966 when the dividend increased substantially. The resulting pattern would not appear appropriate for an investor inference regarding growth.

While the results of this limited test are far from conclusive, it would appear that the model has the flexibility to represent the market prices of most firms achieving patterns of fairly stable growth. Since attention will be focused upon stable processes in this study, the model is considered satisfactory for present purposes.

APPENDIX TO CHAPTER V

Glossary of Symbols for Chapters V, VI and VII

a Proportion of earnings paid in dividends.

b Subscript for "buying" corporation.

c Equity investment per period as a multiple of earnings available to equity.

D Book value of corporate debt.

E Book value of corporate equity.

G_n Ratio of earnings and dividends at any time, t, to their initial values, caused by normal component of growth.

G_x Same as G_n but due to excess component of growth.

g Rate of growth in earnings and dividends per share.

h Proportion of reported earnings not paid in dividends, the "reinvestment ratio."

i "Riskless" rate of interest.

k Market rate of discount for future returns to holders of common stock.

m Price-earnings multiple.

n "Normal" rate of corporate growth.

N Number of common shares outstanding.

p Market price per share.

P Market value of equity for the corporation.

q New (externally raised) equity capital per period as a multiple of current earnings.

r Average after-tax rate of return on invested equity at book value.

r_o Ratio of net operating income to total capital.

s Subscript for "selling" corporation.

t Subscript for periods of time.

U Premium by which price-earnings ratio of buyer exceeds that of seller $U = (m_b/m_s) - 1$.

v Dividends per share.

V Total corporate dividends.

w Decay constant for future rate of per-share growth.

x Ratio of equity to total capital.

y Earnings per common share.

Y Earnings available for common stock.

Y_o Net operating income.

z Rate of increase of outstanding common shares.

α_1 Constant used in valuation expression, equal to $1/(k - n)$.

α_2 Constant used in valuation expression, equal to $1/(k - n)(k - n + w)$.

γ_1 Ratio of standard derivation to mean for net operating income.

γ_2 Ratio of amount by which net operating income exceeds fixed charges to standard derivation of net operating income.

λ Constant in derivation of declining growth-rate valuation model; the multiple of current dividend and earnings ultimately provided by component of "excess" growth equals $(\lambda + 1)$.

CHAPTER VI

A Model of Corporate Performance Through Internal Growth with Continuing External Equity Financing

The inclusion of a chapter on "internal" growth with external equity financing in a study of growth through acquisition may be considered anomalous. The reason for its existence here, in very general terms, is that through the analysis it provides we first began to feel "comfortable" in our understanding of growth through acquisition. For us at least, this provided an important link between existing models of the process of corporate growth and our later discussion of growth through acquisition.

There are two major features which cause the analysis in the present chapter to differ from previous discussions. Neither is necessarily related to acquisition; and we therefore find it preferable to discuss them in the absence of acquisition. Both may simply be considered differences in viewpoint, but they change the conceptual framework in a way that is useful in thinking about growth through acquisition.

First, we know of no previous efforts to model corporate growth that have explicitly taken into consideration the interactive role of market price. For the corporation using little or no external equity financing in its growth process, it is satisfactory to view market price as merely a measure of shareholder wealth and to examine the dependence of market price on measures of corporate performance. But for the corporation employing substantial amounts of external equity financing, as are acquisitive conglomerates, it is essential that market price also be viewed as a major determinant of performance and that the dependence of measures of performance on market price also be examined.

Second, we know of no previous efforts to model corporate growth which have taken what we would consider a "flexible" attitude toward the "investment demand schedule." To limit the discussion of corporate growth to its characteristics for a specified schedule of investment demand is to ignore a large part of the flexibility that exists for the management of a corporation. One might counter that *the* investment demand schedule, properly conceived, includes *all* possible investment opportunities in which the corporation might participate. This viewpoint, we feel, gives an impression that *the* investment opportunities are all perched at the end of the manager's fingertips, waiting to be picked up and transformed into reality. It is more realistic, we suggest, to take into consideration the fact that management time is required for the development of investment opportunities, for searching them out, evaluating them, and planning their implementation. In any given period there is only a limited amount of managerial resources available to do this. We find it helpful to think of the process of deciding what kinds of investment opportunities to pursue and develop as the process of selecting a form of investment demand schedule on which to operate. It is this point of view which we will find useful in explaining the differences in rates of return and rates of expansion which were noted earlier between acquisitive conglomerates and "internal growth" corporations.

In sum, it is primarily (1) the role of market price in performance and (2) the difference in rate of return and rate of expansion employed to achieve performance which differentiate the models of growth through acquisition from other analyses of corporate growth. At the same time, there may be market-price-dependent growth and "low-return, high-expansion strategies" without acquisition; discussion of these characteristics in the absence of "external" investment links the analysis to previous discussions of corporate internal growth and provides a transition to the primary subject: corporate growth through acquisition.

New Equity Financing for Internal Investment

We will proceed through the development and analysis of this model of growth with a minimum of discussion. We will then return to discuss characteristics of this type of analysis in more detail before moving ahead to analyze the growth-through-acquisition cases along similar lines.

The following assumptions are made:

(1) The investment opportunities in any period bear a constant proportional relationship to the scale of then existing activities. In particular, assume that $r = f(c, \ldots)$ for all t, where r is the average after-tax rate of return on equity, c is the annual capital budget expressed as a proportion (or multiple) of annual earnings, and t designates annual periods. Further, the same scale of investment, c, will be made in each period. This is necessarily the case if the firm is assumed to behave optimally at the margin and the optimal marginal rate is assumed to remain constant over time.

(2) The dividend decision is made independently of the investment decision. The relationship between dividends and earnings will be

$$\frac{V_t}{Y_t} = a = (1 - h), \quad \text{for all } t,$$

where V_t is the annual rate of total corporate dividends during t, Y_t is the annual rate of total corporate earnings, a is the dividend payout rate, and h is the rate of retention of earnings.

(3) The capital structure of the corporation consists entirely of equity.[1]

(4) New shares of common stock issued each period will equal a constant, z, times the shares outstanding at the beginning of the period, N_t. The value of z may be positive, negative, or zero, but will be positive in the more interesting case. The issue (or purchase) of shares takes place at the prevailing market price

---

[1] Relaxation of this assumption will be discussed in a later section.

with no costs, discounts, or premiums involved.[2] New equity financing as a pro-portion, q, of earnings will be

$$q = (zN_t p_t)/Y_t = z\frac{N_t p_t}{N_t y_t} = zm \,,$$

where p_t is price per share, y_t is earnings per share, and m is the price-earnings multiple. Thus, the capital budget expressed as a proportion of current earnings will be

$$c = h + zm = h + q \,.$$

Given these assumptions, total corporate earnings in any period $t + 1$ may be written

$$y_{t+1}N_{t+1} = y_t N_t + r y_t N_t h + r(y_t m)(N_t z). \tag{6-1}$$

At the beginning of period $(t + 1)$, the corporation is assumed to reinvest a proportion, h, of earnings during t on which it earns at the average rate r during $(t + 1)$. Further, at the beginning of $(t + 1)$ the corporation issues zN_t new shares at a market price per share of $p_t = my_t$ and earns during period $(t + 1)$ at the average rate r on the newly raised funds.

It is desirable to convert equation (6-1) to continuous form. This may be done in several ways, but since it will be most convenient later to work with difference equations, we will do so now. Equation (6-1) may be written

$$(y + \Delta y)(N + \Delta N) = yN + ryN(h \, \Delta t) + rmyN(z \, \Delta t) \tag{6-2}$$

where the proportion, h, of annual earnings reinvested during Δt depends on the length of Δt, and similarly the proportion z of new shares issued during Δt depends on the length of Δt. All other variables become instantaneous expressions of "flows" on an annual basis or "stocks" at a given point in time.

Observing that $\Delta N = Nz \, \Delta t$, neglecting second order terms, and simplifying, equation (6-2) becomes

$$\frac{\Delta y}{y} = (rh + rmz - z) \, \Delta t \,.$$

Then, letting Δt and Δy go to zero and integrating both sides we have

$$y = \exp\left[(rh + rmz - z)t\right] ,$$

or the continuous rate of growth in earnings per share, $g = d(\ln y_t)/dt$, is

$$g = rh + rmz - z = r(h + q) - q/m \,. \tag{6-3}$$

It is also of interest to examine the growth of total corporate earnings. Observing that $Y_t = y_t N_t$ we may write

$$Y_{t+1} = Y_t + rhY_t + rmzY_t \,,$$

or

$$Y + \Delta Y = Y + Y(rh + rmz) \, \Delta t \,,$$

$$\frac{\Delta Y}{Y} = (rh + rmz) \, \Delta t \,.$$

---

[2] The assumption regarding issue costs is less serious for our primary subject of growth through acquisition, where securities are more frequently exchanged than issued to the public. (Some evidence on this was provided in Chapter II.)

Integrating in the limit, we have

$$Y = \exp\left[(rh + rmz)t\right]$$

or

$$g_T \equiv \frac{d \ln Y}{dt} = rh + rmz ,$$

and substituting into equation (6-3)

$$g = g_T - z ,$$

so that the rate of per-share growth in earnings and dividends equals the rate of growth in total corporate earnings and dividends, g_T, less the rate of growth in number of shares outstanding, z.[3]

Since the dividend payout rate is assumed predetermined, the current earnings *and* current dividend are fixed. Thus the scale of investment only affects the rate of growth of future dividends and earnings. If it is assumed that market price per share is an increasing function of the rate of growth of a given present dividend, *market price will be maximized by maximizing the value of per-share growth, g.*

As has been shown elsewhere,[4] the marginal rate of return on investment, ρ, under the conditions assumed in this discussion will be

$$\rho = \frac{\partial g_T}{\partial c} = \frac{\partial(rc)}{\partial c} = \frac{\partial}{\partial q}\left[r(h + q)\right] .$$

Thus, for the maximum rate of per-share growth, g, we have from equation (6-3)

$$\frac{\partial g}{\partial q} = \rho^* - \frac{m - q\dfrac{\partial m}{\partial q}}{m^2} = 0 .$$

Since current earnings are fixed, the conditions which maximize price will cause $\partial m/\partial q = 0$ and for the optimizing condition we have

$$\rho^* = 1/m ,$$

or the marginal rate of return on equity equals the ratio of current earnings to

---

[3] Lintner, "The Cost of Capital and Optimal Financing of Corporate Growth," p. 300, derives this result in a different and perhaps more concise manner as follows:

$$g = \frac{d \ln y_t}{dt} = \frac{d}{dt} \ln\left(\frac{Y_t}{N_t}\right)$$

$$= \frac{dY_t/dt}{Y_t} - \frac{dN_t/dt}{N_t}$$

$$= g_T - z .$$

[4] Lintner, *ibid.*, pp. 299–301, and with somewhat more discussion in "Optimal Dividends and Corporate Growth Under Uncertainty." Lintner's analysis also provides the other results in the remainder of this section, but in less general form. His derivation relies on the constant-growth-rate valuation model which, as indicated in the text, is not required.

current market price.[5] It should be noted that this result is achieved without reference to a specific valuation system or model. The *essential condition* is that *price be an increasing function of growth rate of a given present dividend, other things being the same.* This, of course, is the case for the J. B. Williams constant-growth valuation model as well as for the valuation model developed in the preceding chapter.

RETURN-EXPANSION COMBINATIONS

We will later be interested in viewing the different ways in which a given rate of per-share growth may be achieved in growth through acquisition, and will therefore do so for the case of internal investment with new equity financing. The role of market price in the growth process is the same here as in the growth-through-acquisition cases.

Initially we make the *assumption* that *for a given rate of growth in earnings per share the price-earnings multiple will not be affected by the combination of rate of return and rate of equity expansion which achieve it.*[6] It may be assumed

---

[5] It may be of interest to note that in the analysis of Modigliani and Miller, "Dividend Policy, Growth, and the Valuation of Shares," an expression is developed for per-share growth under the same assumptions as used here. This takes the form (their equation 25)

$$g = rc\left[\frac{1-h}{1-c}\right] - kq\left[\frac{1}{1-c}\right]$$

and subsumes a price-earnings multiple determined from a constant growth model having the form

$$m = \frac{1-c}{k-rc}.$$

The expression for per-share growth is derived from an expression for valuation where it is assumed that the contribution to value for existing owners of a constant return r on an investment Q_t in a future period t will be $(rQ_t - kQ_t)/k$, discounted to the present. Consequently, Modigliani and Miller profess that "no proposed project would be in the interest of the current owners if its yield were expected to be less than k since investing in such projects would reduce the values of their shares." However, introduction of the constant growth assumption implies dependence of investment demand schedules in successive periods (which they failed to recognize), and it may readily be shown from their above expressions that for

$$\frac{\partial g}{\partial q} = \frac{(1-h)[\rho(1-c) - k + rc]}{(1-c)^2} = 0,$$

$$\rho^* = \frac{k-rc}{1-c} = \frac{1}{m},$$

where

$$\rho = \frac{\partial(rc)}{\partial c}.$$

[6] This would require, as a minimum, that we restrict ourselves to a class of corporations (or a class of growth strategies for a given corporation, as will be discussed later) where the risk of operating flows is the same regardless of rate of return on capital. Operationally, it might be assumed that

$$(\ddot{Y}/\overline{Y}) = \gamma,$$

a constant, regardless of the value of $r = (\overline{Y}/E)$, where E is total capital under the present all-equity assumption.

that for any return-expansion combination the firm in question is behaving optimally at the margin. That is, for any return-expansion combination the rate of return on the marginal project is the same optimal rate, but because of varying shapes of investment demand schedules, the average rate of return and scale of investment differ.

Equation (6-3) may be written in the following form:

$$r = \frac{g + q/m}{h + q} = \frac{g + z}{h + zm}.$$ (6-4)

Under the assumed conditions the rate of earnings retention, h, and the price-earnings multiple, m, are both constant for a given per-share growth rate, g, and the required average rate of return to achieve any specified growth rate is a function of the rate of equity expansion, q, or the rate of new share issuance, z. The required average rate of return as a function of scale of investment will have slope

$$\frac{\partial r}{\partial q} = \frac{(h + q)/m - (g + q/m)}{(h + q)^2} = \frac{(h/m) - g}{(h + q)^2} < 0, \qquad \text{for } m > h/g.$$

The same condition holds for $\partial r/\partial z < 0$. Intuitively, we would expect the price-earnings multiple to exceed the reinvestment rate divided by the per-share growth rate except for very poorly performing companies.[7] Further, if it is accepted that $\partial m/\partial q > 0$, $\partial r/\partial q$ becomes increasingly negative for higher values of g and m.

Figure 6.1 provides an illustration of the relationship between average rate of return, r, and rate of new share issuance, z, and between r and the rate of equity expansion, q. The specified rate of per-share growth, g, is 30% and the dividend payout ratio, a, is assumed to be 50%. Different values of the price-earnings ratio, m, are assumed as shown. Thus, we are not saying what price-earnings multiple, m, is appropriate for a given rate of growth and payout ratio. We are only assuming that, whatever m is, it will be independent of the rate of return-rate of expansion combination which achieves the specified rate of growth and payout ratio. As may be readily observed from equation (6-4) the required average return, r, equals g/h for z or q equals zero and tends toward $1/m$ as z or q increases. Discussion of these curves is provided immediately following the next section.

EFFECT OF THE SYSTEM OF VALUATION

Additional insight is provided by including a valuation model in the analysis. Since the constant-growth model breaks down as the rate of growth approaches the market discount rate, the declining-growth-rate valuation model developed in the preceding chapter is employed. Here, it will be recalled that

$$p = v \left[\frac{1}{k - n} + \frac{g - n}{(k - n)(k - n + w)} \right]$$

---

[7] As an illustration of the relationship which has existed between these variables in recent years, for Moody's Industrial Average (125 common stocks) average values for the 10-year period 1957–1966 were $m = 17.5$, $h = .42$, $g = .055$, or $h/g = 7.7 < m$.

FIGURE 6.1

RATE OF RETURN-RATE OF EQUITY EXPANSION COMBINATIONS FOR SPECIFIED
GROWTH RATE AND VARYING PRICE-EARNINGS MULTIPLES

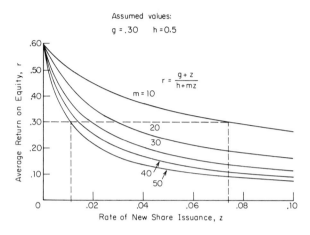

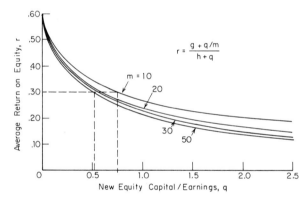

where v is the dividend per share, k the market discount rate, n the expected "normal" rate of growth, w the expected rate of decay of "excess" growth, and other symbols are as defined before.

The initial assumption that valuation is independent of the return-expansion combination may now be made more explicit. Specifically, for a given level of risk of operating earnings, we assume that k, n, and w are independent of g. Then for the present analysis we may write, for a class of firms having a given level of "business risk" but different growth rates, the following expression for the price-earnings multiple

$$\frac{p}{y} = m = a[\alpha_1 + \alpha_2(g - n)], \tag{6-5}$$

where

$$
\begin{aligned}
\alpha_1 &= 1/(k - n) \\
\alpha_2 &= 1/[(k - n)(k - n + w)]
\end{aligned}
\left.\vphantom{\begin{aligned} & \\ & \end{aligned}}\right\}
\begin{aligned}
&\text{remain constant} \\
&\text{for all } g.
\end{aligned}
$$

Then, substituting equation (6-5) for (6-4), the required average rate of return on equity for given growth rate and rate of equity expansion may be expressed

$$r = \frac{g + q/a[\alpha_1 + \alpha_2(g - n)]}{h + q} \, , \tag{6-6}$$

or

$$r = \frac{g + z}{h + az[\alpha_1 + \alpha_2(g - n)]} \, . \tag{6-7}$$

Figure 6.2 portrays families of curves determined by equations (6-6) and (6-7) where r is expressed as a function of either q or z. These are "isogrowth" curves and, at the same time, under the assumed conditions are "shareholder indifference" curves. The assumed values for k, n, w, and h are as indicated in this exhibit. For a discussion of this particular choice of k and n as providing a somewhat meaningful illustration, see the preceding chapter. The payout ratio was chosen to equal 50% for this example because, as was argued in the preceding chapter, the valuation expression makes more sense when the dividend growth

FIGURE 6.2

RATE OF RETURN-RATE OF EQUITY EXPANSION COMBINATIONS
FOR SPECIFIED RATES OF PER-SHARE GROWTH

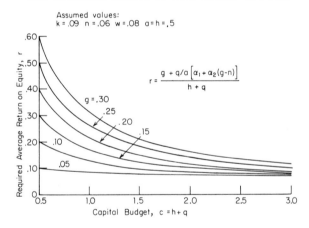

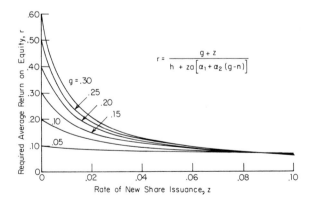

rate may be expected to follow fairly closely the earnings per-share growth rate. That is, the dividend payout ratio is such that it would not be expected to change dramatically as the corporation became larger and more mature. The choice of the decay factor, $w = .08$, was based on a subjective judgment after viewing the results of Table 5.1, regarding "Flexibility of the Declining-Growth-Rate Valuation Model." These values for parameters in the valuation expression will continue to be employed throughout the remainder of this chapter. It may be useful to have a visual representation of the expression we are using for the price-earnings multiple. This is provided in Figure 6.3. Added for purposes of comparison is the price-earnings multiple as represented by the constant growth model where k is assumed independent of g. Parameter values are as shown and are the same as incorporated in Figure 6.2. We turn now to the discussion of these and the preceding set of graphic relationships.

FIGURE 6.3

PRICE-EARNINGS MULTIPLE, DECLINING-GROWTH-RATE, AND CONSTANT-GROWTH-RATE VALUATION MODELS

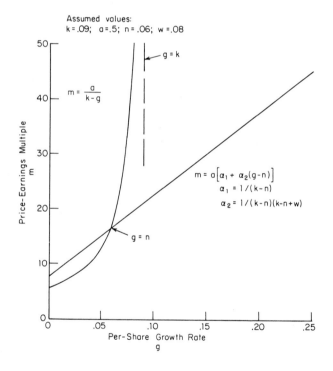

THE RETURN-EXPANSION RELATIONSHIP

Within the framework of the constant-growth-rate model, the nature of the relationship between return and scale of investment for given growth rate has been examined briefly. In Figure 6.1 this relationship was portrayed without reliance upon any specific valuation model. The only assumption regarding value was that it remain unchanged for a given rate of per-share growth as the combination of return and expansion varied.

Figure 6.1 is of interest for two reasons. First, it clearly shows the importance of investment scale to growth rate. *Investment scale and rate of return work together to determine per-share growth rate* in a manner similar to (but more complex than) the determination of rate of return on capital by the combination of sales margin and capital turnover. The discussion of growth has so often been focused upon financing limited to internally generated funds that growth and rate of return on equity are often considered to be similar measures. Such is obviously not the case. As shown in Figure 6.1, the required average rate of return to achieve the specified growth rate (30%) declines rather rapidly as investment scale is increased, even for rather low price-earnings multiples.

Second, Figure 6.1 clearly demonstrates the importance of the price-earnings multiple in growth through equity capital. Looking at the relationship between average rate of return on equity and rate of new share issuance, z, it may be seen that for an average return of 30%, the ratio of new shares per year to outstanding shares required to achieve the specified 30% rate of per-share growth (given the 50% dividend policy and the other assumptions) varies from about 1% to over 7% as the assumed price-earnings ratio varies from 50 to 10 (the lower price-earnings ratio requiring 7 times as many shares).

Scale of investment is more meaningfully expressed in terms of new capital employed than in terms of number of shares required to raise that capital. Since each share provides an amount of capital that is directly dependent upon the price-earnings multiple, the relationship between rate of return and new capital employed is not so striking. It may be observed that achievement of the 30% per-share growth rate with a 30% average return requires an amount of new equity capital expressed as a multiple of current earnings that varies from 0.5 to 0.75 as the assumed price-earnings multiple varies from 50 to 10 (the lower price-earnings requiring 1.5 times the rate of new capital employment of the larger price-earnings multiple). The implied impact of the difference in price-earnings ratios in determining the amount of capital which must be invested at a given average rate of return in order to achieve a given, higher rate of per-share growth is less than we had expected. However, this difference increases as the average rate of return is decreased. For example, at an average rate of return of 20%, the implied scale of new equity capital employment would be 1.1 times earnings for a price-earnings multiple of 50 and 2.0 times current earnings for a price-earnings multiple of 10 (the rate of new capital employment being 1.8 times as large for the lower price-earnings ratio).

Through the introduction of a valuation model into the analysis, a set of iso-growth curves were portrayed in Figure 6.2 for rate of return as a function of capital employed. In terms of a given investment demand schedule for a given firm, the significance of this exhibit is the portrayal of growth potential which may possibly be gained from an increase in the amount of capital employed. It has frequently been claimed that businessmen erroneously feel that internally generated funds have a very much lower "cost" than new equity capital.[8] If investment is restricted to internally generated funds for this reason, management may be falling far short in achieving its potential growth rate. In terms of the graph of average rate of return versus the capital budget expressed as a multiple of current earnings, the firm will reach higher isogrowth curves so long as the slope of the investment demand schedule, expressed in terms of *average* rate of return versus investment scale, is less than the slope of the isogrowth curves. By the earlier analytical demonstration, the point of tangency occurs where the marginal investment (under the assumed constant-growth process) yields a return equal to the earnings-price ratio.

Multiple Investment Demand Schedules

Figure 6.2 is of greater importance, both here and for what is to follow, because it may provide a way of thinking about growth at a broad policy level. The discussion of corporate investment frequently *begins* with the assumption that the firm faces a given investment demand schedule and must solve the problem of deciding which projects among those identified are to be undertaken. It appears more meaningful to say that management has a given amount of time and energy which may be expended in pursuing a variety of corporate strategies. Depending on the knowledge, the expertise, and the special competitive advantages which the firm has developed in the past, each prospective strategy will provide some array of investment opportunities over time. Thus, the firm faces a multitude of investment schedules each of which correspond to a broad corporate strategy for the future of the firm. While the management may think of behaving optimally at the margin in each and every case so that the rate of return on the marginal investment would in all cases be the same, the characteristics of investment demand would differ from case to case so that the scale and average return would be different. *If* a management group could think in terms of the investment demands and returns corresponding to each major alternative strategy, then the types of relationships portrayed in Figure 6.2 would be useful in choosing between alternative strategies. We have argued that the corporation maximizes market value at any point in time and the rate of growth of that market value (for a given dividend rate) by maximizing the rate of per-share growth. Thus the corporate management should strive to select that strategy providing the rate of return-rate of expansion combination which leads to the greatest sustainable rate

---

[8] For example, Gordon Donaldson, from his study of 20 large corporations, reached the conclusions that: (a) "The common practice of these 20 companies with respect to quantitative guides to investment decisions suggested a cost-free concept of retained earnings for the so-called mandatory investments in maintaining traditional product lines and a rough internal opportunity cost standard for 'voluntary' investment opportunities" (*Corporate Debt Capacity,* p. 62); (b) management strongly favored internal generation of external sources except for occasional unavoidable "bulges" in the need for funds (p. 67); (c) management's standards for investment tended to set absolute limits on the rate of investment related to the availability of internally generated funds (p. 67).

of growth in earnings per share; that is, the isogrowth curve or shareholder indifference curve furthest from the origin in Figure 6.2.

"Feedback" Relationship Between Market Value and Growth

It has been observed that for a given rate of per-share growth, under the assumption that valuation is not dependent on the combination of return and expansion which achieves it, the required average rate of return will approach the price-earnings ratio, $1/m$, as the rate of equity expansion, q, increases. For a rapid rate of per-share growth we would expect $1/m$ to be less than k, and the model thus implies that for larger values of q the *average* rate of return could be less than the market discount rate. Why and under what conditions might this be possible?

The only explanation which suggests itself for this is the interdependence of growth rate and market price. That is, the rate of growth of earnings and dividends per share is dependent upon market value per share when new shares are continually being issued over time, and market value per share is dependent upon the rate of per-share growth. The important relationships in this process are displayed in Figure 6.4. Specifically, the price-earnings ratio determines the

FIGURE 6.4

Feedback Relationship Between Market Value per Share and Rate of Growth: Internal Investment with New Equity Financing

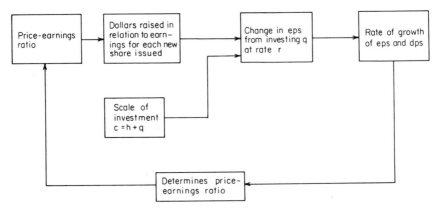

capital which will be obtained from the issue of each share of stock. This amount, invested at some rate, r, determines the earnings that will result from investment of the proceeds of each share. This, in combination with the scale of investment, or the number of new shares being issued, determines the effect on earnings per share for all shares of the company. This change, within the framework of the assumed continuous process, determines the pattern or rate of growth of earnings per share, which in turn is a major determinant of the price-earnings multiple.

The model implies that there may be various equilibrium states for a given growth rate each of which corresponds to some combination of rate of return and scale of investment and that as scale is assumed to become large the required average return may be quite small. The most critical assumption is the one which has been continually emphasized: that is, that the system of market valuation is not sensitive to the combination of rate of return and rate of investment which achieves a particular rate of growth, other things being the same.

The Ridiculous Extreme

The implied set of relationships whereby the *average* rate of return may approach the price-earnings ratio is not credible in the extreme. This may perhaps be seen most easily through an example.

Consider company Z which has somehow (perhaps through internal growth in the past) achieved a price-earnings multiple of 40. The company has decided that present activities are not to be further expanded; it is headed in new directions. Management knows of an area of investment opportunity where the average return will be nominal but the amount invested may be expanded geometrically over time at a rapid rate with little difficulty: municipal bonds. With a price-earnings multiple of 40 each dollar of new equity capital invested at say 5% will make some contribution to earnings per share on outstanding shares and presumably, if the investing public remains insensitive to what specifically is being done with their money, there should be some rate of new equity expansion which would provide a growth rate sufficient to justify the price-earnings multiple of 40 and to allow the process to continue. The model for share price and the specific values we have been using in the examples thus far indicate that a price-earnings multiple of 40 corresponds to a growth rate of 21.5% per annum in earnings per share with a 50 % dividend payout ratio. Equation (6-4) may be written

$$q = \frac{g - rh}{r - 1/m}$$

where we now have specified: $g = .215$; $r = .05$; $h = .5$; and $m = 40$. Solution to this equation indicates that the growth process can continue for a rate of new equity capital employment, q, equal to 7.6 times the rate of annual earnings, or a rate of new share issuance, $z, = q/m$ .19. That is, the rate of new share issuance would be such as to increase outstanding shares by 19% per year. If this process could continue we would have a corporation earning 5% on its equity, with earnings per share growing at a 21.5% annual rate and a price-earnings multiple of 40. Furthermore, the corporation would be continually contradicting shareholders' implied expectations for decline in the growth rate so that the return achieved by shareholders would be the dividend yield of 1.25% ($v/p = ay/p = a/m = .5/40$) *plus* a rate of growth in the market price matching the growth in earnings per share, or 21.5%. The combined return from dividends and capital gains would be 22.75%. Preposterous? It would certainly seem so.

The continuation of this process would be an example of what has been called "the chain letter" effect.[9] The return which justifies the payment of the high price-earnings multiple will be realized only if others continue to pay a high price-earnings multiple in the future. The same types of expectations justify participation in an actual chain letter except that in that case all presumably understand the rules of the game.

This extreme example presumably could not be carried out in reality because at some point attention would in fact begin to focus on the use being made of new equity funds and specifically the rate of return being earned on these funds. At this point the high price-earnings multiple and growth rate would undoubtedly meet with disaster. However, we may state this with some confidence only because the investment media has been designated as 5% municipal bonds. The investor may obviously undertake such investment on his own without the cost of managerial assistance. But what if it were electronics at an average rate of return on equity of 6%, or computer leasing at an average rate of return on investment of 7%? Here, maintaining a high growth rate of earnings per share through a high rate of investment and a high price-earnings ratio appears to be a very real possibility.

The main point of the example in this section has been to point out that while the model we have been discussing seems to have validity for what it says about the ability to achieve a given rate of growth with different combinations of return and investment expansion, at the extreme of very low average rate of return and high rate of expansion, the model cannot be considered to provide a meaningful approximation of reality. That is, at some point price must be expected to be dependent on the rate of return-rate of expansion combination which achieves a given rate of growth.

The "Value" of Growth

Other reasons exist for the dependence of value on the "type" of per-share growth that is being achieved. While we cannot suggest the specific character of the relations involved, the directions of influence seem clear in some cases.

1. For a given rate of per-share growth, the more rapid is the rate of new investment the more rapidly the firm is increasing in total size. As we argued in the preceding chapter, any corporation is to some extent limited in its growth by the external economic environment. It is suggested that as the firm becomes larger this constraint becomes more binding. Per-share growth which involves a more rapid rate of expansion of the total size of the corporation may be expected by the market to be less durable. Thus it may command a lower price.

2. There appear to be different risk characteristics which may be attributable to the returns from investment in productive capacity which has been under the direction of existing management for some significant period of time and to the returns from "new" investment. The latter usually requires the development or expansion of a market position and represents an unfamiliar venture into new

---

[9] See the Introduction.

territory; investors may justifiably consider it more risky.[10] The more of this type of investment there is in any one period in relation to the existing invested capital of the corporation, the more risky do the overall activities of the corporation become. Thus, for a given rate of growth we might expect a high expansion rate to be valued less highly than a lower one.

3. The market is accustomed to considering a high rate of return on corporate investment desirable. Thus, for any particular rate of per-share growth, investors appear to consider a high rate of return more "valuable" than a lower one.[11]

4. The high rate of expansion-growth process contains an extra element of risk in that it is dependent on market price, a variable over which management has considerably less than complete control.

5. From a managerial point of view it might be argued that high-expansion-rate growth is inherently more difficult to maintain. However, this is not at all clear. Rapid expansion increases the problems of managerial control and, perhaps even more important, the problems of procuring additional managerial resources of satisfactory quality for the expanding operations. On the other hand, a high rate of return on capital implies some highly specialized competitive advantage. Unless maintained through patent protection or ownership of some other unique type of resource, such competitive advantages are difficult to maintain because of their attraction to others.

All of the above taken together implies that market price may not be represented $p = f(g, \ldots)$ where r and c may be excluded, but rather, $p = f(g, r, c, \ldots)$. Nonetheless, it should be recognized that there will still be return-expansion combinations which will provide given rates of growth. However, in this case the isogrowth curves will not be shareholder indifference curves as was assumed above, and the model will in general be more complex.

THE ALL-EQUITY ASSUMPTION

In the preceding discussion we have assumed that the capital structure of the corporation was entirely composed of equity. It might seem that it would have been adequate to assume a constant relationship over time between debt and equity in the capital structure. This, however, would have been insufficient for our purposes. Since we have discussed changes in the *average* rate of return on capital, a constant proportion of debt in the capital structure would not provide a constant level of risk; that is, the coverage of any level of fixed charges and hence the "capacity" for debt changes with change in average return on capital. It would be possible to discuss debt in the preceding analysis under the assumption that for each level of average return on capital an amount of debt was included which provided a level of risk for equity holders that would be the same as with other levels of average return. The analysis could then proceed based on average

---

[10] This of course is less true for growth through acquisition, as will be later discussed.

[11] This at least was the conclusion in the preceding chapter from the regression analysis on acquisitive conglomerates.

return on equity and investment opportunities expressed in terms of equity requirements where all investments were assumed to be financed by the predetermined proportions of debt and equity.

For example, the assumption might be made that the risk of *operating flows* for a given set of strategies for growth is the same regardless of return on total capital. That is

$$\frac{\ddot{Y}_o}{\overline{Y}_o} = \gamma_1, \tag{6-8}$$

a constant, regardless of the value of

$$r_o = \frac{\overline{Y}_o}{E + D} = \frac{\overline{Y}_o}{TC}, \tag{6-9}$$

where Y_o is net operating income (subscript "o" for operating income, not a time period as before) and r_o is the ratio of net operating income to total capital, TC. Then, if it is assumed that an equal amount of risk will be perceived in net income if the excess of net operating income over fixed charges is a constant multiple of the standard deviation of net operating income,

$$\overline{Y}_o - iD = \gamma_2 \ddot{Y}_o, \tag{6-10}$$

then we may specify the ratio of debt to total capital which will be "appropriate" for any value of return on total capital, r_o.[12] Specifically, substituting for $\ddot{Y}_o$ from equation (6-8) into equation (6-10) we have

$$\overline{Y}_o - iD = \gamma_1\gamma_2\overline{Y}_o,$$

or

$$\overline{Y}_o = \frac{iD}{1 - \gamma_1\gamma_2}. \tag{6-11}$$

Then substituting for $\overline{Y}$ from equation (6-9) into equation (6-11) we have

$$\frac{D}{TC} = \frac{r_o(1 - \gamma_1\gamma_2)}{i}. \tag{6-12}$$

This equation implies that the "appropriate" amount of debt in relation to total capital will be an increasing function of the rate of return on total capital.[13]

For levels of debt determined in this manner we could then proceed, as indicated above, in terms of return on equity and scale of investment expressed in terms of equity requirements, where all investments were assumed to be financed by the predetermined proportions of debt and equity. The results of such an analysis would of course differ from the case in which an all-equity capital structure is assumed. Viewed in terms of the return on and expansion of total capital

---

[12] The "appropriate" levels of debt/(total capital) which result from these conditions for differing values of return on total capital, r_o, will be such that the variance on an expected dollar of earnings per share will be the same regardless of the value of r_o.

[13] It may also be noted that the implied "appropriate" ratio of debt to total capital is a decreasing function of each of (1) the interest rate, (2) the "riskiness" of net operating income ($\ddot{Y}/\overline{Y} = \gamma_1$), and (3) the required safety in the coverage of fixed charges, γ_2.

(which is the most meaningful way to talk about patterns of investment opportunities) the trade-off relationships would change so that high-return, low-expansion-rate growth could be achieved relatively more easily than before. This may be demonstrated by examining the relationship between rates of return on total capital and rates of return on equity, with and without debt in the capital structure.

First, it may be observed that the rate of per-share growth may be expressed as before

$$g = rh + rq - q/m',$$

where the only difference from the all-equity case is that the system of valuation will reflect the increased risk of returns to equity holders caused by the presence of debt in the capital structure and resultant fixed charges. The price-earnings multiple with debt, m', will now depend on the level of risk implied by γ_1 and γ_2 and the rate of per-share growth, g, but still may be assumed independent of the return-expansion combination which achieves the given growth rate. Thus we may construct isogrowth curves as before, and these will presumably be shareholder indifference curves.

However, in the all-equity case, rate of return on equity bears a constant proportional relationship to rate of return on total capital,

$$r = r_o(1 - t),$$

or

$$r_o = \frac{r}{1 - t},$$

where t in this section refers to the corporate tax rate (rather than time periods as it does elsewhere). As return on equity is assumed to increase, return on total capital must increase proportionately. With the introduction of debt, we have for the rate of return on equity

$$r = \frac{Y}{E} = \frac{(Y_o - iD)(1 - t)}{E}$$

$$= \frac{TC}{E}\left[\frac{Y_o}{TC} - i\frac{D}{TC}\right](1 - t).$$

Substituting from equation (6-12)

$$r = \frac{TC}{E}(r_o\gamma_1\gamma_2)(1 - t).$$

Then, observing that

$$\frac{E}{TC} = 1 - \frac{D}{TC} = 1 - \frac{r_o(1 - \gamma_1\gamma_2)}{i},$$

we may write

$$r = \frac{r_o i \gamma_1\gamma_2(1 - t)}{i - r_o(1 - \gamma_1\gamma_2)},$$

or inverting the relationship

$$r_o = \frac{r}{(1 - t)\gamma_1\gamma_2 + \dfrac{r}{i}(1 - \gamma_1\gamma_2)} \ .$$

Thus, as the rate of return on equity increases, the required rate of return on total capital increases less rapidly. For a given level of risk in the operating flows, the greater the additional risk the corporation wishes to assume with the addition of debt, the more favorable the trade-off relationships become toward high-return, low-expansion growth strategies. That is, the availability of leverage causes "low-return, high-expansion" strategies (such as growth through acquisition) to be *less* desirable relative to "high-return, low-expansion" strategies (such as pursued by the "internal growth" firms we examined) than would be the case in the absence of leverage.

PROBLEMS WITH THE METHOD OF ANALYSIS

Since we will continue with the preceding type of analysis, it may be worth while to point out some of its shortcomings. Quite a few problems have been assumed not to exist. For new equity issues, issue costs and discounts below prevailing market price have been ignored. It has been assumed that the dividend policy decision could reasonably be made in advance of the investment decision, or really before the formulation of strategy regarding what "business" the firm will be in. Also, it has in effect been assumed that the capital structure decision is made (as described in the preceding section) before the strategy or the investment decision. Dividend policy, capital structure policy, and investment policy are of course all interrelated. Only constant-growth processes have been discussed when perhaps of equal interest is the process by which the corporation changes from one growth process to another. It has been assumed that earnings are achieved immediately from the investment of newly raised funds which of course is not the case. Particularly in the assumed case of internal investment, there typically will be a lag of some significant duration between the employment of capital and the initial receipt of returns. Finally, new equity capital has played a relatively minor role in the growth of the average firm.[14]

The last two criticisms and the neglect of new issue costs need not bother us, since we have pursued the analysis in order to be able to apply it to the growth-through-acquisition cases. With acquisition there may be no earnings lag, the reliance on new equity capital clearly is of greater importance, and securities are frequently exchanged rather than issued to the public. As for the other criticisms, we can only say that notwithstanding these objections, it is felt that

---

[14] For the two years 1965 and 1966 new corporate common stock issues totaled $3.5 billion, while corporations retained $53.2 billion of $94.5 billion of total corporate earnings. Thus, while the value of h was .565 the value of q was only .037 or the ratio $q/h = .066$. (*Survey of Current Business*.)

the model provides a useful way of looking at the process of corporate growth with external equity financing and the different ways in which it may be achieved.

SUMMARY OF INTERNAL GROWTH WITH NEW EQUITY

The principal points which we have tried to make in this chapter are the following:

1. A given rate of growth in corporate earnings and dividends per share may be achieved by a variety of combinations of rate of return on equity and rate of expansion of invested capital. The rate of growth in earnings and dividends per share is determined by the combination of rate of return on equity and rate of equity expansion in a manner similar to (but more complex than) the determination of rate of return on capital by the combination of sales margin and capital turnover. The rate of return on equity alone does not tell us very much about the benefits to the shareholder, as some have assumed.

If market price per share is not affected by the return-expansion combination which achieves a particular rate of per-share growth, we may describe a family of isogrowth curves which will also be shareholder indifference curves. For rapid rates of growth and high price-earnings multiples, the required return to achieve a given growth rate declines rapidly for initial increases in the amount of new equity capital employed. This implies that for the firm earning a high rate of return but relying exclusively on internally generated funds because of the belief that new equity is far more "costly" than retained earnings, there may be considerable growth potential which is being ignored.

2. While discussions of the corporate investment decision often begin with an assumed investment demand schedule, the firm actually faces a multitude of investment demand schedules, each of which corresponds to a major alternative strategy. While optimal investment behavior would presumably provide the same return on the marginal project in each case, because of different shapes of the investment demand schedules they may provide quite different combinations of expected rate of return on equity and expected rate of growth of equity employed. We have suggested that a reasonable corporate objective is maximization of the rate of growth of earnings per share which is sustainable over the "long term" for a given dividend policy. The question of choice of strategy then becomes one of choosing that combination of rate of return and expansion which maximizes earnings per-share growth. Or in principle, the objective is one of seeking the highest isogrowth, shareholder indifference curve. According to the model we have employed, this will tend to maximize market price per share and the growth of market price per share over time. In this way maximizing earnings-per-share growth maximizes the return to shareholders *over time* and, so long as the rate of earnings growth is maintained, does so by *continually contradicting the expectations for decline implied in the market price* at any point in time. If, when rapid growth slows down, as it inevitably must, the decline approximately matches the implied market expectation, the shareholder will earn at the market discount rate.

3. Market price per share and growth in earnings and dividends per share are

interrelated. For this reason there is a "feedback" relationship which exists between market price and growth rate in the dynamics of the growth process as it
proceeds over time. This *may* make it possible to achieve a positive contribution
to per-share growth from external equity financing even when the *average* rate
of return is less than the market discount rate. To the extent that this occurs
there are expectations involved (knowingly or unknowingly) which are similar
to those causing individuals to participate in "chain letters." The required underlying conditions for this are (1) that the investing public is primarily interested
in the rate of per-share growth and (2) that they have little or no concern for
the combination of return on equity and rate of equity expansion which achieve
it. To the extent that these conditions hold, market price is dependent primarily
on observed per-share performance and secondarily on knowledge of specific applications intended for new equity funds and specific rates of return expected in
each case. Thus, market price to some extent becomes partially independent of
the firm's future and inevitably becomes, through new equity issues, a force in
shaping that future. Market price is of importance, then, not only because it
provides a measure of *shareholder wealth* at any point in time, as is often assumed, but because it becomes *a determinant of future performance* through the
raising of new equity capital.

4. The lack of attention to the combination of return and expansion which
achieves a particular rate of per-share growth must break down in extreme cases
as the implied rate of return becomes very small and the rate of equity expansion
very large. We suggested no means for determining value in such situations, and
the question of "appropriate" market value in these situations becomes a problem with which we are not prepared to deal. However, for several stated reasons,[15]
it may be expected that market price will to some extent be a function of the
return-expansion combination which achieves a particular rate of growth. Still,
there will be return-expansion combinations which will provide "isogrowth"
curves, but these will not at the same time be "shareholder indifference" curves.

---

[15] And based on our analysis of acquisitive conglomerate market prices in Chapter IV.

CHAPTER VII

Models of Corporate Performance
in Growth Through Acquisition

Having pursued the preceding line of analysis for the firm relying on "continuous" additions of new equity capital for internal investment, we are now ready to discuss growth through acquisition within the same framework.

The principal point to be made at the outset is that the analysis has considerably more relevance for the case of growth through acquisition because of the greater rate of expansion which appears feasible and the consequent greater reliance on new equity capital which will be required. Each acquisition typically brings with it an operational management group so that the "managerial constraint" on growth becomes much less severe. Further, each acquisition typically brings with it a developed market for the goods or services which it produces, avoiding the constraint on expansion often provided by the necessity of taking sales from other producers in order to achieve a market position. Finally, if the acquisition is a profitable going concern, it adds immediately to the stream of total earnings of the parent corporation. All of this has nothing to say about the potential *profitability* of growth through acquisition; only that the constraints, actual or perceived, which are present in the internal growth situation are less severe in growth through acquisition. Thus it makes more sense to talk about the trade-off relationships between rate of return and rate of expansion to achieve a given rate of per-share growth when discussing strategies of internal versus external growth or strategies of external growth with emphasis on different elements of the process (as we shall discuss) than it does in the case restricted to internal investment.

As indicated earlier, in this chapter four "cases" of growth through acquisition are discussed: (1) acquisition without change — isolation of the "feedback relationship" between market value and performance through acquisition; (2) acquisition with possible benefit from change in the financial characteristics of acquired firms; (3) acquisition with operating influence causing change in the profitability of acquired firms; (4) acquisition with operating influence causing change in the rate of growth of acquired firms. In the first case we simply look at equilibrium states where high performance and high price-earnings multiples can be self-supporting through acquisition. In each of the latter three cases we examine the trade-off relationships between scale of acquisition and magnitude of change in acquired company characteristics for specified levels of per-share performance. This is done for extreme possibilities of market valuation for acquisitive conglomerates: (1) market value based on observed per-share performance, as assumed in most of the analysis of the preceding chapter, and (2) market value based on per-share performance which would be achieved through "internal" investment alone (without the effects of acquisition), carrying to the extremes the suggestion of some members of the investment research community that internal growth is more highly valued.[1]

CASE 1: *Acquisition Without Change — Isolation of the "Feedback Relationship" Between Market Value and Performance Through Acquisition*

Consider the case of corporate growth through acquisition where the following conditions and simplifications are initially assumed:

1. A given parent corporation acquires others in a continuing process over time;
2. The expected future investments and earnings of all acquired companies remain the same after acquisition as before;
3. All acquisitions are made on a "stock-for-stock" basis and are treated as poolings of interests;
4. All companies considered have publicly traded securities and all acquisition transactions take place at market price;
5. All acquired corporations come from a population which is homogeneous with respect to profitability, growth, leverage, and accounting scheme; or, in general, it is assumed that all the proportional relationships and rates of change of variables are the same for every firm; however, these firms exist in an infinite variety of sizes so that the parent corporation can make any desired "scale of acquisition" in a given period of time;
6. The homogeneous selling population reinvests internally each period an amount, h, times annual earnings, on which it earns an average rate on equity of r; the remainder of internally generated funds, $a = 1 - h$, is annually paid in dividends;
7. The parent corporation undertakes each period a scale of acquisition which bears a constant proportional relationship to its existing market value.
8. There is no change in leverage or accounting treatment within acquired firms, and for those financial characteristics which inherently change with acquisition, such as size and diversification, there is no market value advantage.

Taken together, these assumptions are intended to imply that there is virtually *no change* in acquired companies. Thus, the parent corporation, being a composite of those it acquires, has the same rate of *internal* investment, average return on equity, and dividend policy as those acquired.

The expected outcome of the parent company's acquisition program may appear obvious. If market prices are accurate representations of the investing public's expectations of future investments and future earnings and of the manner in which these will be financed for each company; and if portfolio diversification is "as good as" corporate diversification, that is, if there is no significant increase in value simply because the parent corporation becomes more diversified or larger; then we would expect the total value of firms involved in such a process to remain unchanged by the fact of acquisition. Our objective is to look at the structure of the process, and at the possibility that this expected outcome might in fact *not* result.

---

[1] See the discussion in Chapter IV regarding the determinants of market values for acquisitive conglomerates.

At the beginning of each period our hypothetical company issues a number of shares equal to some proportion, z, times the number then outstanding, N_t, in the acquisition of companies from the homogeneous population. At a price of $p_t = y_t m_b$ where m_b is the price-earnings multiple of the buying corporation, this will provide a total market value of acquisitions of $y_t m_b z N_t$. If the price-earnings multiple of the selling firms is m_s, then each dollar of market value exchanged in acquisition will provide, on a pooling of interests basis, an amount of earnings equal $1/m_s$. Thus the earnings derived from the issuance of new shares in acquisitions will be $y N_t z m_b / m_s$.

At the same time the parent corporation is assumed to be reinvesting internally a certain portion, h, of annual earnings and paying out a certain portion, $a = (1 - h)$, in dividends. The total earnings, then, of the parent corporation in period $(t + 1)$ will be

$$y_{t+1} N_{t+1} = y_t N_t + rh y_t N_t + z \frac{m_b}{m_s} y_t N_t (1 + rh) .$$

This may be written in the form of a simple difference equation as follows, where h and z *are* dependent on the period of time, Δt:

$$(y + \Delta y)(N + \Delta N) = yN \left(1 + rh \, \Delta t + \frac{m_b}{m_s} z \, \Delta t + \frac{m_b}{m_s} zrh \, \Delta t^2 \right) .$$

Simplifying, neglecting second order terms, and integrating in the limit as Δt and Δy go to zero, we have

$$y = \exp \left[\left(rh + z \frac{m_b}{m_s} - z \right) t \right]$$

or

$$g = rh + z \left[\frac{m_b}{m_s} - 1 \right] \tag{7-1}$$

Thus, the rate of per-share growth equals the return on equity times the proportion of earnings reinvested, plus the rate of new share issuance times the amount by which the ratio of price-earnings multiples of buying to selling firms exceeds unity. Expressed in terms of the rate of equity capital expansion as a multiple of current earnings of the parent corporation, $q = zm_b$, we have

$$g = rh + q \left[\frac{1}{m_s} - \frac{1}{m_b} \right] . \tag{7-2}$$

For an assumed constant average rate of return on equity, the effect on per-share growth of increasing the scale of acquisition will be

$$\frac{\partial g}{\partial q} = \frac{1}{m_s} - \frac{1}{m_b} > 0 \qquad \text{for } m_b > m_s .$$

As noted, we would, under the assumed conditions, expect the price-earnings multiples of the parent corporation and of members of the homogeneous selling population to be the same. The relevant question is whether there might be circumstances where this would not be the case. Given that price per share is an increasing function of the observed rate of per-share growth, and that the observed rate of per-share growth is a function of the relative price-earnings multiples, are there equilibrium states where a high price-earnings multiple permits the acquisition process to generate a rate of per-share growth which "justifies" the price-earnings multiple?

This is certainly what some observers appear to think is going on,[2] and *mathematically*, given the assumptions of the present analysis, such states may be readily defined.[3] The counterpart of such states in reality is suggested by the previously discussed regression data. In a later chapter we will demonstrate the reality more convincingly for a single corporation.

The behavior of the growth model depends on the system of market valuation which is asumed. We shall look first at the J. B. Williams constant-growth model, as a basis for comparison, and subsequently at the declining-growth-rate valuation model.

With the constant-growth valuation model the price-earnings multiples of the buying and selling companies may be expressed

$$m_b = \frac{a}{k-g}, \qquad m_s = \frac{a}{k-rh}, \tag{7-3}$$

where valuation for the homogeneous group of selling companies is assumed to be determined by their internally generated growth, equal to rh, and the valuation of the parent corporation is assumed to be determined by their observed but as yet undefined rate of per-share growth, g. Substituting equation (7-3) into (7-1) provides

$$g - rh = z\left[\frac{k-rh}{k-g} - 1\right],$$

which, upon simplification, may be found to have the solution

$$(g - rh)(g - k + z) = 0,$$

$$g = rh,$$

or

$$g = k - z.$$

That is, either the rate of growth of the parent corporation is equal to that of the selling firms, and consequently their price-earnings multiples are the same, *or* the rate of growth and price-earnings multiple of the parent will differ and the growth rate will be $g = (k - z)$. It may be observed that

$$\frac{\partial g}{\partial z} = -1$$

in this case. This reflects the nature of the *equilibrium states* implied by the equations of the system. Price per share and resulting new equity capital from each share issued increase sufficiently rapidly with growth rate that higher growth rates and price-earnings ratios correspond to *smaller* rates of new share issuance.

---

[2] See references cited in the introduction.

[3] It is also possible, under the assumed conditions, that a low price-earnings ratio and growth trend could be sustained through purchase of like companies having growth rates which justified higher price-earnings ratios. It may be safely assumed that no one will find this desirable.

It might be inferred from this that, given any equilibrium position, an attempt to increase the scale of acquisition would result in a reduction of per-share growth rate. However, our ability to say anything at all about the transient characteristics of the system is subject to question.

Viewed in terms of the rate of equity expansion as a multiple of existing earnings, q, substitution of equation (7-3) into (7-2) provides

$$g - rh = q \left[\frac{k - rh}{a} - \frac{k - g}{a} \right],$$

which may be simplified to provide the following solution

$$(g - rh)(q - a) = 0,$$
$$g = rh$$

or

$$q = a.$$

The implication is that for any given value of z, if the per share growth rate remains *unequal to rh*, the rate of equity expansion will adjust so that $q = a$. The peculiar implications of this analysis presumably result from the rapid rate at which price increases (toward infinity) as the rate of growth increases toward the market discount rate.

A somewhat different result is achieved when the declining-growth-rate model is included in the analysis. The price-earnings multiples may be expressed

$$m_b = a[\alpha_1 + \alpha_2(g - n)]$$
$$m_s = a[\alpha_1 + \alpha_2(rh - n)] \tag{7-4}$$

where it will be recalled that

$$\alpha_1 = \frac{1}{k - n}, \qquad \alpha_2 = \frac{1}{(k - n)(k - n + w)}, \qquad \text{all } g.$$

Substitution for m_b and m_s in equation (7-2) provides either $g = rh$, or

$$g = \frac{q}{m_s} - \frac{\alpha_1}{\alpha_2} + n = \frac{q}{m_s} - (k - 2n + w),$$

and the implied effect on g of an increase of scale of acquisition is

$$\frac{\partial g}{\partial q} = \frac{1}{m_s} > 0.$$

Substitution of (7-4) into (7-1) provides an expression having solution of the form

$$(g - rh) \left(z - \frac{m_s}{a\alpha_2} \right) = 0,$$
$$g = rh,$$

or

$$z = \frac{m_s}{a\alpha_2}.$$

In general *it is implied* that increasing the rate of equity expansion for acquisition, q, results in an increase in g in such a way that $\partial g / \partial q = 1/m_s$; however, for any particular rate of growth, g, *greater than rh* the value of shares will adjust so that the number issued each period will be $z = m_s / a\alpha_2$ in the equilibrium state.

Although the implications of the declining-growth-rate model appear more reasonable, the rigidity of implied equilibrium states in both cases is unrealistic. The point of significance, however, is that for any system of valuation where market price per share is an increasing function of the rate of per-share growth, and it is the *rate* of per-share growth rather than *how it is achieved* which is given primary consideration, there will be implied equilibrium states where the per-share growth rate of the parent corporation will exceed that of corporations acquired, even though there is no operating change in acquired companies. It is worth reemphasizing these two properties which make this result possible: (1) that market price be an increasing function of the *observed* rate of per-share growth, and (2) that the investing public have little or no concern for the manner in which a particular rate of growth is achieved.

Regarding the dynamic properties of this system we have little to offer. That is, assuming that this process of g greater than rh can be achieved under the assumed conditions through acquisition, how may the process be initiated, how does the growth process change from one state to another, what would be the characteristics of decline if investors became unwilling to pay a price which ignores the process by which growth is achieved? On this we have no suggestions except to say that *intuitively* the solution to the above systems of equations which implied $g = rh$ appears to be a more *stable* one than the respective solutions in each case which indicate that equilibrium states exist where g may exceed rh. Certainly, if the investment research community were to succeed in its apparent attempt to value acquisitive conglomerates based on *internal growth*, the type of acquisition process described in this section, in which there is no change whatsoever in acquired companies, would add to neither earnings-per-share growth nor market value per share. However, as implied in Chapter IV, and as will be seen later in more detail for one corporation, actual internal performance and the image of that performance may be quite different.

CASE 2: *Change in Financial Characteristics — Possible Impact on Market Value and Hence on Performance Through Acquisition*

In this section we consider the potential impact on market value and performance of changing the financial characteristics of acquired firms but not their operating performance. We focus attention on the question of changing leverage and then generalize the discussion to include other changes in financial characteristics.

Initially we continue with all the assumptions of the previous section *except* the assumption that leverage remains unchanged within acquired companies. Specifically we assume that there is some ratio of book value of equity to total capital for the parent or buying firm, x_b, which is different from the ratio of book value of equity to total capital for the homogeneous group of selling firms, x_s.

Consider the acquisition of a firm with book value of equity equal E_s and book value of debt D_s. The change in the leverage of this firm at the point of acquisition will permit borrowing an amount for its purchase equal to

$$E_s - \left[\frac{E_b}{E_b + D_b} \right] (E_s + D_s)$$

where E_b and D_b are the book values of the buying firm's equity and debt respectively. Thus in terms of the *existing* earnings of the selling corporation, each dollar of market value of the buying corporation exchanged in acquisition will provide an amount of earnings equal to

$$\frac{Y_s}{P_s - \left[E_s - \dfrac{E_b}{E_b + D_b} (E_s + D_s) \right]} = \frac{1}{\dfrac{P_s}{Y_s} - \dfrac{1}{r_s E_s} \left[E_s - \dfrac{E_b}{E_b + D_b} (E_s + D_s) \right]}$$

$$= \frac{1}{m_s - \dfrac{1}{r_s} \left(1 - \dfrac{x_b}{x_s} \right)}.$$

However, with the change in the leverage of the selling corporation the earnings after interest and taxes will of course change. For what we wish to show, however, it will be sufficient to speak in terms of average return on equity. The earnings of the selling corporation after acquisition and change of leverage, Y_s', may be expressed

$$Y_s' = Y_s \left(\frac{Y_s'}{Y_s} \right)$$

so that *each dollar* of pre-acquisition earnings will now be

$$\frac{Y_s'}{Y_s} = \frac{r_b E_b [(E_s + D_s)/(E_b + D_b)]}{r_s E_s} = \frac{r_b x_b}{r_s x_s}.$$

Thus, each dollar of market value given up provides in earnings, after the change in leverage, an amount equal to

$$\frac{(r_b x_b / r_s x_s)}{m_s - \dfrac{1}{r_s} \left(1 - \dfrac{x_b}{x_s} \right)}.$$

We assume that at the beginning of each period the parent corporation reinvests a proportion of current earnings, h, internally at an average rate of r and in addition issues a number of new shares equal to some constant proportion, z, times the number outstanding, N_t, in the acquisition of other companies. Of the earnings of acquired companies a proportion, h, of these are also invested at an average rate of return r. The total earnings of the corporation in period $(t + 1)$ will thus be

$$y_{t+1} N_{t+1} = y_t N_t (1 + r_b h) + \frac{y_t N_t z m_b [(r_b x_b / r_s x_s) + r_b h]}{m - \dfrac{1}{r_s} \left(1 - \dfrac{x_b}{x_s} \right)}.$$

Expressing this as a difference equation where h and z depend on the length of the period in question, simplifying, neglecting second order terms, and integrating in the limit, we have for the rate of per-share growth

$$g = r_b h + z \left[\frac{m_b(r_b x_b / r_s x_s)}{m_s - \frac{1}{r_s}\left(1 - \frac{x_b}{x_s}\right)} - 1 \right].$$

It may be observed that the acquisition process will add to per-share performance only if

$$\frac{\partial g}{\partial z} > 0,$$

or

$$\frac{m_b r_b x_b / r_s x_s}{m_s - \frac{1}{r_s}\left(1 - \frac{x_b}{x_s}\right)} > 1.$$

This will be the case if

$$m_b r_b x_b > m_s r_s x_s - x_s\left(1 - \frac{x_b}{x_s}\right),$$

$$m_b r_b x_b - x_b > m_s r_s x_s - x_s,$$

$$\frac{P_b - E_b}{E_b + D_b} > \frac{P_s - E_s}{E_s + D_s},$$

where it will be recalled that $m = P/Y$, $r = Y/E$, and $x = E/(E + D)$. For this inequality to hold for the parent corporation with respect to those which are being acquired, it must hold for all the parts within the parent corporation. That is, in the transition from an independent operating entity to a part of the parent corporation, with a greater amount of debt in the capital structure, we must have for the *selling company*

$$\frac{P_s' - E_s'}{E_s' + D_s'} > \frac{P_s - E_s}{E_s + D_s},$$

where the primed variables indicate post-acquisition values. Under our assumptions, the total book value of the acquired enterprise will not change upon acquisition so that $(E' + D') = (E + D)$, and if we multiply through both sides by this quantity and then add it to each side, we have

$$P_s' + D_s' > P_s + D_s.$$

That is, the total market value of equity plus the book value of debt for the selling company must increase when it becomes a part of the parent with different capital structure. Since we may assume that the book value and market value of debt are the same in our hypothetical situation, the requirement for the acquisition process to contribute to per-share performance is that the total market value of the acquired company increase as a result of the acquisition and change in leverage. That is *not* to say that the price-earnings multiple of the parent must be larger than that of selling companies. Indeed we would expect that it would almost surely be less if there is a substantial increase in leverage upon acquisition. Still, the *total market value* of acquired firms may increase with

acquisition, and in that event there will be a contribution to per-share performance.[4]

The preceding analysis of leverage is somewhat complicated because acquisition
and the change in leverage are treated simultaneously. Through an artificial
separation of the change in financial characteristics and the acquisition we can
greatly simplify the analysis without in any way changing the meaning.

Let us assume, artificially, that the change in leverage is made *before* the
acquisition but that the change in market value (if any), due to the change in
leverage, occurs after acquisition. The assumption that the change in leverage
occurs before acquisition does not alter the economic relationships involved but
does allow us to work with variables in the form they will take within the
parent corporation after the acquisition.

Recalling our assumption that operating performance characteristics are the
same for all firms (see the assumptions of the preceding section), we may now
work with equation (7-2), which we repeat for convenience:

$$g = rh + q\left(\frac{1}{m_s} - \frac{1}{m_b}\right), \qquad (7\text{-}2)$$

where the price-earnings ratio for the seller, m_s, now is *after* the change in
leverage but *before* any market price reaction to that change. Here we have

$$\frac{\partial g}{\partial q} > 0 \qquad \text{for } m_b > m_s,$$

as previously discussed.

The implied condition is the same as that provided by the more complicated
analysis. Since m_s is after the leverage change, we do not have to worry with
changing levels of equity capitalization, fixed charges, and earnings. Any change
in market value will be reflected in change in the price-earnings ratio. Since m_b
reflects the market's reaction to the composite of previously acquired firms, for
which like changes in leverage are assumed to have been made, we will have
$m_b > m_s$ only if the market's reaction to the acquisition and change in leverage
increases the market value of the acquired firm.

Viewed in a similar manner, we may also examine the potential impact of
other changes in financial characteristics. For example, we may assume that m_s
in equation (7-2) is after any changes in accounting treatments at the time of
acquisition but before the market's reaction to those changes. As in the case of
leverage, the change of accounting treatments in acquired firms will add to per-
share performance through acquisition if such changes lead to increased market
values for the acquired firms.

For increases in size through acquisition and decreases in earnings variability
based on diversification through acquisition, the analysis is the same. However,
there is no change here in financial characteristics *within* the acquired firm.

---

[4] Under the argument of Modigliani and Miller in "Corporate Income Taxes and the Cost
of Capital: A Correction," we would expect that total value would in fact increase upon acquisition with an increase in the leverage of the selling company, other things being the same and
"within limits," because of the deductibility for taxes of the interest on debt.

The changes in size and diversification are inherent in the act of combination. In these cases, m_s in equation (7-2) is before market reaction to the acquisition. But there is no preceding change in financial characteristics within the acquired firm to alter the previous price-earnings ratio, as was the case for leverage and accounting change.

Since we may use equation (7-2) to represent each of the changes in financial characteristics, we may examine their potential impact on performance simultaneously. In Figure 7.1 we examine the relationship between per-share growth

FIGURE 7.1

ACQUISITION WITH CHANGE IN FINANCIAL CHARACTERISTICS
PERFORMANCE WITH AND WITHOUT FEEDBACK

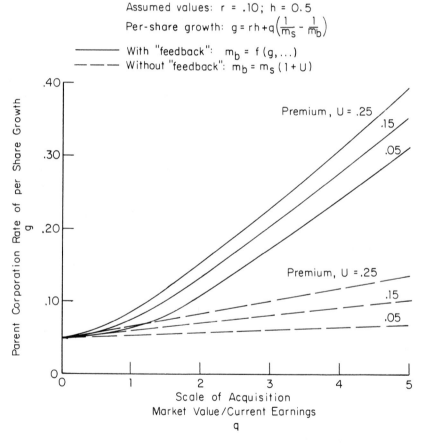

Assumed values: $r = .10$; $h = 0.5$

Per-share growth: $g = rh + q\left(\dfrac{1}{m_s} - \dfrac{1}{m_b}\right)$

—————— With "feedback": $m_b = f(g, \ldots)$

— — — Without "feedback": $m_b = m_s(1 + U)$

rate and scale of acquisition for various assumed premiums resulting from the change in leverage, accounting treatment, size, and/or diversification. The premium, U, is assumed to reflect the difference in prices resulting from the change in financial characteristics only. In order to clarify this, consider a firm in the selling group which is not acquired. We leave the operating performance exactly as is but change one or more of the discussed financial characteristics. The market's reaction to this change will alter the price-earnings ratio, m_s, to provide a new price-earnings multiple, m_s', such that

$$m_s' = m_s(1 + U) .$$

Figure 7.1 was prepared under two extreme sets of assumptions regarding valuation of the parent or acquiring corporation. In both cases valuation is based on the declining-growth-rate model. However, in one case, it is assumed that $m_b = m_s'$, the price-earnings ratio for the acquired firms, increased only by the premium caused by the change in financial characteristics. Valuation, therefore, is based upon the per-share growth rate provided by the "internal performance" of the parent which is the same as the demonstrated per-share performance of selling firms, $g_s = rh$. As previously discussed, "the feedback loop is open" under these assumptions; there is no valuation benefit for the parent from the immediate effects of acquisitions on earnings-per-share growth.

In the other case, market value of the parent is based on the observed rate of per-share performance, which of course includes the immediate effects of acquisitions. Here the "feedback relationship" between market value and performance is in operation.

Expressing the above in equation form, we have for the selling corporations the price-earnings ratio

$$m_s = a[\alpha_1 + \alpha_2(r_s h_s - n)] .$$

For the parent corporation, *without* the feedback relationship between value and performance, we have

$$m_b = m_s' = m_s(1 + U) .$$

And for the parent corporation, *with* the feedback relationship between per-share performance, we have

$$m_b = a[\alpha_1 + \alpha_2(g - n)](1 + U) ,$$

where g is of course the observed rate of per-share growth as defined by equation (7-2). For purposes of the illustration, the value of the rate of return on equity r_s is 0.10 and the assumed dividend payout ratio is 0.5. The values for α_1, α_2, and n are the same as used previously (see Figure 6.3).

Looking first at the set of dotted lines, we may discuss the potential impact on performance of changes in financial characteristics in the absence of any contribution to market value from the feedback relationship. Assume for the moment that the parent corporation can continually sell at a 25% premium, or can buy firms at a 25% discount, simply because of the change in financial characteristics of acquired firms (leverage, size, diversification, accounting treatment). Based on our market value estimate of q from Table 4.5 of about 3.5 for the "average" acquisitive conglomerate (and based on the parameter values assumed in Figure 7.1), such a premium would be expected to add about six percentage points to the per-share growth rate. While this could add a much more substantial amount to the per-share growth rate for those acquisitive conglomerates with much larger rates of expansion (larger values for q), for the "average" acquisitive conglomerate such a market value premium would explain only a small proportion of an average per-share growth rate of 50% per year.

In addition, the realism of a premium as large as 25%, due only to changing financial characteristics, appears subject to question. We noted in Chapter III that the evidence on the relationship between market value and leverage, size, diversification (variability), and accounting treatment is either mixed or unavailable, except for size where the findings appear fairly consistent. Also, except for size where we discussed some data regarding the sizes of acquiring and acquired firms, we know very little of the extent to which other changes in financial characteristics actually occur. There is a minor amount of evidence that acquisitive conglomerates are increasing the leverage of acquired firms. We noted in Figure 4.4 that the "average" member of the group had a ratio of debt to total capital over 1962–1967 equal to 0.34 ($x_b = 0.66$). For the average manufacturing firm in 1967, the comparable figure was 0.24.[5] However, it may be noted that the leverage estimate for acquisitive conglomerates becomes an overstatement through the bringing in of new equity at less than market value in poolings transactions.

In the area of change in accounting treatment we have very little meaningful data regarding what has occurred. And for those two corporations we later discuss in detail, the observed changes, as noted earlier, are in the direction of greater conservatism. There is unquestionably an increase in diversification for most firms joining an acquisitive conglomerate. However, the extent to which variability is actually reduced is unknown; and the evidence regarding market value advantages of diversification seems no stronger than the evidence and argument regarding its disadvantages (see Chapter III).

All of the above leads us to find it extremely difficult to believe that changes in the financial characteristics of acquired firms, considered in isolation, have provided more than a small proportion of the preformance achieved by acquisitive conglomerates.

On the other hand, when it is assumed that the parent company's market value is based on *observed* per-share performance, when market value and performance through acquisition are interdependent, the picture looks rather different. It is obvious from the solid lines in Figure 7.1 that the per-share growth which may be achieved through the combination of changes in financial characteristics and the feedback relationship is much more attractive. In this case, however, it might be said that the market value premium, from changing the financial characteristics for acquired firms only, plays a reinforcing and stabilizing role for the feedback relationship, and that the latter plays the dominant role in contributing to per-share performance for the parent corporation.

The potential importance of the feedback relationship may be measured by the difference between the dotted and solid lines for any given value of the assumed market price premium, U. Measured horizontally, it is the difference in scale of acquisition required to achieve a given per-share growth rate. Measured verti-

---

[5] From Securities and Exchange Commission–Federal Trade Commission, *Quarterly Financial Report for Manufacturing Corporations,* First Quarter, 1968.

cally, it is the difference in per-share growth rate which will be provided by a given scale of acquisition.

While our regression analysis concerning valuation for acquisitive conglomerates was not very conclusive, it implied that the feedback relationship should be at least partially effective. But regardless of how acquisitive conglomerates are in fact valued, it is clear from Figure 7.1 that the manner in which they are valued should be of very substantial importance for the management pursuing growth through aggressive acquisition. In addition, the manner in which management thinks values are determined should have a considerable impact on their acquisition strategy. Finally, it is obvious that the importance of the "feedback effect" between value and growth is directly related to the scale of acquisition. Thus, we would expect the level of management concern for market price to be directly related to the scale of expansion involved in their growth strategy. Such expectations will to some extent be borne out by our later study of Contek Incorporated in Chapter VIII.

While we will not discuss it in as much detail in the two following cases, the importance of the feedback effect may be similarly measured and the relationships which exist again lead to the expectations discussed above.

CASE 3: *Acquisition with Improvement in Profitability — Influence on the "Management Process"*

We next consider the case in which all the initial assumptions hold except that the parent corporation is assumed to change the rate of return on equity of acquired companies. However, it is not assumed to change the rate of growth of sales or of capital employed. The underlying idea is that we are examining a corporation which has an impact on the internal operating efficiency of acquired companies, but does not have an impact on the nature of goods or services produced. That is, by changing *how* existing activities are *managed* it has an impact on *efficiency* and hence on *profitability*, but because it has no impact on *what* goods and services are produced, it has no effect on *demand*, so that the rate of growth of sales and consequently *the rate of growth of capital employed* will be expected to continue the same as before acquisition.[6,7] The increase in rate of

---

[6] This case is not nearly so clear cut as we would like to imply. The inherent and somewhat unrealistic assumption involved is that with an increase in operating efficiency and hence a reduction in unit costs, our hypothesized firm either (1) *chooses* not to lower prices or (2) knows it could not increase its profits if it did.

[7] The more simple assumption from an analytical point of view is that the rate of internal reinvestment of earnings, h, is the same for the parent and selling corporations. Then we would have

$$y_{t+1}N_{t+1} = y_t N_t \left[1 + r_b h + \frac{q\, r_b}{m_s r_s} \left(+ r_b h \right) \right],$$

or

$$g = r_b h + \frac{q}{m_s} \left[\frac{r_b}{r} - \frac{m_s}{m_b} \right],$$

but in this case it is obvious that the scale of internal investment changes when the rate of return on equity of selling corporations is changed, which does not permit us to make the distinction between the two cases in which the parent firm has an impact on *either* the rate of return on equity *or* the scale of investment.

return is assumed to occur within the first period after acquisition.[8] In addition, we return to the assumption that the leverage and accounting scheme of the homogeneous selling group remain unchanged upon acquisition, and that there is no market value advantage for those financial characteristics (size and diversification) for which change is inherent with acquisition.

For the capital budget of the selling corporation to remain unchanged when the rate of return on equity is increased, we must have

$$h_b Y' = h_s Y ,$$

where Y and Y' are the total earnings of the selling corporation before and after acquisition respectively, that is, before and after the increase in rate of return on equity. This implies

$$h_b r_b E_s = h_s r_s E_s ,$$

$$r_b h_b = r_s h_s ,$$

$$h_s - h_b = h_s - \frac{r_s}{r_b} h_s = h_s \left(1 - \frac{r_s}{r_b} \right) ,$$

where the latter two expressions shall be of use to us below. Since the parent corporation earns a higher rate of return on equity but has the same rate of growth of capital employed, internal investment as a proportion of current earnings for the parent corporation will be smaller than for the selling companies. Analytically we could deal with this under two different types of assumptions. It could be assumed that the dividend payout ratio of the parent exceeds that of acquired companies and is dependent on rate of return, or it may be assumed that some portion of current earnings is used in making acquisitions (or is used for the repurchase of stock to be used in acquisitions) so that the dividend payout ratios of parent and acquired corporations are the same. We have chosen to follow the latter alternative because we consider it conceptually more desirable to assume that the dividend policy is predetermined and does not depend on the characteristics of the acquisition program.

Then the total earnings of the parent corporation in any period $(t + 1)$ may be expressed

$$y_{t+1} N_{t+1} = y_t N_t + r_b h_b y_t N_t + [(h_s - h_b) + z m_b](y_t N_t / m_s)\left(\frac{r_b}{r_s} + \dots \right) \qquad (7\text{-}5)$$

where it is assumed that $r_b > r_s$ and consequently that $h_b < h_s$. That is, at the beginning of period $(t + 1)$ the parent corporation is assumed to reinvest a proportion h_b of its earnings during period t on which it earns at a rate r_b during period $(t + 1)$. Also, it invests a proportion of earnings $(h_s - h_b)$ in the acquisition of other companies. At the same time it is assumed to issue a number of shares $z N_t$ at a market price $p_t = y_t m_b$ for the purpose of acquisitions. That is, a proportion $q = z m_b$ of total earnings $y_t N_t$ is employed in making acquisitions. For each dollar of market value of acquisition the parent corporation obtains an amount of earnings equal $1/m_s$, and through the improvement of the rate of

---

[8] This unrealistic assumption is made because it is felt to add more in analytical simplicity than it subtracts in meaning.

return on equity, these earnings are increased by the ratio r_b/r_s. The continuing series of terms indicated in the last parenthesis results from the reinvestment of the earnings of acquired companies both internally and in other acquisitions, the earnings from which will be reinvested internally and in acquisition, and so on. Since all these terms vanish in going to an expression for per-share growth rate in continuous form (because of second-order and higher-order terms), we need not be bothered about their specific character.

Relying on the relationships specified above between r_b, h_b, r_s and h_s we may rewrite equation (7-5) in the form

$$y_{t+1}N_{t+1} = y_t N_t \left[1 + r_s h_s + \frac{1}{m_s} \left[h_s \left(1 - \frac{r_s}{r_b} \right) + q \right] \left(\frac{r_b}{r_s} + \dots \right) \right].$$

Then, writing this as a difference equation, observing that $y \, \Delta \, N = yN \, z\Delta t = yN (q/m_h) \, \Delta t$, integrating in the limit as Δy and Δt go to zero, we have for the rate of growth

$$g = r_s h_s + \frac{h_s}{m_s} \left(\frac{r_b}{r_s} - 1 \right) + \frac{q}{m_s} \left(\frac{r_b}{r_s} - \frac{m_s}{m_b} \right). \tag{7-6}$$

An illustration of the relationship between the rate of per-share growth of the parent corporation and the scale of acquisition undertaken for different levels of improvement in the rate of return of the acquired companies is provided in Figure 7.2. The assumed rate of return of the acquired companies is 10% and the assumed rates of return of the parent corporation are as shown. The illustration again includes the declining-growth-rate valuation model for the price-earnings multiples of parent and selling corporations. That is

$$m_s = a[\alpha_1 + \alpha_2 (r_s h_s - n)], \tag{7-7}$$
$$m_b = a[\alpha_1 + \alpha_2 (g - n)].$$

It should be noted that the rate of per-share growth is again dependent on the price-earnings multiple of the parent corporation which is, in turn, dependent on the rate of per-share growth.

As before, we also examine the system under the assumption that valuation for the parent corporation is based only on internal performance, that the "feedback loop" is open. In this case the price-earnings multiple for the parent corporation would be:

$$m = a[\alpha_1 + \alpha_2 (g_o - n)],$$

where g_o is as expressed in equation (7-6) with $q = 0$, that is,[9]

$$g_o = r_s h_s + \frac{h_s}{m_s} \left(\frac{r_b}{r_s} - 1 \right).$$

---

[9] In the form specified g_o represents growth through internally generated funds rather than simply through internal investment. We have assumed that the parent corporation is not having any effect on the scale of internal investment within acquired companies, but that it does increase average rate of return. It could be assumed that additional earnings were used either to increase dividends or in *external* investment. Since we prefer to allow dividends to remain independent of growth strategy and of impact of the parent on average rate of return, we are forced to the latter assumption.

The difference between per-share performance under the two sets of assumptions, while substantial, is much less than in the preceding case. The process of improving the profitability within acquired firms can provide attractive performance without the benefit of the feedback relationship.

FIGURE 7.2

Acquisition with Profitability Improvement

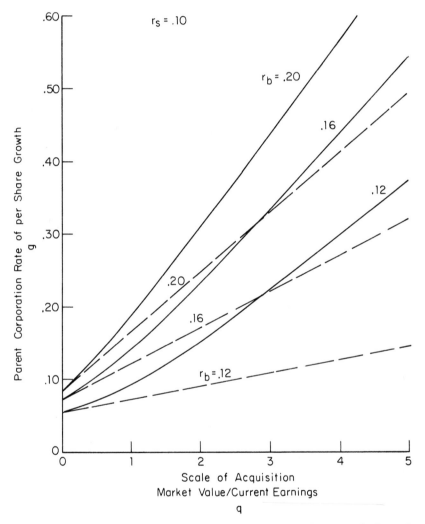

We can measure the importance of the feedback effect, as before, by the difference between the solid and dotted curves for a given value of r_b. Measured horizontally, it is the difference in scale of acquisition required to achieved a given per-share growth rate. Measured vertically, it is the difference in rate of per-share growth which will be provided by a given scale of acquisition.

We may look at this in a slightly different manner. It will be recalled that in the discussion of growth through internal investment with continuing use of new equity capital, we examined isogrowth or "shareholder indifference" curves as a possible means of "thinking about" alternative broad strategies which a company might pursue. Here we may examine alternative strategies in terms of trade-off relationships between the extent of profitability improvement in acquired companies and the scale of acquisition. That is, a given rate of per-share growth for the parent corporation could be achieved by a continuing acquisition program which involved a relatively small scale of acquisition each period but a large improvement in the rate of return of acquired companies, or a continuing acquisition program which involved a relatively small improvement in the profitability of acquired companies but a large-scale of acquisition each period. All the combinations of profitability improvement and scale of acquisition which would provide a given rate of per-share growth form an "isogrowth curve" or, again, under our assumptions, a "shareholder indifference curve." Figure **7.3** provides a family of such curves where the underlying expressions and assumed parameter values which provide the data are exactly the same as in Figure 7.2. The solid curves are based on the assumption that $m_b = f(g, \ . \ . \ .)$, so that there is an interaction between growth and valuation, whereas the dotted curves are based on the assumption that $m_b = f(g_o, \ . \ . \ .)$, where g_o is the "internal rate of growth" as defined above. Here we may measure the impact of the feedback effect between valuation and growth as the distance between the isogrowth curves for a given growth rate under the two assumptions. This, of course, may be measured either vertically as the difference in profitability improvement required for a given scale of acquisition or horizontally as the difference in scale of acquisition for a given amount of assumed profitability improvement.

It should be noted that the distance between the dotted and solid lines, for a given level of per-share performance, increases with scale of expansion through acquisition. That is, for a given level of performance (a given isogrowth curve), those strategies which involve higher expansion rates and less operating change are more dependent on market price behavior. Hence, they may be considered to offer greater uncertainty. In addition, the firm is increasing its size more rapidly under such strategies, so that there may be less promise of durability.

CASE 4: *Acquisition with Improvement in Growth — Influence on Technologies, Products, Markets*

The final case we wish to examine is that of an acquisition program in which the parent corporation increases the rate of growth of sales and hence of capital employment in acquired firms but leaves unchanged the average rate of return on equity. Here the underlying idea is that the acquiring company has an impact on *what* goods and services the acquired companies produce and sell in *what* markets, and in doing so has an influence on demand, causing the rate of growth of sales and hence the rate of new capital employment to increase. This may be expected to occur when the acquiring company influences the technologies, products, and/or markets of those acquired. With changes of this variety in the product-service stream of a company it would be coincidental if the rate of

FIGURE 7.3

Acquisition with Profitability Improvement: Isogrowth
of "Shareholder Indifference" Curves

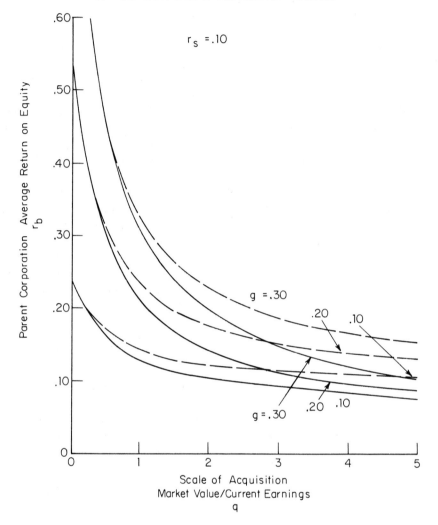

return on equity remained the same as before. However, there is no particular
reason to assume that it should be either higher or lower, so it does not appear
objectionable for this case to assume that it remains the same.

In general, then, we have a situation in which rate of return on equity, leverage, and dividend policy of acquired companies remain the same after acquisition
as before, and the only change is the rate of new capital employment. Members
of the homogeneous selling group are assumed to have an internal reinvestment
rate of h times annual earnings and an average rate of return r. The parent firm
is assumed to issue some number of shares, $z_1 N_t$, each period at a market price,

$p_t = y m_b$, in the acquisition of firms from the homogeneous group. Each dollar of market value exchanged in acquisition provides $1/m_s$ dollars in earnings. The parent corporation is assumed to increase the rate at which new equity capital is employed by acquired companies. Specifically, while the same proportion, h, of annual earnings will be reinvested internally and the same proportion $a = (1 - h)$ paid out in dividends annually, there will also be some number of shares, $z_2 N_t$, issued annually at a price, $p_t = y_t m_b$, to raise funds for additional internal investment. This change in the rate of expansion of internal investment is assumed to occur immediately upon acquisition. The average rate of return r earned on all equity employed by the parent is assumed to be identical to that of the selling corporations.

Under these assumptions the total annual earnings of the parent corporation in period $(t + 1)$ may be expressed

$$y_{t+1} N_{t+1} = y_t N_t + r h y_t N + r m_b z_2 y_t N_t + z_1 y_t N_t \frac{m_b}{m_s} (1 + rh + rmz_2) .$$

Following the by now familiar procedure of forming a difference equation, neglecting second order terms, and integrating in the limit as Δy and Δt go to zero, we have for the per-share growth rate

$$g = rh + z_1 \left(\frac{m_b}{m_s} - 1 \right) + z_2 (m_b r - 1) ,$$

or

$$g = rh + q_1 \left(\frac{1}{m_s} - \frac{1}{m_b} \right) + q_2 \left(r - \frac{1}{m_b} \right) , \tag{7-8}$$

where $q_1 = z_1 m_b$ and $q_2 = z_2 m_b$.

In this case it may be noted that the contribution to growth from the expanded scale of internal investment will be positive for

$$\frac{\partial g}{\partial q_2} = r - \frac{1}{m_b} > 0 ,$$

or for

$$r > \frac{1}{m_b} .$$

If this is the case,[10] and if market valuation is an increasing function of growth rate, it is assured that

$$m_b > m_s ,$$

and

$$\frac{\partial g}{\partial q_1} = \frac{1}{m_s} - \frac{1}{m_b} > 0 ,$$

or the contribution to per-share growth from an expanded scale of external investment will also be positive.

---

[10] And based on recent *average* figures of approximately .10 for r and 14 to 18 for m, we would expect this inequality to hold in the majority of cases.

Figure 7.4 illustrates the relationship between the rate of per-share growth of the parent corporation, g, and the scale of acquisition, q_1, for different levels of increase in the scale of equity expansion for internal investment, q_2. The price-

FIGURE 7.4
ACQUISITION WITH EXPANSION IMPROVEMENT: VALUATION BASED ON OBSERVED GROWTH

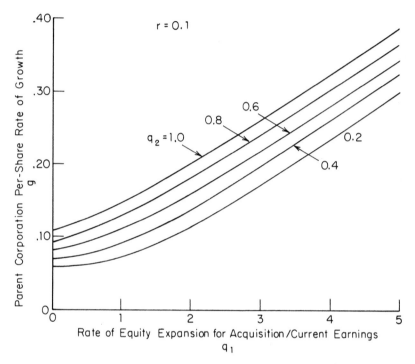

earnings multiples of buying and selling corporations are assumed to be determined in accordance with equations (7-7). That is, it is assumed that valuation of the parent corporation is based on the *observed* rate of per-share growth.[11]

We may again think in terms of a trade-off relationship between the level of change in acquisitions and the scale of acquisition, and of the managerial problem of deciding how their efforts may best be employed to achieve that combination of change and scale which provides the greatest rate of per-share growth. Figure 7.5 illustrates isogrowth, shareholder indifference curves for this case, showing the combinations of acquisition scale and internal expansion improvement which provide selected rates of per-share growth. As is readily apparent from equation (7-8), $\partial q_2 / \partial q_1$ is a constant under the assumed conditions.

---

[11] Another set of curves could be provided for Figure 7.4 in this case as was done in the two preceding cases. It suffices to say, however, that there is again a substantial difference between the required change in acquired companies for a given acquisition scale, or in the required scale of acquisition for a given level of change, to achieve a given rate of per-share growth under the two assumed systems of valuation.

FIGURE 7.5

ACQUISITION WITH EXPANSION IMPROVEMENT

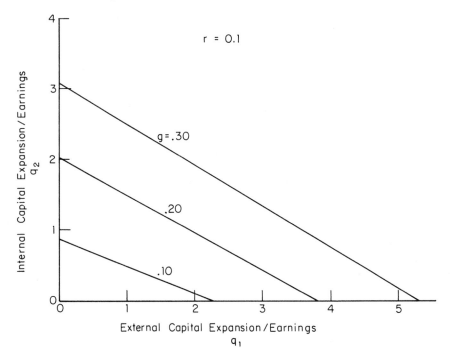

A HYPOTHETICAL "CASE" EXAMPLE

This completes the symbolic representation of the four "pure" cases which we have proposed as covering the most important characteristics of the acquisition process as pursued by the population of "acquisitive conglomerates." However, for several reasons it is considered desirable to represent the mechanics of the growth-through-acquisition process with a hypothetical case example where the method of representation is numerical rather than symbolic.

First, we find that a numerical example facilitates getting a "feel" for the mechanics of this type of growth process and, therefore, assume that it will serve this purpose for the reader. Second, the "pure" cases we have discussed are clearly far from reality. We can achieve somewhat more realism by examining a "combined case" where several of the previously discussed characteristics of the process are in operation simultaneously. While an attempt to portray such a growth process in symbolic form would be sufficiently complex to be meaningless, it is readily tractable in numerical form. Third, presentation of a "combined case" permits discussion of the difficulty of differentiating between the various effects in actual cases. And finally, the example will permit comparison of what can be ascertained regarding the acquisition process from published corporate financial data and from data available "within" the corporation. The latter will have implications for the nature of our detailed company studies.

Consider the case of Mr. Outside and Mr. Inside who have decided to pursue wealth, prestige, and power by building through diversified acquisitions a major industrial corporation.

Messrs. Outside and Inside can put together five or six hundred thousand dollars between them. They establish as an objective a rate of growth in the value of their initial investment of at least 30% per year. This, they feel, will be achieved if the earnings and dividends per share of their "conglomerate" grow at a rate of at least 30% per year. They plan to proceed on the theory that an attractive "per-share performance" can be achieved through a process of corporate growth in which there is a substantial increase in size each period through acquisition accompanied by a small improvement in the profitability and growth of those firms acquired. Others have demonstrated, they feel, that a per-share growth rate can be sustained which far exceeds the rates of internal growth of the operating companies.

Since the plan involves a rapid rate of expansion in total corporate size, they consider it desirable to acquire companies where existing management has demonstrated an ability to run a profitable organization and thus will not have to be replaced. Corporations to be acquired are envisioned as being of about "average"

TABLE 7.1

CONSTANT CHARACTERISTICS OF ACQUIRING AND ACQUIRED CORPORATIONS

	Acquired Corporations	Acquiring Corporation
Operating income as % of total capital	16.00%	18.00%
Ratio of debt to total capital	.30	.50
Interest cost on debt	6.67%	6.00%
Tax rate	50.00%	50.00%
Net income after tax as % of equity	10.00%	15.00%
% of earnings paid in dividends	40.00%	40.00%
Internal growth rate	6.00%	9.00%
Price-earnings ratio	15.00	28.00
ACQUIRING CORPORATION ONLY:		
Premium paid in acquisition		12.00%
Growth rate in number of shares		22.03%
Growth rate of total sales, earnings, market value		59.99%
Growth rate in earnings, dividends, and market price per share		30.95%

profitability and growth with roughly the characteristics shown in Table 7.1 under the heading, "Acquired Corporations." Through increased managerial efficiency (presumably based upon enlightened management practice, improved motivation, etc.) they expect to achieve a minor increase in operating income as a percent of total capital (from 16% to 18%). This, in combination with the indicated change in leverage and an anticipated small decrease in the cost of debt, will cause net income after tax as a percent of book value of equity to increase from 10% to 15%. With a 40% dividend payout ratio and the remaining 60% reinvested, the implied "before" and "after" internal rates of growth are (.60 × 10%) = 6% and (.60 × 15%) = 9% respectively. It is expected that the price-earnings ratios of the "average" firms to be acquired will be about 15 times. Further, it is assumed that acquisition of such firms can be achieved through payment of a premium of about 12% over market value.

Initial plans are to be based on the assumption that this acquisition and improvement process will proceed on a continuing basis so that the characteristics (profitability, internal growth rate, etc.) of the parent firm will be those of the improved "average" companies which have been acquired. For simplicity, it is assumed that all acquisitions will be "stock-for-stock" transactions treated as poolings of interests.

Needed to initiate the acquisition program is of course a base corporation. Desirable characteristics include sufficient size to permit an active market for the corporation's securities and a relatively high price-earnings ratio. Our planners decide that a base firm with sales of about $10 million would be an appropriate initial size and that a growth rate of 30% per annum (in per-share terms) would support a price-earnings ratio of about 28.

At the same time, it would be desirable not to have to pay 28 times earnings for stock in the base corporation. If a corporation with the "average acquired corporation" characteristics can be found and purchased for 15 times earnings, implementation during the first year of those improvements contemplated for all future acquisitions will cause a sharp increase in per-share earnings and presumably in the price-earnings ratio.

Specifically a corporation is sought with the characteristics shown in Table 7.2 under the heading "year −1." That is, in order to begin an acquisition program in "year 1" with a $10 million firm, an investment is to be made at the start of "year 0" in the base corporation having operating characteristics as shown for "year −1." In accordance with the anticipated "average" characteristics, this firm would be growing at an annual rate of 6% in total size and in per-share terms. It is assumed that under new management capital turnover will remain unchanged so that in the transition year sales will again increase by 6%, but improvement in return on capital from 16% to 18%, increase in the ratio of debt to total capital from .30 to .50, and the reduction in debt cost will cause an increase in earnings per share of 39% from $0.72 to $1.00. This, in combination with effective communication to the investing public of the growth objectives of the new management, will, it is hoped, raise the price-earnings ratio to the desired 28 times.

With a 12% premium over market (as is to be assumed in all purchases) 50,000 shares of common in the base corporation can be purchased for (50,000 × 10.82 × 1.12) = $605,900. The anticipated alteration of the capital structure will provide $1,333,000 which may be used in the purchase of outstanding shares and (at a market price of $10.82 × 1.12 = $12.12) will reduce the number outstanding to 500,000. Messrs. Outside and Inside would thus own 10% of the base corporation. Obviously, achievement of managerial control with a 10% ownership position will require that the existing controlling interests desire the management transition.

TABLE 7.2

BASE CORPORATION FOR ACQUISITIVE GROWTH

	Year − 1	Year 0 Old Capitalization	Year 0 As Recapitalized
Beginning Capital (in thousands)			
Equity	$4,402	$4,667	$ 3,333
Debt	1,887	2,000	3,333
Total capital	6,289	6,667	6,667
Operations (in thousands)			
Sales	$9,433		$10,000
Operating income	1,006		1,200
Interest	126		200
Earnings after tax	440		500
Dividends	176		200
Retained earnings	264		300
Ending Shares Outstanding (in thousands)	610		500
Ending Per-Share Data			
Earnings per share	$ .72		$ 1.00
Dividends per share	.29		.40
Price-earnings ratio	15		28
Market value per share	10.82		28.00

Table 7.3 illustrates that given (1) the characteristics of the "average" acquired firms, (2) the improvement of their internal growth rate from 6% to 9% as discussed, (3) the price-earnings ratios of acquiring and acquired firms of 15 and 28 respectively, and (4) the required 12% premium; acquisition each year of firms having sales equal to 48% of those of the parent will provide a per-share growth rate slightly in excess of 30% per year (30.95% to be exact). The 48% size increase through acquisition combined with the internal growth of the acquiring and acquired firms cause the total size of the parent corporation to increase by 59.9% each year. To effect the indicated acquisitions an increase in outstanding shares of the acquiring corporation of 22.0% per year will be required. As can be shown to be the case in any constant growth process, these different growth rates are related by the expression, $(1 + g) = (1 + g_T)/$

$(1 + z)$, where g is the per-share growth rate, g_T is the rate of growth in total size of the corporation, and z is the rate of growth in shares outstanding.[12]

Table 7.4 shows for the first year the sources of the increase in earnings per share. In percentage terms these sources will be the same each year. The exact amounts will vary somewhat depending on the order in which they are calculated, but the difference is quite small.

TABLE 7.3

FINANCIAL RESULTS: FIRST YEAR OF ACQUISITION PROGRAM

	Acquiring		Acquired		Consolidated
	Year 0	Year 1	Year 0	Year 1	Year 1
Beginning Capital (in thousands)					
Equity	$ 3,333	$ 3,630	$2,240	$1,696	$ 5,329
Debt	3,333	3,630	960	1,696	5,329
Total capital	6,667	7,260	3,200	3,392	10,658
Operations (in thousands)					
Sales	$10,000	$10,900	$4,800	$5,088	$15,987
Operating income	1,200	1,308	512	611	1,919
Interest	200	218	64	102	320
Earnings after tax	500	545	224	254	799
Dividends	200	218	90	102	320
Retained earnings	300	327	134	153	480
Ending Shares Outstanding (in thousands)	500				610
Ending Per-Share Data					
EPS	$ 1.00				$ 1.31
DPS	.40				.52
MVPS	28.00				36.68

Table 7.5 portrays the combined size of the firms which must be acquired in each of the first five years in order to keep the process going (all have the "average" company proportional relationships), and Table 7.6 projects this acquisition-based growth process for a ten-year period. If these plans were actually met, it is implied that ten years hence Messrs. Outside and Inside would be managing a billion dollar corporation and their 50,000 shares would be valued at $(50,000 \times 419.50) = \$20,975,000$.

Three aspects of this example should be noted. First, the projected performance is a straightforward expression of the accounting implications and the resulting financial position which will be achieved at periodic intervals if the

---

[12] This expression holds when rates of growth represent the discrete change from period to period as they do in the above example. As we have previously observed, when expressed as continuous rates of change, these quantities follow the somewhat simpler relationship, $g = g_T - z$.

TABLE 7.4

SOURCES OF GROWTH IN EARNINGS PER SHARE FOR ACQUIRING CORPORATION
ILLUSTRATED FOR FIRST YEAR

	Increase in Earnings Per Share — 1st Year	
	Incremental Effect	Cumulative
1. Internal growth of acquiring corporation only, at rate of 9% per annum.	$ .09	$1.09
2. Acquisition if no premium paid and no change in acquired firm (return on capital, debt/equity, debt cost), and if p/e of acquiring firm were equal that of acquired (15 times).	−.01	1.08
3. Differential in p/e ratios of acquiring and acquired firms (28 v. 15).	.18	1.26
4. Change in ratio of debt to total capital of acquired firm from .30 to .50.	.02	1.28
5. Lower cost of debt for acquiring firm (6% v. 6 2/3%).	.01	1.29
6. Improvement of return on total capital from 16% to 18%.	.05	1.34
7. Payment of 12% premium in acquisitions.	−.03	1.31

Notes corresponding to numbered items above:

1. Earnings of acquiring corporation increase 9% to $545,000 bringing earnings per share to $545,000/500,000 = $1.09.

2. Issuance of shares for acquisition at market value if price-earnings ratio of acquiring company were 15 times requires 224,000 shares. Acquired earnings at end of first period will be ($1.06 × 224,000) = $237,440, based on previous growth rate, providing total earnings of ($237,440 + $545,000) = $782,440 and total shares of (500,000 + 224,000) = 724,000. This provides earnings per share of ($782,440/724,000) = $1.08 or $.01 less than without acquisition.

3. Decreases shares required in acquisition to (224,000 × 15/28) = 120,000 so that acquisition provides earnings per share of ($782,440/620,000) = $1.26, an increase of $.18 per share.

4. Change in debt to total capital from 0.3 to 0.5 increases debt in acquired firm from (960,000 × $1.06) = $1,017,600 to $1,696,000 which permits borrowing $678,400 in the acquisition and reduces market value of acquired shares to ($244,000 × 15 − $678,400) = $2,681,600. The required number of shares is thus (2,681,600/28) = 95,770, bringing the acquiring firms total to 595,770. Interest cost would increase to (.0667 × $1,696,000) = $113,000 reducing net before tax to ((512,000 × $1.06) − $113,000) = ($542,720 − $113,000) = $429,720 or net after tax to $214,860. This provides earnings per share of ($545,000 + $214,860)/595,770 = $1.28, or an additional $.02 per share.

5. Reduction of cost of debt from 6⅔% to 6% reduces interest to ($1,696,000 × .06) = $102,000. Net after tax is ($542,720 − $102,000)/2 = $220,360. Earnings per share are ($545,000 + $220,360)/595,770 = $1.29, or an additional $.01 per share.

6. Improvement of return on total capital from 16% to 18% increases operating income of the acquired corporation to $611,000. This provides net after tax of ($611,000 − $102,000)/2 = $254,000. Earnings per share are ($545,000 + $254,000)/595,770 = $799,000/595,770 = $1.34 or an additional $.05 per share.

7. Payment of 12% premium requires issuance of (224,000 × 15 × 1.12 − 678,400)/28 = 3,084,800/28 = 110,170 shares in the acquisition. Earnings per share will be $799,000/610,170 = $1.31 or a decrease of $.03 per share.

TABLE 7.5

CORPORATIONS ACQUIRED AT BEGINNING OF YEARS
(in thousands)

Years	1	2	3	4	5
Previous Year's Operations					
Sales	$4,800	$7,675	$12,275	$19,628	$31,405
Operating income	512	819	1,310	2,094	3,351
Interest	64	104	164	262	419
Earnings after tax	224	358	573	916	1,466
Dividends	90	143	229	366	586
Retained earnings	134	215	344	550	880
Beginning Capital					
Equity	$1,696	$2,712	$ 4,336	$ 6,934	$11,086
Debt	1,696	2,712	4,336	6,934	11,086
Total capital	3,392	5,424	8,673	13,867	22,173

specified plans for the acquisition program can be implemented and if the "market" reacts in the manner anticipated. Second, we have represented only *one* means through which the stated objective might be realized. It should by now be obvious that the objective of a 30% rate of growth in dividends and earnings per share could be achieved through an infinite variety of combinations of internal performance, scale of acquisition, and degree of improvement in companies acquired. Our hypothetical planners might find it worth while to consider the trade-off relationships implicit in alternative means of achieving their objective. Third, when the planned expansion rate is high, as in this example, the "market" becomes a major element in the planning process. That is, any meaningful projection of the performance which will result from implementation of a given high-expansion-rate growth strategy requires explicit consideration of the manner in which the "market" can be expected to evaluate that strategy.

TABLE 7.6

ACQUIRING CORPORATION

	Year 0	Year 1	Year 2	Year 3	Year 4	Year 5	Year 10
				(in thousands)			
Beginning Capital							
Equity	$ 3,333	$ 5,329	$ 8,521	$13,625	$21,786	$ 34,837	$ 364,041
Debt	3,333	5,329	8,521	13,625	21,786	34,837	364,041
Total capital	6,667	10,658	17,042	27,250	43,573	69,673	728,083
Operations							
Sales	$10,000	$15,987	$25,563	$40,875	$65,360	$104,510	$1,092,234
Operating income	1,200	1,919	3,068	4,905	7,843	12,541	131,068
Interest	200	320	511	818	1,307	2,090	21,842
Earnings after tax	500	799	1,278	2,044	3,268	5,225	54,613
Dividends	200	320	511	817	1,307	2,110	21,845
Retained earnings	300	479	767	1,227	1,961	3,115	32,768
Ending Shares							
Outstanding	500	610	745	909	1,109	1,353	3,661
Ending Per-Share Data							
EPS	$ 1.00	$ 1.31	$ 1.71	$ 2.25	$ 2.95	$ 3.87	$ 14.98
DPS	.40	.52	.68	.90	1.18	1.55	5.99
MVPS	28.00	36.60	47.90	63.00	82.60	108.40	419.50

The feedback relationship between market price and performance requires that they be considered simultaneously.

The combination of elements in this mythical scenario, as well as its numerical form, will, it is hoped, help to bridge the gap between the abstract representation of the "pure" cases and the actual growth patterns demonstrated by members of the "population" examined in Chapter IV and by Contek in the next chapter. However, notwithstanding this objective, the hypothetical case does provide a framework for discussing (1) the difficulty of accurately measuring the significance of the various determinants of performance in actual cases and (2) the limitations for the observer who must rely on published financial data.

Regarding the determinants of performance, several of the effects discussed in the "pure" cases were included in the example. The parent was assumed to increase the profitability of companies acquired. Then, since the payout percentage of an increased earnings stream remained unchanged, it was implicitly assumed that the rate of growth of capital employment was increased. Further, there was an immediate impact on the per-share financial position of the parent corporation both from change in leverage of acquired companies and from the difference in assumed price-earnings ratios of acquiring and acquired firms. The direct effect of each of these elements (as well as the interest rate reduction and the required acquisition premium) on per-share performance was presented in Table 7.4. As is typically the case in systems where elements of feedback are present, the *direct* effect of any causal factor is less than the whole story.

We may focus on the problem through examination of the increase in earnings per share shown to result from the continuing differential between price-earnings ratios of acquiring and acquired firms. The "real" sources of this gain are the sources of the price-earnings ratio differential. Three factors appear probable reasons for the higher price-earnings multiple of the acquiring company. First, the demonstrated internal growth potential of the acquiring firm exceeds that of those companies assumed to be acquired; the parent has achieved a higher rate of return on capital and a higher rate of new capital employment for internal investment. Since the parent has demonstrated an ability to improve the performance of companies acquired to match its own, the expectations regarding the future earnings of a given company may increase at the time of the announcement of the merger. In this way the acquirer may achieve a "capital gain" which permits it to obtain the immediate per-share gain of acquiring a lower price-earnings ratio company while at the same time maintaining the previous, higher price-earnings ratio.

Second, the parent corporation may be thought to "justify" a higher price-earnings ratio not only because it *maintains* a higher rate of internal growth and presumably will *maintain* that same internal performance for other companies after acquisition, but also because of the impact on earnings of the one-time change in the performance of each company acquired. *If* the investing public is willing to project into the future increases in earnings of the parent which would result from a continuing series of one-time changes in the performance of companies acquired, *if* the "market" projects demonstrated capability to *acquire and improve* other companies, then the acquiring company may be thought to "justify" a price-earnings ratio *exceeding* that "justified" by its internal growth capability.

Finally, it can be argued that, as in the case with no operating change, the high market price of the parent simply supports itself. That is, the gains in earnings per share resulting from the price-earnings ratio differential in a series of acquisitions provides a pattern of growth in earnings per share which "justifies" in the eyes of the investing public the market price which makes the process possible.

It would be useful for any party interested in the value of the corporation to know the significance of each of these possible sources of growth because their "durability" may differ as discussed previously. However, in order to accurately determine the significance of each of these three factors in causing a higher price-earnings ratio for the company in our example, we would need additional information. This should be viewed in perspective of the information we have assumed available: (1) the financial characteristics of the parent; (2) the financial characteristics of all companies prior to their acquisition; (3) the change in financial characteristics of acquired companies and hence their post-acquisition performance; (4) the scale on which the parent firm acquires others; (5) the manner in which the "market" is assumed to react. The additional information needed obviously concerns market price. In the preceding discussion of cases we assumed a particular model of the relationship between the expected pattern of growth in earnings and dividends and the level of market price. In our numerical example, as in reality, there is a growth process and there is a market price, but we do not know the "model" by which they are related; models of this aspect of reality are notoriously unreliable.

In order to partition the earnings growth provided by the price-earnings differential we must know in detail the expectations for future growth implied by the existing market price. Does the market price imply expectation of a growth rate no greater than internal growth potential; does it include continuing contributions to growth from improvement of companies acquired; or does it represent some equilibrium state determined in part by the feedback relationship between price and the contributions of price to growth through the acquisition process? To answer this question would, of course, require a level of understanding of the determinants of market price which never has been and probably never will be achieved.

This negative conclusion is enlightening for several reasons. First, it tells us clearly that we cannot achieve what we had once naively hoped to achieve: a quantitative measure of the importance of the feedback effect in providing performance for particular corporations. Second, it clearly points to the type of situation which will permit convincing conclusions that this feedback relationship has in fact provided some significant contribution to performance. As long as there have been *any* significant improvements in the profitability or growth of firms acquired by a given acquisitive conglomerate, it is very difficult to make a convincing argument that the price-earnings ratio differential (if any) between parent and average acquisition results from something else. As noted, we simply do not know enough about the determinants of market values to know what differential is "justified" by any particular level of performance improvement. Only if we study a corporation where attractive per-share performance has resulted from the immediate effects of acquisition and *without any improvement* of operating performance in acquired firms, can we provide a compelling argument regarding the importance of the feedback effect in an individual situation. Contek Incorporated, the subject of the next chapter, turned out to be such a situation.

Our approach to studying the feedback relationship again emphasizes the general importance of studying the change, or lack thereof, in the operating performance of acquired firms and the difficulty of measuring that change. Regarding its importance, we discussed in the introduction the controversy in this area and, in the discussion of the "population," narrowed the likely sources of such change to influences without operating integration. In this chapter we have argued (a) that without operating change performance exceeding internal growth appears unstable and likely to "collapse" to the internal rate of growth, and (b) that for a given level of performance, the proportion of that performance dependent on market price and therefore subject to the vagaries of the market system was inversely related to the degree of improvment in acquired operations. Regarding the former, it is eminently appealing on an intuitive basis that unless there is some operating improvement which results from the combination of firms, benefits for shareholders cannot continue indefinitely. The potential for operating improvement in this type of growth process is thus of prime importance, and we are directed toward an investigation of the nature and significance of change that corporations have found it possible to achieve.

Regarding the difficulty of measuring such change, our hypothetical example may have been misleading. In the example, the magnitude of change in acquired companies was readily apparent because we knew *by assumption* what their performance *would have been* had they remained independent companies. The need to compare *what is* with *what would have been* has plagued previous merger studies and we shall not escape this dilemma. However, we meet it with the conviction that an approach providing a combination of financial *and descriptive* data will be more enlightening regarding the structure of change and its impact on performance than more statistical approaches have been in the past.

The importance of change in the growth-through-acquisition process and the problems of measuring that change have interesting implications for the external observer. If our example were an actual company, the observer relying on published information would have available little more financial data than that exhibited in Table 7.6. Limited to this amount of information it is impossible to determine the proportion of total growth which is "external," the characteristics of companies prior to their acquisition, the terms of acquisitions and hence their immediate effects on financial performance, the change in operations of acquisitions and hence their longer term impact on financial performance — in short, anything about the manner in which internal and external growth "fit together" to determine performance for the stockholder. In particular, we have argued that the magnitude of change in acquisitions may be an important indicator of the risk and durability of any level of performance, and the external observer is completely "in the dark" regarding this aspect of the growth process.

For the investing public this clearly implies a need for better information. Information of the type provided for our hypothetical example in Table 7.4, regarding the sources of earnings-per-share growth, would be desirable but difficult to provide as discussed above. Nonetheless, the information must relate to the "before" and "after" performance of acquired companies to be really helpful; financial data reported by product line or product group, as currently sought by some,[13] would serve this purpose only by coincidence.

For the present study, the implication is a clear need for "internal" corporate data. This means "in-depth" studies of individual corporate acquisition programs and, of necessity, a small number of such studies. As indicated, our sample for detailed study consists of two acquisitive conglomerates.

SUMMARY AND IMPLICATIONS OF THE GROWTH-THROUGH-ACQUISITION CASES

We have examined the characteristics of growth through acquisition by a representation of the system within which it occurs. The elements in this system are three: the acquiring firm, companies acquired, and the market system of valuation. Attention has been confined to constant growth processes where rates of change follow constant geometric progressions and financial variables maintain constant proportional relationships. As in the discussion of internal growth, the question of transient behavior between growth states has been sidestepped.

The behavior of the system is determined by the characteristics of the elements and the nature of their interaction. Specifically, based upon (1) the performance characteristics of the parent, (2) the performance characteristics of potential acquisitions, (3) the scale of acquisition undertaken by the parent, (4) the type and magnitude of change in acquired companies achieved by the parent, and (5) the market reaction to this growth process, a particular level of per-share performance is generated. Primarily, the analysis has focused upon the parent corporation per-share performance which will result from implementation of given strategies for growth through acquisition and upon the trade-off relationships between strategies for any given level of per-share performance. Secondarily, the analysis has focused upon the manner in which these relationships are affected by the nature of the market system of valuation. Several characteristics and conclusions of the analysis are to be noted.

1. We have provided an analysis of corporate growth through acquisition which treats acquisition as a continuing *process*. We have argued that for the population of acquisitive conglomerates the purchase of other companies is viewed as an

---

[13] Discussion of the requirement for conglomerate companies to report on a product group or divisional basis is widespread. For example, this was the subject of Part 5 of the U.S. Senate *Economic Concentration* Hearings before the Subcommittee on Antitrust and Monopoly of the Committee on the Judiciary, September 1966 (*Concentration and Divisional Reporting*).

integral part of the growth strategy and that these discrete investments are sufficiently similar to discrete internal investments that useful insight can be gained from viewing both internal *and external* investment as a process.

2. In the analysis there has been an attempt to isolate four categories of potential sources of performance through acquisition based on the discussion of four "cases." These four categories result from the elimination of some of the potential sources of performance originally listed in Figure 1.1 of the introduction and from the grouping of others.

We reached the conclusion in preceding chapters that operating economies requiring substantial operating integration and taxation advantages are not likely to be of primary importance for acquisitive conglomerates. The remaining "immediate financial effects" of acquisition we treated in two categories: (1) the feedback effect; (2) "everything else," including leverage, size, diversification, and accounting treatments. These two categories provided the first two "cases." The remaining two were provided by the two suggested categories of operating influence without integration: (1) influence on the "management process," which we have associated with a change in profitability; (2) influence on technologies, products, and markets, which we have associated with a change in rate of growth.

3. In our preceding analysis of growth through internal investment it was shown that, given the system of market valuation, the rate of growth in earnings per share for a given dividend policy is a function of the rate of return on equity, r, and the rate of new capital employment, c. In our analysis of the growth through acquisition process, we have been concerned not only with the r and c for internal investment, both within parent and acquired companies, but also with the change in r and c assumed to result from acquisition. Primarily, it is still these two variables which, given the market system, determine the level of per-share performance. However, we are now concerned not only with their level but with the change in level assumed to be achieved by the parent corporation.

4. In our examination of the performance that will result from the implementation of any assumed strategy there is one speculative feature, the reaction of the market to the growth process. *Given* the nature of that reaction, the projection of the performance resulting from a given strategy is a straightforward, mechanical process. It is in essence a projection of the accounting implications and future financial positions which will inevitably result given the rates of change of variables and the relationships between variables assumed to be achieved. Expression of these relationships between performance and the financial variables in symbolic form simply provides a convenient means for investigating the relationships between strategies for growth and resulting performance. The abstract, deductive argument says little regarding the ease or difficulty of implementing any of the types of strategies discussed. It is primarily an argument which says *if* a given strategy, implying rates of change of and relationships between financial variables, can be achieved, and *if* the market is assumed to react in a given manner to that strategy, *then* the character of the resulting per-share performance will be as described.

5. The major assumptions regarding market price which have provided a basis for the conclusions reached have been that (1) price is an increasing function of

rate of growth in earnings per share for a given degree of variability of that growth and for a given dividend policy and (2) for given growth rate, variability, and dividend policy, market price is not a function of the rate of return on capital and the rate of capital expansion which achieve that growth rate. If the latter assumption does not hold, as we presume it does not at the extremes, in the growth through acquisition cases as in the internal growth analysis there will still be isogrowth curves; but these will not at the same time be shareholder indifference curves. If the former assumption does not hold, then much of the analysis loses its meaning. However, this assumption has so consistently been a part of theoretical discussions and has so consistently been supported by empirical tests (including our own) that its credibility does not appear subject to serious question. We have chosen to work with our particular model of the system of market price determination because it is capable of representing, in what we consider a believable manner, the market prices of rapidly growing firms. Any other model capable of representing the prices of rapidly growing corporations in an equally credible and compact manner and conforming to the above two assumptions would be equally acceptable in the preceding analysis and would yield the same conclusions.

6. We have examined the nature and importance of the feedback relationship between growth and valuation (1) by analyzing the possibility of positive per-share benefits for shareholders without any change in companies acquired and (2) through examining the difference between growth curves in situations with change in operating and financial variables of acquired firms where market price is based on either the rate of "internal" growth (without feedback) or on the observed rate of per-share growth (with feedback).

In the former analysis we discussed the conditions under which such benefits could be achieved. We argued that if (1) market value is an increasing function of the rate of per-share growth for a given dividend policy and (2) it is the rate of growth rather than the manner in which it is achieved that is of primary concern to investors, there are equilibrium growth states where a high market price and a high per-share growth rate can be mutually supporting in the process of growth through acquisition. At the same time we argued that this process is likely to be unstable and to collapse to a market valuation based upon the internal growth potential of the acquiring corporation and to an absence of per-share benefits from the process of acquisition without change.

In looking at the difference between growth curves where market valuation is assumed to be based upon either "internal" or observed growth, we argued that the significance of the feedback effect could be measured graphically as the distance between these curves.

For the cases involving improvement in operating performance, we suggested that the distance between isogrowth curves can be interpreted as either the difference in required scale of acquisition for a given level of improvement in acquired operations or as the difference in required improvement for a given scale of acquisition. We observed that this distance between isogrowth curves under the two assumed systems of valuation increases with increase in scale of acquisition. Since this distance is also a measure of the degree to which the growth process is subject to the vagaries of the system or market price determination, we argued that for a given level of per-share performance (hence, a given iso-growth curve) those strategies which require higher expansion rates and less operating change will provide greater risk and less promise of durability. This is in addition to the relationship, also noted for the process of internal growth, that high expansion growth rate strategies lead the firm to be more quickly hindered by whatever constraints exist in the external economic environment for firms of increasing size.

7. We examined the potential impact on performance of those "immediate financial effects" other than the "feedback relationship" (leverage, diversification, size, accounting treatments). Here we demonstrated that the critical question regarding the contribution of such changes in financial characteristics to per-share performance is whether market value increases as a result of the change. We showed that the magnitude of this contribution to performance is dependent on the market value premium which is achieved and the scale with which such acquisitions are undertaken. Based upon the scale of expansion demonstrated by the "average" acquisitive conglomerate and the magnitude of the market value premium which we consider credible, we argued that it is unlikely that changes in the financial characteristics of acquired firms, viewed in isolation, have provided a major portion of the performance achieved by the "average" acquisitive conglomerate. On the other hand, such changes in financial characteristics may reinforce and stabilize the feedback effect in such a way that attractive performance is provided. In that event, however, it is the feedback effect and not the other changing financial characteristics that provide the major contribution to performance.

8. We demonstrated that if improvement in the profitability and growth of newly acquired firms can be continually achieved by the parent corporation, attractive per-share performance should result. Such performance is enhanced if there is also in operation the interdependence of market value and demonstrated performance. We have suggested nothing, however, regarding the extent to which or the manner in which such operating improvements have been achieved within the acquisitive conglomerate environment. These questions will receive substantial attention in the remaining chapters.

9. Realistically speaking, all programs of diversified corporate growth through acquisition are "combined cases" and do not proceed at constant rates of change over time. The latter we have consistently avoided, but the combination of elements we have sought to represent through a hypothetical, numerical case example. Through the combination of diverse assumed effects and the numerical form of the presentation, it was sought to bridge the gap between the preceding abstract discussion and reality.

10. In the discussion of the hypothetical example and throughout the more abstract discussion of internal and external growth, normative implications have periodically been mentioned. It is desirable to piece these together briefly. We have argued that a meaningful, logical goal for the corporate management seeking to provide the greatest possible benefits to ownership interests is maximization of the rate of growth in earnings per share for a given dividend policy. The market

value established for any rapidly growing company may be considered to imply expectations for decline in the growth rate. If management can maintain a high, relatively constant rate of growth, the implied expectations of the "market" will continually be contradicted, and the expectations for decline, although they will continue, will be shifted into the future. In this manner market price will maintain approximately the same relationship to earnings, and a return for shareholders will be generated which equals the sum of the per-share growth rate plus the dividend yield.

If per-share performance is the objective, it must be realized that any given level of performance can be achieved in a variety of ways. We argue that this is of importance because any *individual firm* may pursue a variety of paths of expansion. This implies that there are a variety of investment demand schedules on which any firm may operate. The obvious idea is that no corporation can expand in all directions at once because of limitations, managerial or otherwise, on the rate of expansion. A corporation must choose between alternative strategies for expansion, each of which will in principle define sets of opportunities which are feasible. Therefore, management is faced not only with the question of selection of investment opportunities from a given demand schedule, as is typically assumed in financial management theory, but with the question of which investment demand schedule to pursue.

In the internal growth process we have discussed two dimensions, rate of return on capital and rate of expansion of capital employed, which determine per-share performance. Maintenance of a relatively higher level on either of these dimensions requires a relatively greater amount of managerial effort. In principle, at least, management should seek that strategy for expansion such that its efforts, when applied to the combination of these two dimensions, will provide the highest level of per-share performance. One of the major difficulties of such a process, as we have noted, is that "strategy" in this context must include estimates of rates of return and rates of expansion which will be feasible.

In the growth-through-acquisition process we have not only the trade-off between rate of return on investment and rate of capital expansion. There are in addition trade-offs between internal and external growth and between scale of acquisition and level of improvement in acquired operations. This complicates the conceptual process of choosing a growth strategy, but the actual trade-off relationships seem somewhat more in tune with reality in growth through acquisition than in strictly internal growth. Each acquisition provides an operating management and a market and may add immediately to earnings. Further, in most transactions requiring additional common stock, new shares go to former owners rather than the investing public so that many of the costs associated with a new issue are avoided. This means that relatively high-expansion-rate growth strategies are more feasible and more closely follow our assumptions about market price.

In selecting a "most desirable" strategy management might examine the performance implications which result from the various growth strategies which are deemed feasible. It is important to note that the resulting performance will depend upon the assumed market reaction to each proposed strategy. That growth strategy which both appears feasible and promises the highest level of per-share performance over the long term is, under our assumptions, most desirable.

11. Discussion of our hypothetical example has provided a clear indication of what we may and may not hope to learn about the determinants of performance in individual situations. Specifically, our attention has been directed toward "in-depth" studies of financial characteristics and of the structure and significance of change in acquired operations in a small number of acquisition programs. It is to such studies that we now direct our attention.

CHAPTER VIII

Financial Strategy and Performance
of the Acquisitive Conglomerate: A Study
of Contek Incorporated

The financial character of acquisitive conglomerates may be somewhat illuminated by taking one apart and looking at it piece by piece, by "dissecting" it. That is the purpose of this chapter. In part, the objective is to illustrate through an actual case history the financial strategy and mechanics for a growth process where outstanding per-share performance has been achieved with a relatively low rate of return on capital and a high rate of capital expansion through aggressive, diversified acquisition. In part the objective is to illustrate the problems of determining the sources of per-share performance and their relative importance within the acquisitive growth process. Throughout, the emphasis is financial: financial strategy and its implementation; financial performance and its derivation.

We suggest three reasons for pursuing these objectives. First, the illustration of financial strategy and mechanics provides an opportunity to analyze in detail some of the propositions resulting from the earlier deductive analysis of growth through acquisition. Specifically, we have discussed: the importance of growth in earnings per share as a corporate objective; the role of market price as a major determinant of performance; the consequent attention to the perceived determinants of market price; "financial" and "operating" sources of performance expected to be of most significance for acquisitive conglomerates; the importance of operating improvement in acquired subsidiaries for the process of growth through acquisition to benefit per-share performance over the long term. While the analysis of one corporation hardly provides a basis for generalization regarding these propositions, it does provide an opportunity for refinement and for some discussion of their potential relevance in other situations.

The second reason is quite simple. The illustration of financial strategy and mechanics for an actual situation should add to the understanding of performance achievement through acquisition for those who are not familiar with this type of corporate growth.

The third reason relates to the analysis per se. In broad terms the analysis seeks to do two things: (1) to partition the per-share performance into that provided by the internal profitable growth of existing operations and that provided by the immediate effects of new acquisitions and (2) to explain the underlying reasons for the immediate financial effects which result from acquisition. We are interested in the extent to which these immediate effects have been achieved because of (1) demonstrated ability to improve performance in previously acquired subsidiaries, (2) the interdependence of valuation and per-share growth, and (3) other reasons relating to differences in corporate size, leverage, marketability of securities, degree of diversification, etc. Based on the experience of the analysis we will discuss (1) the conditions under which this kind of analysis will be feasible; (2) the sources of data and methods of analysis which will be meaningful; and (3) the kinds of conclusions which may be reached.

We suggest that the analysis of sources of acquisitive conglomerate financial performance should be of interest for both management and investor groups. For corporate management we have argued that per-share performance "should be" the financial objective and that there are many combinations of profitability and of internal and external growth which may be employed to achieve any given level of such performance. We have further argued that management should address the problem of using available resources to pursue a growth strategy which will over the long run provide the highest level of sustainable per-share performance. Certainly it would appear that the starting point for such an analysis is an accurate picture of the ingredients of performance achieved in the past.

Among investor groups the controversy about acquisitive conglomerates concerns not only what the sources of performance are; there has been much discussion but no agreement on how one should go about finding out. We have earlier discussed the concern of various groups over the appropriate financial information to be received by the investing public regarding conglomerate performance. Most of the discussion has revolved around approaches to product line reporting which inherently is focused on better analysis of the future internal growth and profitability of the corporation as it stands at any point in time. While this is obviously important, we suggest that additional and perhaps more useful information regarding the acquisitive conglomerate may be derived from analysis of the internal and external contributions to per-share performance and of the reasons for the external contributions. The sources of past performance appear important in assessing future performance because different sources are dependent upon different corporate resources and have different attendant risks. It should be helpful to know what factors, what competences have provided demonstrated performance in order to reach a truly intelligent judgment regarding the maintenance or improvement of that performance in the future.

We hasten to add, however, that we have no intention of making specific policy recommendations regarding the kinds of information to be provided to the investing public for acquisitive companies. We will only seek to illustrate how far it is possible to go, given access to internal information and, equally important, to illustrate the numerous assumptions and approximations which are required to get there.

THE SUBJECT CORPORATION

In the selection of a subject corporation several criteria had to be satisfied. We sought a corporation which clearly exceeded our established criteria for expansion rate, acquisition, shareholder performance, and diversity. Further, a history was needed which was long enough to be meaningful and yet short enough to be manageable. These criteria were met through the analysis of the early stages of development of an acquisitive conglomerate company.

Certainly by our definition, and probably by most, Contek Incorporated [1] is eminently qualified as an acquisitive conglomerate. During the six calendar years 1962 through 1967 Contek made 15 acquisitions in diverse fields and increased sales from $1.2 million to $43.2 million. Earnings after taxes increased from $51,000 in 1962 to $2.92 million in 1967 for an average annual change of 154%. At the same time the average annual increase in shares outstanding was only 34%. As a result, earnings per share increased from $.15 to $2.30 during the period, providing an average annual increase of 87%. Market price per share increased at approximately the same rate. This per-share performance was achieved through an unusually high rate of expansion of invested equity coupled with a moderate rate of return. On the average, the annual increase in the book value of invested equity was 4.94 times annual earnings after tax.[2] After-tax earnings averaged 18.9% of the book value of invested equity. These and other publicly available financial details are shown in Table 8.1.

A Brief Overview of Contek Incorporated

Contek Incorporated was organized with Mr. David Augustus as president in 1961 to carry on the contract government research of a predecessor company. From its incorporation through the better part of 1964 Contek concentrated on expansion of its contract research. By the end of 1964 work was in progress on 17 contracts for six different government organizations.

At an early stage it became apparent to Mr. Augustus that strict concentration on government research offered a limited future for the firm. His ambitions were to create a major industrial organization based on technology — a technology-based "enduring institution" — and to build personal financial independence for himself and other major stockholders in the process. This ambition evolved from a dream to a three-phase plan.

The goals of the first phase were (a) to build a solid basic research business, (b) to assemble an effective management team, and (c) to develop financial strength. This phase began with the company's incorporation and culminated in the first public issue of Contek in April 1964.

The second phase was envisioned as a transition phase. Contek financial strength would be used to acquire companies with basic skills in engineering, manufacturing, and marketing to complement Contek's strength in research and

---

[1] All names, dates, and financial data for Contek Incorporated have been disguised. What remains are the accurate proportional relationships between financial variables, within each time period and across time periods.

[2] Had all acquisitions been treated as purchases, so that increases in equity came in at market value, this measure of expansion rate would have been very much higher, the rate of return correspondingly lower.

TABLE 8.1

CONTEK INCORPORATED: FINANCIAL CHARACTERISTICS OF GROWTH[1]

(Fiscal Years Ended December 31)

	1967	1966	1965	1964	1963	1962	Average
SALES[2]	$43,207	$17,174	$5,801	$2,579	$2,221	$1,186	
EARNS	2,919	881	392	92	98	51	
DEBT	17,158	4,049	156	100	82	0	
EQUIT	15,785	5,984	2,665	1,528	336	169	
EPS	2.30	1.32	0.76	0.25	0.31	0.15	
DPS	0.00	0.00	0.00	0.00	0.00	0.00	
MKTLO	26.26	20.36	11.80	11.65			
MKTHI	136.59	30.09	22.57	12.69			
NOACQ	8	4	2	1	0	0	
C	3.357	3.769	2.900	12.982	1.700	*	4.942
G	0.741	0.750	2.048	−0.192	1.000	*	0.869
GT	2.315	1.247	3.268	−0.067	0.935	*	1.540
Z	0.904	0.284	0.400	0.156	−0.032	*	0.342
R	0.185	0.147	0.147	0.060	0.293	0.301	0.189
M	35.385	19.085	22.754	49.107	**	**	31.583
H	1.000	1.000	1.000	1.000	1.000	1.000	1.000
XB	0.479	0.596	0.946	0.939	0.804	1.000	0.794

[1] The variables calculated from the financial data in this exhibit are discussed in more detail in earlier chapters. Summary definitions only are provided here.

[2] See footnotes to Table 4.2, p. 70.

* Not available; these items based on year-to-year change.

** No market for company's stock until 1964.

development. Acquired firms were to have product lines which involved technologies in which Contek excelled so that Contek technical expertise could be employed to bring the acquired subsidiary to the forefront of its field. At the same time companies were sought with a record of profitability indicating entrepreneurial and managerial competence which could be used not only within the acquired operation but to the benefit of other parts of the Contek organization. The criteria for an attractive acquisition candidate were thus (a) that the company be in a technically relevant area, (b) that it have a strong, active management, and (c) that it be profitable. The first acquisition was made in December 1964 and, as previously mentioned, by the close of the fiscal year ending December 31, 1967, Contek had acquired 15 small but profitable companies.

The goals for the third phase of Contek's development were (a) continued growth both internally and through acquisition as a vertically integrated, technically based corporation and (b) increased managerial expertise throughout the organization and particularly at the corporate level. Mr. Augustus felt that Contek was moving into this stage of its development close to the end of the period we are studying.

As we shall discuss in some detail, Contek management was constantly concerned about building growth in earnings per share as a financial performance objective. Mr. Augustus discussed the potential contribution to earnings per share from the acquisition process in three parts. One was the immediate financial effect which resulted from the purchase of a company with a lower price relative to its earnings, from "doing a good deal." The other two were of an operating nature and were concerned with improved internal performance. The first he referred to as "trimming" which he viewed as a "surgical procedure" for improving profitability through cutting out expendable people and hence overhead in the acquired organization. The second encompassed all the truly "constructive interactions" which led to sustained positive changes in technology, marketing management, financial management, and other operating characteristics of the acquired subsidiary. The objective was to provide contributions to earnings per share through the acquisition process from all these sources.

Given this brief statement of what Contek was all about in a general sense, we proceed to concentrate on financial strategy and the financial analysis of performance. We shall analyze the Contek operating strategy for providing a positive influence on acquired subsidiaries in the next chapter.

FINANCIAL STRATEGY

The financial strategy of Contek Incorporated is of particular importance since, as we shall observe, it was the dominant factor in the per-share performance the company achieved. Mr. Augustus, while trained as a scientist, demonstrated a canny understanding of the financial ingredients in the acquisitive growth process.

The underlying financial objective was and continued to be the building of wealth for shareholders of Contek. This required an increase in the market value of Contek common stock, and in Mr. Augustus' words, "earnings per share is how the investment community keeps score." Thus growth in equity values demanded growth in earnings per share. The explicitly stated corporate financial objective was a 40% annual rate of increase in per-share earnings. As has been noted, this was on the average far exceeded.

The series of events beginning with the first issue of Contek common stock led to the evolution of a well-defined financial strategy for growth in earnings per share. This was based on the perceived interrelationships between market value and its determinants. Contek stock was initially offered to the public at $11.75 per share, approximately 40 times per-share earnings for the preceding fiscal year of $.31 and approximately 50 times earnings per share of $.25 for the fiscal year of the offering. It rapidly became apparent that Contek stock could be used to advantage as a medium of exchange in the acquisition of smaller, privately held companies. Purchased at prices which were lower in relation to their earnings, such acquisitions could provide attractive immediate contributions to the earnings per share of Contek. At the same time it was evident to Mr. Augustus that maintenance of the Contek price-earnings ratio at a level which permitted continued acquisition on an attractive basis was largely dependent on a rapid rate of growth in Contek earnings per share and an appropriate image of the corporation. An image was sought which would cause the investing public to believe that the demonstrated per-share performance could be continued or improved in the future. The financial strategy which evolved was diagrammed by Mr. Augustus as presented in Figure 8.1.

FIGURE 8.1

A CONCEPTUAL MODEL UNDERLYING FINANCIAL STRATEGY

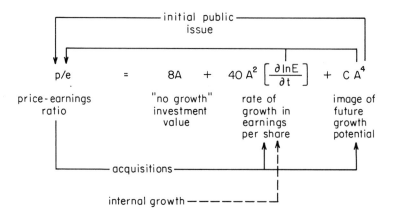

TABLE 8.2

A SAMPLE OF PRICE-EARNINGS RATIO VALUES
FROM THE MODEL OF FINANCIAL STRATEGY

$$\frac{\partial \ln E}{\partial t} = .40; \quad C = 7$$

A	$8A + 40A^2 \left[\dfrac{\partial \ln E}{\partial t} \right] + CA^4 = p/e$			
1.4	11	31	27	69
1.0	8	16	7	31
.8	6	10	3	19

As shown, the price-earnings ratio was perceived as being determined by a linear combination of three elements: (1) "no growth" investment value, or the value the corporation would have if earnings were expected to continue at their present level indefinitely; (2) the rate of growth in earnings per share, or Contek's demonstrated ability to perform in the past (viewed by Contek as an important ingredient in the formation of investor expectations regarding future performance); (3) the corporate image of potential for future growth.

Obviously, Mr. Augustus thought quite specifically about the relative importance of the factors involved. In the expression the variable A represents the stock market climate. This was viewed as ranging from .75 to 1.5 where 1.5 represents a very speculative period and .75 represents a depressed period of stock market prices. This was the one element completely outside corporate management control. The variable E is earnings on a per-share basis and the differential is the logarithmic slope or the annual percentage rate of change. This was viewed as the investing public's perception of the "normalized" or average rate of per-share earnings growth. Finally, C is the "glamour factor" or the image of future growth potential. It ranges from 0 to 10 where zero might be a "nuts and bolts" manufacturer and 10 is the company that has found "the cure for cancer" or some other such exciting and growth promising activity. It should be noted that investment value, growth, and the image of growth were viewed as being increasingly sensitive to market climate in that order. As may be observed, dividends play a nonexistent role in financial strategy. They were never paid and were viewed by Mr. Augustus as irrelevant for the investing public's determination of market price for a company such as Contek.

The arrows in Figure 8.1 represent the dynamic interrelationships between price-earnings ratio and its determinants as the growth process proceeds over time. In the initial issue of Contek common stock the corporation had no public record of demonstrated growth in earnings per share. The company did have a highly developed research competence which could be used to present an image of great potential for future growth in areas of advanced technology. Thus, the company first used its image or "C" to provide a high price-earnings ratio. Subsequently, Contek used its price-earnings ratio through the acquisition process to build earnings per share and to buy companies which would permit maintenance of an image of advanced technology and of great potential for future growth. The development of an attractive pattern of growth in earnings per share and the maintenance of an exciting image provided the ingredients for maintenance of a high price-earnings ratio so that the process could continue.

Contek management called the transaction which permits an increase in earnings per share through the trading of equity securities having different price-earnings ratios "levered acquisitions." The continuing financial strategy was to build earnings per share by maintaining the dynamic relationships portrayed by the model through an expanding scale of "well-levered acquisitions" while at the same time adding to earnings per share through the internal growth of those companies acquired. The stated objective was to achieve half of the annual increase in earnings per share through "levered" acquisitions and half through internal growth. As we shall observe, the balance leaned toward increasing per-share earnings through the acquisition process.

As we have noted, this model of financial strategy takes a very specific form. The variables are well defined; they are limited to specified ranges; and, if not measurable, they could at least be assessed. The coefficients are specified in numerical form. It will be of some interest to look at the quantitative implications of the model.

Given the objective of 40% per year for the rate of growth in earnings per share and Mr. Augustus' assessment of $C = 7$ for the measure of the Contek corporate image, we examine in Table 8.2 values of the price-earnings ratio for three selected values for A, the measure of market climate. This model has never been tested in any statistical sense and no such test is intended here. Still, the specific form of the model is important for two reasons. First, it illustrates that

Contek management was sensitive to the fact that during times of high stock market prices generally (large values of A) they would be in a relatively better position to purchase firms which had less demonstrated growth and less image for future growth. We doubt that many firms have thought so specifically about the relative position of price-earnings ratios based on the "market climate." But if a significant number have even a vague understanding of this, it could provide some explanation of the positive correlation between merger activity and stock market prices which we have discussed earlier.

Second, the amount of thought obviously given to development of this model in such specific form is one indication of the importance attached to the price-earnings ratio by Contek management.

At the same time, the specific numerical form of the model appears to be of little consequence for the decision-making process. It is the belief in the basic nature of the relationship and the elements which comprise that relationship which have a major impact on management action. It is the knowledge that earnings-per-share growth can be achieved with a high price-earnings multiple through the acquisition process and the belief that the price-earnings multiple is largely dependent on rapid per-share growth and on an image of continuing future per-share growth.

A better understanding of the practical significance of the model of Contek financial strategy can be achieved through discussion of management thinking about variables it contains and of actions it promotes.

We have mentioned that the primary financial objective for Contek was growth in earnings per share and the resulting growth in market value per share. This could be achieved through the internal growth of those businesses which were a part of Contek or through the immediate financial effects of new acquisitions. Internal growth was achieved through the combined effects of various kinds of resources which existed within the firm — technical competence, managerial expertise, familiarity with various markets, etc. Growth in earnings per share resulting from the immediate effects of acquisitions was dependent primarily on one of Contek's resources: its high market multiple. Indeed, the high market multiple which Contek was able to maintain was viewed by Mr. Augustus as the firm's most important single resource for achievement of the established per-share performance objective. Maintenance of this resource was considered to require the continuing purchase of companies which would enhance or at least not significantly diminish the image of potential for future growth, and to demand rapid and steady growth in earnings per share, quarter after quarter, year after year.

We have mentioned that internal growth and acquisition were viewed as working in combination to achieve the objective per-share growth rate. Their respective roles, however, differed to some extent. Internal growth necessarily proceeded on a best efforts basis governed by the quality of Contek resources, industry conditions, actions by competitors, and so forth. That part of the target per-share growth not achieved internally was sought through the immediate effects of acquisitions. It could be said that the acquisition program served as the driving force in a servo-mechanical-like system. There was a periodic assessment of the difference between the target end-of-period per-share performance and the anticipated per-share performance based upon internal profitability and growth and upon acquisitions to date. The process of "levered" acquisition was then geared into action to close the gap.

In order to accomplish this there was a continuing search for acquisitions which met the criteria of technical relevance, managerial competence, and demonstrated success. Attractive acquisitions had to be found which could be made on the proper "scale" and with the proper timing to provide the supplement to internal growth required to meet the performance objective. As might be expected, this was a demanding assignment. At times there was some trade-off between desired acquisition characteristics and the earnings-per-share objective. That is, in order to "fix" earnings per share for some particular period, an acquisition might be made which otherwise would be only marginally desirable or perhaps undesirable. These trade-off considerations played a continuing role in acquisition decisions but became particularly important at the end of the fiscal year when previous earnings predictions had to be realized. To quote Mr. Augustus, "Everyone in this [acquisitive conglomerate] business is familiar with the 'acquisition fix' for earnings per share."

This concern for the maintenance and effective use of the multiple through the acquisition process is not one of the more frequently discussed management functions. Yet at Contek it was considered a major requirement for success through the acquisitive growth process. To quote Mr. Augustus again:

> The classical entrepreneur was marked by his abilities to match ideas to products, products to market needs. The entrepreneur in the acquisitive conglomerate must have an additional ability of equal importance. This is his ability to use one resource creatively: his market multiple.

The perceived relationship between per-share growth and the multiple is further illuminated by the approach taken in "selling" the prospective acquisition on becoming a part of Contek. If Contek common stock was to be used as the medium of exchange, as it typically was, the selling principals had to be favorably disposed to Contek ownership. While the market value of Contek common stock increased rapidly, the price remained high relative to earnings and was quite volatile. The latter was evident from the yearly high-low ranges displayed in Table 8.1. The high multiple and high volatility were natural causes of concern for the potential seller. Very likely, an individual in this position is disturbed that his earnings-per-share position will be diluted, is concerned over ownership in a widely fluctuating security, and is afraid that the high price-earnings multiple may decline.

If the prospective seller was to become enthusiastic about accepting the market value of Contek common stock as value received in an exchange, he had to become sold on the idea that there was a strong likelihood of capital appreciation to offset his previously mentioned worries. The selling argument revolved around future growth in Contek earnings per share and may be paraphrased as follows:

> The Contek price-earnings ratio is high because there has been rapid growth in earnings per share. However, it is likely to remain high because Contek management

is dedicated to the maintenance of rapid growth. This is to be accomplished through internal growth such as the prospective acquisition has achieved in the past and, it is hoped, will improve upon with the benefit of Contek technical and managerial resources. However, this internal growth will be supplemented by future "levered" acquisitions which will continue to contribute to earnings per share. Just as the present acquisition will provide some increase in Contek per-share earnings, so will others in the future.

Moreover, and of greater importance, the growth of Contek's market value per share will follow the growth in earnings per share. This of course will provide capital appreciation for the selling parties.

Unfortunately, high growth, high multiple stocks are almost inevitably accompanied by volatility. Yet, the price-earnings ratio of Contek's stock has typically varied within a range that has been fairly well defined even though fairly wide. Therefore, if the selling principal is willing to assume the position of long-term investor in Contek and can resist the temptation of worry about short-term fluctuations, he will eventually be rewarded by attractive capital appreciation.

In making this argument, Mr. Augustus frequently used a diagram such as that shown in Figure 8.2. In the typical case the price-earnings ratio for the prospective acquisition was lower and less volatile than that of Contek, and therefore appeared somewhat less risky. However, attention was drawn to the more steeply rising earnings trend which was likely for Contek. Then, since market price equaled the multiple times per-share earnings, price would follow the per-share earnings trend, making Contek ownership look substantially more attractive over the long run.

This whole approach and the argument which underlies it is illustrated by the following portion of a letter from Mr. Augustus to the principals of Microwave Devices with whom he was negotiating regarding the consideration for acquisition of Microwave:

> . . . Obviously, the one reason that we can justify this kind of an investment is the high price-earnings ratio placed on Contek by the market, which reflects continued confidence in our growth program. . . . I have every reason to believe that we will continue to maintain a high ratio in years to come. Because of our high multiple and because of the relative size of our respective operations, this projected earnings [of Microwave] will strongly enhance our market value. This in turn will make it possible for us to raise additional capital to acquire other companies and generally to fulfill the growth which is expected of us.
>
> An interesting consequence of the transaction is the fact that this projected earnings of $225,000 added to our current earnings alone would raise total earnings per share from $.61 to $1.00. At our current multiple, the effect would be to raise our stock price to $30 per share from its current value of $18. Your equity position would rise consequently from $1,350,000 to $2,250,000. Moreover, even this figure is unrealistically low since it assumes no further growth in earnings per share through the growth of Contek exclusive of Microwave. In view of the great progress which we are making in many areas within the company and in view of our expectations of making several well-levered acquisitions within the near future, I can assure you that Contek is not standing still.

Thus it was argued that the prospective seller would receive gains through capital appreciation in a transaction where his earnings benefited the earnings-per-share position of the parent and at the same time would pave the way for more of the same in the future.

FIGURE 8.2

CONCEPTUAL MODEL FOR "SELLING" POTENTIAL ACQUISITIONS ON DESIRABILITY OF OWNERSHIP IN CONTEK

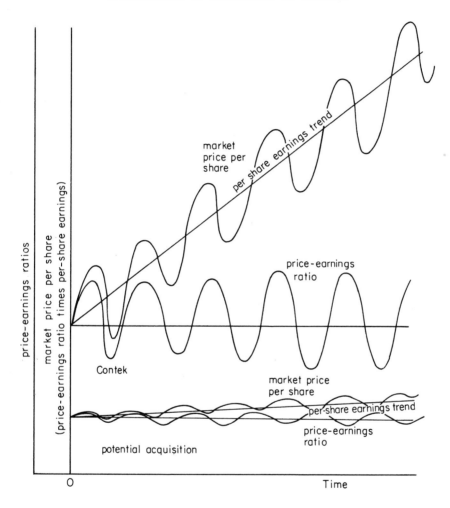

QUANTITATIVE ANALYSIS OF THE SOURCES OF PERFORMANCE

In the analysis of Contek's performance we begin by looking at the internal and external components of growth in total size of the company. We will then examine the nature of the 15 acquisition transactions to determine the "mechanics" by which the external component of growth in size contributed to per-share growth. This will be followed by an analysis of the "before and after" performance of the seven companies which were a part of Contek for at least a full year. The objective here is to see if performance changes in these companies provide an explanation of the multiple differentials between Contek and its acquisitions. An attempt is then made to adjust the "before-after" performance analysis for changes in the industry environment to see if a significant impact on previous conclusions resulted. Finally we analyze the contributions to annual growth in earnings per share provided by internal growth and provided by the acquisitions made in each fiscal year.

GROWTH IN TOTAL SIZE

As previously noted, total sales of Contek increased from $1.2 million in 1962 to $43.2 million in 1967. Sales in 1962 were provided by the original company and were increased to $2.22 million in 1963 through internal growth. In the following fiscal year the original company increased its sales to $2.36 million and the first Contek acquisition, which was a purchase late in 1964, provided an additional $216,000 in consolidated sales. In the remaining three years of the relevant period, sales growth was achieved almost entirely through acquisitions. In 1967 sales for the original company, now called the Corporate Research Division, were $3.16 million and the remaining $40.0 million of the $43.2 million total was provided by the 15 acquired subsidiaries.

From various corporate records, income and balance sheet data for all the companies acquired during the relevant period were "pieced together" for the six Contek years 1962–1967. The histories of sales revenues for the original company and the 15 acquisitions are shown in Table 8.3. One immediately apparent complication is that the fiscal years for the previously independent companies were different from that of Contek in almost every case. For each subsidiary the top row of data represents the previous fiscal year basis and the bottom row of data represents sales based on the Contek fiscal year after becoming part of the parent company. The spacing of the data on the old and new fiscal years has been carried out to represent the respective positions in time. The horizontal lines which precede the first data items for several of the subsidiaries indicate that the companies were not yet in existence during those periods. Seven of the 15 acquired companies were less than six years old at the end of 1967.

While detailed study of Table 8.3 can reveal the pattern of sales growth for Contek, it is more easily grasped when Table 8.3 is presented in graphical form. This has been done in Figure 8.3. Here "P" is the original or parent company, and "A1" through "A15" are the 15 subsidiaries in chronological order of their acquisition. The vertical scale is based on 100% of Contek consolidated sales in 1967 so that all sales are expressed relative to the Contek total at the end of the relevant period. The exhibit was constructed by first representing to scale the sales of the parent or original company. Sales of the subsequent acquisitions for each year of the period were converted to percentages of total fiscal year 1968 sales and "added to" the preceding sales line. Because of the differing fiscal years, interpolation "around the corners" was required in numerous cases. The dotted line represents Contek consolidated sales, and in a very rough sense the various other companies can be viewed as becoming a part of Contek at the time the dotted line crosses the region which represents their sales volume.

The top solid line in Figure 8.3 represents the sales volume which these companies would have had over the six-year period if they had been joined together throughout. Obviously there was a very substantial amount of growth in the companies which became a part of Contek. However, it may also be observed that much of this growth occurred before these companies became a part of Contek.

While the linear scale of Figure 8.3 accurately represents the proportional relationships between the parent company and the acquired subsidiaries, it cannot provide a meaningful representation of the rates of growth of Contek consolidated sales and of the sales of the component parts of Contek. Figure 8.4 is the same as Figure 8.3 in every respect except that the percentage of 1967 consolidated sales is represented on a logarithmic basis. Here it is apparent that the growth in Contek consolidated sales provided by the original company in 1962 and 1963, after slowing in 1964, was continued at approximately the same rate through acquisitions in 1965, 1966, and 1967. Also, the sharp drop in the rate of growth of sales for the original company after 1963 is apparent.

Sales growth of the subsidiaries after becoming part of Contek can be observed from the breakdown of consolidated sales for the six fiscal years. This is displayed in Table 8.4. It should be noted that some of the acquisitions were purchases so that their first-year contribution to consolidated sales covers less than a full twelve-month period. This makes the growth from the first to the second year as a part of Contek appear larger than was actually achieved. For Environmental and Electromek this is particularly evident. Regardless, it can be said that on balance the picture is a positive one. For the seven acquisitions represented by at least two years of data there were eleven year-to-year changes in sales volume. Eight of these annual changes were positive; three were negative.

Also of interest is the proportion of consolidated sales for each fiscal year provided by acquisitions during that period. While the acquisition of Environmental in 1964 provided only a small proportion of consolidated sales, as previously noted, the proportions added by acquisitions were large in subsequent periods. Acquisitions during 1965 almost doubled the sales volume of the previously existing company. In 1966 and 1967 acquisitions more than doubled the sales volume of the company as it existed at the beginning of those fiscal years.

As a measure of profit for the companies that became a part of Contek we look to net profit before tax. This is because the tax situations of some of the companies changed significantly upon becoming a part of the parent. This happened both because Contek was larger and for other reasons. Table 8.5 displays the histories of net profit before tax for the original company and for the 15 subsidiaries. Here the picture is very mixed. For example, a cursory examination

TABLE 8.3

REVENUE HISTORIES FOR CONTEK SUBSIDIARIES: FISCAL YEARS 1962–1967

(Companies Acquired Prior to December 31, 1967)

(annual revenues in thousands of dollars)

Subsidiary	Date Acquired	Fiscal Year Ends	1962	1963	1964	1965	1966	1967
Original Company		Dec. 31	1,186	2,221	2,362	2,230	2,836	3,162
Environmental Controls	12/64	July 31		449	579	697		
		Dec. 31				805	882	1,043
Electronic Enclosures	4/65	June 30	874	1,077	1,471	2,383		
		Dec. 31				2,567	3,160	3,032
Electromek Controls	10/65	Nov. 30	612	722	753	845		
		Dec. 31					946	1,050
Microwave Devices	4/66	May 31	1,932	2,988	3,988	4,077	5,327	
		Dec. 31				4,581	6,140	5,458
Digital Instrument	5/66	Mar. 31			390	940	1,235	
		Dec. 31				749		2,020
Micronet	12/66	Sept. 30		43	661	1,091	1,440	
		Dec. 31				1,220	1,548	1,650
Diodyne	12/66	Mar. 31		408	390	628	779	
		Dec. 31					951	738

Company		Date						
Custom Audio	3/67	Dec. 31	4,625	3,270	1,553	341		
Stratton	4/67	July 31						
		Dec. 31	1,830	2,084	1,968	1,214	674	
Spectra	6/67	Jan. 31						
		Dec. 31	3,000	3,908	536			
Computex	9/67	May 31		4,859				
		Dec. 31	6,183	5,036	4,056	2,109	1,968	
Melcast	9/67	Dec. 31	417	38				
Fletcher	9/67	Dec. 31	2,037	1,502	815	789	615	
Autocircuit	12/67	Jan. 31						
		Dec. 31	2,340	1,674	1,612	507	157	
Ferromagnetics	12/67	Feb. 28						
		Dec. 31	4,866	5,007	4,382	5,712	4,792	3,392
Consolidated		Dec. 31	43,207	17,172	5,801	2,578	2,221	1,186

of Environmental and Electromek reveals that profits increased substantially after joining Contek. At the same time, it is obvious that Electronic Enclosures and Diodyne changed from a profit to a loss situation after acquisition.

FIGURE 8.3

SALES OF ACQUIRED SUBSIDIARIES AND CONSOLIDATED SALES
OF PARENT CORPORATION
(% of consolidated sales for 1967)

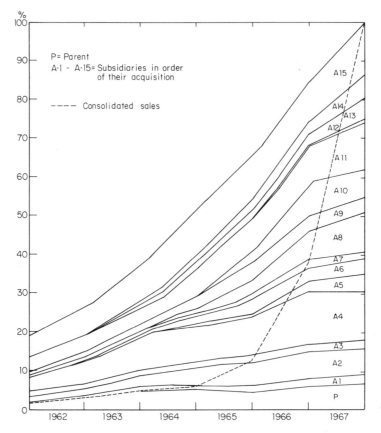

An attempt to portray the profit before-tax histories graphically, as was done for sales, provides an incomprehensible spiderweb of intersecting lines. This is caused by frequent changes from negative to positive profitability and vice versa. However, the breakdown of consolidated profit before tax is enlightening.

Table 8.6 exhibits Contek consolidated net profit before tax and the contribution of each of the subsidiaries to the total. While the one 1964 acquisition provided growing contributions to consolidated net before tax, this was not the case for the 1965 and 1966 acquisitions. The positive contribution of $476,000 from 1965 acquisitions changed to losses of $126,000 and $33,000 in the two following years. The positive contribution of $1,310,000 from 1966 acquisitions declined to $484,000 in the following year. For the 1967 acquisitions we have of course only one year of data.

What may at first appear as inconsistency between the declining profits of the 1965 and 1966 acquisitions, on the one hand, and the rapidly increasing consolidated net before tax, on the other, is explained by the expanding scale of acquisitions. For example, while the company as it existed at the end of 1965 declined in net before tax from $645,000 to $190,000 in 1966, the first year earnings of companies purchased during 1966 brought the consolidated total to $1,466,000. That is, the acquisitions during 1966 provided 87% of the consolidated profit before tax for that period. The figures for 1965 and 1967 were 74% and 86% respectively.

FIGURE 8.4

SALES OF ACQUIRED SUBSIDIARIES AND CONSOLIDATED SALES
OF PARENT CORPORATION
(% of consolidated sales for 1967 — logarithmic scale)

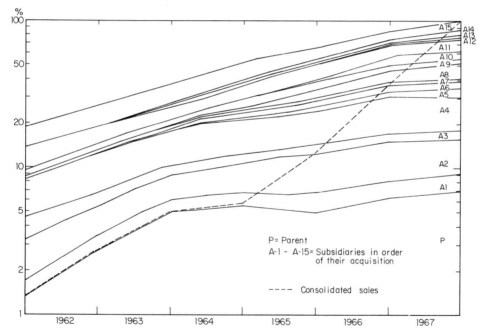

At this point, the performance on a per-share basis that Contek achieved may appear somewhat perplexing. Accordingly, we turn to an analysis of the mechanics of the acquisition transactions. This provides a partial explanation for the contribution of profits gained through acquisitions to the growth of per-share earnings. It is a "mechanical" explanation, however, rather than an "economic" one. That is, it says nothing regarding the *reasons* for the valuations placed on buying and selling companies, which is at the heart of the matter and which will be addressed later.

TABLE 8.4

Contek Incorporated
Sources of Growth in Consolidated Sales

(in thousands)

	1962	1963	1964	1965	1966	1967
Original Company	$1,186	$2,221	$2,362	$2,230	$ 2,836	$ 3,162
1964 acquisitions						
Environmental[1]			216	805	866	1,043
			$2,578	$3,036	$ 3,718	$ 4,205
1965 acquisitions						
Electronic Enclosures				$2,567	$ 3,160	$ 3,032
Electromek[1]				198	946	1,050
				2,765	4,107	4,082
				$5,801	$ 7,824	$ 8,287
1966 acquisitions						
Microwave					$ 6,143	$ 5,458
Digital Instrument[1]					707	2,020
Micronet					1,548	1,650
Diodyne					951	738
					9,348	9,866
					$17,172[2]	$18,153
1967 acquisitions						
Custom Audio						$ 4,625
Stratton[1]						1,830
Spectra						3,000
Computex						6,183
Melcast						417
Fletcher						2,037
Autocircuit						2,340
Ferromagnetics						4,866
						25,297
Consolidated	$1,186	$2,221	$2,578	$5,801	$17,172[2]	$43,207[2]

[1] Treated as purchase for accounting purposes. First-year sales figure covers less than full 12-month period.

[2] Smaller than total of preceding sales figures because of $243,000 of intercompany sales eliminated in consolidation.

The Acquisition Transactions

The terms for each of the 15 Contek acquisitions are listed in Table 8.7. Common stock was the primary medium of exchange; 11 of the 15 combinations were based entirely on common stock. Of the remaining four, two were part common stock and part cash. One of the transactions was based on convertible preferred and one on cash.

As has been previously discussed, for a stock transaction the primary determinant of the immediate financial effect is the relationship between the price-earnings ratios for the buying and selling firms. The relationship between price or value and earnings is also of significance for transactions not directly involving stock since equity capital will ultimately be required to finance some proportion of total capital employed. It is consequently of interest to examine this relationship for each of the Contek acquisitions and for the "average" transaction. This requires measures of value and measures of earnings relevant for each combination.

For the stock transactions, measures of value for both the parent and the acquired subsidiary may be based on the market value of Contek common stock at the time of the merger. The appropriate time to measure the market value is presumably the time that the "deal" was negotiated and agreed upon. However, this varies from a few weeks to several months before the merger transaction was completed and announced. Further, it would be difficult to get agreement even from the parties involved regarding exactly which market price formed the basis for the transaction. To avoid confusion and maintain consistency, we have arbitrarily taken the market price for the close of the week preceding the completion of the merger transaction as the basis for valuation. The cash and preferred stock were included at face values. The resulting total market values are shown in the next to the last column of Table 8.7. (The "equivalent number of shares" in the last column will be of use later.)

It may be observed that 5 of the 15 transactions were dependent on future earnings, and two values are listed for each of these. The first is the initial payment and the second is the maximum possible payment under an "earnings formula." This kind of transaction has typically been used where the principals of the selling firm have rather optimistic projections for increased levels of future earnings. The earnings formula approach allows the buying firm to pay an initial price which it feels appropriate for a conservative projection of future earnings, while at the same time agreeing to a higher price if more rapidly increasing earnings should be realized. In addition an attractive incentive for improved performance is provided.

This creates an unavoidable problem regarding the purchase price. Each of the five transactions were contingent on earnings over periods which had not yet ended so that the ultimate price was uncertain. Our approach to this problem was simply to look at shares issued through 1967. While hardly an elegant solution it had the advantages that (1) it was objective and (2) it is the shares issued through 1967 which were used in the earnings-per-share calculation.

In four out of five cases the initial payment had not been exceeded. It appeared appropriate to use these initial figures since they were presumably based on what Contek management considered a "reasonable" earnings projection. In the one remaining case, Custom Audio, earnings had increased dramatically and the initial exchange of 118,000 shares had been increased to 215,000 based on

TABLE 8.5

HISTORY OF NET PROFIT BEFORE TAX FOR CONTEK SUBSIDIARIES: FISCAL YEARS 1962–1967

(Companies Acquired Prior to December 31, 1967)

Subsidiary	Date Acquired	Fiscal Year Ends	1962	1963	1964	1965	1966	1967
			(annual profit before tax in thousands of dollars)					
Original Company		Dec. 31	77	167	149	128	182	172
Environmental Controls	12/64	July 31		38	66	67	100	136
		Dec. 31				41		
Electronic Enclosures	4/65	June 31	54	79	123	497	(130)	(108)
		Dec. 31				474		
Electromek Controls	10/65	Nov. 30	2	13	21	3	4	75
		Dec. 31						
Microwave Devices	4/66	May 31	361	107	138	(25)	728	333
		Dec. 31				302	918	
Digital Instrument	5/66	Mar. 31				(66)	125	162
		Dec. 31				52	115	
Micronet	12/66	Sept. 30		(175)	(2)	97	172	159
		Dec. 31				134		
Diodyne	12/66	Mar. 31		26	(61)	112	146	(171)
		Dec. 31					154	

Custom Audio	3/67	Dec. 31			69	605	868	1,976
Stratton	4/67	July 31	(3)	116	151	(16)		
		Dec. 31						166
Spectra	6/67	Jan. 31				(67)	751	
		Dec. 31						371
Computex	6/67	May 31	(115)	(125)	572	543		
		Dec. 31					367	646
Melcast	9/67	Dec. 31					(8)	41
Fletcher	9/67	Dec. 31	49	121	187	466		292
Autocircuit	12/67	Jan. 31	(157)	(182)	121	(82)		
		Dec. 31						508
Ferromagnetics	12/67	Aug. 31	443	625	477	548		
		Dec. 31						858
Consolidated		Dec. 31	77	102	156	645	1,466	5,428

TABLE 8.6

CONTEK INCORPORATED

SOURCES OF GROWTH IN CONSOLIDATED NET PROFIT BEFORE TAX

(in thousands)

	1962	1963	1964	1965	1966	1967
Original Company	$77	$167	$149	$128	$ 216	$ 172
1964 acquisitions						
Environmental[1]			74	41	100	136
			$156	$169	$ 316	$ 308
1965 acquisitions						
Electronic Enclosures				$474	$ (129)	$ (108)
Electromek[1]				2	3	75
				476	(126)	(33)
				$645	$ 190	$ 275
1966 acquisitions						
Microwave					$ 918	$ 333
Digital Instrument[1]					66	162
Micronet					172	159
Diodyne					154	(170)
					1,310	484
					$1,466[2]	$ 759
1967 acquisitions						
Custom Audio						$1,976
Stratton[1]						165
Spectra						370
Computex						646
Melcast						41
Fletcher						292
Autocircuit						508
Ferromagnetics						858
						4,856
Consolidated	$77	$167	$156	$645	$1,466[2]	$5,428[2]

[1] Treated as purchase for accounting purposes. First-year net profit before tax covers less than full 12-month period.

[2] Less than total of preceding net profit before-tax figures because of under-allocation of corporate level expenses by $34,000 and $187,000 in 1966 and 1967 respectively.

the first year's performance. While the management expectation was that the maximum of 236,000 shares would be earned, we used the 215,000 share figure. The market values for each of the transactions, determined as described above, are listed in the first column of Table 8.8. For the subsidiary price-earnings ratio we used these transaction market values relative to the total earnings of the

TABLE 8.7

CONTEK INCORPORATED
TOTAL MARKET VALUE OF TRANSACTIONS AND EQUIVALENT NUMBER OF SHARES

Acquisition	Date Acquired[1]	Market Price of Contek Common Stock[2]	Cash[3]	No. of Shares	Market Value of Shares	Total Market Value[4]	Equiv-alent No. of Shares[5]
			(000)		(000)	(000)	
Environmental	11/30/64	$ 19 6/8	$ 62	14,600	$ 288	$ 349	17,700
Electronic	4/1/65	19 6/8		125,100	2,472	2,473	125,100
Electromek	10/2/65	23		13,900	320	320	13,900
Microwave	4/1/66	25 5/8	2,952[6]			2,952	125,100
Digital	5/30/66	21 7/8	649	27,800	607	1,256	57,500
Diodyne	12/12/66	55 4/8		13,600	752	751	13,600
Micronet	12/19/66	51 3/8		34,800	1,784	1,784	34,800
Custom Audio	3/8/67	73 1/8		139,000	10,169	10,168	139,000
				278,000	20,336	20,336	278,000
Stratton	4/5/67	66 1/8	697			697	10,600
			1,312			1,312	19,700
Spectra	6/13/67	102 5/8		97,300	9,988	9,988	97,300
				166,800	17,122	17,122	166,800
Melcast	9/14/67	112 4/8		7,000	782	782	7,000
				13,900	1,564	1,565	13,900
Computex	9/14/67	112 4/8		55,600	6,257	6,257	55,600
Fletcher	9/14/67	112 4/8		27,800	3,128	3,129	27,800
				55,600	6,257	6,257	55,600
Autocircuit	12/28/67	124 5/8		39,300	4,896	4,895	39,300
Ferromagnetics	12/31/67	124 5/8		55,600	6,929	6,929	55,600

[1] Contract date or announcement date depending on information available.

[2] Bid price or closing price for end of week preceding acquisition date, as shown.

[3] Where two figures are shown for either cash or number of shares, the first represents the initial payment and the second the maximum possible payment under a purchase plan contingent on increased future earnings.

[4] Sum of cash and market value of shares, as shown.

[5] Cash is converted to number of shares by dividing by market price per share, except for transaction using convertible preferred, see note 6.

[6] Face value of preferred, convertible into 125,000 shares of common stock.

subsidiary. For Contek we used market value and earnings on a per-share basis, where the share value was based on the same price employed in measuring market value for the acquisition transaction. This provided consistent measures for market values; that is, for each acquisition we were measuring the value of the subsidiary (in the transaction) and the market value of Contek based on the same market price per share.

Needed was a consistent measure for earnings. Fortunately what was needed was consistency between parent and acquisition for each transaction and not

TABLE 8.8

CONTEK INCORPORATED

RELATIVE PRICE-EARNINGS RATIOS FOR CONTEK AND ACQUIRED COMPANIES

Acquisition	Total Market Value of Transaction[1]	Earnings before Tax for Fiscal Year of Acquisition	Earnings after Tax at Contek Tax Rate[2]	Equivalent p/e for Acquisition[3]	Contek p/e[4]	Ratio of Contek p/e to Acquisition p/e[5]
	(000)	(000)	(000)			
Environmental	$ 349	$ 66	$ 39	9	80	9.0
Electronic	2,473	474	289	9	26	3.0
Electromek	320	3	2	195	30	.2
Microwave	2,952	918	551	5	19	3.5
Digital	1,256	115	69	18	17	.9
Diodyne	751	154	92	8	42	5.1
Micronet	1,784	172	103	17	39	2.3
Custom Audio[6]	18,506	1,976	1,063	17	32	1.9
Stratton	697	166	89	8	29	3.7
Spectra	9,988	371	200	50	45	.9
Melcast	782	41	21	37	49	1.3
Computex	6,157	646	348	18	49	2.7
Fletcher	3,129	292	157	20	49	2.5
Autocircuit	4,895	508	274	18	54	3.0
Ferromagnetics	6,929	858	461	15	54	3.6
Average					41	2.9
Weighted Average[7]					41	2.3

[1] Total market value taken from Table 8.7. For those acquisitions having purchase plans contingent on future earnings, no payments beyond initial payment were made through end of 1967 except in case of Custom Audio Systems; see note 6 below.

[2] Contek federal income tax rate for fiscal year during which acquisition occurred.

[3] Total market value divided by earnings after tax, as shown.

[4] Market price per share of Contek stock of acquisition date, as shown in Table 8.7, divided by Contek earnings per share for fiscal year during which acquisition occurred.

[5] Calculated before rounding preceding two columns.

[6] Total market value of transaction based on 215,000 shares issued under purchase plan with 118,000 shares initial payment and a maximum additional payment of 118,000 shares contingent on future earnings.

[7] Weighted by total market value of transactions. For those acquisitions involving contingent purchase plans the market value and ratio based on the initial payment were used in calculating the weighted average (except for Custom Audio, see note 6).

consistency across transactions. The former could be achieved simply by measuring the earnings of parent and subsidiary over the same period of time. The latter would require that price and earnings have the same relationship in time for each transaction. Data were available for the former; they were not for the latter. For both Contek and the subsidiary we used earnings for the Contek fiscal year during which the transaction occurred, regardless of when during the year it occurred. For the subsidiary we eliminated taxation differences with Contek by using the reported before-tax profits and treated them as though taxed at the Contek federal income tax rate for the full fiscal year.

To summarize, we measured the Contek price-earnings ratio as the market price per share at the time of the acquisition divided by the earnings per share for the fiscal year during which the transaction occurred. For the subsidiary we measured the price-earnings ratio as the value of the transaction, based on the same market price, divided by reported before-tax earnings of the acquisition for the Contek fiscal year, assumed to be taxed at the Contek federal income tax rate. These price-earnings ratios and the relationships between them are shown in the last three columns of Table 8.8.

Two qualifications are necessary to understand the meaning of these figures. First, what is the significance of relative price-earnings ratios for a transaction based entirely or in part on cash or for a transaction based on controvertible preferred which is not used in the normal earnings per-share calculation? For the transaction which is part or all cash the assumption inherent in our analysis is that the cash used in acquisitions has been supplied by or will later require the issuance of common stock. Strictly speaking, this in turn implies that Contek on the average was not altering the capital structures either in companies purchased or in the parent company and was using internally generated funds for "internal" investment. For the convertible preferred the inherent assumption is that it is more appropriate to look at the financial impact on a converted basis since conversion will ultimately occur. While the accuracy of these assumptions is subject to question, the approach taken does provide a relatively conservative measure of the initial financial impact of acquisitions. Also, exchange media other than common stock have been used in particular situations primarily because of strong preferences of the selling parties. Contek management preferred to use common stock and had generally done so. Of the total market value of all transactions listed in the first column of Table 8.8, which equals $61.0 million, $57.4 million or 94% represents market value of common stock. The distortion caused by our assumptions is therefore reasonably small.

The second qualification relates to the treatment of purchases. We looked at price relative to subsidiary earnings for a full 12-month period even in those cases where purchase accounting was involved. While earnings actually consolidated would provide a better measure of the financial impact in the *first* fiscal year, earnings for a 12-month period provide a better measure of the earning power which Contek acquired and which will contribute to consolidated earnings in future periods.

Given these qualifications, we may turn to the interpretation of the values in the last three columns of Table 8.8. The ratio of value to earnings for Contek exceeded that of companies purchased in 12 of 15 cases. In the case of Electromek, where the price-earnings ratio was substantially higher than that of the parent, Contek purchased a company with essentially no earnings because of the perceived technical expertise of the former owner and general manager. For the two other cases where the subsidiary price-earnings ratio was slightly higher, Digital and Spectra, strong technical competence and the promise of future growth compensated for the lack of contribution to earnings per share.

On the average the Contek price-earnings ratio far exceeded that of companies acquired. For the average acquired company the Contek price-earnings ratio was 2.9 times as large. On the basis of an average weighted by market values of the transactions, the Contek multiple was 2.3 as large.

Making use of the weighted average Contek price-earnings multiple, which equaled 41 times, we may view this in a slightly different manner. For every $100 of market value given up by Contek in acquisitions, Contek had $100/41 = $2.44 in earnings. For that $100 in market value given up it received $2.44 × 2.3 = $5.61 in earnings which served to "average up" the earnings per share of the parent.

Since these relationships are averages which obtained over a period of four years, we may say something about the change in value of the subsidiary upon becoming a part of Contek. Because the average and weighted average multiples of the Contek price-earnings ratio times the subsidiary price-earnings ratio are 2.9 and 2.3 times respectively, we can say that the average subsidiary was appraised by the market at 290% of its purchase price after becoming a part of Contek, an increase of 190%. Or we can say that the average dollar of market value acquired was appraised by the market at 230% of its purchase price for an increase of 130%. And when one can equal 2.90, or even 2.30, who can doubt that two plus two equals at least five?

The Analysis of Before and After Performance

The preceding analysis of relative values sheds some light on the per-share performance of Contek. However, it provides understanding only at a superficial level. There remain the all important questions: Why this disparity in prices relative to earnings? Why this increase in subsidiary value upon joining the parent corporation?

As has been discussed previously, some have suggested that for acquisitive conglomerates generally the answer lies in the change of subsidiary performance upon becoming a part of the parent corporation. That is, if the investing public thinks that a given acquirer has demonstrated an ability to improve the profitability and growth of companies purchased in the past, it will be inclined to believe that the same will be achieved in the future. Thus, when it is announced that a given subsidiary has been acquired, the expectations for future performance increase and the value of the subsidiary increases. In this way the acquirer is continually able to "transfer" its higher price-earnings ratio to the companies that it acquires and thus to achieve a "capital gain" on the transaction.

Our examination of this possible explanation, as things turned out, may be viewed as the first step in an elimination process. We consider improvement in subsidiary performance the most important of the possible explanations for acquisition-based performance which has "real" economic content and therefore a "rational" foundation. If such improvement has not been achieved, we can then look to other possible explanations of lesser importance which may be considered "rational" to the extent that more desirable combinations of risk and return may be achieved (differences in size, diversification, capital structures, marketability, etc.). If these are judged inadequate to explain the observed differences in valuation, we must look to the interrelationships between performance and value which appear to exist in high expansion-rate growth strategies. That is, we must look to the kind of explanation provided by the Contek financial strategy model (Figure 8.1) but with "internal growth" playing an insignificant or negative role.

Our brief discussion of the consolidated statements of sales and earnings before tax earlier in this chapter provided some tentative conclusions regarding internal performance. Specifically, we noted that sales appeared to have increased for most subsidiaries after joining Contek but that earnings before tax presented a very mixed picture, with some subsidiaries achieving increases but others making dramatic changes from positive to negative profit contributions upon becoming a part of Contek. In this section we will pursue two objectives: (1) to provide a more adequate analysis for the individual subsidiaries which had been acquired and (2) to compare the post-acquisition performance with previous performance as an independent company.

This kind of analysis is feasible only because of the operating characteristics of Contek. There was almost no integration of acquired subsidiaries; each previously independent company operated as a largely separate part of Contek. Intercompany sales were nonexistent prior to 1967 and in that year amounted to $243,000 or 0.6% of total sales. The corporate management and staff group was small and provided few operating functions for the subsidiaries. The allocation of corporate expenses was based on a flat 2% of subsidiary sales volume. Changes in accounting treatments for acquisitions were relatively few and for the most part susceptible to adjustment. In general, the ingredients are present for obtaining reasonably meaningful financial data for the comparison of subsidiary performance before and after acquisition.

This initial, unadjusted approach to comparing "what was" with "what would have been" inherently assumes that "what would have been" was more of the same in terms of previous profitability and growth. While this approach is fraught with shortcomings, we will ultimately conclude that this is about as good as can be done with any possible adjustments. It is therefore reasonable to pursue the analysis in some detail.

We have continually emphasized that the key ingredients of performance for shareholders are the efficient use of invested capital and the rate of expansion of invested capital, or more simply: profitability and growth. Accordingly, it is measures of these two dimensions of performance that we examined for the acquired subsidiaries.

The choice of items of financial data was based both upon the chosen measures of performance and upon availability. The performance analysis required at a minimum some measure if capital employed in the business as a function of time and some measure of profitability of the employment of that capital. Further, since the proportional relationships between gross revenues, profits, and capital obviously did not remain the same over time in reality as they do in our abstract models, it is helpful to bring some measure of sales into the picture. This allows us to partition efficiency in the use of capital into margin on sales and capital turnover. In addition we are interested in the growth of sales since ultimately it is sales expansion which permits profitable expansion of capital employed.

We focused on three items of financial data for each subsidiary: (1) net sales, (2) profits before taxes, and (3) total capital. We chose to look at total capital rather than net worth because there were significant changes in capital structure over time. The corresponding measure of profitability is, of course, profit before interest and taxes. Unfortunately, information regarding interest expenses for some of the pre-acquisition periods was not available, and the only measure of profitability available on a consistent basis was profit before tax. Thus, our measure of profitability has a flaw of some significance, but we had no choice but to use it.

Table 8.9 provides financial data for each of the seven acquired subsidiaries which had been a part of Contek for at least a full year by the end of 1967. Data on sales, profit before tax, and total capital are given for each fiscal year after acquisition and for fiscal years before acquisition going back as far as possible or for five years. At least three years of pre-acquisition data were available for each of the seven subsidiaries except Digital which had been in existence for only two full years when it was acquired. A given fiscal year was considered before or after acquisition depending on whether the subsidiary joined Contek after or before the midpoint in that 12-month period. On this basis, there were two subsidiaries with three years of post-acquisition data, three subsidiaries with two years, and two subsidiaries with one.

Adjustments to the original data were made for three of the seven subsidiaries. Environmental was a purchase involving a significant increase in stated value of depreciable assets at the time of acquisition. Based on an estimate[3] of average depreciable life for the change in asset values, post-acquisition balance sheet and income data were adjusted to be comparable with pre-acquisition data. Digital underwent changes in the accounting treatment of certain expense items. In this case adjustments to pre-acquisition data were made by Contek for evaluation of pre-acquisition performance based on the parent company's accounting policies. The figures as adjusted by the parent appear in Table 8.9. Digital was also a purchase, as was Electromek; however, in neither case were there significant increases in the stated values of tangible assets. For Diodyne a large portion of the pre-acquisition inventory was written off by Contek and the accounting policies for valuing inventory changed to a more conservative basis.

---

[3] This estimate and other information for the required adjustments were provided by Contek management. We therefore consider the adjusted data about as close to being comparable as can be achieved. It should be appreciated, however, that when accounting changes alter taxable income or operating decisions, in either case causing *real* changes, no adjustment is entirely adequate.

The one year of post-acquisition data was adjusted to correspond with the pre-acquisition inventory policy. For the other subsidiaries adjustments were not required.

As has been mentioned, expenses incurred by corporate management and staff were covered by a charge against each subsidiary amounting to 2% of their respective sales volumes.[4] Post-acquisition earnings before tax listed in Table 8.9 were net of this corporate level expense.

Measures of performance calculated and displayed in Table 8.9 are (1) GS — the rate of growth in sales; (2) GNBT — the rate of growth in net profit before tax; (3) NBT/S — net profit before tax as a percentage of sales; and (4) NBT/TC — net profit before tax as a percentage of total capital. The growth rate of sales is defined as the annual change in sales volume measured as a percentage of the sales figure for the earlier year. Growth in profit before tax had to be treated somewhat differently. Because the profit figure changed from negative to positive and vice versa in a number of instances, an annual percentage change would be difficult to interpret if not meaningless. As a substitute, growth in profits before tax was measured as the year-to-year change taken as a percentage of total capital in the latter year. The measures of net profit before tax as a percentage of sales and as a percentage of total capital are self-descriptive. In all cases the averages which were calculated are simple averages of the annual figures.

The results of this analysis are summarized in Tables 8.10 and 8.11. In Table 8.10 profit before tax as a percentage of sales and as a percentage of total capital is shown for the average of the periods before and after acquisition and for the first years before and after. In Table 8.11 the rates of growth in sales and net before tax are shown for the average of periods before and after acquisition and for the year-to-year change covering the transition from independent company to Contek subsidiary. For all the performance measures in the two tables, simple averages for all subsidiaries and averages weighted on the basis of 1967 total capital for the respective subsidiaries were calculated. Both the simple and the weighted average calculations were made, first including all subsidiaries and then excluding Digital. As mentioned earlier Digital had only two years of pre-acquisition data. The first of these represented the initiation of operations, and the profitability for that year as well as the year-to-year growth to the next year would not appear appropriate for comparison with post-acquisition performance. In particular, it would not be reasonable to expect the initial dramatic growth to continue. Therefore, while the averages based on all subsidiaries provide a better absolute measure of post-acquisition performance, the averages exclud-

---

[4] This resulted in under-allocation of corporate level expenses by $34,000 in 1966 and $187,000 in 1967, 2.1% and 3.4% of consolidated net profit before tax for 1966 and 1967 respectively. This under-allocation of expenses was not distributed to the subsidiaries for the earnings figures shown in Table 8.9. This provides a slight *overstatement* of post-acquisition earnings, but we prefer a consistent basis for allocation of this expense, and in any event an overstatement of post-acquisition subsidiary earnings only strengthens the conclusions which will develop.

TABLE 8.9

COMPARISON OF PERFORMANCE[1] BEFORE AND AFTER ACQUISITION
CONTEK SUBSIDIARIES ACQUIRED PRIOR TO DECEMBER 31, 1966

(dollar figures in thousands; performance data in percents)

	Pre-Acquisition						Post-Acquisition			
	1961	1962	1963	1964	1965	Average	1965[2]	1966	1967	Average
Environmental 11/30/65			*July 31*					*December 31*		
S			449	579	697		805	882	1,043	
NBT			38	66	67		49	108	144	
TC			203	271	300		323	415	323	
GS				29	20	25	28	10	18	19
GNBT				10	*	5	(4)	14	11	7
NBT/S			8	11	10	10	6	12	14	11
NBT/TC			19	24	22	20	15	26	45	29
Electronic 4/1/65			*June 30*					*December 31*		
S	690	874	1,077	1,471	2,383		2,567	3,160	3,032	
NBT	75	54	79	123	497		474	(130)	(108)	
TC	197	554	528	584	802		877	2,076	2,053	
GS		27	23	36	62	37	16	23	(4)	12
GNBT		(4)	5	8	47	14	(3)	(29)	1	(10)
NBT/S	11	6	7	8	21	11	18	(4)	(4)	3
NBT/TC	38	10	15	21	62	29	54	(6)	(5)	14
Electromek 10/2/66			*November 30*					*December 31*		
S	597	612	722	753	845[4]			946	1,050	
NBT	(20)	2	13	21	3			3	75	
TC	225	226	235	249	248			328	339	
GS		3	18	4	12	9		11	11	11
GNBT		9	5	3	(7)	3		*	21	11
NBT/S	(3)	*	2	3	4	*		*	7	4
NBT/TC	(9)	1	6	9	1	2		1	22	12

	1961	1962	1963	1964	1965	1966	Average	1966	1967	Average
Microwave 4/1/66				*May 31*					*December 31*	
S	1,468	1,932	2,998	3,988	4,077	5,327		6,143	5,458	
NBT	148	361	107	138	(25)	728		918	333	
TC[5]	431	567	881	1,169	1,171	1,589		1,914	1,837	
GS		32	55	33	2	31	31	26	(11)	8
GNBT		38	(29)	3	(14)	48	9	17	(32)	(8)
NBT/S	10	19	4	3	(1)	14	8	15	6	11
NBT/TC	34	64	12	12	(2)	46	28	48	18	33
Digital 6/30/66				*March 31[6]*					*December 31*	
S					390	940		1,235	2,020	
NBT					(66)	(40)		115	162	
TC					48	72		495	689	

TABLE 8.9 (continued)

	Pre-Acquisition						*Average*	*Post-Acquisition*		*Average*
	1961	*1962*	*1963*	*1964*	*1965*	*1966*	*age*	*1966*	*1967*	*age*
GS						141	141	41	64	53
GNBT						264	264	(2)	7	3
NBT/S					(17)	13	(2)	9	8	9
NBT/TC					(138)	173	18	23	24	24

Micronet
12/19/67

	September 30							*December 31*		
	1961	*1962*	*1963*	*1964*	*1965*	*1966*	*Average*	*1966*	*1967*	*Average*
S			43	661	1,091	1,440			1,650	
NBT			(175)	(2)	97	125			159	
TC[7]			16	231	372	462			800	
GS[8]					65	32	49			
GNBT					26	6	16		13	13
NBT/S				*	9	9	6		10	10
NBT/TC				(1)	26	27	17		20	20

	1963	*1964*	*1965*	*1966*	*1967*	*Average*	*1967*	*Average*
Diodyne 12/30/67	*March 31[9]*						*December 31*	
S	408	390	628	779	951		738	
NBT	26	(61)	112	146	154		(46)	
TC[10]	254	180	289	359	394		392	
GS		(4)	61	24	22	26	(30)	(30)
GNBT		(48)	40	10	2	1	(68)	(68)
NBT/S	6	(16)	18	19	16	9	(6)	(6)
NBT/TC	14	(34)	39	41	39	20	(12)	(12)

[1] The symbols used in this table are defined as follows: S equals annual sales volume; NBT equals annual net before tax; TC equals total capital, net worth plus long-term debt; GS equals the year-to-year percentage change in sales; GNBT equals the year-to-year change in net before tax as a percentage of total capital in the latter year; NBT/S equals net before tax as a percent of sales; NBT/TC equals net before tax as a percent of total capital.

[2] Performance measures for growth in sales and growth in net before tax linearly adjusted to reflect change over a 12-month period from pre-acquisition financial data. For example, in the case of Environmental, sales and profit growth for the fiscal year ending May 31, 1966, were calculated in the usual way using the fiscal year ending December 31, 1964, as a base and the results were multiplied by 12/17.

[3] Post-acquisition data adjusted to be approximately comparable with pre-acquisition data. Environmental was a purchase and depreciable assets were increased by $82,000 to their fair value at the time of acquisition.

[4] Sales and net before tax as of November 30, 1965; total capital as of December 31, 1966.

[5] Total capital for 1961–1964 not available. Figures shown are estimates based on assumption that (sales/total capital) for these years was same as average for 1965–1966.

[6] As restated by parent company for purposes of comparison on consistent basis with post-acquisition accounting. Sales were insignificant before year ending March 31, 1965.

[7] Pre-acquisition figures for total capital estimated based on balance sheet data available for fiscal years ending December 31 of 1964, 1965, and 1966.

[8] Data for fiscal year 1963 represent initiation of operations and are not used for measures of profitability and growth in pre-acquisition period.

[9] Fiscal years ending March 31 with exception of 1967 which is data for annual period ending December 31, 1966.

[10] Estimated for 1963–1966 based on the relationship between sales and total capital for 1967.

* Less than 0.5%.

ing Digital provide a better basis for comparison of before and after performance.

Net before tax as a percentage of sales for the average period after acquisition increased for five of the seven subsidiaries in comparison with the average

TABLE 8.10

SUMMARY OF PERFORMANCE BEFORE AND AFTER ACQUISITIVE
MEASURES OF PROFITABILITY IN RELATION TO SALES AND TOTAL CAPITAL:
CONTEK SUBSIDIARIES ACQUIRED PRIOR TO DECEMBER 31, 1966

	Net Profit before Tax as % of Sales				Net Profit before Tax as % of Total Capital			
	Aver-age before	1st Year before	1st Year after	Aver-age after	Aver-age before	1st Year before	1st Year after	Aver-age after
Environmental	10	10	6	11	20	22	15	29
Electronic	11	21	18	3	29	62	54	14
Electromek	*	*	*	4	2	1	1	12
Microwave	8	14	15	11	28	46	48	33
Digital	(2)	13	9	9	18	173	23	24
Micronet	6	9	10	10	17	27	20	20
Diodyne	9	16	(6)	(6)	20	39	(12)	(12)
Average	6	12	7	6	19	53	21	17
Weighted average[1]	7	15	12	7	24	58	36	20
Excluding Digital								
Average	7	12	7	6	19	33	21	16
Weighted average[1]	9	15	13	6	24	44	38	20

* Less than 0.5%.
[1] Weighted on the basis of 1967 total capital for each subsidiary.

period before acquisition. However, the increases were relatively small and the two decreases large, so that there was no improvement in profit margins on the average. Indeed, excluding Digital, there was a minor decline. In the first-year–first-year-after comparison the picture is more negative. There was an increase in only two cases and no significant change in one case; all the average figures declined.

The story for net before tax as a percentage of total capital is much the same. In the average-before–average-after comparison there were five increases, but the two declines were large causing all the "average subsidiary" figures to decline. In the first-year-before–first-year-after comparison there was only one subsidiary for which there was an increase and one for which there was no change. Again all the average figures declined.

In general, it may be said that in terms of the average profitability of subsidiaries after acquisition there were increases in a majority of the cases. However, these increases were relatively small and the substantial declines in the case of two subsidiaries, Electronic and Diodyne, resulted in no improvement or declines on either a simple or weighted average basis. The picture for the transition years is more negative with the majority of the subsidiaries declining and all the average figures declining. This would lend credence to the frequently discussed difficulty of the transition from an independent company to a subsidiary or operating division.

TABLE 8.11

SUMMARY OF PERFORMANCE BEFORE AND AFTER ACQUISITION
MEASURES OF GROWTH FOR SALES AND EARNINGS BEFORE TAX:
CONTEK SUBSIDIARIES ACQUIRED PRIOR TO DECEMBER 31, 1966

	Annual Rate of Growth of Total Revenues (%)			Annual Change in Net Profit before Tax as % of Total Capital		
	Average before	*1st Year before to 1st Year after*	*Average after*[1]	*Average before*	*1st Year before to 1st Year after*	*Average after*[1]
Environmental	25	28	19	5	(4)	7
Electronic	37	16	12	14	(3)	(10)
Electromek	9	11	11	3	*	11
Microwave	31	26	8	9	17	(8)
Digital	141	41	53	264	(2)	3
Micronet	49	13	13	16	4	4
Diodyne	26	(30)	(30)	1	(68)	(68)
Average	45	15	12	45	(8)	(9)
Weighted average[2]	45	19	13	38	*	(8)
Excluding Digital						
Average	30	11	6	8	(9)	(11)
Weighted average[2]	34	16	8	11	*	(9)

* Less than 0.5%.
[1] Includes transition year.
[2] Weighted on the basis of 1967 total capital for each subsidiary.

For the growth of sales and profits, summarized in Table 8.11, the comparison is still more negative. For only one subsidiary, Electromek, had the average rate of sales growth after acquisition exceeded that before. In two cases, Environmental and Electromek, the transition sales increases exceeded the average before. All the "average subsidiary" measures showed declines; in every case the average after was less than the transition which in turn was less than the average before.

Most important and most dramatic is the before and after comparison for the measure of growth in net profit before tax. There were increases in the "average after" relative to the "average before" for only two subsidiaries, again Environmental and Electromek. For three of the five cases where the "average after" was less, the "growth rate" became negative. In those three subsidiaries, profits were declining sufficiently rapidly to offset those cases where profits were increasing, so that the "average subsidiary" measures show declining profits after acquisition. The growth of net before tax in the transition year was little better, and for all the "average subsidiary" figures the "average after" was smaller than the transition which in turn was smaller than the "average before."

The analysis provides substantial evidence that for the seven subsidiaries which had been with Contek for at least a year aggregate performance declined after acquisition. It seems fair to say that this is not the kind of evidence that would inspire the investing public to greatly increase their expectations regarding the performance of a new acquisition joining Contek. Therefore it would appear possible at this point to rule out the change in performance of acquired companies as a major cause or "justification" for the disparity between price-earnings ratios of Contek and the companies which were purchased.

At the same time it seems desirable to go one step further in the quantitative analysis. We concluded that subsidiary performance declined after acquisition, but it does not necessarily follow that acquisition by Contek was the cause. As we pointed out earlier, the possible causes for changes in performance include (1) the influence of Contek, (2) change in the economic environment for the various industries, and (3) forces at work within the subsidiaries either before or after acquisition which would have led to changes in performance without any external influence.

In the next chapter we will make some effort to differentiate between the influence of Contek and those forces internal to the subsidiary. For the moment we shall be content to pursue an analysis of the effects of changing industry environments. As will soon become apparent this is as much an analysis of the problems for this type of comparison as it is an analysis of the effects of changing conditions.

ANALYSIS OF EFFECTS OF CHANGING INDUSTRY ENVIRONMENTS

The difficulty in the analysis of changing industry environments is caused not so much by the methodology as by the inadequacy of available data. Data on growth and profitability are only available for industry categories which are much broader than the "industries" in which our seven subsidiaries participated. This disparity between breadth of industry covered by the data and breadth of subsidiary product line is sufficient to make it questionable whether the analysis has significance. The problem is best understood by examination of one situation in some detail.

As an example we will discuss the analysis of Electromek Controls Corporation which was probably about average among the seven subsidiaries in terms of adequacy of available data. The bulk of Electromek revenues were derived from the assembly and sale of controls for process machinery rate control systems. These controls were built to customer specifications around several basic models. They were composed of an electromechanical transducer providing input to an electronic control circuit which maintained the rate of flow within a narrowly specified range. This type of control device permits a smaller number of workers to supervise processing machinery than is otherwise possible.

The proper question is: What happened to profitability and growth over the relevant period in the "industry" that produces and sells electronic controls for process industry machinery? Not surprisingly no one has collected a wealth of data on this "industry."

It is typically data on sales which are available for the most narrow product categories. These are frequently collected and published by industry associations.[5] The data most closely aligned with the Electromek product line are a series on annual sales volume of "electronic controls" provided by the Electronic Industries Association.[6] This series appropriately includes electronic controls for various production processes but also inappropriately includes electronic controls for aerospace applications.

The data available for performance ratios are less adequate. Needed is a timely source of periodic data providing performance ratios, or income and balance sheet data from which performance ratios can be derived, for narrow industry classifications and for groups of firms in different size categories. None of the possible sources is entirely satisfactory.[7] However, when timeliness, industry coverage, and size classifications are considered, the best source for our particular purposes in most cases was provided by Robert Morris Associates in their *Annual Statement Studies*. This series provides detailed balance sheet and income statement data for 209 industrial categories and within each category for four size classes under $10 million in total assets. There is approximately a one-year delay between the end of the annual period covered and publication. The 209 industrial categories approximate but do not follow exactly the Standard Industrial Classification at the three-digit level.

The industry category most closely aligned with Electromek is "Manufacturers of Engineering, Laboratory, Scientific and Research Instruments" which includes a wide range of electronic, mechanical, and optical instruments. While this ap-

---

[5] Another important source of detailed sales data where timeliness is not important is provided by the U.S. Department of Commerce, *Census of Manufactures;* years for which these census figures have been compiled include 1963, 1958, 1954, 1947; in the most recent census there was approximately a delay of four and one-half years between the end of the period covered and publication; among the wealth of information included is annual value shipped (in each census going back to the preceding census) for industry categories corresponding to the Standard Industrial Classification at the five-digit level.

[6] *Electronic Industries Year Book, 1968.*

[7] Some of the better sources for the specified type of information are the following:

(1) U.S. Treasury Department, Internal Revenue Service, *Statistics of Income, Corporation Income Tax Returns;* prepared annually but with approximately a four-year delay between the end of the period covered and publication; provides balance sheet and income data for 68 industry categories based on Standard Enterprise Classification, established by Office and Statistical Standards, Bureau of the Budget; prior to 1963, categories based upon Standard Industrial Classification; each category broken into 16 size groups, 11 of them for firms with less than $10 million in total assets.

(2) Dun and Bradstreet, *Key Business Ratios;* prepared annually with approximately a one-year delay between end of period covered and publication; performance ratio data for 125 selected SIC categories at the three- and four-digit level; no breakdown by size.

(3) FTC-SEC, *Quarterly Financial Report for Manufacturing Corporations;* prepared quarterly with approximately six-month delay between end of latest period covered and publication; balance sheet and income data for industry categories at the two-digit level of the Standard Enterprise Classification with no size breakdown; or broken down into groupings based on size of total assets with no industry breakdown.

(4) Robert Morris Associates, *Annual Statement Studies.*

pears marginally appropriate at best, the fact remains that the Electromek electronic controls more closely resembled electronic instruments than any other product category for which data were available.

Since the Robert Morris Associates data are published with a one-year delay, another source of profitability data had to be used for the last fiscal year. This was provided in all cases by the Federal Trade Commission-Securities and Exchange Commission's, *Quarterly Financial Report for Manufacturing Enterprises.* Profitability data from this source were "spliced" to the Robert Morris data so that FTC-SEC data established only the direction and magnitude of change in the profitability measures for the last fiscal year, not their absolute levels. The FTC-SEC series most appropriate for Electromek is based on firms of all sizes within Standard Enterprises Classification No. 38, "Instruments and Related Products."

Results of the analysis of Electromek Controls are shown in Table 8.12. First the industry sales series was scaled to match actual Electromek sales in 1967. The source of balance sheet and income data was then used to establish appropriate amounts of Net Before Tax and Total Capital relative to Sales for each period. Both sales and profitability data were linearly adjusted to match the fiscal years shown. Performance measures for the "comparable" industry data were then calculated in the same manner as for the subsidiary. Averages of the annual figures for the periods corresponding to subsidiary operations before and after acquisition were also calculated for the industry data. The differences between the average figures for the subsidiary and for the "industry" provide measures of performance relative to the industry.

For example, in terms of the rate of growth of sales, Electromek improved in the periods after acquisition relative to those before while the "industry" slowed down. The rate of growth of Electromek sales before acquisition averaged 7 percentage points below that of the industry while the average rate of growth in the periods after acquisition equaled that of the industry. Thus, while Electromek sales growth improved from 9% to 12% per year in the periods before and after acquisition, it may be said that relative to the industry the rate of growth in sales improved from minus 7 percentage points to zero.

Taking a broader view, it will be recalled from the earlier analysis that average performance improved for Electromek on all four performance measures. However, the "industry" performance moved in the same direction for three of the four measures, all but the sales growth measure discussed above. Therefore, when the change in Electromek performance is viewed relative to the industry, it appears somewhat less positive. Still, on all four performance measures the relative figures became more positive (or less negative) so that, to the extent that the "industry" data are meaningful, we can say that improved industry conditions accounted for some but not all of the post-acquisition improvement in Electromek performance.

Similar analyses were carried out for each of the other six subsidiaries[8] and

---

[8] These tables are included in Harry H. Lynch's doctoral dissertation, "Acquisitive Conglomerate Performance," pp. 410–416, on file in Baker Library, Harvard Business School (1969).

the results are summarized in Table 8.13. This table shows, for each of the four performance measures, the average performance for periods before and after acquisition for the subsidiary, the industry, and the subsidiary relative to the

TABLE 8.12

Example Comparison of Subsidiary and "Industry"
Performance Data: Electromek Controls
(dollar figures in thousands; performance measures in percent)

		Pre-Acquisition						Post-Acquisition		
		1961	*1962*	*1963*	*1964*	*1965*	*Average*	*1966*	*1967*	*Average*
Company[1]				November 30					December 31	
S		597	612	722	753	845		946	1,050	
NBT		(20)	2	13	21	3		3	75	
TC		225	226	235	249	248		328	346	
"industry"										
S[2]		428	489	531	654	835		974	1,050	
NBT[3]		20	18	13	10	38		72	71	
TC		225	257	280	312	464		487	556	
GS	company		3	18	4	12	9	13	11	12
	industry		7	8	23	27	16	14	9	12
	difference						(7)			*
GNBT	company		9	5	3	(7)	3	*	21	11
	industry		(1)	(2)	(1)	5	*	7	*	4
	difference						3			7
NBT/S	company	(3)	*	2	3	*	*	*	7	4
	industry	5	4	3	2	5	4	7	7	7
	difference						(4)			(3)
NBT/TC	company	(9)	1	6	9	1	2	1	22	12
	industry	9	7	5	3	8	6	15	13	14
	difference						(4)			(2)

* Less than 0.5%.

[1] All data for company same as shown in Table 8.9.

[2] Sales data based on sales of "Electronic Controls" as listed in *Electronics Industries Year Book 1968*, linearly adjusted to match fiscal years shown, and scaled so that 1967 sales equal company sales.

[3] Net before tax and total capital based on financial data provided for "Engineering, Laboratory, Scientific and Research Instruments" in Robert Morris Associates, *Annual Statement Studies*, 1961–1966 editions; interpolated linearly to match fiscal years shown; NBT and TC for fiscal year ending December 31, 1967, based on financial data from FTC-SEC *Quarterly Financial Report for Manufacturing Corporations*, Standard Enterprise Classification No. 38, "Instruments and Related Products"; the FTC-SEC data have been "spliced" to the Robert Morris Associates data.

industry. The sources of data for the industry comparisons are listed in the notes to Table 8.13. Averages weighted on the basis of total capital for each subsidiary in 1967 were calculated for each performance measure for the periods before and after acquisition. These are shown first for all subsidiaries and then,

TABLE 8.13

PERFORMANCE OF CONTEK SUBSIDIARIES BEFORE AND AFTER ACQUISITION:
COMPARISON WITH INDUSTRY PERFORMANCE DATA
(Percent)

| | | GS^1 | | $GNBT$ | | NBT/S | | NBT/TC | |
| | | Average | | Average | | Average | | Average | |
		before	after	before	after	before	after	before	after
Environ-									
mental	company[2]	25	19	5	7	10	11	20	29
	industry[3]	10	9	4	1	4	5	15	19
	difference	15	10	1	6	6	6	5	10
Electronic	company	37	12	14	(10)	11	3	29	14
	industry[4]	6	9	2	2	3	7	7	12
	difference	31	3	12	(12)	8	(4)	22	2
Electromek	company	9	12	3	11	*	4	2	12
	industry[5]	16	12	*	4	4	7	6	14
	difference	(7)	*	3	7	(4)	(3)	(4)	(2)
Microwave	company	31	8	9	(8)	8	11	28	33
	industry[6]	8	(5)	2	(1)	6	9	10	13
	difference	23	13	7	(7)	2	2	18	20
Digital	company	141	53	264	3	(2)	9	18	24
	industry[7]	21	9	7	1	5	7	10	13
	difference	120	44	257	2	(7)	2	8	11
Micronet	company	49	13	16	4	6	10	17	20
	industry[8]	18	(15)	6	(3)	9	7	12	13
	difference	31	28	10	7	(3)	3	5	7
Diodyne	company	26	(30)	1	(68)	9	(6)	20	(12)
	industry[9]	18	(9)	5	(1)	4	7	9	13
	difference	8	(13)	(4)	(49)	5	(12)	11	(22)
Weighted									
Average[10]	company	45	13	38	(8)	7	7	24	20
	industry	11	1	3	*	5	7	9	13
	difference	34	12	35	(8)	2	*	15	7
Excluding Digital									
Weighted									
Average	company	34	8	11	(9)	9	6	24	20
	industry	10	*	3	*	5	8	9	13
	difference	24	8	8	(9)	4	(2)	15	7

for reasons discussed earlier, excluding Digital. As previously argued, the before
and after comparisons are probably more meaningful with Digital omitted.

We have noted that the "average subsidiary" figures declined after acquisition
on all performance measures. The industry figures also declined for the growth
measures, lessening the decline in the growth rates of the subsidiaries relative to
their respective industries, but not reversing the change to a positive one. For

FOOTNOTES TO TABLE 8.13

* Less than 0.5%.

[1] Definitions for performance measures provided in notes to Table 8.9.

[2] Performance ratios for each of the seven subsidiaries are the same as shown in Table 8.9.

[3] Environmental derived over 90% of sales volume from subassemblies for industrial temperature and humidity control systems. Such equipment is typically installed in a nonresidential, nonfarm structure at the time of its construction. Sales series based on Department of Commerce data for New Construction Expenditures: Commercial, Industrial and Public Structures. Income and balance sheet information based on data for all manufacturing corporations of less than $1 million in total assets as provided by FTC-SEC, *Quarterly Financial Report for Manufacturing Corporations,* various editions. No profitability information on an individual industry basis was available which could be considered even marginally appropriate.

[4] Electronic Enclosures fabricated precision sheet metal components to customer specifications. Production is composed primarily of chassis and special enclosures for electronic and associated equipment. More than 80% of the end products for which Electronic sheet metal components are produced are sold to the U.S. Government. The industry sales series is based on total annual purchases of electronics and electronics-related equipment by all branches of the U.S. Government as compiled by the Electronics Industries Association, *Electronics Industries Handbook, 1968.* Profitability data, with the exception of 1967, from Robert Morris Associates, *Annual Statement Studies,* "Manufacturers of Metal Stampings." Data for 1967 from FTC-SEC, Standard Enterprise Classification No. 34, "Other Fabricated Metal Products."

[5] For the sources of data employed in the analysis of Electromek, see the text.

[6] Microwave Devices produced microwave filters and other passive microwave components. The sales series is based on total annual sales of "Passive Electronic Components" as compiled by the Electronics Industries Association, *Electronics Industries Handbook, 1968.* Profitability data based on Robert Morris Associates, "Manufacturers of Electronic Components and Accessories" and on FTC-SEC, Standard Enterprise Classification No. 36, "Electrical Machinery, Equipment, and Supplies."

[7] Digital produced digital readout electronic counting modules and digital instruments primarily or the measurement of position, time, and voltage. Sales series based on total annual sales of "Time Measuring and Counting Instruments" as compiled by the Electronics Industries Association. Profitability data based on Robert Morris Associates, "Manufacturers of Engineering, Research, Scientific Laboratory Instruments" and on FTC-SEC, Standard Enterprise Classification No. 38, "Instruments and Related Products."

[8] Micronet produced microwave components similar to that produced by Microwave Devices. Sources of industry data for sales and profitability are the same.

[9] Diodyne was engaged primarily in the production of silicon high-speed switching diodes. Sales series is based on total annual sales of "Silicon Diodes and Rectifiers" as compiled by the Electronics Industries Association. Profitability data are based on Robert Morris Associates, *op. cit.,* and FTC-SEC, Standard Enterprise Classification No. 36, "Electrical Machinery, Equipment, and Supplies."

[10] Average weighted on the basis of 1967 total capital for each subsidiary.

the profitability measures the industry figures improved, worsening the relative performance. Thus, on all measures the weighted average subsidiary performance, relative to the respective industries, declined after acquistion. And while we prefer the omission of Digital in this comparison, the same holds true with Digital included.

We have taken the position that, because of the character of available sources of data, the industry comparison is only suggestive, certainly not exact. Also, we have not dealt with the argument regarding the effects of forces operating within the various subsidiaries which might have changed performance without any external influence. These qualifications notwithstanding, conclusions appear possible regarding the demonstrated influence of Contek on the aggregate financial performance of subsidiaries for which we have at least a full year of post-acquisition data. Certainly, the position that the demonstrated influence was positive appears untenable. And the argument that the influence was, on the average, negative is a strong one.

OTHER POSSIBLE REASONS FOR THE PRICE-EARNINGS DIFFERENTIAL

While the preceding analysis eliminated subsidiary performance improvement as an explanation for the price-earnings differential between parent and acquired companies, a variety of possible explanations remain. In addition to the elements in the Contek financial strategy model, the feedback relationships between valuation and both performance and imagery, there are differences in capital structure, size, diversification, and marketability of securities to be considered. Unfortunately, only the differences in capital structure between parent and acquisitions are susceptible to analysis.

We demonstrated in the earlier conceptual development that if changing the capital structure of acquired firms increases their market value (as part of the parent), the process of acquisition will add to growth in earnings per share. There was some change in the financing for companies acquired by Contek. Based on the last year before acquisition for each of the respective subsidiaries, the aggregate acquired capital was financed with 63% equity and 37% debt. At the same time the parent capital structure changed from 100% equity in 1962 to 49% equity and 51% debt in 1967. As a rough measure[9] we can say that debt financing for the capital of acquired subsidiaries increased from 37% to 51%. While this is useful in a descriptive sense, it tells us little about the impact of debt financing on values and hence on per-share performance.

As things turned out, a more helpful approach is provided by analysis of the performance which would have resulted from continuation of the 1962 Contek capital structure of 100% equity financing. In Table 8.14 we analyze performance based on the assumption that additional shares of common stock had been issued each period as a substitute for the increases in outstanding debt less the required interest payments. This resulted in an increased number of shares outstanding each period and an increase in the earnings available for common by the after-tax cost of interest. The required number of shares was based on an average of actual market prices for each period, an assumption which must be questioned. However, based on these market values the assumed replacement of debt with equity resulted in earnings-per-share figures which were essentially the same as those actually reported, with the amount for the final period reduced only from $2.30 to $2.25. Because of this, the use of actual market prices in the calculation does not appear unreasonable. If anything, we might expect the price-earnings multiples to be higher with all equity financing, so that less shares would have

---

[9] Among other things, purchase accounting treatments increase the proportion of equity in the capital structure of the parent relative to the pre-acquisition figures.

TABLE 8.14

ANALYSIS OF THE INFLUENCE OF DEBT ON GROWTH IN EARNINGS PER SHARE

Year	Debt Outstanding	Increase over Previous Year (in thousands)	Interest at 6 1/2% on Average Debt[1]	Increase in Debt Less After-Tax Cost of Interest	Average Market Price per Share[2]	Required Shares to Reduce Outstanding Debt to Zero (in thousands)
1962	—	—	—	—	—	—
1963	$ 82	$ 82	$ 2	$ 80	$12	7
1964	100	18	7	15	12	1
1965	151	51	8	46	21	3
1966	4,049	3,898	138	3,818	38	101
1967	16,776	12,726	672	12,369	87	142

Year	Cumulative Additional Shares[3]	Actual Shares Outstanding[4] (in thousands)	Actual plus Additional Shares Outstanding	Earnings Available for Common plus After-Tax Interest Cost[5]	Earnings per Share without Outstanding Debt	Earnings per Share as Reported
1962	—	322	322	$ 51	$ .15	$ .15
1963	7	322	322	100	.31	.31
1964	8	379	387	95	.25	.25
1965	11	318	529	397	.74	.76
1966	63	598	661	872	1.32	1.32
1967	183	1,234	1,417	3,195	2.25	2.30

[1] Used in lieu of reported interest expense because the latter includes interest on current debt. Average debt was calculated as the simple average of amounts outstanding at the beginning and end of each fiscal year.

[2] Simple average of the market prices at the beginning and end of each fiscal year. During 1964 there was no publicly held stock and the price for 1965 was used for that period.

[3] Shares used in the earnings-per-share calculation as reported.

[4] Earnings for 1966 and 1967 were based on average shares outstanding. Accordingly only half of the "additional" shares which would have been required to reduce debt to zero were added to the actual figures for these years. For example, the figure for 1967 is based on the sum of required shares for previous periods, 112,000, plus half the amount required for that year, 71,000, for a total of 183,000 shares.

[5] Based on interest cost as shown in column four of the upper level of figures and the actual Contek tax rate for the respective fiscal years.

been required and the reduction in earnings per share would have been even smaller.

This is a finding of some significance. Because of Contek's unusually high price-earnings multiple, the increase in debt financing for acquisitions and, in fact, the use of debt financing in general had little impact on the per-share performance that was achieved. It therefore appears possible to eliminate the change in capital structures of acquired subsidiaries as a significant element in providing the difference in earnings multiples between parent and subsidiaries and hence in providing performance.

Certainly there was a differential in size between Contek and its acquisitions at any point in time. This may be observed by referring back to the consolidated sales figures of Table 8.4. Certainly Contek was more diversified than its acquisitions. While not previously discussed, the product lines of each company were quite narrow. At the same time, only two pairs of companies were in approximately the same fields so that the parent became increasingly diversified. Certainly the securities of Contek were more marketable than those of its acquisitions; most of these companies were previously very closely held. The effects on value of these differences between parent and subsidiaries are impossible to ascertain. However, based on the evidence from market value studies discussed in an earlier chapter, it would seem that they can explain only a small part of a Contek multiple 2.9 times that of the average subsidiary.

It is our judgment that this differential is explained primarily by the interdependence between value and per-share performance achieved through the acquisition process. The conveyed image of technology-based growth undoubtedly had a significant effect on value. However, we suspect that its principal effect was on the evaluation and projection into the future of achieved performance and that the image without the performance would have had little value. The investing public seems to satisfy those previously specified conditions required for the value-performance "feedback relationship" to be of importance: the investing public's attention is focused on per-share performance with little attention toward (or simply an inability to determine) the manner in which it is achieved.

"INTERNAL" AND "EXTERNAL" GROWTH IN EARNINGS PER SHARE

Before relating the preceding evidence to our earlier conceptual discussion of the growth-through-acquisition process, it will be useful to attempt a direct analysis of the "internal" and "external" sources of growth in earnings per share.

Once again we are forced to make assumptions and approximations. In order to determine the contribution to earnings per share from acquisitions in any given fiscal year, we need to know the earnings made available for consolidation by acquisitions during that period and the required increase in outstanding shares. Because of the lack of operating and accounting integration for acquired Contek subsidiaries, the earnings resulting from each acquisition may be ascertained. The problem lies in relating increases in shares outstanding to particular subsidiaries.

While the "equivalent number of shares" of Contek common stock issued for each acquisition was calculated and listed in Table 8.7, this unfortunately does not provide an accurate measure of the required increase in outstanding shares. The increase in number of shares outstanding in each period was greater than the "equivalent number of shares" for acquisitions during the period. Outstanding shares increased for a variety of reasons other than acquisitions. Contek common stock had been issued in the conversion of debentures and preferred, in the exercise of options, and directly to the public. It is difficult to determine the extent to which funds derived from such issues in any period were used in connection with (1) purchase and expansion of new acquisitions and (2) expansion or changes in financing for existig businesses. Accurate answers are impossible.

Our approach was to treat the increase in outstanding shares of common stock each fiscal year as though it were related only to the acquisitions in that period. It is important to note that, to the extent that outstanding shares were increased for purposes other than new acquisitions, this provides an *understatement* of the earnings-per-share contribution of acquisitions in the respective fiscal years and an *overstatement* of the contribution to earnings per share from internal growth.

Following this assumption, Table 8.15 was developed to provide an analysis of the contribution to earnings-per-share growth from acquisitions. Some explanation of the table may be helpful. Tracing the first line, "end of 1962," across the six fiscal years provides an estimate of the contribution to earnings per share provided by that part of the parent corporation which existed at the end of 1962. This might be considered a rough measure of what earnings per share would have been if Contek management had followed the unlikely course of restricting its activities to the business existing at that time and had made no acquisitions. Since no acquisitions were made in 1963, the "end of 1963" figures are the same as for 1962. The "end of 1964" figures pick up the earnings from Environmental and the increase in outstanding shares during 1964.[10] The row entitled "acquisitions 1964" shows the contributions of Environmental each fiscal year to earnings available for common. The accompanying earnings-per-share figures are simply the difference between the earnings-per-share calculation for the company as it stood at the end of 1963 and 1964. The remainder of the table provides similar figures for acquisitions made during 1965, 1966, and 1967. The left diagonal of course shows earnings available for common and earnings per share as reported.

The difference between the per-share performance "down the diagonal" and across any of the horizontal rows is dramatic. While acquisitions added nothing to per-share performance in 1963 and 1964 according to our calculation, the contributions to earnings per share from acquisitions during 1965, 1966, and 1967 were 64%, 83%, and 77% of the total earnings per share during those respective periods.

If the acquisition program had not been aggressively pursued in any of these latter years so that performance moved (in our table) "horizontally" rather than "along the diagonal," it appears likely that both market price and market multiple would have dramatically declined. Had this occurred Contek would have lost part or all of its major resource (the market multiple) for achieving continuing per-share growth through the acquisition process.

---

[10] The approximation on which the table is based is at its worst at this point: while outstanding shares increased by 57,000 in 1964, the acquisition of Environmental required the equivalent of only 18,000 shares.

TABLE 8.15

CONTRIBUTIONS TO EARNINGS PER SHARE FROM ACQUISITIONS
IN EACH FISCAL YEAR: AN APPROXIMATE CALCULATION[1]

Stage of Company Growth	Number of Common Shares[2] (000)	1962 E[3] ($M)	1962 e[4] ($)	1963 E ($M)	1963 e ($)	1964 E ($M)	1964 e ($)	1965 E ($M)	1965 e ($)	1966 E ($M)	1966 e ($)	1967 E ($M)	1967 e ($)
End of 1962[5]	322	51	.15	98	.31	89	.27	77	.24	130	.40	93	.30
Acquisitions 1963[6]				—	—	—	—	—	—	—	—	—	—
End of 1963	322			98	.31	89	.27	77	.24	130	.40	93	.30
Acquisitions 1964						3	(.02)	25	.04	61	.10	74	.14
End of 1964	379					92	.25	102	.27	190	.51	167	.44
Acquisitions 1965								290	.48	(75)	(.28)	(18)	(.15)
End of 1965	518							392	.76	115	.22	149	.28
Acquisitions 1966[7]										677[8]	1.10	182	.25
End of 1966	598[9]									792	1.32	348	.53
Acquisitions 1967												2,490[10]	1.77
End of 1967	1,234											2,837	2.30

[1] Assumes that the increase in number of common shares outstanding in each year is attributable solely to acquisitions in that year. This ignores shares issued through options or to the public which might have been issued regardless of acquisitions in order to provide capital for the expansion of existing businesses or for other purposes. To the extent that the increase in outstanding shares may not be attributed to acquisitions, the table provides an *understatement* of the earnings-per-share contribution of acquisitions in the respective fiscal years and an *overstatement* of the contribution to earnings-per-share from "internal growth."

[2] Number of common shares used in earnings-per-share calculation at end of the fiscal year shown. For the first four fiscal years this is the number of shares outstanding at the end of the fiscal year; for the last two fiscal years it is the average shares outstanding.

[3] Earnings available for common stock. Typically, this is profit after tax, excluding extraordinary items, less the dividends paid on preferred stock.

[4] Earnings per common share. For each end-of-year entry the earnings-per-share calculation is based on the earnings contribution provided by the company as it existed at that point in time. The one exception is "end of 1966" where the average shares outstanding of 598,000 were used in the 1966 calculation and the shares outstanding at the end of 1966, amounting to 656,000, were used in the 1967 calculation. The latter figure would, of course, have been the number outstanding in 1967 if no additional shares had been issued.

[5] Each end-of-year entry follows the earnings contributions of the original business and the acquired subsidiaries which were part of the parent corporation at the end of the indicated fiscal year.

[6] Each acquisitions-year entry traces the contribution to earnings available for common from subsidiaries acquired in the indicated fiscal year. The earnings-per-share figures under these headings are simply the difference between the corresponding end-of-year figures.

[7] The earnings contribution from Microwave Devices is listed excluding the $66,400 in dividends on the preferred stock issued specifically for the acquisition of Microwave.

[8] Under allocation of $34,000 of corporate level expenses for 1966 subtracted from this figure.

[9] The change in this fiscal year from an end-of-year to an average shares outstanding measure for the earnings-per-share calculation reduced the relevant number of shares from 656,000 to 598,000 and increased earnings-per-share by 12 cents. The end-of-year figure is used for the 1967 earnings-per-share calculation as discussed in note 4 above.

[10] Under allocation of $187,000 of corporate level expenses for 1967 subtracted from this figure.

SYNTHESIS

As stated at the outset we have pursued this analysis of Contek Incorporated for two reasons: (1) to examine in light of our previous conceptual discussion financial strategy and its implications for one corporation which far exceeds our minimum criteria for an acquisitive conglomerate; (2) to investigate the kind of analysis that can be carried out to determine sources of per-share performance within this growth process.

The Contek financial strategy is a remarkable example of the pattern of thinking discussed in the earlier conceptual development: remarkable both because it exists in such explicit detail and because elements of it conform so closely to the conceptual framework we found useful for discussing the acquisition growth process. At the same time, there are some interesting differences which can be observed. These result primarily from the sources of the two conceptual frameworks, Contek's and the one developed earlier here. We have attempted to proceed within a framework of deductive logic about economic relationships. The Contek strategy was developed from shrewd observation of the "rules of the game," the way others had played it, and the way the investing public "keeps score."

We have argued at length that the rate of growth in earnings per share for a given dividend policy and a given degree of uncertainty about future growth is a logically sound measure of corporate performance for shareholders. Contek management took a more pragmatic view: "Earnings per share is the way the investment community keeps score." The corporate financial objective was established accordingly.

We have argued that per-share performance is basically dependent on rate of return on capital, rate of expansion of invested capital, and the market system of valuation; that as a given level of performance is achieved with combinations of these elements which lean more heavily on expansion rate, as through the acquisition process, market price becomes more important as a determinant of performance. We have talked in terms of the feedback relationship between market value and performance in those situations where there is significant, continuing dependence on additions to invested equity. Such ideas are integral parts of the Contek conceptual model underlying financial strategy which we examined in Figure 8.1. This model incorporated one of the assumptions which was basic to our analysis and which indeed has been employed by many previous writers: that the price-earnings ratio will be an increasing function of the rate of growth in earnings per share. Also integral to this model is the idea that market value is a primary determinant of performance through the acquisition process. The feedback process is explicity conceived.

We have argued that the high expansion rate firm will evidence particular concern over the perceived determinants of market value. This is symbolized by the one element in the Contek conceptual model that is noticeably absent from the models employed in the analytical representation of the growth process: the corporate image or "glamour factor." The perceived importance of this image is demonstrated in part by the insistence on acquisitions having product lines which will allow the parent to maintain the aura of advanced technology and growth potential. And while not discussed, it is also demonstrated by the time and energy of top management which are consumed in the preparation of the annual report and other communications to the investment community.

At a broader level, potential elements of the acquisition process have been discussed which were expected to be most important for increasing earnings per share: (1) the price-earnings differential; (2) the operating impact on profitability through change in managerial efficiency; (3) the operating impact on growth through change in technology and entrepreneurial intensity. While the view of this matter by Contek top management was somewhat different, it appears of some significance that there was a structured concept of the potential contributions to earnings per share through the acquisition process and that it was similar. Mr. Augustus, in what he called his "standard lecture on the subject," also talked of three potential components for building earnings per share through acquisition. As has been previously discussed, these were (1) the "well-levered" acquisition; (2) "trimming"; and (3) "constructive interactions" in technology, marketing management, financial management, and other operating areas. The two conceptual frameworks differ only in the structure of potential areas for operating improvement. The primary difference between expectations and findings in this area is that we originally expected these categories of influence on performance to apply in reality as well as in management thinking. As has been observed, in the case of Contek through the end of 1967, the reality was difficult to achieve outside the immediate financial effects.

Finally, we have discussed the logic for arguing that if the acquisition process is to contribute to the earnings-per-share growth of the parent corporation over the long run, there must on the average be improvement in the performance of companies purchased. At the same time we argued that over the short term it appeared *possible* to contribute to per-share performance through the acquisition process without performance improvement in companies acquired. The requirements for this possibility to become a reality are (1) that market price per share be an increasing function of rate of growth in per-share earnings and (2) that the investing public be concerned primarily with growth in earnings per share with little or no attention to the manner in which it is achieved (or no way to find out how it is achieved).

The performance of Contek provides some rather surprising evidence which, depending on what is considered to be the long run, either contradicts the former proposition or dramatically confirms that the latter possibility may indeed become a reality. At the same time Contek management felt very strongly that continued superior performance would require improved performance for acquired subsidiaries and it was directing increasing attention toward the realization of such internal performance, of which more later.

While the analysis of Contek financial strategy in comparison with the previously developed conceptual framework follows the central argument of this study, much of this chapter has been concerned with details of the quantitative analysis of sources of per-share performance for the acquisitive conglomerate. It has been our belief that the analysis *per se* provides some insight into several questions. Specifically, we are concerned with (1) the conditions under which this kind of analysis will be meaningful, (2) the sources of data and methods of analysis which will be useful, and (3) the kinds of conclusions which may be reached.

The required conditions for the analysis include the presence of certain operating characteristics in the corporation's development. The analysis of sources of per-share performance cannot be meaningfully pursued if there is significant integration in either the operations of acquired subsidiaries or the accounting for those operations. Operating integration would include the parent corporation's assuming responsibility for all or most of the staff functions of the acquired subsidiary under some scheme of expense allocation.

The data which ideally would be available include (1) meaningful financial information on the performance of all acquired subsidiaries both after joining the parent and for a period before sufficient to provide a basis for comparison, (2) the participation of subsidiaries in various industries, (3) industry performance data for corresponding periods so that subsidiary performance can be evaluated relative to respective industries, (4) the details of all acquisition transactions, (5) the allocation to specific subsidiaries of funds raised through increases in shares outstanding not directly connected with acquisition transactions, (6) the change in capital structures of acquired subsidiaries.

The development of such data for Contek required numerous assumptions: that the mechanical system of corporate expense allocation was "economically" meaningful; that adjustments could be made for purchase accounting and other changes in accounting treatments to put the before-after comparison on a meaningful basis; that inadequate industry data were adequate as a basis for comparison; that the increase in shares outstanding in any one period was attributable to acquisitions in that period; that changes in capital structure could, in effect, be ignored. For Contek these assumptions did not appear to provide sufficient distortion to preclude an analysis which was meaningful in an economic sense. However, it is easy to imagine situations where the required assumptions would render such an analysis worthless.

By way of conclusions we have been able to partition the annual change in earnings per share into the proportions resulting from internal growth and from immediate effects of acquisitions. This has permitted conclusions regarding the heavy dependence of past Contek performance on the market price of common stock and the use of that stock as a medium of exchange in a continued, expanding scale of acquisition. More important and more difficult are conclusions regarding the reasons for the immediate financial effects of these acquisitions. The conclusions we are able to reach are perhaps best discussed using as an outline a rearrangement of part of the earlier exhibit (Figure 1.1) regarding sources of performance through acquisition. In Figure 8.5 we expanded upon the possible sources of immediate effects on earnings per share from acquisitions.

At the first stage we indicated that the immediate effects of acquisitions on earnings per share may result from at least four kinds of sources: the differential between price-earnings ratios of buying and selling firms; changes in capital structure of acquired firms; changes in taxation; changes in accounting. We have argued that on a relative basis the effect of capital structure changes is small and can be ignored. Contek had a tax loss carryforward during the earlier years of the period studied, which we did not discuss. However, the tax reduction from this source was treated as an extraordinary gain and was not entered into the earnings-per-share calculation. The other tax change was to the higher tax rate of a larger company, a negative effect on per-share earnings. Observed accounting changes were in the direction of conservatism. On the other hand we have demonstrated that the price-earnings differential was extremely large, providing the major contribution to growth in earnings per share.

FIGURE 8.5

REASONS FOR THE IMMEDIATE EFFECTS OF ACQUISITIONS
ON EARNINGS PER SHARE

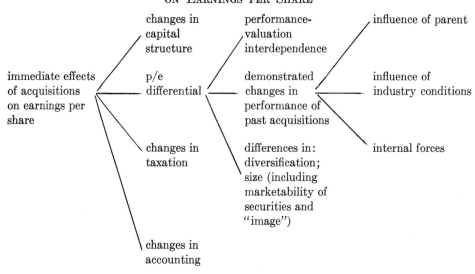

We suggest that the most important potential reasons for the price-earnings differential are (1) the interdependence between valuation and per-share growth; (2) demonstrated ability to improve performance in subsidiaries acquired; and (3) differences between parent and acquisition in diversification and size (including marketability of securities and ability to portray an "image"). It has been shown that the average effect on performance of companies acquired was negative. The analysis of performance relative to the industry suggests that changes in the respective industry environments explains part but not all of this decline. The existence of internal forces which might have led to decline in performance regardless of acquisition may have been of some significance, partly because of the frequent practice of "plumping" prior to acquisition. While we have offered no analysis of this, it is our judgment that it cannot explain the magnitude of the decline which occurred and that the influence of Contek up to this time on subsidiary financial performance cannot be considered positive. It is important to note that this lack of positive influence permits much stronger conclusions than would otherwise be possible regarding the dependence of performance on the feedback relationships in the acquisition process. As we discussed in an earlier chapter, where there is significant improvement in acquired companies there will be a "justified" increase in subsidiary value which cannot be distinguished from any caused by the valuation-performance interdependence.

The differences in size and diversification between parent and acquisitions probably accounted for some part of the price-earnings differential. And almost certainly part of the explanation is to be found in the marketability of Contek securities in comparison with the largely closely held companies which were acquired, along with the image of Contek which was conveyed to the market for its securities. The closely held firm without a market for its securities has no media through which to convey a value-enhancing image. When offering itself for sale it must base arguments regarding value on internal strengths and accomplishments. Contek, on the other hand, was highly skilled in the press release and produced an annual report that was magnificent in its imagery, providing possible additional sources of value.

We conclude, however, that it is the performance backing up the imagery which provides the dominant factor. That is, the Contek price-earnings ratio, and hence the differential over companies acquired, was based largely on Contek's demonstrated performance. And as we have discussed in detail, it was the price-earnings ratio which provided the performance through the acquisition process. As suggested in the Contek conceptual model of financial strategy and as suggested in our earlier conceptual discussion of the process of acquisition without performance improvement, for the period through 1967 it was the feedback relationship between valuation and per-share growth which allowed this acquisitive conglomerate to achieve its exceptional performance.

The one element in the analysis most limited by the quantitative approach is the operating influence of Contek on its acquired subsidiaries. Given the relatively short time span studied, the quantitative analysis must be supplemented by a descriptive approach. In Mr. Augustus' words, the process of growth through acquisition "combines a short-time constant financial process with a long-time constant management problem." Despite the decline in the performance of subsidiaries, positive things appeared to be happening; the technical and managerial strength of Contek was beginning to be felt and increasing effort was being focused in this direction. In order to analyze this we will examine in the next chapter the operating strategy of Contek for having a positive influence on its subsidiaries. As a basis for comparison we follow a parallel analysis for Walter Kidde & Company, an equally aggressive acquisitive conglomerate which is of much greater size and which puts much less emphasis on technology.

CHAPTER IX

Potential for Improvement in Sudsidiary Operating Performance: A Comparative Analysis of Two Companies

What is the potential for the acquisitive conglomerate to exert a positive influence on the operating performance of its acquired subsidiaries? What is the nature of the influence that is most likely to occur within this corporate environment? These two rather complex but related questions provide the basis for the investigation of this chapter. We attempt to learn something indirectly about the first by dealing directly with the second. We begin with a brief review of why we are interested in these questions in the first place and some indications of what we expect to find.

We began this study with a systematic discussion of sources of acquisitive conglomerate performance which have been given some attention in recent literature. For current purposes these have been grouped in four categories: (1) operating economies requiring integration; (2) operating influence without significant operating integration; (3) the feedback relationship between market value and performance through acquisition; (4) "immediate financial effects" other than the feedback relationship. In the development of the study, through the analysis of evidence provided by others, the characteristics of the population, and models of growth through acquisition, we reached some preliminary conclusions regarding the relative importance of the various sources of performance. We concluded that the feedback relationship is likely to be of greater importance than the other immediate financial effects. Also, we concluded that operating economies requiring substantial integration are not likely to be of importance, with the exception of scale advantage in management and staff functions. If operating improvements are to be considered of significant importance, our attention, through a process of elimination, is directed toward those influences not requiring operating integration.

In order to study in more detail the financial strategy of acquisitive conglomerates and the importance of "immediate financial effects" an anlysis of Contek Incorporated was presented. While we attempted to provide a general examination of the financial characteristics of the acquisitive growth process, our expectation, as stated, was that the feedback relationship would be of more importance than other immediate financial effects. Expectations in this direction were more than fulfilled.

In the present chapter, through the study of two firms, we pursue a general analysis of the operating influence of acquisitive conglomerates on their acquired subsidiaries. Our expectations, as stated, are that improvements, if achieved, will not be based on substantial operating integration.

We build in this chapter on some previous evidence regarding operating influence. In the study of Contek financial data on subsidiary operating performance were described, and these data provided evidence of one situation where the impact of an acquisitive conglomerate on the operating performance of its "average subsidiary" was a negative one. At the same time, we ended with a dissatisfied feeling regarding the strictly quantitative nature of the analysis. Positive things appeared to be happening in this corporation that could only be appreciated through a descriptive analysis. We can learn about the structure of influence even where the net effect has been negative. Also, the apparent impact of Contek on its "average subsidiary" may well be the exception. Clearly needed, we suggest, is a somewhat broader and more careful examination of the nature of influence on subsidiary operating performance within this type of corporate environment and, indirectly, of the potential for positive influence to occur. We attempt not only to reach some meaningful conclusions about the nature of influence but to give the reader a better understanding, a "feel," for the kinds of interactions that develop.

Expanding on our expectations, we have argued that operating advantages appear most likely from the more effective utilization of resources which may be most easily transferred across the organizational boundaries within the acquisitive conglomerate: knowledge; expertise; personnel; funds. The idea of commonality leads to some expectations regarding the kinds of influences that these resources are most likely to provide. That is, we expect the specialized human resources to flow more effectively and understandably across the boundaries of diverse subsidiaries when they are used to influence areas and functions which the subsidiaries have in common. These, we suggest, are more the "managerially" oriented areas than the "technology-product-market" oriented areas. We expect influence more on the management process for subsidiary operations, generally the area of efficiency and hence profitability, than on the basic nature of subsidiary products and markets, generally the area of demand and hence growth.

APPROACH

In the introductory discussion of the current, "informal" literature regarding the impact of acquisitive conglomerates on subsidiary performance we reached several conclusions. First, most of the discussion has either dealt in generalities about such things as "better management" or "technological cross-fertilization," with little discussion of what these terms mean in a more detailed operating sense, or where specifics have been offered they have come in random bits and pieces without any structured attempt to deal with the whole. Second, those discussing the question have generally been expressing judgments based on their personal experience and exposure either without evidence or with occasional examples to support particular points. Third, almost without exception those making a case for the operating advantages of acquisitive conglomerates have been in positions which would very likely cause them to have biased opinions. These are individuals at the corporate level of the companies in question. As has been discussed, it is clearly to the advantage of the corporation to create as favorable an image as possible in the eyes of the investing public. In addition, everyone wants to believe that his own activities make a positive contribution. To the extent that the corporate level executive devotes his attention to subsidiary operations, he would like to believe that positive changes have resulted.

We have sought to improve upon the quality of available evidence in three ways. First, and probably most important, we have sought information from a source which has experience and exposure but less bias or at least a different point of view, the subsidiary manager who in most cases was in the same position when the subsidiary was an independent company. Second, we have sought to pursue explanations and examples which would indicate in more detail and hence more clearly the nature of influence that exists and have sought to back these up with quantitative data. Third, we have sought to bring more structure and organization to the evidence on the question. It will be worth while to elaborate briefly on these three aspects of our approach.

From the review of the published discussions on operating advantages of acquisitive conglomerates we concluded that the subsidiary manager is a neglected source of information. As has been noted, there is a preference for retaining management of the acquired company, and in most of the cases we shall discuss this was done. The subsidiary general manager then, more often than not, was previously president of his company as an independent entity or at least as a member of its management. If the parent company is to influence subsidiary performance, some aspects of operations must change with respect to their previous state. We suggest that no one is in a better position to observe that change than the company president who retains his position after the company becomes an acquired subsidiary. The question of bias obviously remains. Favorable comments filtering back to the parent company would seem preferred to unfavorable ones. Also, people are somewhat inclined to tell you what they think you want to hear, a constant problem in presenting judgments as evidence. At the same time the company-president-become-subsidiary-manager is by nature a proud, independent individual. We found him quite willing to point out where he thought accomplishments were his own, quite willing to identify areas where he thought the parent company had provided no positive influence, and, on occasion, areas where he thought the influence was negative. The bias, if not smaller, was at least different and the combination of the subsidiary view with the parent company view provides, we feel, a substantial improvement in objectivity.

The generality and lack of evidence in previous discussions of our question have influenced two decisions regarding approach. First, in order to diminish generality we decided that available time would be better spent in the study of a small number of situations in depth than in a more superficial examination of a larger segment of the population. We have focused attention on two acquisitive companies (one of them Contek Incorporated) and on five acquired subsidiaries within each of these. This allowed us to pursue the nature of influence in some detail and to be more specific regarding what we find.

Second, in order to improve the quality of evidence we tapped four sources: (1) as discussed above, the judgments of the subsidiary manager; (2) the judgments of the corporate level manager; (3) published and internal descriptive material; and (4) the financial record of actual performances.

In order to provide a more structured and organized approach to our analysis, we have provided a comparison of two corporations which differed significantly along two important dimensions: size and emphasis on technology. Assuming that the influence of the management process at the corporate level upon subsidiary operations is important, we expected the larger corporation, which might accommodate a corporate level organization of greater scale and quality, to demonstrate advantages over the smaller acquisitive conglomerate. Assuming that the cross-fertilization of technological processes is an important source of advantage, we expected the firm pursuing such activities to exhibit a different structure of influence from the firm that is not. In general, we expected to emerge better informed from the study of two firms that were quite different than from the study of two firms much the same.

The subject of our preceding chapter, Contek Incorporated, is a relatively small acquisitive conglomerate with a strong technical orientation. We considered it desirable to use Contek for this chapter as well because the detailed financial analysis presented earlier and the descriptive material presented here are of course complementary. It remained to select an acquisitive conglomerate of relatively large size and with substantially less emphasis on advanced technology. The choice was Walter Kidde & Company.[1]

The decision to study five subsidiaries in each company was based on the belief that this would be sufficient to obtain a representative picture of the nature of influence within a particular corporate environment and that diminishing returns would result from substantially increasing the number. In the selection of subsidiaries in each corporation we sought to satisfy several criteria. These included (1) at least two years since acquisition by the parent company, (2) little or no operating integration with other subsidiaries,[2] and (3) some continuity of management personnel before and after acquisition. We found that nearly all subsidiaries in the two firms satisfied the second criterion and most satisfied the third. In order to satisfy the first criterion at Contek we looked at its first five acquisitions. At Kidde there were 15 acquisitions which had been made more than two years before the time of the study. Here our selection of subsidiaries was based on the desire to provide a diversity of product-market orientations and to avoid acquisitions of relatively insignificant size. There is a potential problem in studying acquisition influence if the subsidiary has been part of the parent for too long. The base for comparison, the subsidiary as an independent company, becomes of increasingly less relevance as time passes. The subsidiaries we studied had been part of the parent for no more than four years. Finally, it is important to note that in both cases the choice of subsidiaries for detailed study was ours, not theirs.

---

[1] The material on Walter Kidde & Company is presented in undisguised form.

[2] Otherwise, meaningful subsidiary financial data would not be available.

OUTLINE OF THE ANALYSIS

We begin with a brief overview of each company covering (1) the pattern of development of the corporation and (2) the objectives and strategy for financial performance, products, and new acquisitions. (Having already discussed much of this for Contek, we give it little emphasis here.) We then briefly describe the organization and resources at the corporate level in each company in an attempt to get some initial idea of the potential for operating influence. This is followed by a summary discussion of the opinions of corporate level management regarding the structure and significance of operating changes that they have been able to achieve. We then provide a more detailed discussion of the findings at the subsidiary level. Finally, we review the financial record of changes in observed performance for the five subsidiaries in each corporation.

CONTEK — A BRIEF OVERVIEW

The financial strategy and performance of Contek are familiar from the last chapter. A brief review is provided here for convenience. This is followed by a short discussion of product strategy which has not been previously covered.

During the six years 1962 to 1967 Contek made 15 acquisitions and increased sales from $1.2 million to $43.4 million. During this period the annual average rates of increase for total earnings, shares outstanding, and earnings per share were 154%, 34%, and 87% respectively. The average annual increase of book equity was 4.94 times after tax earnings; after tax earnings averaged 18.9% of book equity over the period. In general, exceptional per-share performance was achieved with a very rapid rate of expansion and a moderate rate of return.

Contek was strongly oriented toward growth in earnings per share as a financial objective and displayed a keen appreciation of the contribution to this objective which could be provided by the immediate financial effects of acquisitions. The explicit earnings-per-share objective was a total annual increase of 40%, with half of this achieved internally. The overall objective was far exceeded; the internal growth objective had not yet been met.

The strategy for Contek's development was to build from technological strength toward strength in finance, engineering, manufacturing, and marketing, relying on acquisition for the major part of the transformation. In terms of broad market areas Contek emphasized control systems, communication systems, and specialty materials. In terms of broad product types the emphasis was on materials, devices, and instruments. Mr. Augustus, Contek president, frequently spoke of Contek products in terms of a matrix composed of advanced technologies and market needs. The intersection of an advanced technology and a market need defined a product possibility (although not necessarily an economically feasible one). Given a particular advanced technology currently used in one Contek product area, it is possible to think about other potential products by examining the "intersection" of this advanced technology with other potential markets. Contek management suggested that this line of thinking was helpful in seeking new product areas that would be logical either for internal development or for acquisition. Through 1967 almost all the expansion into new product areas came through external rather than internal growth. The 15 Contek acquisitions with their principal product areas are shown in Table 9.1.

TABLE 9.1

Contek Incorporated
Acquisitions: 1964–1967

Company	Acquisition Date	Principal Product Areas
Environmental Controls Corporation	Nov. 1964	Subassemblies for industrial and commercial temperature and humidity control systems
Electronic Enclosures Incorporated	Apr. 1965	Custom metal fabrication of chassis and special enclosures for electronic and associated equipment
Electromek Controls Company	Oct. 1965	Electromechanical rate control systems for process industry machinery
Microwave Devices Corporation	Apr. 1966	Microwave filters and other microwave passive components
Digital Instrument Company	May 1966	Digital counting and timing modules and instruments
Micronet Incorporated	Dec. 1966	Microwave filters and other microwave passive components
Diodyne Corporation	Dec. 1966	High-speed silicon switching diodes
Custom Audio Systems Company	Mar. 1967	Commercial high fidelity audio systems
Stratton Corporation	Apr. 1967	Specialty hardware and fabricated metal parts for the electronics and other industries
Spectra Incorporated	June 1967	Precision spectrometers and other instruments based on measurement of radiation diffraction patterns
Computex Corporation	Sept. 1967	Ferrite components for high speed computer memory application
Melcast Corporation	Sept. 1967	Castings of specialty metals for aerospace industry applications
Fletcher Transducer Corporation	Sept. 1967	Precision temperature and other transducers
Autocircuit Corporation	Dec. 1967	Printed circuit boards
Ferromagnetics Incorporated	Dec. 1967	Ferrite components for high speed computer memory application and other ferrite devices

Kidde — A Brief Overview

From 1963 through the end of 1967 Walter Kidde & Company made 29 acquisitions in diverse fields and increased annual sales from $40.9 million to $423.7 million. Earnings after tax increased from $275,000 in 1963 to $17.7 million in 1967 for an average annual increase of 188%. At the same time the average annual increase in shares outstanding was 69%. As a result, earnings per share increased from $.39 to $3.20 during this period, providing an average annual increase of 73%. Market price per share increased somewhat more slowly, from a high of $13 7/8 in 1963 to a high of $79 in 1967. This performance was achieved

TABLE 9.2

WALTER KIDDE & COMPANY: FINANCIAL CHARACTERISTICS[1]
(corporate figures in thousands of dollars, per-share figures in dollars)

Fiscal Years Ending December 31

	1967	1966	1965	1964	1963	Average
SALES[2]	423,661	273,698	109,494	49,280	40,888	
EARNS	17,730	8,005	3,123	903	275	
DEBT	63,000	40,103	4,658	5,428	5,751	
EQUIT	129,119	72,117	31,498	19,289	15,592	
EPS	3	2.43	1.56	0.92	0.39	
DPS	0.00	0.00	0.00	0.00	0.00	
MKTLO	46.25	40.25	14.63	11.38	10.38	
MKTHI	79.00	72.13	47.50	20.38	13.88	
NOACQ	11	5	11	2	0	
C	3.215	5.074	3.909	4.094	*	4.073
G	0.317	0.558	0.696	1.359	*	0.732
GT	1.215	1.563	2.458	2.284	*	1.880
Z	0.682	0.646	1.040	0.392	*	0.690
R	0.137	0.111	0.099	0.047	0.018	0.082
M	19.570	23.122	19.912	17.255	31.090	22.190
H	1.000	1.000	1.000	1.000	1.000	1.000
XB	0.672	0.643	0.871	0.780	0.731	0.739

* Not available; these items based on year-to-year change.

[1] The variables calculated from the financial data in this exhibit are discussed in more detail in earlier chapters. Summary definitions only are provided here.

[2] See footnotes to Table 4.2, p. 70.

with a very rapid rate of expansion of invested equity and a moderate rate of return. On the average the annual increase in book value of invested equity was 4.07 times annual earnings after tax. After-tax earnings as a percentage of the book value of invested equity increased each year, from 1.8% in 1963 to 13.7% in 1967, and averaged 8.2% for the period. These and other publicly available financial details are shown in Table 9.2.

For the five years ending in 1963 Kidde performance had been uninteresting at best. Sales approximated $40 million throughout this period, ranging from a low of $36.1 million to a high of $41.3 million. Earnings during the period ranged from a deficit of $500,000 to a profit of $753,000, and earnings per share from a deficit of $.75 to a profit of $1.13. Kidde was closely held during this period with fewer than 600 stockholders, and more than 50% of the stock was held by two family groups.

The transition began with the selection of Fred R. Sullivan as president and chief executive of Kidde in January 1964. Sullivan had been president of Monroe Calculating Machine Company from 1953 to 1958 and moved to Litton Industries when Monroe was acquired by Litton. He was a senior vice president of Litton and chairman of their Business Equipment Group at the time of his departure for Kidde. With Sullivan came Franc M. Ricciardi who had been president of the Kimball Systems division at Litton and who directed the acquisition program for the Business Equipment Group. Both Sullivan and Ricciardi became significant stockholders in Kidde and in 1968 they were chairman and president of the corporation respectively.

When Sullivan and Ricciardi joined Kidde it was known primarily as a producer of fire extinguishing, detection, and alarm equipment and systems. Other product lines of lesser importance were burglar alarm systems; products for the aerospace industry based on pressurized fluids, including oxygen systems, fuel handling systems, and pneumatic components; consumer products based on pressurized fluids, including gas cylinders, cream whippers, and soda water siphons; and specialized textile machinery. In planning the future expansion of Kidde, Sullivan and Ricciardi viewed the strengths of the existing corporation as lying in four broad areas: safety, security, and protection; aerospace systems and equipment; consumer products; and textile machinery and equipment. The expansion program began in August 1964 with the acquisition of Cocker Machine and Foundry Company, a manufacturer of textile machinery and equipment. Many of the subsequent acquisitions through the end of 1967 were related to the four initially identified areas. However, as the acquisition program evolved new areas were entered. These included merchandising equipment, automotive parts, business machines, lighting equipment and fixtures, and materials handling equipment. Acquisitions through the end of 1967 and their principal products and services are listed in Table 9.3. Between the end of 1967 and the time of this writing Kidde entered additional product areas. These included firearms with the acquisition of Harrington and Richardson; furniture manufacturing with the acquisition of American Desk Manufacturing Company; and intermodal transportation with the acquisition of U.S. Lines Company.

From the start Sullivan and Ricciardi viewed the objectives and strategy for Kidde in terms which parallel our definition of an "acquisitive conglomerate." [3] In this connection it will be worth while to quote at some length from a par-

---

[3] In fact some of the formative thinking for this thesis was influenced by Sullivan's speech quoted below, another reason for the choice of Kidde as a subject for detailed study.

TABLE 9.3

WALTER KIDDE & COMPANY: ACQUISITIONS: 1964–1967

Company	Acquisition Date	Principal Product Areas
Cocker Machine & Foundry	Aug. 1964	Textile machinery and equipment
Safety Development Corporation	Sept. 1964	Fire extinguishing equipment
Associated Testing Laboratories	Feb. 1965	Environmental and reliability testing services and equipment
Audio Equipment Company	Feb. 1965	Power megaphones
Fyre Safety Incorporated	Feb. 1965	Fire alarm distribution
Air-Tech Industries	Mar. 1965	Air supported protective enclosures
Columbian Bronze Corporation	June 1965	Marine propellers and propulsion systems; marine communications and safety equipment
Pathe Equipment Company	June 1965	Automatic sewing and stitching machinery
Weber Showcase & Fixture Company	July 1965	Merchandising fixtures and equipment; aerospace equipment
Park Products Company	Aug. 1965	Electromagnetic components primarily for color television
M & D Store Fixtures Incorporated	Oct. 1965	Merchandising display fixtures
Morris Manufacturing	Oct. 1965	Merchandising fixtures and refrigeration equipment
S. W. Farber Incorporated	Dec. 1965	Consumer products including cookware and electric appliances
LeFebure Incorporated	May 1966	Banking and office security equipment including vaults and safety deposit boxes
Globe Security Systems	May 1966	Security guard services and other security services
Dura Corporation	Nov. 1966	Automotive parts; business machines
Fenwal Incorporated	Nov. 1966	Temperature control and fire detection equipment
Interstate Security Services	Dec. 1966	Guard and other security services
Modern Refrigeration Services	Jan. 1967	Refrigeration equipment
Merit Protective Services	Feb. 1967	Guard and other security services
Cardinal Electronics Company	Apr. 1967	Quartz crystals and crystal devices
Sargent & Company	Apr. 1967	Locks and architectural hardware
Lighting Corporation of America	June 1967	Residential and architectural lighting fixtures; theatrical and television lighting equipment and systems; offset printing
Wright Light Incorporated	Aug. 1967	Fluorescent lighting fixtures
Piezo Technology Incorporated	Aug. 1967	Quartz crystals and crystal based electronic equipment and devices
Toledo Commutator Company	Aug. 1967	Commutators and slip rings for electrical motors and generators
Houston Electronics Corporation	Oct. 1967	Glass-to-metal hermetically sealed components for electronics industry
Carpenter Manufacturing Company	Oct. 1967	Emergency lighting equipment
Grove Manufacturing Company	Nov. 1967	Mobile hydraulic cranes and fire ladders
Jade Corporation	Dec. 1967	Electronic components and measuring devices
Morrison Industries	Dec. 1967	Numerically controlled machining of specialty metals for high temperature applications in aerospace industries

ticularly lucid speech[4] by Mr. Sullivan regarding the objectives and strategy of Kidde as a "conglomerate" company:

> The Walter Kidde Company is a conglomerate. . . . A conglomerate company is not only a company involved in many industries but also one engaged in an active, continuing acquisition program. Further, it is a company which either is, or strives to be, a growth company in terms of compound annual percentage increase in earnings per share as well as absolute dollar sales and profits.
>
> . . . In many respects the conglomerate company appears to be quite similar to the diversified company. But I submit there are essential differences. First: motivation. The diversified company seeks to diversify. . . . Its acquisitions and moves into new industries are defensive moves. The acquisition program of the conglomerate, on the other hand, is offensive. . . . It tries to anticipate the opportunities of the future, and it tries to take advantage of the opportunities of today, wherever they may be and whenever it makes sense. Each potential acquisition is weighed on its own individual merits. . . . Second, the diversified company, more often than not, does not view a continuing acquisition program as part of its routine activities. . . . The conglomerate, in contrast, . . . views its acquisition program as a continuing part of its day-to-day operations.
>
> . . . I mentioned earlier that our own definition of conglomerate includes: One: operating in many industries. Two: a record of, or attempts to achieve, a rapid rate of growth, of sales, profits, and especially earnings per share. Three: a continuing acquisition program. . . . Let me review our acquisition guidelines which tie all three together. These are the things we look for: One: growth industries, industries whose markets are growing or will grow faster than the economy. . . . Two: companies which outperform their industries, either technologically, or in profit margins, sales growth, profit growth, or management capabilities. Three: good in-place management, with a proven record of superior profit performance. Four: proprietary products and services.

In a similar listing of acquisition criteria Ricciardi added one more: ". . . Of course, it's always nice to acquire a company with a lower price-earnings multiple, but it's not necessarily a rule with us." [5]

In terms of broad financial characteristics of corporate development, Kidde and Contek were quite similar. Both provided exceptional performance for shareholders based on (1) a rapid rate of expansion of invested capital through diversified acquisition and (2) a moderate return on invested capital. The immediately obvious differences at this point are those which influenced their selection. Kidde was approximately ten times the size of Contek and leaned toward proprietary products rather than products heavily dependent on advanced technology.

CORPORATE LEVEL ORGANIZATION AND RESOURCES

The corporate level organizations for Contek Incorporated and for Walter Kidde & Company are shown in Figures 9.1 and 9.2 respectively. Because of the

---

[4] Fred R. Sullivan and Franc M. Ricciardi, remarks before The New York Society of Security Analysts, October 27, 1967.

[5] Fred R. Sullivan and Franc M. Ricciardi, remarks before The Investment Society of Chicago, September 21, 1967.

FIGURE 9.1

CONTEK INCORPORATED: CORPORATE LEVEL ORGANIZATION

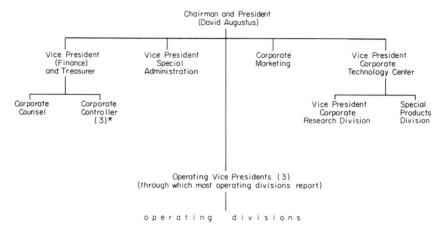

*Indicates number of professional personnel.

rates of growth of both of these corporations they were frequently in a state
of transition. Also, there was little emphasis on formal organization in either
corporation. As a result these representations of corporate organization can only
be considered indicative of approximate structure and content at mid-1968.

The structures of the corporate level organizations are of interest because they
tell us something of the importance attached to various functional areas and of

FIGURE 9.2

WALTER KIDDE & COMPANY: CORPORATE LEVEL ORGANIZATION

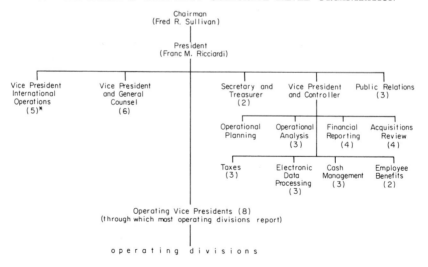

*Indicates number of professional personnel.

the time and energy allocated to them. In this way they are indicative of the areas in which we may expect to find significant corporate level influence.

In the Contek organization most of the listed titles represented one professional or managerial individual. Exceptions were the Controller's organization and the two organizations reporting to the Vice President of the Corporate Technology Center. One of the latter organizations, the Corporate Research Division, represented the original company and was perhaps better thought of as a subsidiary operation. It contained approximately 100 technicians and research professionals including about 25 with PhD degrees. Almost all the work of this group was government contract research. The Special Products Division operated on a task force basis, drawing largely on the Research Division for personnel, to solve subsidiary technical problems and to work toward the development of new products.

The Financial Vice President had an organization of four professional people. These were a legal counsel, a controller, and, reporting to the controller, an internal corporate auditor and an accounting manager. The group had a broad set of responsibilities, and there appeared to be unanimous agreement that additional people were needed. It was responsible for internal planning and control throughout the corporation; financial reporting to the public and to regulatory agencies; new financing; cash management; all acquisition work. The president of course was involved in some of these functions and was the principal individual in the acquisition area.

The Vice President for Special Administration, after joining Contek, was directly involved in the management of Electronic Enclosures, a subsidiary which had post-acquisition operating difficulties as discussed in the preceding chapter. In effect, this vice president had been a subsidiary general manager for the entirety of his employment by the parent corporation.

The Director of Corporate Marketing was a one-man effort to realize potential complementarities that existed within subsidiary marketing systems and to develop a corporate-wide advertising and promotion scheme taking advantage of and enhancing the corporate name where possible.

Three vice presidents played an operating role. One was a group vice president for the two microwave component subsidiaries and the switching diode subsidiary. The other two were the same people as the Vice President of the Corporate Technology Center and the Vice President of the Corporate Research Division. These latter two individuals filled the role of what they called "sponsors" rather than group operating vice presidents. This appears to mean that they were more in an advisory role than an operating role with direct responsibility and authority. One was "sponsor" for subsidiaries in the "measurements and controls" areas, the other for subsidiaries in "materials technology." Most of the subsidiaries reported through one of these three vice presidents to the President.

Omitting the staff members of the Research Division and the Special Products Division, the Contek corporate organization, including operating vice presidents, was composed of eleven people plus secretarial and clerical support.

The Kidde corporate organization had a somewhat different orientation. Kidde had decided not to establish corporate level positions for research, development, or engineering which, as we discussed earlier, appears more typical of "acquisitive conglomerates." Also, Kidde had not established a position for company-wide marketing.

At the same time, the vice president in charge of international activities was in a marketing role. This group of approximately five men was responsible for assisting Kidde subsidiaries to develop markets outside the United States, taking advantage of existing marketing structures within Kidde wherever possible. The remaining groups outside the Controller's organization were concerned with the legal and financial environment and with problems that were largely related, directly or indirectly, to new acquisitions. Much of the legal work was in connection with new acquisitions. The Secretary-Treasurer was concerned with new financing and with the nature of financial transactions, much of which was occasioned by new acquisitions. The public relations function was oriented primarily toward the investment community and hence the price of the company's common stock, of prime importance for the acquisition program.

The Controller's organization was composed of 24 professional people. About half of these were certified public accountants with both industry and public accounting firm experience. Others had backgrounds in such areas as electronic data processing, tax law, insurance, and pension planning. This organization was grouped in eight functional areas each of which will be briefly described.

The Acquisitions Review group was responsible for reviewing the financial statements and operations of companies with which Kidde had reached an initial acquisition agreement. This group went to work "when a handshake had taken place" to perform a detailed analysis of historical and forecasted results, of the impact of the acquisition on operations of parent and subsidiary, and of the impact on Kidde's corporate and per-share financial position. This group drew on others inside and outside the corporate organization for needed competence to evaluate special financial and technical features.

The Operational Planning and Operational Analysis groups worked closely together. Both were involved in assisting the new acquisition to adapt to the parent company's planning and control system. Then on a continuing basis the Operational Planning group worked with the subsidiary in the preparation and evaluation of operating and financial plans. The Operational Analysis group was responsible for the accumulation and analysis of periodic financial statements, prepared by the subsidiaries, which compared performance against the previously established plans.

The Financial Reporting group was concerned with preparation of consolidated financial statements for reports to the public, for reports to lenders, and for reports to regulatory agencies, principally the Securities and Exchange Commission. The numerous acquisitions and their associated financing created a particularly heavy load in terms of major proxy statements and registration statements required by the SEC.

The Tax group provided advice and assistance in the preparation of subsidiary tax returns and reviewed them for technical competence and mathematical accuracy. During a recent year the various operating groups within Kidde were required to file over 1,100 Federal, state, and local tax returns. This group also was involved in tax work in connection with acquisitions and associated re-organizations.

The Electronic Data Processing group was involved in the planning and coordination and approved the selection of data processing equipment throughout the corporation. This group provided advice regarding the development of new systems and occasionally did programming work for subsidiaries. In addition, this group was involved in some accounts payable and payroll processing for subsidiaries too small to have their own computer installations.

The Cash Management group coordinated with all the subsidiaries and with the other corporate level organizations in the preparation of corporate forecasts of cash inflows and requirements. All receipts and disbursements and all borrowing requirements were centrally controlled. Divisions that were net users of new borrowed funds obtained such funds through the Cash group and paid interest at a corporate-wide rate. Subsidiaries that were net providers of cash invested these funds, in effect, in other Kidde subsidiaries through the Cash group and received interest at the corporate-wide rate. This was the one area in which the parent corporation assumed complete operating responsibility for every subsidiary at the time of acquisition.

Finally, the Employee Benefits group had responsibilities in the areas of insurance, pension plans, and union agreements. Kidde, with its numerous acquisitions, had a total of about 40 pension plans. This group was attempting to achieve some consistency and uniformity among these plans and to improve their investment performance. Casualty, liability, and group insurance programs for all subsidiaries were centrally arranged by this group. This changed the position of the average subsidiary with respect to the insurance company from small buyer to large buyer.

The Operating Vice Presidents primarily were individuals who were operating heads of companies acquired by Kidde. In addition to their respective original subsidiaries they had been given responsibility for other acquisitions in similar product areas having management groups of lesser strength, frequently acquisitions which to a greater or lesser degree they had arranged. Most of the subsidiaries reported through one of these vice presidents to the President and Chairman.

Including the Operating Vice Presidents the corporate management and staff people numbered 50. This was almost five times as many as in the Contek organization but it was for a corporation ten times as large. The Kidde charge to subsidiary operations to cover corporate level expenses averaged about 0.5% of subsidiary sales volume compared with a charge of 2% of sales volume for Contek. This comparison provides an initial indication of the possible economies in the utilization of specialized staff personnel within this kind of organization.

Further, the amount of time and effort required at the corporate level was as much determined by the number of subsidiaries and the acquisitions made in any period as it was by the size of these entities. In fact there was some feeling in both corporations that a small acquisition may take more time than the larger one. From this point of view Kidde, with between two and three times as many acquisitions and hence operating subsidiaries as Contek, may have had a significantly larger management and staff group at the corporate level relative to its requirements than did Contek. In general it would appear that because of (1) economies of staff specialization and (2) the dependence of required corporate level effort on numbers of acquisitions and subsidiaries as much as their size, Kidde was able, at a lower proportional cost, to operate a corporate organization that was stronger, more highly specialized, and generally better equipped for the requirements for diversified growth through acquisition.

At the same time the areas of emphasis within the two corporate organizations were clearly quite different. The Kidde organization was strong in those functions which served to shield the subsidiary from the problems of coping with the legal, tax, regulatory, and financial environments and in those functions required to support the planning and control process within the acquired subsidiary. The one function in which the corporate organization was specialized in a product-oriented area was in international marketing. Contek, on the other hand, while not nearly as deep in those areas where Kidde was strong, had made the effort to develop a company-wide marketing competence and had a great deal of technical competence in its research organization. The ability to use these resources for the benefit of the acquired subsidiary are of course questions which we shall further explore.

Corporate Judgment Regarding Influence on Subsidiaries

The discussions of influence on acquired subsidiaries took place within somewhat different frameworks at Contek and Kidde. The "hard-nosed" appraisal at Contek was that all the potentially "constructive interactions" resulting from acquisition either were not significant enough or had not progressed far enough to be discernible in the financial data at the time. The discussion was thus in terms of those influences and changes that were easiest to bring about and those which were potentially most important. At Kidde the judgment was that, in addition to a variety of potentially important influences, significant influence had occurred in several functional areas which had brought about discernible results. These different points of view are partially but not entirely borne out by the financial data to be examined later.

Below we discuss the views of the corporate level managers and provide some representative examples. The examples used here either relate to subsidiaries other than those we studied or suggest a different view from that subsequently provided by the subsidiary manager.

Influences on the acquired subsidiary at Contek were viewed in terms of a conceptual framework similar to the technology-market matrix discussed earlier for new product definition. This is shown in Figure 9.3. The principal resources at the corporate level were thought of in three categories: financial, marketing, and technology. Financial resources are further broken down in terms of the supply of funds and the financial communication and control system. These resources have potential or actual "intersections" with needs in the various subsidiaries. The intersections may provide a basis for "constructive inter-

FIGURE 9.3

CONCEPTUAL FRAMEWORK REGARDING USE OF CORPORATE RESOURCES
FOR CONSTRUCTIVE INTERACTIONS WITH AND BETWEEN
ACQUIRED SUBSIDIARIES

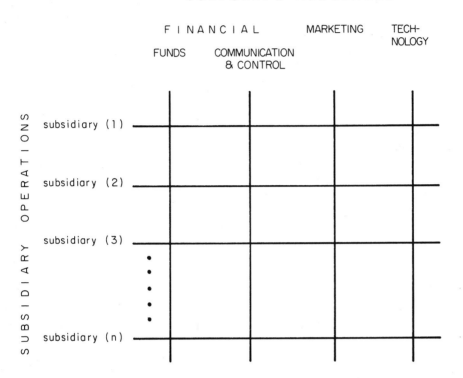

actions." Such interactions may take place between the subsidiary and the corporate organization, or, particularly in the marketing and technology areas, the corporation may initiate or promote interactions between subsidiaries. The subsidiaries, in principle, are to lean toward an operating and marketing orientation with the corporate organization assuming much of the responsibility for coping with problems in the financial, legal, and regulatory environments, for major resource allocation decisions, particularly those leading to expansion in new product areas, and for provision of technology required by such new products. At the same time, the corporate group encourages the subsidiary manager to operate much as he had as an independent, aggressive businessman; the corporate group does not seek to change any "formulas that have proven successful."

The provision of needed additional funds for expansion and the improvement of communication and control are considered the *easiest* resources to employ, the easiest interactions to accomplish. Finance is the common denominator. The financial control system is the common language throughout the corporation for setting objectives and measuring performance against those objectives. Cash or funds is the common resource and is viewed as frequently providing a constraining force on small, closely held corporations. The next easiest interactions to achieve are in the marketing area. Distributors, representatives, and marketing channels can sometimes be usefully shared by subsidiaries whose products differ functionally but are similar in terms of customer group. These interactions can occur outside the internal structure of the subsidiary and thus without major operating change. Most difficult to achieve are the technological interactions, providing advanced technology for major improvement of an existing product or for development of a new product. This demands major internal change and considerable resources in terms of time and energy. Measured by the potential impact and importance for performance, the three areas are viewed in reverse order: technology; marketing; finance (funds and control). Other corporate resources and functions were discussed as significant but of lesser importance than those covered above. These included cash management and the management of banking relationships, insurance management, tax management, staffing assistance, and legal work.

Examples were frequently cited in the marketing and technology areas. Periodic meetings had been initiated between marketing personnel in all subsidiaries to discuss marketing cooperation, and such cooperation was encouraged in other contacts with the corporate organization. Some effort had been made to develop corporate-wide promotional schemes which took advantage of and enhanced the Contek name. In terms of specifics, examples were cited which suggested the imperfection of information regarding customers and supplies in the markets for technical products and the importance of personal contacts. Spectra, which made radiation-based instrumentation, brought a major customer to Fletcher, which made transducers. Fletcher and Spectra cooperated in a joint marketing effort for wind tunnel instrumentation. Electronic Enclosures introduced the Microwave Group to a large customer. Autocircuit helped find customers in the computer industry for Computex, which made ferrite memory devices. Computex found customers for Autocircuit in the aerospace industry and for Spectra and Fletcher in the commercial aircraft industry.

In the technology area, Fletcher needed a high temperature transducer for potential market applications with which they were familiar. Also, they had been buying semiconductor devices for the transducers they manufactured and were concerned about the few sources of supply. Developing the internal capability to produce semiconductor devices for their current line and for the new application looked like an impossible job in terms of financing and finding the necessary technical competence. After acquisition a five-man research team was organized by Contek to work on the project. Progress was reported but the new items had not yet reached the production stage. The corporate research group knew of a crystal slicing machine that it considered far superior to those then employed by Microwave Devices Corporation. The new machine was purchased and installed with considerable savings expected. Spectra needed a smaller, less expensive radiation detector for certain "distributed" instrumentation applications. The corporate research group initiated work on this project and within a matter of months an operating prototype had been developed. A production model was expected in a short time. At the time this was written the story was much the same for all the new product technical interactions between Contek subsidiaries and the parent corporation. Opportunities had been recognized, work initiated, and progress reported, but profitable products had not yet resulted.

At Kidde the subject of influence on the acquired subsidiary was not viewed within so clearly defined a conceptual framework as it was at Contek. There was a basic philosophy about the place of the acquired subsidiary in the Kidde corporate environment and from this areas emerged where the influences of that environment appeared most important.

Basically it was an environment where adequate performance provided a wide degree of subsidiary autonomy. Corporate management made a concerted effort not to appear to consider themselves "experts" in new business areas they entered. "You know how to run your business," Ricciardi was known to have said to the manager of the acquired subsidiary, and as long as he performed he was given freedom and encouragement to run it. The advantages provided by resources at the corporate level and the interactions with other subsidiaries were not forced upon the adequately performing subsidiary manager. "We use the best form of intellectual persuasion we know," suggested Sullivan, "but the decision is theirs." Sullivan viewed Kidde as "kind of a democratic company" in contrast to what he considered more rigid, institutionalized companies such as General Motors and IBM: "Industrially speaking there is room for everyone's view, approach, and style."

We would characterize the philosophy along the following lines. Create an environment where because of the structure of psychological and real rewards people are motivated to perform, an environment where the structure of resources and complementarities are such that subsidiary interaction with the corporate group and with other subsidiaries will be advantageous for performance; then things will begin to happen. If an individual proves he can't perform in this environment, don't change the environment; replace him with an individual who can.

It is difficult to provide a meaningful ordering of the importance of various influences on the acquired subsidiary as viewed by Kidde corporate management. We feel comfortable dividing them into two groups, however: those clearly viewed as of primary importance and those considered to be of significantly lesser importance.

Kidde management felt that the interactions of greatest importance were those between subsidiaries with some similarities in markets or technologies, some "common thread." Generally speaking these included those situations where one subsidiary could benefit from the established marketing channels and contacts of another or from the expertise of another in production or distribution technology. Also discussed as being of substantial importance were influences on subsidiary operations resulting from provision of needed financing. Discussed as being of lesser importance were influences on the planning and control process; on subsidiary management motivation; and on the management of cash, insurance, taxes, and so on.

A variety of examples of marketing cooperation can be cited. Lighting Corporation of America, which made fluorescent lighting fixtures, and Sargent, which made architectural hardware, cooperated in jointly obtaining new distribution and in taking advantage of each other's customer contacts. U.S. Lines, which was described as an "order taker," was temporarily joined by an executive from Dura to develop a more aggressive marketing program. The Kidde division (the original company), which marketed fire protection equipment to the marine industry, had begun to represent Columbian Bronze for certain of its marine safety and communication equipment items. LeFebure, which manufactured bank vault and teller equipment and other bank security systems, gained several major bank customers through Kidde's various banking connections and through Globe Security Systems. Intercompany sales were cited as being of significance. Associated Testing Laboratories provided testing services for other Kidde divisions. More important, it was suggested that Globe Security Systems had gained "two or three million dollars of additional business" by supplying guard services to other Kidde subsidiaries.

Viewed as perhaps the greatest marketing influence was selling in international environments. As we have discussed, a specialized group for this function existed at the corporate level. Also, Kidde had various divisions which had had marketing operations in England, West Germany, Australia, and Japan for a number of years. Other divisions could take advantage of these established marketing systems. Houston Electronics, Cardinal Electronics, and Jade Corporation — companies which independently had been too small to initiate international marketing efforts — could jointly, with the help of Kidde, begin marketing efforts abroad. Associated Testing Laboratories, which also had been too small to market abroad, could take advantage of the 500 to 600 Kidde people in England, their contacts, the market position that had been established, and the expertise at the corporate group to begin marketing test equipment in Great Britain. Kidde had a major distributor in Australia who was "building a small marketing conglomerate of his own" selling Kidde products. Each year he came to the United States to learn what new Kidde products he could market. In doing so he opened new markets for several subsidiaries.

In the technical area, the Group Vice President in charge of those subsidiaries in the aerospace industries had assembled a group of design and production specialists. These men were regularly a part of the aerospace subsidiaries but were on call for assignments elsewhere. Cocker Machine and Foundry had tried with limited success to develop a new knitting machine. Design specialists from the Aerospace Group were temporarily assigned to Cocker. They developed a quality, reliable machine which was finding good market acceptance. The president of Columbian Bronze was a highly trained metallurgist. He assisted Dura, an automotive parts manufacturer, in the design of a new foundry. Because of its work and contacts in various areas, Kidde was able to locate skilled technical employees for various subsidiaries where they were needed for specialized functions.

In the financing area the most frequently discussed example was S. W. Farber, a manufacturer of cooking utensils and electrical appliances. A family business for more than 60 years, Farber was very conservatively managed. Farber reportedly had not fully satisfied the demand for its products in most years prior to acquisition. By making available additional funds and encouraging Farber to employ them, Kidde was able to induce a rate of expansion that "steepened their sales curve significantly."

The Kidde financial planning and control system was viewed with mixed emotions as far as the impact on subsidiary performance was concerned. Overall it was an obvious necessity. Establishment of financial goals and excellent visibility of the progress against those goals were mandatory for the management of a company such as Kidde. This did not necessarily mean that the system provided a major, positive influence on subsidiary performance. The corporate controller, as might be expected, felt that this was an important positive force. Sullivan was less optimistic. In the "democratic" kind of company that Kidde was, it was necessary to maintain the spirit of independence and motivation. The control system was the one uniform overlay on a very heterogeneous group of people and operations; it must be a "fragile thing." Maintaining proper relationships while maintaining excellent control was a matter of "delicate balance." In general, Sullivan suggested that the net impact on subsidiary performance was a positive one. For subsidiaries the system provided better information about where they were going and about where they had been. It provided danger signals and time to react. At the same time, the subsidiary manager inevitably felt that it encroached somewhat on his management prerogatives; it was time-consuming and somewhat costly; it demanded some degree of conformity.

The corporate views at Kidde and at Contek were somewhat similar. Both viewed influences in the marketing and technology areas as being most important (*potentially* most important at Contek). The provision of additional financing seemed to be considered of somewhat more importance at Kidde than at Contek, which was a bit unexpected since the Kidde acquisitions had been larger, some of them with publicly traded securities, and should have had better access to new financing pre-acquisition. Both Kidde and Contek seemed to view influences on the subsidiary planning and control process and influences in the areas of other staff specialization and personal motivation and stimulation as being of relatively less importance.

Influences viewed as being more important seemed to be of the variety that would influence subsidiary growth rate: influences on what was being produced and sold; influences on the rate of expansion through provision of needed financing and better marketing contacts or systems. Influences of the variety that would promote internal efficiency and hence profitability seemed to be considered of somewhat less importance.

Subsidiary Judgment Regarding the Nature of Influence

Opinions of the subsidiary manager were different. This was no surprise; we expected them to be different. The subsidiary manager is different in orientation, background, and experience. His priorities are different: his subsidiary's operations are foremost in his thinking; for the corporate level man it is the corporation. Further, the subsidiary manager, typically president of his company before acquisition, is proud of what he has accomplished, views himself as a more or less independent agent, and is reluctant to think that improved operations have resulted from the influence of the parent corporation rather than his own. At the same time, the interviews had been arranged with parent corporation sponsorship in both cases. So the subsidiary manager was inclined to search out those things where he could say without reservation that positive influences had in fact resulted from acquisition. We suggest that the opposing forces of individual pride and corporate sponsorship of this study caused the subsidiary manager to be fairly objective. All of this is not to suggest that people at the corporate or subsidiary level were not making an honest effort to be objective; almost without exception we think they were. It is simply that after living with one point of view for a long time, objectivity is a difficult thing. We expected the subsidiary manager to be generally less optimistic about the importance of those influences resulting from acquisition, and he was. What we did not expect was that, in the composite, the subsidiary manager appeared to have a rather different view regarding the nature of those influences which are important.

We take a more structured approach for analyzing the subsidiary manager's judgment. Twenty-three individuals were interviewed in the ten subsidiaries. This included the top man in every case and, on the average, one other individual in a responsible position who had been with the subsidiary prior to acquisition. In every interview we discussed the nine functional areas listed below in terms of changes and their significance resulting from acquisition. This provided detailed information and examples and forced the interviewee to think through the whole range of possible influences. We then asked him to go back and summarize the discussion by listing, in decreasing order of importance for improved performance, significant influences on his subsidiary resulting from acquisition.

The ordering of influences by the various subsidiary managers is shown in Tables 9.4 and 9.5 for Contek and Kidde respectively. These are the judgments of the top man in each subsidiary; we considered these more meaningful than those of other managers in the subsidiary. The column of numbers listed under each subsidiary represents the order in which influences were listed. In some cases this ordering was carried out with an obvious attempt to be precise. In others the response was more like, "I don't think it's possible for me to order these things, but the important influences in my view are. . . ." In cases of the latter variety, we made the tenuous assumption that the order in which they were discussed was the order of importance. This indicates that the specific numbers associated with the various influences in each column are not entirely meaningful. Of significance, we suggest, is whether an influence is listed for a given subsidiary and, if listed, whether it is toward the top or bottom of the list. The number of times each influence was mentioned is listed in the righthand column in each of these tables.

At Kidde the planning and control process and the personal influence of managers at the corporate level and in other subsidiaries were at the top of the list; financing was midway down; marketing, technological innovation, manufac-

TABLE 9.4

CONTEK INCORPORATED: SUMMARY OF POSITIVE INFLUENCES RESULTING FROM ACQUISITION, JUDGMENT OF SUBSIDIARY MANAGERS

Perceived Order of Importance of Acquisition Influences

Area of Influence	Environmental Control	Electronic Enclosures	Electromek Controls	Microwave Devices	Digital Instrument	Times Cited
Planning, reporting, and control		2	5	1	2	4
Manufacturing and distribution						—
Miscellaneous staff specializations and economies		3		3		2
Personal influence				2	3	2
Staffing		1	4			2
Financing			1		1	2
Marketing	3				5	2
Strategic decisions	2		2			2
Technological innovation	1		3		4	3
					Total influences cited	19

TABLE 9.5

WALTER KIDDE & COMPANY: SUMMARY OF POSITIVE INFLUENCES RESULTING FROM ACQUISITION, JUDGMENT OF SUBSIDIARY MANAGERS

Perceived Order of Importance of Acquisition Influences

Area of Influence	Associated Testing Laboratories	Columbian Bronze	S. W. Farber	Globe Security Systems	Fenwal	Times Cited
Planning, reporting, and control	2	1	3	2	1	5
Manufacturing and distribution		4				1
Miscellaneous staff specializations and economies	4		2	1	2	4
Personal influence	3	2	1	4	5	5
Staffing	1					1
Financing	5			3	6	3
Marketing	6	3			3	3
Strategic decisions						—
Technological innovation					4	1
					Total influences cited	23

turing, and distribution were toward the bottom of the list. At Contek the distribution was closer to being flat. The standouts were the planning and control system and technological innovation. It is significant to note that Contek influences in technology were typically discussed in terms of *potential* change; influences on planning and control were discussed in terms of *actual* change.

We suggest that it is difficult to have an adequate comprehension of the subsidiary view from these titles and numbers, and we proceed to discuss each area of influence in more detail. We will discuss a few examples from the subsidiaries and will draw from the two corporations somewhat interchangeably. So that the reader will not have to refer to the tables, we will follow the name of each subsidiary with a (C) for Contek or a (K) for Kidde.

1. The Planning and Control Process

The planning and control systems at Contek and at Kidde are quite similar, at least in terms of their mechanics. We will briefly sketch the elements of these systems. Each quarter the subsidiary manager prepares a 12-month operating and financial plan which, after corporate level review and approval, becomes the established set of financial objectives for the coming four quarters. This plan or budget describes objectives in terms of sales by major product lines, expenses, earnings, capital expenditures, personnel, and associated performance ratios describing relationships between financial quantities. Performance against the established objectives is reported in several ways. Cash position is reported weekly, and at Contek this report includes working capital status, bookings, shipments, and backlog. There are two reports each month. A preliminary or "flash" report a few days after the end of the month shows sales and profits for the period. Ten days after the end of the month complete financial statements are provided by each subsidiary. Quarterly detailed reports are provided showing performance against all items in the previous budget, a new 12-month budget is prepared, making changes where appropriate in the preceding one, and the cycle begins again. Particular attention is given to the operating and financial plan for the period matching the corporate fiscal years. Periodically the subsidiary manager meets personally with corporate financial and management personnel to discuss performance against budget for the preceding period and the operating and financial plans for the coming period. At Kidde this occurs semiannually, at Contek quarterly.

We feel that there is nothing particularly unusual about this scheme of planning and control. Based on our examination of the literature regarding other "acquisitive conglomerates," many of the systems seem quite similar. Sullivan of Kidde suggested: "Any well-managed company has this kind of planning and control; the really important thing is the kinds of relationships you are able to develop within it."

But the small and sometimes not so small acquisition appears very often not to have developed this kind of planning and control. Each new acquired subsidiary is required to adapt to this system as soon as possible, and for some it is a major transition. Many simply are unable to do it with their existing personnel, and temporary assistance from the corporate group is combined with the hiring of a controller and perhaps other financial personnel. In such situations it is rare that the subsidiary manager is initially pleased. Preparing an annual financial plan for the first time is not only time-consuming and frustrating; without any experience in the process it is probably not meaningful when completed. However, once the transition is finally made and the new system in operation, typically after three of four quarterly cycles, many of the subsidiary managers appear to consider it very valuable.

Influence of acquisition on the planning and control system was listed as significant by nine of the ten subsidiaries. Of course in some cases it was considered more important than others. At Columbian Bronze (K) quarterly financial statements had previously been prepared by outside accountants, usually one or two months after the end of the quarter. Once a year a forecast of sales for the coming year was prepared and then usually given little attention. Columbian was completely unprepared to cope with the Kidde control system and initially argued strongly against it. A man from the corporate controller's office provided temporary assistance to the Columbian treasurer and was eventually hired as controller. After a difficult transition the president of Columbian seemed pleased by the system and "what it has made us do for ourselves." He suggested:

> When we were operating by ourselves, if we made a few bucks more or less, so what? Now we're competing against our own goals with lots of interested people looking on. . . . It's made professionals out of us.

The situation at Fenwal (K) was somewhat similar. The company had been owned by four men who set their own standards for performance. This subsidiary apparently had a fairly adequate system of budgeting and control pre-acquisition; however, the chairman suggested that moving from their former system to Kidde's was "like moving from the sand lot to the National League." The president of Fenwal felt that they now were doing a much better job of thinking out where they wanted to go, of getting more rapid feedback on how they were doing, were having more time to react when things did not go as planned, and were receiving better information on which to base decisions.

At Microwave Devices (C) the president suggested that the really major contribution resulting from its acquisition was that the Contek financial management system "has made us organize ourselves internally." Microwave had never had a budget; "for the first time we have to sit down and think things out ahead of time, to plan."

This kind of judgment was of course not universal. It was the top men in the subsidiaries, those who interacted personally with people at the corporate level, who were, at least ultimately, most pleased by the system. At Fenwal, for example, the marketing manager feared that the control system was causing an internal orientation at the expense of a previous externally oriented spirit of constantly reaching for new markets and products. The controller naturally thought that his system had always been a good one and saw little need for change.

In general, however, this is clearly the area perceived by the subsidiary manager as being most important. In some cases the change was neither large nor very important; but in others it was dramatic.

2. Personal Influence

The manager of the acquired subsidiary finds himself involved in a new set of interpersonal relationships with individuals at the corporate level and with individuals in other subsidiaries. Some of the subsidiary managers we talked with considered these relationships quite important; they found them a new source of motivation, stimulation, and ideas.

Sullivan and Ricciardi made a concerted effort to establish informal relationships between the top managers of the various Kidde subsidiaries. An annual meeting brought all the top subsidiary people together for a management conference; other interaction was continually encouraged. At both Contek and Kidde there was frequent interaction between subsidiary managers and certain individuals in the corporate group. This resulted from the periodic operational reviews and discussion of other opportunities and problems. Possibly because of the greater effort in this direction at Kidde, personal relationships resulting from acquisition were viewed as a greater influence there.

At Columbian Bronze (K) the president felt that his relationship with Sullivan and Ricciardi had helped him to grow in his understanding of and ability to deal with management problems. He suggested that it had broadened his exposure and raised the level of his thinking; he was willing to consider opportunities and approaches that he would not have before. At Fenwal (K) the chairman cited the importance of interaction with other subsidiary managers. The entrepreneur who has built his own company tends to trust no one, he suggested, and therefore proceeds down a long, lonely road. He found that he could not even trust some professional consultants and advisors. "If you've got any worthwhile technical ideas, the first thing you know your consultant is using them to start a new firm." After acquisition by Kidde he felt he still had the independence to run his own company, but suddenly there was a large group of people with other divisions and subsidiaries who were on the same team. These people had proved to be a source of inspiration and ideas. Feelings similar to those discussed above were expressed by all the subsidiary top managers with whom we talked at Kidde.

At Contek the relationships appeared to be more limited to those between the subsidiary manager and top management of Contek. Two of the subsidiary presidents were quite enthusiastic about these, however. The president of Microwave Devices (C), Dan Johnson, had been entirely happy with the existing size of his business at the time of acquisition. David Augustus raised his sights to new objectives. Johnson suggested that a business had to have a source of inspiration, enthusiasm, confidence, feeling; it had to have "soul." Augustus provided that "soul." "If he appreciated the kind of enthusiasm he injects when he visits a subsidiary," Johnson suggested, "he would do it more often."

The president of Digital Instrument (C) suggested that one of the most important influences resulting from acquisition had been his personal growth resulting from working with the Contek management group. Digital was a subsidiary of another corporation before acquisition, and although he was head of the Digital operation, he was basically an engineer. Through the exposure to Contek management and their policies and practices he now felt confident in his abilities as a general manager.

In contrast to these examples, it should be clear that at the time of acquisition there is a great danger of loss of motivation on the part of the subsidiary manager. Previously he had been in a position of much greater risk but much greater potential monetary reward, and it was all his show. Afterward, he shared his risk, had greater security, and had his wealth in marketable form. The potential rewards were greater in the psychological category, smaller in the real category. Some top managers moved on a short time after the acquisition; some sold because they wanted to. Within a two-year period after acquisition the top men either left voluntarily or were asked to leave at Electromek (C), Associated Testing Laboratories (K), and Electronic Enclosures (C). Many, however, seemed to thrive in the new environment. And to maintain or possibly increase the motivation which the independent situation engenders was no mean feat.

It might be argued that for something as intangible as personal impact on motivation, enthusiasm, and confidence to appear high on the list of important influences is in itself indicative of how little the parent corporation can contribute to the acquired subsidiary in this kind of corporate growth. At the same time, few worthwhile things are accomplished without someone wanting them very badly and having the confidence that they can be achieved.

3. Miscellaneous Staff Specializations and Economies

This is the "catch-all" category and was listed as frequently cited for that reason. It included some influences that we expected to find, some that we did not. With the exception of functions discussed elsewhere it included all influences resulting from highly specialized human resources and other economies available through the corporate level organization.

As we noted earlier, acquisition by a large conglomerate changes the position of the subsidiary from small to large insurance buyer. Associated Testing Laboratories (K) frequently conducted nondestructive tests on extremely valuable batches of electronic devices and equipment. They had tried repeatedly to obtain insurance coverage for such items during testing and were quite concerned over their inability to do so. After joining Kidde adequate coverage was obtained. Several subsidiaries at Kidde and Contek suggested that their ability to obtain wider insurance coverage at lower cost was a significant advantage.

The president of Farber cited the greater knowledge at Kidde of the economic environment and its probable future trends as an important resource. Sullivan reacted modestly to this: "I'm afraid Isidor Farber thinks our encouraging him to go ahead and spend a couple of million dollars to expand into a new plant is evidence of our abilities in economic forecasting." In fact, operation in many industries does seem to provide an exposure and awareness of social and economic change that the company in a narrow field does not have. Both Contek and Kidde are attempting to identify areas in which most rapid future economic growth is likely to occur and to be at the right places at the right times.

Globe (K) and Fenwal (K) cited the assistance they received in finding, evaluating, and making further acquisitions as factors high on the list of important influences. Since we are attempting to evaluate the potential to influence the operations of the acquired subsidiary positively, the ability to make further acquisitions is an influence of questionable importance here.

Electronic Enclosures (C) which, as we have mentioned, had major post-acquisition operating difficulties was being temporarily managed by the Vice President for Special Administration. His abilities in organization appeared to have been particularly useful in completely changing the personnel structures for the marketing, estimating, and job shop functions.

The president of Microwave (C) simply cited the caliber of the staff professionals at Contek as an influence that had raised his standards of business practice.

4. Financing

The importance of the parent corporation providing needed financing for the acquired subsidiary is perceived in several ways, depending largely on the position of the previously independent company. Where additional financing was badly needed, was sought, and was not found available on anything approaching reasonable terms, the provision of funds by the parent corporation was viewed as easily the most important element in the acquisition relationship. Where financing had been difficult to obtain and therefore expensive in terms of both money and, more importantly, management time, assumption of this responsibility by the parent corporation was considered an important factor, largely in terms of freeing management to cope with pressing operating problems. For corporations of some strength but without attractive marketable securities, parent corporation securities were viewed as important because of the ability to use them in acquisition transactions. In the above-mentioned situations it is difficult to separate the importance of the financial strength of the parent corporation *per se* from the importance of its expertise in dealing with the sources of new financing and in encouraging the acquired subsidiary to take advantage of this financing. Each of these factors is important.

In some cases the financial resources of the parent corporation are considered important for operations for reasons that have little to do with supplying funds needed for expansion. These reasons are as follows: (a) the size and diversity of the parent corporation and the resulting financial strength permit reduction in the risk of failure for the smaller firm, through what is essentially a risk-sharing arrangement, and thus is thought to insure the survival of the acquired firm as an institution; (b) the marketability and, to some extent, potential for capital appreciation of parent corporation securities make them more desirable for investment and estate purposes. In our view these factors are questionable operating influences, but they were mentioned in a few cases as providing sources of security and peace of mind in the new environment which were important for operations. At the same time, when we talked about why the corporations were sold in the first place, the factors cited above were the principal ones for nine of the ten subsidiaries.

Digital Instrument (C), as previously mentioned, had formerly been the subsidiary of another corporation. That corporation was engaged primarily in the engineering consulting field which was the prime area of interest for the chief executive. This parent corporation was already pressed for funds and had no desire to pump additional money into the Digital subsidiary. Outside financing was sought for Digital, but venture capital and other potential suppliers of funds either wanted control or wanted no part of it. Selling to Contek seemed a good solution to the problem. The former parent received needed funds from the transaction and Digital was insured a continuing source of new financing. With funds provided by Contek, Digital was able to undertake a major development program for a new instrument that was receiving good market acceptance.

At Electromek (C) the orientation of management was and continued to be very much toward operations: engineering, production, to some extent marketing. Electromek was small, closely held, and not extremely profitable. Obtaining necessary funds, maintaining banking relationships, and otherwise dealing with the external financial environment had been difficult and was viewed as a major nuisance. Assumption of this responsibility by Contek was welcomed by the present manager of Electromek as a major blessing. Also of much importance to the manager of Electromek was the environment of financial security.

These two subsidiaries were the only ones which felt acquisition was of substantial importance for performance through provision of needed funds. That this should occur only in the minority of cases was due, we suggest, to the preference by acquisitive conglomerates for companies with demonstrated profitability and capable management. As we have argued in an earlier chapter, it is not feasible to replace management in every situation in the aggressive acquisition program; and the acquired company must be profitable to contribute to the earnings-per-share position of the parent. Those characteristics which make the company desirable as an acquisition candidate are not those which would make other sources of financing unavailable.

At Globe (K) and Fenwal (K) the attractiveness of parent corporation securities as acquisition instruments was cited as an important influence on operations. Globe had made several acquisitions; Fenwal was negotiating its first.

It is also important to note that in some cases where the parent corporation thought needed financing was an important force, the subsidiary manager felt otherwise. As noted, Kidde top management felt that provision of needed financing and the encouragement to use it had had a significant impact on the rate of sales expansion for Farber. The president of Farber suggested that it was able to generate internally all the funds Farber could use for expansion. If anything, he suggested, it had become more conservative now that it was "gambling with someone else's money"; after acquisition it held back a little, seeking the encouragement and commitment of the parent corporation before going ahead with new projects. As will be observed later, the financial data support to some extent the subsidiary view in this case.

Finally, the provision of additional financing can be a source of difficulty. The problems at Electronic Enclosures (C) were largely caused by the parent corporation's being overly permissive in making available funds for expansion. In fact, it may be more accurate to say that the parent corporation was the prime source of encouragement for the expansion moves that were attempted. The former president of Electronic Enclosures was a highly skilled craftsman who could inspire and lead a team of job shop machinists by maintaining frequent contact with them and their work. All the work of Electronic prior to acquisition had been according to customer specifications. The firm had grown rapidly and was quite profitable. This was the second Contek acquisition, and with little experience behind them at the time Contek management was inclined to feel that the people at Electronic Enclosures "could do no wrong."

Shortly after acquisition, plans were made to (1) begin manufacturing a standardized line of instrument enclosures in competition with some very large and well-established manufacturers; (2) build and move into a new and enlarged facility; (3) install an automated information system regarding job shop activities; (4) increase the level of supervisory personnel in the job shop so it could operate on a more independent basis and have the capability to increase rapidly in size. The president of Electronic spent less and less time with the custom metal fabrication activities, more and more time with the various plans for expansion and associated problems. Operating efficiency and profitability declined; annual profits slipped from half a million to a loss of half a million; things became chaotic; the president lost control and panicked; the parent corporation moved in. The Contek Vice President for Finance assumed responsibility until the Vice President for Special Administration joined Contek to deal with Electronic Enclosures as his first "temporary" assignment; he was still there in 1967. Within a few months nine of the previous top management group at Electronic Enclosures, including the president, had been released.

5. Marketing

The subsidiary manager appears to view the influence on marketing as significant but less so than the corporate manager. Still, the several examples cited below as well as those cited earlier suggest several underlying reasons why there may be significant marketing cooperation in the acquisitive conglomerate.

First, there may be economies in the use of marketing channels where products are quite different but some similarities exist in customer groups. Second, the established marketing system may be a valuable resource. The examples suggest that the customer is to a significant degree a creature of habit; there is industrial as well as consumer "brand loyalty." As one manager suggested, "Repeat business must provide the major part of the sales in this world." The customer who is reasonably satisfied with the product is most likely to return to the same source. When that source offers another product, it is easier and there is less uncertainty in buying from that source than in going elsewhere. There is a lot of rigidity or friction in product markets; to have "been around a long time" as a quality supplier may be a valuable thing. Third, information about customers and suppliers may be quite imperfect in the markets for specialized products. Through a diversified operation there can be significant cooperation in the interchange of contacts and market information. Finally, the corporation with substantial marketing experience and thus expertise may be able to transfer some of this or use it to the advantage of the smaller subsidiary. The frequently discussed "market power" of the conglomerate, achieved through reciprocal, tying, exclusive, or other agreements, seemed to be of lesser importance. When we examine the financial data the resulting significance of all of the above will not appear very great. Still it seems worth while to consider the apparent reasons for the influence that existed.

Fenwal (K), which manufactured temperature controls and fire protection equipment, was one of the corporations whose products were being carried by the previously mentioned Australian distributor. They formerly had had weak representation there and felt the new relationship to be a significant advantage. The Kidde division, which also manufactured fire protection equipment, was representing Fenwal in Canada. Further, Fenwal hoped to enter a distribution arrangement with Columbian in the domestic marine field for a new line of explosion suppression equipment. Fenwal had had considerable international experience and indicated that it had been able to provide significant assistance to others. It had good representation in Scandinavia and expected to be helpful to another subsidiary operation in England that manufactured escape slides, oxygen bottles, and extinguishers. Fenwal had a joint venture in Japan which had begun to represent other Kidde products and expected to become more heavily involved in such activities. All these relationships were mutually agreed upon by the subsidiaries; that is, they resemble "arm's length" agreements. While there was cooperation, there was also competition. Fenwal and the Kidde division had recently competed in providing fire protection systems for a new Boeing commercial aircraft. This did not appear to be frowned upon by the parent corporation.

Digital Instrument (C) felt that it was receiving some significant support from the corporate marketing function. An outside group engaged by the corporate marketing director provided a study of Digital markets which changed the direction of some of its marketing efforts. The president of Digital suggested that he would never have got around to securing such a service. At Environmental Controls (C) the general manager indicated that he got significant benefit from the Contek name in enhancing the image of technical expertise behind his product.

Intercompany sales were mentioned in several cases but were not seen as very significant. At Globe (K), for example, which was mentioned by the corporate group in this connection, the subsidiary president discussed arrangements to provide guard and other security services for some of the other Kidde subsidiaries, but suggested that this provided an insignificant part of his sales volume. The financial data we later examine support this view.

6. Technological Innovation

By technical innovation we refer to influence where one subsidiary, acting jointly with another subsidiary or with the parent corporation, introduces a new or improved product based on a technical advance that it could not or would not have achieved by itself. As we indicated earlier, there were significant achievements that appeared to be in the making at Contek but little that had come to fruition. Most of what we discussed earlier for Kidde fell in the manufacturing process area rather than the new product area.

At Fenwal (K) a high sensitivity combustion detector developed by a recent Kidde acquisition allowed Fenwal to produce an advanced fire protection system. Nothing else of significance was discussed in the other Kidde subsidiaries we interviewed.

For Environmental Controls (C) the Special Products Division of Contek developed a new semiconductor-based control device that could permit Environmental to move from manufacturing subassemblies for its customers to manufacturing a major part of the system. The new device was technically superior to competitive products but could not at the time be manufactured at a competitive price. The product was being sold in limited quantities but was still under the control of the Special Products Division and had not yet become profitable. While the general manager at Environmental was optimistic about the future potential of this product, more development effort was needed.

Electromek (C) had been profitably manufacturing process machinery rate control systems based on electronic circuitry that was years behind "the state of the art." The Contek Special Products Division had developed a new system based on integrated circuit technology. At the time of the study the new product was expected to be introduced in the fairly near future. In both of these cases the subsidiary general managers were concerned that the technical expertise backing up these products would lie with the corporate level research group and outside their control.

At Digital Instrument the Contek research group provided design assistance for two instruments now part of the Digital line. In both cases the extent of the parent contribution was difficult to ascertain.

The technological innovation area was a particularly interesting one at Contek. Both publicly and privately the professed strategy for operating management included as an important element use of corporate technical expertise to benefit the acquired subsidiary. There was much concern over the fact that at the time of this study there had not been a very significant payoff. This was the area that most clearly should affect the rate of sales expansion. But as we noted in the preceding chapter and will examine more carefully later, the Contek "average subsidiary" had a substantially slower rate of sales growth post-acquisition than pre-acquisition. It may well be that the post-acquisition time period was simply too short; the product development cycle is frequently a rather lengthy one. There was some optimism for the future about the situations described above and about other situations that were only beginning to take shape. It could be that Contek would eventually be able to achieve significant benefit from such "technological transfusions." We would argue, however, that there were some problems with Contek's technology strategy for an acquisitive conglomerate. One of the principal keys to successful operations in this environment appeared to be the independent, aggressive subsidiary general manager, motivated to perform, rewarded on the basis of his performance, and in control of the ingredients of his performance. For the corporate group to maintain control over his technical resources did not appear a feasible strategy over the long term. Also, at Contek the corporate research group was primarily in the "research business," government contract research. It was primarily oriented toward sophistication of technology and very little oriented toward marketability of product. Competence in the application of new technology to marketable products was a missing ingredient at the Contek corporate level.

7. Staffing

By influence in the staffing area we refer to the parent corporation or another subsidiary playing a significant role in the location and employment of managerial, professional, and technical personnel needed in the acquired subsidiary. Two kinds of resources which may exist at various points in the organization seemed important. First, much industrial hiring is based on established personal relationships and referrals. To some extent the acquisitive conglomerate provides a network of information about available people. Second, individuals with expertise in a given area are better equipped to evaluate a potential employee in their own area. If, for example, the subsidiary manager is attempting to hire a controller for the first time or someone in a technical area that is new to his subsidiary, expertise in evaluating potential candidates may prove valuable.

The subsidiary general manager considered influence in the staffing area of some significance in two kinds of situations: (1) where he had received help in hiring specialized people; (2) where he had been hired to replace the pre-acquisition subsidiary manager who had either left or been asked to leave. In the former category the corporate groups appeared to have been most helpful in the area of hiring needed controllers and other financial people. This was particularly true at Contek where the acquisitions were smaller and several had almost no financial management capability prior to acquisition. Contek had either hired or was looking for controllers in 9 of the 15 acquisitions. We have cited earlier some cases where assistance was provided in employing needed technical or research personnel.

In the second category, for two of the five Contek subsidiaries and one of the five Kidde subsidiaries the present general manager had replaced a previous owner-manager after acquisition. In two cases, Associated Testing Laboratories (K) and Electromek (C), the present subsidiary manager was formerly next in command and his predecessor had left at least partly on a voluntary basis. This kind of transition could have happened but would not have occurred without the acquisition. The extent to which it provides "better management" is an open question. The third case is the now familiar situation of Electronic Enclosures (C) where several management people were asked to leave. The new general manager brought in by Contek appeared to have substantially improved the unpleasant situation that developed and to have eliminated the loss position of the subsidiary. In the midst of some very negative changes, the staffing influence was the one positive factor that changed the direction back toward a healthy operation. In all three of the cases discussed above, the new general managers naturally felt that the change in top management was a needed change, a change for the better, a change in the direction of more professional management, and so forth.

8. *Strategic Decisions*

In the periodic operational reviews each subsidiary discusses plans for the future with the corporate group. Particularly at these times, but obviously at any time, the parent corporation may, if it so chooses, play a major role in determining the future direction for the subsidiary. We were interested in the extent to which the parent corporation can help the subsidiary manager to make, or can make for him, better decisions about such major things as what products to manufacture and which markets to sell them in. Contek, it may be recalled from discussion of the corporate view, expressed more interest in playing this role than did Kidde.

Most of the subsidiary managers suggested that acquisition had provided no significant contribution[6] to the process of making so-called strategic decisions. In some cases such decisions simply had not been made after acquisition. Elsewhere it was suggested that the parent corporation made them think it all out more carefully but generally had permitted them to make and carry out their own plans. In two Contek subsidiaries where the corporate group was working on new product lines, Environmental and Electromek (see *Technological Innovation*), the general managers felt that the parent organization was having a major influence on their strategic decisions. We would agree. The difficulty lies in evaluating whether the influence was a positive or a negative one. This usually can be determined only after the passage of a substantial amount of time and perhaps not even then.

If nothing else, we may conclude that the infrequent mention of this area is evidence of the independence which the subsidiary manager perceived for himself in these two companies, Kidde in particular.

9. *Manufacturing and Distribution*

Our discussion of the corporate level view suggests that even where subsidiaries manufacture quite different products there may exist similarities in the methods and the technology of manufacturing and distribution that permit the expertise of one subsidiary to be used to the advantage of another. We earlier discussed some examples in this area provided by Kidde management; these related primarily to subsidiaries other than those we studied. The subsidiary manager's discussion of this influence, in our sample of ten subsidiaries, was notable by its absence. Outside the assistance provided by the metallurgist-president of Columbian in foundry operations, which was mentioned earlier, there was no discussion of significant influence in the area of manufacturing and distribution. This may have simply been a result of the particular subsidiaries we chose to study. It may have resulted from the relatively short period of time as part of the parent. But in nine of ten cases the feeling seemed to be that it takes a long time to get to know the peculiarities of any particular manufacturing-distribution system and that

---

[6] We could discuss as an example of negative influence in this area the decisions made at Electronic Enclosures (C); see the section on "Financing."

substantial assistance from other subsidiaries would be difficult within this type of corporate environment.

The preceding discussion of subsidiary management judgment presents a complex picture. A variety of relationships develop between the acquired subsidiary and other parts of the acquisitive conglomerate. The relative and absolute importance of various influences is different in each situation. Still, a couple of related generalizations seem possible for our sample of ten. First, there appeared to be some difference between subsidiary and corporate management judgment regarding the relative significance of various areas of influence. Second, in the aggregate the subsidiary managers clearly felt that the most significant acquisition influence in terms of operating performance came in the area of the planning and control process.

In general, those areas perceived as more important by the subsidiary manager are those which have much in common for any business corporation and those in which influence flows most easily across the organizational boundaries within the acquisitive conglomerate: planning and control; personal influence; financial support. Viewed as less important are those influences which demand specialized knowledge and expertise about the products and markets of a given subsidiary: manufacturing and distribution; technological innovation for new or improved products; marketing. We would characterize the areas viewed as most important by the subsidiary manager as those which tend to influence the efficiency of internal operations (influence in the planning and control area in particular) and therefore influence profitability. The areas viewed as of lesser importance are more externally directed influences concerning what is being produced and to whom it is being sold, influences we would expect to affect the rate of expansion of the acquired subsidiary.

ANALYSIS OF FINANCIAL DATA ON SUBSIDIARY PERFORMANCE

Some indication of the nature and significance of influence on the ten subsidiaries is provided by financial data covering operations before and after their acquisition. In general, profits relative to sales increased after acquisition; rate of growth of sales volume declined. We will argue that this tends to support the subsidiary view regarding the nature of acquisition influence and, in particular, the importance of influence on the planning and control process.

We have discussed in detail in the preceding chapter the data collected on the Contek subsidiaries. More complete data were made available for the five Kidde subsidiaries than we were able to collect at Contek. We will look at Associated Testing Laboratories as an example. Table 9.6 shows financial data for the five years preceding acquisition by Kidde and three years afterward. These data have been coded so that sales in the last pre-acquisition year equal 100. All items of data have been similarly adjusted so that the proportional relationships within each period and across periods are accurate. Some analysis of

TABLE 9.6

ASSOCIATED TESTING LABORATORIES — WALTER KIDDE & COMPANY:
FINANCIAL PERFORMANCE BEFORE AND AFTER ACQUISITION
(coded data; sales in last pre-acquisition year = 100)

	Pre-Acquisition Fiscal Years Ended May 31					Post-Acquisition Fiscal Years Ended December 31		
	1960	*1961*	*1962*	*1963*	*1964*	*1965*	*1966*	*1967*
Selected Income Items								
Total sales	33.34	58.43	66.78	75.96	100.00	102.80	124.90	140.25
Intercompany sales	—	—	—	—	—	1.03	.59	1.77
Gross margin	10.15	16.56	14.01	13.92	25.31	27.52	36.61	44.11
Operating profit	3.55	8.19	3.27	1.87	12.11	13.54	18.37	23.07
Profit before interest and tax	3.70	8.00	3.46	.87	12.27	13.79	18.55	23.35
Selected Expense Items								
Research and development	—	—	—	—	—	—	.16	.47
General administration[1]	6.57	8.37	10.74	12.05	13.20	7.28	9.87	10.87
Net interest expense	.06	.03	.12	.25	.50	(.12)	(.31)	(.75)
Home office charge	—	—	—	—	—	—	.59	.65
Selected Balance Sheet Items								
Total capital[2]	18.62	44.89	46.54	46.85	53.08	56.41	67.21	80.07
Total assets[2]	26.56	63.23	60.86	64.47	76.62	71.60	85.36	103.51

[1] Pre-acquisition data include selling expenses; detail breakdown not available.

[2] Post-acquisition data exclude certain assets retailed by Walter Kidde & Company upon merger and cash left behind to wind up old Associated Testing Laboratories legal entity.

these data is shown in Table 9.7. As before, attention is focused on *profitability* relative to both sales and total capital and *growth* in sales and in profits. We use profits before interest and tax (PBIT) here rather than profits before tax as before because it is a more appropriate measure for profitability relative to total capital and the interest data were made available.

The only measure requiring special mention is that for the rate of growth of profits before interest and taxes. Because of the large fluctuations which occasionally occur in this figure relative to its size and in order to be consistent with the analysis of Contek, we measured the year-to-year change in profits relative to total capital rather than to the profit figure itself. The measure of growth in profit is thus not in any way similar to a compound growth rate but does provide a consistent measure for comparing pre-acquisition and post-acquisition periods. The measure for growth in sales is simply the year-to-year change taken as a percentage of the prior year's sales. Average figures are shown for pre-acquisition and post-acquisition periods for profitability relative to sales and capital, for capital turnover, and for growth in sales and profits. These average figures are simple averages of the annual performance measures.[7]

Given the greater level of detail in the data on Kidde subsidiaries a few additional observations are possible. First there has been some tendency for the level of research and development expenditure to increase in post-acquisition periods for Kidde subsidiaries. For the three that listed research and development expense, the post-acquisition amounts, relative to sales, exceeded amounts for

---

[7] Similar data for the other four Kidde subsidiaries are presented in Lynch's doctoral dissertation, "Acquisitive Conglomerate Performance," pp. 502–510, on file in Baker Library, Harvard Business School, and certain adjustments to the financial data on two subsidiaries that were made are described on pp. 483–484.

TABLE 9.7

ASSOCIATED TESTING LABORATORIES — WALTER KIDDE & COMPANY: ANALYSIS OF FINANCIAL PERFORMANCE BEFORE AND AFTER ACQUISITION
(Acquired February 1965)

	Pre-Acquisition Fiscal Years Ended May 31						Post-Acquisition Fiscal Years Ended December 31			
	1960	1961	1962	1963	1964	Avg.	1965	1966	1967	Avg
						(percent of annual sales)				
Selected Income Items										
Total sales	100.00	100.00	100.00	100.00	100.00		100.00	100.00	100.00	
Intercompany sales	—	—	—	—	—		1.00	.47	1.26	
Gross margin	30.44	28.34	20.98	18.33	25.31		26.77	29.31	31.45	
Operating profit	10.65	14.02	4.90	2.46	12.11		13.17	14.71	16.45	
Profit before interest and tax	11.10	13.69	5.18	1.15	12.27	8.68	13.41	14.85	16.65	14.97
Selected Expense Items										
Research and development	—	—	—	—	—		—	.13	.34	
General administration	19.07	14.32	16.08	15.86	13.20		7.08	7.90	7.75	
Net interest expense	.18	.05	.18	.33	.50		(.12)	(.25)	(.53)	
Home office charge	—	—	—	—	—		—	.47	.46	
						(performance measures in percent)				
Other Performance Measures										
PBIT/total capital	19.87	17.82	7.43	1.86	23.12	14.02	24.45	27.60	29.16	27.07
PBIT/total assets	13.93	12.65	5.69	1.35	16.01	9.93	19.26	21.73	22.56	21.18
Sales/total capital	179.05	130.16	143.49	162.13	188.39	160.64	182.24	185.84	175.16	181.08
Sales/total assets	125.53	92.41	109.73	117.82	130.51	115.20	143.58	146.32	135.49	141.80
Growth-sales		75.25	14.29	13.75	31.65	33.74	1.77	21.50	12.29	11.85
Growth-PBIT		9.58	(9.75)	(5.53)	21.48	3.95	1.70	7.08	5.99	4.92

the years immediately preceding acquisition. This may imply corporate management influence on subsidiary preparation for the future in terms of new product research and development. This would seem a logical extension of the increased emphasis on planning.

Second, it may be noted that intercompany sales were quite small, almost negligible in every case. While this was discussed as an advantage of some significance resulting from acquisition, the level of intercompany sales as a percentage of total sales ranged from zero to 1.26% in 1967 and averaged 0.48% for the five Kidde subsidiaries. In particular at Globe, where intercompany sales of guard services were discussed as significant, 1967 intercompany sales were 0.64% of that subsidiary's total sales.

Third, in only one case, Columbian Bronze, had the level of interest expense as a proportion of sales increased. Post-acquisition interest expense averaged 1.6% of sales as compared with 1.2% pre-acquisition, indicating some reliance on the parent corporation as a source of funds. In the other four cases interest had either changed from an expense to an income item or had become a larger income item since acquisition. This means that four of the five subsidiaries were net suppliers of capital to other parts of the corporation; they were generating more funds internally than were needed for their own expansion. While this may be an indicator of increased profitability, it implies that the supply of needed funds for expansion had not been an important acquisition influence for those subsidiaries. In the case of Farber, for example, interest, which had traditionally been an expense item, became an income item in 1967. At the same time the average figure for rate of post-acquisition sales growth was slightly less than the pre-acquisition figure (17.6% v. 18.4%). This lends some support to the Farber president's argument that the supply of needed funds for more rapid expansion had not been among the more important acquisition influences.

Fourth, the rate of capital turnover (sales divided by total capital) decreased for four of the five Kidde subsidiaries and declined on the average from 3.27 pre-acquisition to 2.99 post-acquisition. While a change in this direction would normally be considered undesirable, these may be instances of smaller firms becoming more "adequately" capitalized.

TABLE 9.8

CONTEK INCORPORATED: SUMMARY OF SUBSIDIARY PERFORMANCE
BEFORE AND AFTER ACQUISITION
(all figures in percent)

	Environmental Control	Electronic Enclosures	Electromek Controls	Microwave Devices	Digital Instrument	Average With Digital	Average Without Digital
PBT/sales							
Average after	11	3	4	11	9	8	7
Average before	10	11	*	8	(2)	5	7
Difference	1	(8)	4	3	11	3	*
PBT/total capital							
Average after	29	14	12	33	24	22	22
Average before	20	29	2	28	18	19	20
Difference	9	(15)	10	5	6	3	2
Growth-sales							
Average after	19	12	11	8	53	21	13
Average before	25	37	9	31	141	49	23
Difference	(6)	(25)	2	(23)	(88)	(28)	(10)
Growth-PBT							
Average after	7	(10)	11	(8)	3	1	*
Average before	5	14	3	9	264	59	8
Difference	2	(24)	8	(17)	(261)	(58)	(8)

* Less than 0.5%.

Turning to our primary concern of comparing profitability and growth before and after acquisition, we show in Tables 9.8 and 9.9 the summary of performance measures for the ten Kidde and Contek subsidiaries. Again, the performance measures are profitability relative to sales and total capital, growth of sales, and profits before tax. The figures shown are averages for the five (in some cases less) annual periods before acquisition and the annual periods after acquisition (ranging from three years to only one). The data on Contek were presented in different form (and for different purposes) in the preceding chapter but are reproduced here for convenience. It will be recalled that Digital Instrument was omitted in some of the before-after comparisons because of the company's extremely short pre-acquisition history; we will continue to discuss performance with and without Digital. For Kidde also there is one subsidiary that is questionable for inclusion in any before-after acquisition performance comparison. Fenwal, in the last pre-acquisition year, had a major contract for temperature instrumentation in military aircraft. This contract was completed prior to the beginning of the one post-acquisition year for which financial data were available. Absence of this contract had a significant negative impact on financial performance (relative to the year before) which had little to do with the fact that Fenwal was acquired. Therefore, we show the averages of the performance measures with and without Fenwal included. For both Contek and Kidde the average figures

TABLE 9.9

WALTER KIDDE & COMPANY: SUMMARY OF SUBSIDIARY PERFORMANCE
BEFORE AND AFTER ACQUISITION
(all figures in percent)

	Associated Testing Laboratories	Co- lumbian Bronze	S. W. Farber	Globe Security Systems	Fenwal	Average	
						With Fenwal	Without Fenwal
PBIT/sales							
Average after	15	7	14	10	17	13	12
Average before	9	6	8	10	14	9	8
Difference	6	1	6	1	3	4	4
PBIT/total capital							
Average after	27	15	48	59	33	36	37
Average before	14	15	30	56	34	30	39
Difference	13	1	18	3	(1)	6	8
Growth-sales							
Average after	12	14	18	16	(5)	11	15
Average before	34	12	18	16	16	19	20
Difference	(22)	(2)	(1)	(1)	(21)	(8)	(5)
Growth-PBIT							
Average after	5	3	14	8	(7)	5	8
Average before	4	5	10	8	12	8	7
Difference	1	(2)	4	*	(20)	(3)	1

* Less than 0.5%.

are for the "average subsidiary"; that is, they are not weighted by any measure of subsidiary size.[8]

First, on an absolute basis profit before interest and tax relative to sales and total capital averaged 13% and 36% respectively for all five Kidde subsidiaries in post-acquisition periods. On the same basis the average percentage increase in sales was 11% per year and the index of profit growth was 5% per year. This index of profit growth can be transformed to an approximate measure of annual percentage increase by multiplying times the ratio of total capital to profit before interest and tax. That ratio is approximately equal to three, so the post-acquisition

---

[8] Weighted average figures could not be calculated since data on the absolute size of subsidiaries were not made available by Walter Kidde & Company.

profit growth approximates 15% (3 × 5%) per year, 24% (3 × 8%) per year without Fenwal. Regardless of what the before-after comparison implies about the *nature* of influence, this post-acquisition record of earnings growth is clearly quite respectable.

For the first five Contek acquisitions the average post-acquisition performance was slightly better than for the first seven, which we discussed in the preceding chapter. Post-acquisition profit before tax relative to sales and total capital averaged 8% and 22% respectively. The average annual increase in sales was 21% and the index of profit growth was 1% per year, negligible without Digital.

A comment by the Kidde chairman provides an interesting prelude to the analysis of performance before and after acquisition. He was somewhat surprised, as we were, by the degree of emphasis which the subsidiary manager placed on improved planning and control. He suggested:

> If it's really important, it should be possible to prove it in some way. If improved information permits better decisions about which activities to emphasize, which activities not to emphasize, if the system provides better control over costs or more efficient operations generally, all of this should show up somewhere. . . . It should show up in the increased profitability of these subsidiaries.

We agree. We also suggest that if better marketing and better products, resulting from better technology and better manufacturing, are really important, it should show up in an increased rate of sales growth.

Profit growth for the Contek "average subsidiary" slowed from a fairly rapid pace before acquisition to a standstill after acquisition. For the Kidde "average subsidiary" profit growth increased slightly or decreased somewhat, depending on whether Fenwal was included, from what was previously a fairly rapid pace. At Contek this resulted from a small increase in profitability relative to sales and capital and a significant decrease in rate of sales growth. The earnings trend at Kidde resulted from a significant increase in profitability and a small decrease in rate of sales growth. That is, despite an apparent acquisition impact on earnings trend that was quite different in these two cases, the average profitability relative to sales and capital *increased* for both corporations and the average rate of sales growth *decreased* for both corporations. The record is more impressive when the individual subsidiaries are examined. In nine of the ten subsidiaries profitability relative to sales increased;[9] in nine of the ten subsidiaries the rate of sales growth declined.[10] There is some question whether all these changes were of great enough magnitude to be considered significant. In particular, the pre-acquisition and post-acquisition rates of sales growth for two of the Kidde subsidiaries were different by between one-half and one percentage point. Nonetheless, we find

---

[9] The record was slightly less consistent for profitability relative to total capital where there was an increase for eight of the ten subsidiaries.

[10] The record would be slightly less consistent if the two later Contek acquisitions which we discussed in the last chapter were included here. While the rate of sales growth declined in both cases, profitability relative to sales increased in only one.

the record sufficiently uniform to pursue a statistical argument regarding its possible meaning in the next section.[11]

First, a few words are in order regarding the relationship between subsidiary financial performance and corporate per-share performance. We demonstrated in the preceding chapter that the 87% average annual increase in earnings per share achieved by Contek over the period studied resulted primarily from the interdependence of price-earnings ratio and earnings-per-share growth through the acquisition process. We suggested that since profits for the Contek "average subsidiary" declined after acquisition, improved subsidiary financial performance can in no way explain the dramatic difference in price-earnings ratios between parent and acquisitions and hence the per-share earnings performance. At Kidde the situation was more complex, and because of more limited information any arguments are necessarily tenuous. Post-acquisition profit growth for the subsidiaries we have studied had been rather impressive. In addition to the data examined earlier on five Kidde subsidiaries, some information of a more general character is provided in the 1967 Kidde Annual Report. The sales and profit growth for companies acquired in each fiscal year is shown in Table 9.10. This

TABLE 9.10

Financial Performance of Kidde Acquisitions

Operations and Base Year	1967 Sales Increase over Base Year	1967 Pretax Profit Increase over Base Year	Equivalent Compound Growth Rate for Profits
Original Kidde operations, 1963	38%	736%	69%
Companies acquired during 1964	75	75	20
Companies acquired during 1965	54	12	6
Companies acquired during 1966	(5)	11	11
Average of compound growth rates for profits			26%
Average of compound growth rates for profits, excluding original Kidde operations			12%

Source: Walter Kidde & Company, 1967 Annual Report.

is as shown in the Annual Report except for the last column where we have shown equivalent annual compounded growth rates for profits. Including the original Kidde operation the average of the compound figures is 26% per year. Excluding original Kidde operations, which were small in the total scheme of things, the average of the compound figures is 12%.

For the five subsidiaries discussed above, the average annual increase in profits before interest and tax was 15% to 24% depending of whether or not Fenwal was included. Let us assume that the average annual increase in profits for all subsidiaries was in the range of 15% to 20%. Since the average annual increase

---

[11] We will assume that the reader has some statistical background regarding sample information.

in earnings per share for the corporation was 73% for the period studied, it seems safe to say that a substantial part of corporate per-share performance (roughly the difference between 73% and 15% to 20% growth per year) had been achieved through the immediate financial impact of acquisitions. This of course means that, on the average, the parent corporation market value relative to earnings was substantially higher than that of companies acquired. While post-acquisition performance of Kidde subsidiaries was attractive, based on the sample studied here, it does not appear substantially different from pre-acquisition performance in terms of rate of growth and profitability. We still do not have any evidence, we suggest, that would explain a dramatic increase in subsidiary market value at the time of acquisition based on justified expectations by the investing public that subsidiary financial performance would substantially improve as a result of the acquisition. For the difference between corporate per-share performance and subsidiary earnings growth, the kind of explanation pursued in the preceding chapter regarding the relationship between price-earnings ratio and earnings-per-share growth through the acquisition process seems to be of primary importance.

A STATISTICAL ARGUMENT ON THE NATURE OF ACQUISITION INFLUENCE

Consider for a moment the assumption that the ten subsidiaries are a random sample from the rather large total population of acquisitive conglomerate subsidiaries. Also, assume for the moment that the post-acquisition rate of growth in sales volume and the post-acquisition profit margin on sales were either *greater* than or *less* than they were before acquisition — we will not worry about insignificant change.[12] Then there are four possible states in which we might find a given subsidiary in terms of growth rate of sales after acquisition relative to before acquisition and in terms of profit margin on sales after relative to before

TABLE 9.11

POSSIBLE STATES AND THEIR DISTRIBUTION
IN SAMPLE OF SUBSIDIARY PERFORMANCE

State	Rate of Sales Growth	Profit Margin on Sales	Distribution
1	+	+	1
2	−	+	8
3	−	−	1
4	+	−	0

acquisition. These are shown in Table 9.11 where the plus sign indicates improved post-acquisition performance, the minus sign indicates a decline. In our sample of ten we found the distribution shown in the righthand column of this table.

---

[12] In this section we focus on profit margin on sales as the measure of profitability because the net impact on profit may more appropriately be viewed as resulting from the combination of sales growth and profit margin on sales.

Based on the sample we can talk probabilistically about the "true" proportion of the total population of acquisitive conglomerate subsidiaries with increased post-acquisition profitability, those in states one or two which we shall denote p_{12}, the "true" proportion with decreased rate of sales growth, p_{23}, and the "true" proportion with both increased profitability and reduced sales growth, p_2. For the proportion in a given state, we would like to know the probability that the "true" value for the total population is less than any given fraction. Our assumptions stated above imply that we are sampling from what may be considered a "Bernoulli process." Thus, the desired probabilities may be determined from appropriate left-tail cumulative Beta distributions.[13] Table 9.12 shows for values

TABLE 9.12

ASSUMING THAT SAMPLING IS FROM BERNOULLI PROCESS:
LEFT-TAIL CUMULATIVE BETA DISTRIBUTIONS
ON "TRUE" PROPORTIONS

| | Probability that "True" Proportion Is Less than Stated Amount | | | |
	0.01	0.05	0.10	0.20
Proportion*				
p_{12}	0.5302	0.6356	0.6898	0.7514
p_{23}	0.5302	0.6356	0.6898	0.7514
p_2	0.4277	0.5299	0.5848	0.6499

* p_{12} is the proportion in states 1 or 2; i.e., increased profitability. p_{23} is the proportion in states 2 or 3; i.e., decreased sales growth. p_2 is the proportion in state 2; i.e., both increased profitability and decreased sales growth.

of the relevant proportions the probabilities that these values are not exceeded by the "true" proportions. For example, it is indicated that there is less than one chance in a hundred that the "true" proportion of acquisitive conglomerate subsidiaries with increased profitability on sales[14] is smaller than one-half, less than one chance in five that the "true" proportion is smaller than three-fourths; likewise for decreased growth in sales. Further, our statistical argument implies that there is less than one chance in twenty that the "true" proportion with *both* increased profitability and decreased growth is smaller than one-half, one chance in five that it is smaller than 65%.

Certain aspects of this analysis are clearly subject to question. In particular, the reader will inevitably be skeptical about accepting our sample of ten as anything very close to a random sample of acquisitive conglomerate subsidiaries; this despite our arguments regarding the strong similarities among the members of the acquisitive conglomerate population. So the analysis stretches the imagina-

---

[13] Assuming no prior information regarding the true proportions, we are interested in the Beta distribution with parameters $(r + 1,\ n + 2)$, where r is the number of outcomes in a given state, equal nine for p_{12} and p_{23} and eight for p_2, and n is the sample size, equal 10 in this case.

[14] Presumably based on financial data covering not more than three post-acquisition periods, since that is the nature of our sample.

tion, yet we think it strengthens the argument on the nature of acquisitive conglomerate influence.

Summary

We have been interested in the nature of operating influence on the acquired subsidiary of the acquisitive conglomerate and, indirectly, on the potential for that influence to improve the subsidiary's financial performance. Based on the characteristics of acquisitive conglomerates generally, we argued at the outset for the importance of economies in the use of specialized human resources. Further, we argued that those functional areas in which such economies should be most important are those which are common to business corporations generally, areas where influence flows most easily and understandably across the organizational boundaries of diverse subsidiaries within the acquisitive conglomerate. We expected those areas to be of less importance which demand specialized knowledge and expertise elsewhere in the organization regarding the technology, products, and markets relevant to a given subsidiary's operations. We expected influence to be more on the nature and quality of the management process, on profitability, and to be less on the basic nature of subsidiary products and markets, on growth.

We have investigated the proposed question by studying two acquisitive conglomerates with particular attention to five subsidiaries in each case. The two parent corporations differ primarily in that one is substantially smaller and more technically oriented than the other. Each of the ten subsidiaries studied had been part of the parent for between two and four years at the time of the study.

After an overview of the development of each corporation, we discussed the corporate organizations and the resources they contain, corporate and subsidiary management opinions regarding the nature and significance of operating influence, and the financial record of performance before and after acquisition.

The corporate organizations differ in several respects. The Kidde organization is strong in those functions required to support the planning and control process within the acquired subsidiary and in those functions which shield the subsidiary from the problems of coping with the legal, tax, regulatory, and financial environments. Contek has less depth in financial management and in functions related to common problems of the external environment, but in contrast to Kidde has made an effort to develop a corporate level marketing competence and has substantial technical resources in its central research organization. Partly because of (1) functional orientation, (2) economies in staff specializations, and (3) dependence of corporate level effort on numbers of acquisitions and subsidiaries as well as size, Kidde appears able at lower proportional cost to operate a corporate level organization that is stronger, more highly specialized, and better equipped for the requirements of growth through aggressive acquisition.

The corporate and subsidiary views regarding the influence of acquisition appear somewhat different. We have attempted to be careful not to overemphasize this. Managers at both levels talk about all the same kinds of influences, which is certainly to be expected since they spend considerable time talking to each other.

However, the subsidiary managers are generally less optimistic regarding the degree of significance of acquisition influence and indicate a somewhat different view from the two corporate groups regarding which influences are more important.

At both Contek and Kidde, corporate managements suggest that influences in "technology-product-market" areas are of relatively greater importance, either potentially or actually. For Kidde in particular, given the composition of resources in the corporate level organization and the management philosophy regarding the independence of the subsidiary manager, this was somewhat surprising. At the subsidiary level, managers tended to emphasize influences in more "managerially" oriented areas, particularly the planning and control process and their own personal development as better general managers. Both the subsidiary and corporate groups discussed the provision of needed funds as important for the performance of potential acquisitions unable to obtain capital for expansion on "reasonable" terms. However, because of the preference of acquisitive conglomerates for acquisitions with demonstrated profitability and capable management, these situations were in the minority.

The analysis of operating influence on the acquired subsidiary, based on opinions and descriptions provided by managers at the corporate and subsidiary levels, provides some differences of opinion regarding which kinds of things are more important. We turn to the financial data to attempt to learn something further of the nature of acquisition influence.

At Kidde the "average subsidiary" studied in this chapter had a respectable rate of profit growth after acquisition. At the same time, this growth rate had not been substantially different from the rate of growth before acquisition. It resulted from a significantly increased profitability relative to sales and capital and a slightly decreased rate of sales growth. At Contek the "average subsidiary" studied in this chapter had virtually no growth in profits after acquisition compared to a fairly rapid rate of growth pre-acquisition. This resulted from slightly increased profitability relative to sales and capital and a significant decline in rate of sales growth. It is to be noted that in both corporations profitability relative to sales and capital improved for the "average subsidiary"; rate of growth in sales declined. More convincingly, in nine of the ten subsidiaries studied in these two corporations profitability relative to sales increased; in nine of ten subsidiaries the rate of sales growth declined after acquisition. We have provided a probabilistic argument that it is unlikely this would have occurred "by accident." At the outset we had argued: (1) that influence in technology-product-market areas should be reflected primarily in expanded demand and hence in a greater rate of growth in sales than was achieved pre-acquisition; (2) that influence on the management process should be reflected primarily in the efficiency of operations and hence in profits relative to sales. The financial data, the subsidiary manager, the characteristics of the acquisitive conglomerate in general, all argue for the importance of influence in the latter area.

In general the data on Kidde subsidiaries would indicate that it is possible for the acquired subsidiary to thrive in the acquisitive conglomerate environment if not to improve its performance dramatically. We still do not have any evidence, we suggest, that would explain a dramatic increase in subsidiary market value at the time of acquisition based on justified expectations by the investing public that subsidiary financial performance will substantially improve. The kind of explanation pursued in the preceding chapter seems the more important. The conclusions regarding the nature of influence would indicate that it is the potential acquisition that (1) is strong in product technology and marketing, (2) deficient in planning and controlling its operations and deficient in expertise for dealing with the external financial, legal and regulatory environment, and (3) has management personnel with the ability to "grow" that will receive the greatest performance benefit from the acquisitive conglomerate. The company badly in need of funds for expansion will also benefit, but it probably is not a very likely prospect for the acquisitive conglomerate.

CHAPTER X
Summary of Conclusions

In this study we have sought greater understanding of the outstanding shareholder performance achieved by a group of firms growing through continuing programs of aggressive, diversified acquisition. These are the "acquisitive conglomerates," a corporate form of growing importance in the 1950s and 1960s.

Our concept of performance for shareholders has included (1) the rate of market price appreciation or, as a "proxy" for this, the rate of growth in earnings per share plus (2) the dividend yield. Together these two elements determine the rate of return over time for the owners of equity securities.

Our motivation for studying the superior shareholder performance of acquisitive conglomerates stemmed from two sources. First, the existing evidence about past industrial acquisitions and mergers would lead one to expect inferior performance for the corporation engaged in numerous acquisitions. Second, there has been a substantial amount of controversial discussion in recent years regarding the determinants of the performance that has been achieved by this group of corporations.

In the introductory chapter we began with a systematic discussion of the recent controversy about acquisitive conglomerate performance. We suggested that it is possible to view the potential contributions of the aggressive acquisition program to per-share performance in two categories: (1) those which result from the immediate financial effects of business combinations; (2) those which depend on longer term operating improvement in companies acquired. We will briefly review the argument regarding the potential role of these two categories in providing per-share performance through acquisition.

The immediate effects of a continuing series of acquisitions may lead to increased per-share performance because of (1) the interdependence of market value and performance in high-expansion-rate growth; (2) the alteration of risk and return for the shareholder in combination with market imperfections; (3) accounting flexibility; and (4) the structure of tax laws. The basic idea is that for one or more of these reasons, the market values of acquired firms may increase when they join the parent.[1] This would allow the parent to maintain a market value advantage over those acquired. Such a valuation differential permits acquisitions on a basis which provides an immediate favorable effect on the per-share position of the buying corporation. A series of such acquisitions is translated into an increased rate of per-share growth.

---

[1] Except for tax reduction advantages which increase cash flow as well as possibly increasing market value.

On the other hand, increased per-share performance may result from operating improvement in acquisitions based on (1) integration of operations providing advantages of horizontal scale, vertical transfer efficiencies, better "balance," and market power or (2) influence on operations without integration, either on the technologies, products, and markets in which the acquisition participates or on the management process within the acquired company. In either event, if there is an improvement in the profitability or growth of the acquired company after acquisition, there is a corresponding increase in the present value of future returns for shareholders. If the acquiring corporation has demonstrated, or the investing public thinks it has demonstrated, an ability to improve the performance of companies acquired in the past, there may be an upward revision of expectations for future returns from a new acquisition. As a result there may be an increase in actual market value of the acquired company at the time of acquisition announcement, and the parent corporation thus may achieve an immediate "capital gain." Because of its demonstrated or perceived ability in performance improvement the parent corporation will be valued relatively higher than companies acquired. For this reason it may be possible to continually make acquisitions on terms that will contribute immediately to per-share performance.

Certainly there is no uniform explanation for the performance of acquisitive conglomerates. All the factors discussed above (and summarized in Figure 1.1 of the introductory chapter) undoubtedly are involved to varying degrees at different times in different acquisition programs. Further, any realistic explanation must be a complex one. None of the discussed factors can be viewed independently of all others. In particular, all are intertwined with the feedback relationship between market value and performance. We have made no pretense of being able to partition demonstrated performance precisely over the possible sources of that performance even for one acquisitive conglomerate, much less for acquisitive conglomerates as a class. Nonetheless, some of the factors we have discussed appear more important than others in achieving the outstanding performance demonstrated by acquisitive conglomerates. Our objective has been identification and greater understanding of those factors which appear to have been most important.

Our approach has been exploratory and eclectic. A major part of the study has been concerned with (1) providing background and perspective based on previous studies, (2) discussing the characteristics and valuation of the population of acquisitive conglomerates, (3) achieving better understanding of the manner in which financial variables interact to provide per-share performance in growth through acquisition. At the same time these three parts of the study allowed us to focus attention on those sources of performance which appeared more important: (1) the improvement in operating performance of acquired companies without operating integration and (2) the interdependence of market value and performance in growth through acquisition. We then proceeded to the detailed investigation of these two sources of performance through the study of two acquisitive conglomerates. We will briefly review the evidence and argument regarding the "financial" and "operating" aspects of performance.

STRUCTURE OF THE ARGUMENT

We begin with the immediate financial effects of acquisitions. Based on evidence developed in other studies we made two kinds of arguments. First, previous studies have indicated that aggregate merger activity is most closely associated with the general level of stock market prices. At the same time, there has been no adequate explanation for this. We have associated this correlation with the immediate effects on per-share financial position of acquisitions with lower price-earnings ratios. The market prices of "growth stocks" tend to be more highly volatile than the market prices of corporations growing at more "normal" rates. The ratio of the price-earnings multiples for rapidly growing and "average" corporations is positively related to the general level of market prices. Based on the evidence that share exchange ratios are primarily determined by market values, it is likely that the high price-earnings company can acquire the lower price-earnings company on more favorable terms when market prices are at relatively high levels. We suggest that the aggregate studies provide an initial argument regarding the importance of the motivation to achieve immediate improvement in per-share financial position through acquisition.

Second, evidence from previous studies was used to argue that other immediate financial effects appear of lesser importance. If those factors which potentially alter the structure of risk and return for the shareholder are to be significant sources of per-share performance in acquisition programs, they must provide substantial increases in market value through acquisition. The evidence on the relationship between leverage and valuation is sufficiently mixed and inconclusive to suggest that this is not a major source of performance. The evidence and argument regarding the effect on market values of reduced earnings variability through diversification are also mixed. The one area where the evidence is reasonably strong and convincing is in the area of corporate size. For corporations of increasing size, other things being the same, market prices per share are higher, capital costs are lower. At the same time, the evidence indicates that large differences in relative size are required for relatively small differences in capital costs. While size clearly seems of some importance in performance through acquisition, it does not seem possible to associate a major part of acquisitive conglomerate performance with the increases in size which inevitably result from acquisitions. Evidence regarding the effects of taxation on corporate mergers indicates that in general this has been an important influence in only a small proportion of cases. And evidence discussed below leads us to conclude that tax reduction mergers are infrequently pursued by acquisitive conglomerates. We found no studies which attempt to relate market valuation to accounting treatment. Adequate analysis of the relationship between accounting treatments and acquisitive conglomerate performance would require a separate, comprehensive study. We can only state that within the two companies studied in detail all observed changes in accounting treatments were in the direction of greater conservatism and could not be considered sources of performance.

We extend the analysis of the "feedback relationship" in our discussion of the characteristics of the population of acquisitive conglomerates. Information regarding these companies suggests that (1) the principal financial objective is growth in earnings per share, (2) an immediate contribution to earnings per share is sought in acquisition transactions, (3) the price-earnings multiple is viewed as an important resource for growth. Taken together these characteristics argue for behavior oriented toward taking advantage of the feedback relationship between value and performance if in fact it is possible to do so. Among the "common" operating characteristics discussed is a preference for acquisition of profitable, successful companies. This provides a strong argument that taxation effects are not important for the performance of acquisitive conglomerates.

The significance of the feedback relationship is dependent upon the extent to which expectations for future performance and hence price-earnings ratios are based on past per-share performance and the extent to which they are based on the manner in which past per-share performance has been achieved. Based on discussions with members of the investment community and regression analysis, we argued that (1) for acquisitive conglomerates, as has been demonstrated for other classes of corporations, price-earnings ratios are positively related to measures of past per-share performance; (2) at the same time investors show some preference for growth strategies that involve higher rates of return on invested equity and larger amounts of internal (versus external) growth; this causes "low return, high expansion" growth strategies to be less attractive than would otherwise be the case.

Through the development of models of the determinants of performance in growth through acquisition we further analyzed the importance of immediate financial effects. First, we demonstrated that the "feedback relationship" may provide attractive performance without any change in acquired firms if (1) the investing public is primarily concerned with the level of per-share performance, and (2) it is not concerned with or is unable to determine the manner in which it is achieved. At the same time, performance based only upon this effect is entirely dependent upon market price behavior and appears unstable. We also examined the potential interaction of the feedback relationship with other sources of performance by assuming that market values were based either on "internal" or "observed" performance. In all cases the feedback relationship strongly enhanced contributions from other sources of performance.

We also employed models to demonstrate the manner in which other immediate financial effects may be reflected in improved per-share performance through acquisition. The critical question is whether they lead to increased market values for acquired firms. However, either the increase in market values would have to be very substantial or the scale of acquisition would have to be very large for any of these effects to independently provide major sources of performance. The complicating feature is that these effects may interact with and therefore may initiate or reinforce the feedback effect between valuation and performance. In that event, however, it appears that the feedback relationship and not the other changes in financial characteristics must be considered the primary source of performance.

Contek Incorporated provided an opportunity to study in detail a corporation where the explicit strategy has been to take advantage of the feedback relationship between price-earnings ratio and growth in earnings per share through acquisition. The evidence strongly supports the argument that exceptional performance for shareholders has been achieved in this manner. Contek has continually been able to acquire other companies on terms which are very attractive for the immediate effect on per-share earnings. At the same time, the post-acquisition performance of acquired companies can in no way explain the differential in price-earnings ratios between buying and selling companies which persisted over the period studied. In addition, we demonstrated that the use of leverage over the period studied offered minor if any advantage. Tax reduction through merger was not involved in the achieved performance, nor was change in accounting treatments. In the case where there were accounting changes they were in the direction of conservatism. Diversification possibly added some value, but this was not part of the performance strategy and appeared unimportant. Certainly size and what it offered in terms of the marketability of securities and the ability to portray a favorable "image" played a significant role in achieving performance. However, the perceived function of the "image" was to cause investors to project past per-share performance into the future. Without the acquisition-based performance, the "image" likely would not have had a major impact on the price-earnings ratio and hence on the ability to make acquisitions on attractive terms. We emerged from the analysis convinced that the feedback relationship between price-earnings ratio and earnings-per-share growth through acquisition was the major determinant of the performance that was achieved.

While our analysis of Kidde was oriented toward operating influence on subsidiaries, it appeared that the feedback effect was important here as well. A major portion of Kidde's performance has been derived from the immediate effects of acquisitions. Post-acquisition performance of subsidiaries (at least for our sample) was attractive but not significantly better than it had been before acquisition. Performance improvement could not offer an explanation for the valuation differentials required for that part of Kidde's performance achieved through the immediate effects of acquisitions. Again tax reduction through acquisitions was not of importance. Accounting changes which we encountered were in the direction of more conservatism. We made no attempt in the case of Kidde to deal with any of those effects related to the alteration of risk and return or the imperfection of capital markets.

In general, the most important conclusions regarding the feedback relationship between valuation and growth come from the analysis of Contek. The fact that it has been possible for a corporation to achieve exceptional performance over a significant time period based on this relationship and without any improvement in the financial performance of acquired companies permits a generalization about the nature of the present corporate environment. The feedback relationship between market value and performance is potentially very important for any company pursuing a "low return, high expansion" growth strategy because of (1) investor concern primarily with demonstrated per-share performance and (2) lack of concern with or lack of sufficient information in most cases to accurately determine the manner in which that performance has been achieved.

Regarding the other immediate effects of acquisitions the only one where we found convincing evidence of significant importance is increased size and what is offered in terms of marketability of securities, ability to portray a favorable image in the market for securities, and higher market prices generally. Our evidence does not justify general conclusions regarding the other immediate effects. However, it is possible to state that in our limited study of acquisitive conglomerates we found no evidence to suggest significantly increased market values and hence per-share performance through acquisition based on increased leverage or diversification or based on tax reduction or change of accounting treatments. That is the essence of the argument regarding the immediate financial effects of acquisitions on acquisitive conglomerate performance. We return now to trace through the argument regarding the contribution to acquisitive conglomerate performance of operating improvement in acquired subsidiaries.

Existing studies of mergers and acquisitions do not provide an optimistic outlook regarding the impact on operating performance. Early studies, which traced the performance of particular combinations over significant time periods, have provided pessimistic conclusions. More recent studies, which have indicated a negative relationship between merger activity and shareholder performance, are at least in part indicative of poor post-acquisition performance of merging firms.

Traditional discussion of merger economies has focused on advantages possible through the operating integration of merging firms. However, the trend in merger activity has been strongly away from mergers that offer opportunities for operating integration toward those of the "conglomerate" variety. Certainly this is the kind of merger typical of the "acquisitive conglomerate." While conglomerate mergers appear frequently to have some vertical, horizontal, or "complementary" aspects, the extent to which such integration opportunities exist has certainly diminished from previous merger periods. At the same time, the evidence on the relationship between operating performance and vertical or horizontal integration is not very encouraging. That is, even where there are opportunities for operating integration, existing evidence would not lead us to be very optimistic about the achievement of improved operating performance. More recently there has been discussion of possible merger advantages that do not require operating integration. We found little existing evidence, however, of the extent to which such advantages have been achieved.

Examination of the characteristics of the population of acquisitive conglomerates provided implications regarding the nature of operating improvement where in fact it occurs. Acquisitive conglomerates indicate common tendencies of the following variety: (1) profitable, successful companies are sought; (2) there is a strong preference for capable management which can be retained after the acquisition; (3) operations are conducted on a decentralized management philosophy; (4) "visibility" of diverse operations is maintained through a highly developed system of planning and control; (5) there is no significant integration of the operations of acquired subsidiaries. Taken together these characteristics imply that if significant improvement in operations is to be achieved, it will necessarily result from influencing the operations of the acquired company while it continues as a separate operating entity. Our later two-company analysis of operating influence is, therefore, a study of influence without operating integration.

Modeling the process of performance achievement in growth through acquisition provides a small note of optimism for the role of operating improvement. In the achievement of a given level of per-share performance there is a trade-off relationship between the required improvement in acquired companies and the scale of acquisition. Significant though relatively small improvement in the internal operating performance of companies acquired at a rapid pace can result in attractive per-share performance. In addition, there may be interaction and mutual reinforcement between internal performance improvement in acquired companies and the feedback relationship between market price and per-share performance through acquisition. The potential importance of this interaction appears to be quite significant.

We studied the potential for positively influencing subsidiary operating performance through the analysis of Contek Incorporated and Walter Kidde & Company. We expected no significant advantages from the traditionally discussed combination of physical resources. To the extent that operating advantages could be said to exist, we expected to find them in the combined use of resources that can be transferred easily across the organizational boundaries within the acquisitive conglomerate: primarily specialized human resources and to some extent financial resources. We have continually thought of the opportunities for operating influences without operating integration in two categories: (1) influences on the technologies, products, and markets in which the acquired subsidiary participates; influences more on *what* products and services are being provided in *what* markets; influences that would be more likely to affect the demand for the acquired subsidiary's products and hence more likely to affect its rate of growth; (2) influences on the "management process" within the acquired subsidiary; influences more on *how* the chosen set of goods and services are produced and distributed to their markets; influences on the management process of planning, decision making, reporting, reviewing, controlling; influences more likely to affect internal operating efficiency and hence profitability relative to sales or capital.

Evidence regarding Walter Kidde & Company and Contek Incorporated was gathered in the form of: (1) opinions of corporate level managers, (2) opinions of subsidiary level managers, (3) internal corporate documents, and (4) financial data regarding subsidiary operations. Structurally we looked at resources in the corporate level organizations, opinions regarding the nature and importance of various categories of possible operating influence, and data regarding the nature of change in financial performance. The managers at the corporate level indicated that influences on subsidiary technologies, products, and markets had been of significant importance. However, the subsidiary managers, the resources in the corporate level organizations, the financial data, and the nature of acquisitive conglomerate organization and management all argued that influences on the "management process" were of greatest importance.

Implications for Management

There are implications for management both from the conceptual framework that has been developed in this study and from the empirical findings. We turn first to the conceptual framework.

We have argued that a logical and operational goal for corporate management seeking to provide the greatest benefits for shareholders is maximization of the rate of growth in earnings-per-share for a given dividend policy. The market value for any rapidly growing company may be considered to imply expectations for decline in the growth rate. However, if management can maintain a high, relatively constant rate of growth, the implied expectations of the "market" will continually be contradicted, and the expectations for decline, although they will continue, will be shifted into the future. In this manner the trend in market price will follow the trend in earnings per share, and a return for shareholders will be generated which approximates the sum of the earnings-per-share growth rate plus the dividend yield.

If per-share performance is the objective, it must be realized that given levels of performance can be achieved in a variety of ways. This is of importance because an individual firm may decide to pursue any of a number of paths for expansion. The discussion of corporate investment frequently begins with the assumption that the firm faces a given investment demand schedule and must solve the problem of deciding which projects among those identified are to be undertaken. It appears more meaningful to say that management has a given amount of time and energy which may be expended in pursuing any of a variety of corporate strategies. Depending on the knowledge, the expertise, and the special competitive advantages which the firm has developed in the past, each prospective strategy will provide some array of investment opportunities over time. Thus, the firm faces a multitude of investment demand schedules each of which corresponds to a broad corporate strategy for the future of the firm.

In the internal growth process we have discussed two dimensions, rate of return on equity and rate of expansion of invested equity, which determine per-share performance. Maintenance of a relatively higher level on either of these dimensions requires a relatively greater amount of managerial effort. In principle at least management should seek that strategy for expansion such that their efforts, when applied to the combination of these two dimensions, will provide the highest level of per-share performance. One of the major difficulties of such an approach, as we have noted, is that "strategy" in this context must include estimates of rates of return and rates of expansion which will be feasible.

In the process of growth through acquisition we have not only the trade-off between rate of return on investment and rate of investment expansion. There are in addition trade-offs between internal and external growth and between scale of acquisition and the level of improvement in acquired operations. This complicates the conceptual process of choosing a growth strategy. However, the trade-off relationships implied by the conceptual models are more realistic for growth through acquisition than for strictly internal growth. Each acquisition provides an operating management and a market and may add immediately to earnings. Relatively high-expansion-rate growth strategies are, therefore, more feasible.

In selecting a "most desirable" strategy management might examine the performance implications which result from the various growth strategies considered feasible. In each case the resulting performance will depend upon the market reaction to the proposed strategy, and the evaluation of alternatives must therefore include explicit assumptions regarding the market system of valuation. That growth strategy which both appears feasible and promises the highest level of per-share performance over the "long term" is, under our assumptions, most desirable. While the selection and pursuit of such a strategy may sound like an extremely difficult problem, we suggest that it is the nature of the problem which, consciously or unconsciously, managements face.

The empirical findings provide indications of what specific strategies will and will not prove successful within the general strategy of growth through aggressive, diversified acquisition. At the broadest level, there is a fairly uniform pattern of objectives and operations which we have observed within 28 companies achieving outstanding shareholder performance through strategies of aggressive acquisition. These "common characteristics" we first observed in studying acquisitive conglomerates as a group and later confirmed through the study of two in detail. While 28 successful conglomerates could be wrong, it appears unlikely.

These companies have explicitly established and communicated objectives in terms of per-share performance. Management and shareholder interests in these corporations are well aligned because most of the chief executives are major shareholders. There is an acute awareness of the determinants of high market prices and of their importance for the acquisition program. Major, continuing efforts are made to provide the stable performance and the favorable image of future performance which seem to cause high multiples to be established in the market. In the aggressive pursuit of acquisitions, efforts to maintain a high market multiple are combined with the search for attractive companies which can be purchased to provide immediate favorable effects on per-share performance. This and the aggressive pace of acquisition demand that those companies be successful with demonstrated profitability. It is the exceptional case where the objective is "taking over" the poorly managed or "sick" company and "running it" better. Also, because of the aggressive pace of acquisition, companies are sought with operating management that can be retained. The successful conglomerate is interested primarily in motivating and assisting the acquired subsidiary to manage itself better, in shielding it from aspects of the external environment, in helping to provide needed resources for improved performance; it is interested in moving in new people to assume "day-to-day" operating management only when it becomes necessary because of demonstrated lack of ability by the existing management. In order to utilize the existing subsidiary management personnel effectively, those who served as the chief executives and frequently the founding entrepreneurs of their own companies, there is a management philosophy of decentralized authority and responsibility. And with frequent acquisitions in diverse fields there is no feasible alternative.

Effective management at the corporate level for such a highly decentralized and diversified enterprise demands excellent "visibility." This has been achieved through systems of planning and control which provide for the specification of detailed financial and operating plans and objectives and rapid feedback of comprehensive information regarding progress relative to those plans and objectives.

All of this means that there is little integration of the operations of acquired subsidiaries; typically the acquired company continues as a separate operating entity, with the parent corporation assuming operating responsibility only for some staff functions. The parent corporation does, of course, acquire ultimate responsibility for subsidiary performance and, therefore, becomes involved in major decisions which shape the subsidiary's future. However, the parent corporation appears more frequently to provide a "screening" function rather than an "initiating" function in the strategic decision-making process.

Taken individually none of these characteristics is unique for acquisitive conglomerates; taken together they form a unique pattern. These characteristics certainly are indicative of only a small part of what is required for success in conglomerate building. However, their degree of consistency indicates that they are not to be ignored by those who aspire to success in this area.

The detailed analysis of two corporations provided further conclusions regarding what may and may not be expected to prove successful in aggressive acquisition strategies. Managements must appreciate what can be achieved for shareholders through high-expansion-rate growth strategies because of the feedback relationship between market value and performance. The study of Contek and the analysis of market values for the population provide evidence of the potential importance of this relationship. Those who can demonstrate sustained performance and can maintain the image of its continuance will have available to them a relatively high market multiple as a resource for further performance. At the same time, in the evaluation of high-expansion-rate growth strategies managements must realize that some penalty is paid in terms of market multiple for growth strategies which achieve performance with rates of return on equity and rates of internal growth which are relatively small.

The feasibility of capitalizing on the feedback relationship between market value and performance adds to the rationality of seeking acquisitions which contribute immediately to per-share performance. However, as we have emphasized and as should be obvious, the long-term success of the acquisition program also demands improved performance and substantial internal growth within companies acquired. This almost inevitably means that there will be trade-off considerations between the short-term and long-term desirability of various acquisition candidates. The most attractive acquisition for the immediate effect is one which has good earnings but little promise of improvement so that the multiple at which it may be purchased is low. The most attractive acquisition for longer-term improvement probably is one where the promise for the future looks unusually great and which consequently sells at an unusually high multiple relative to earnings. Rational solution of this short-term long-term dilemma demands detailed projections of expectations regarding both performance and market response. Such projections must, of course, include the short-term impact on market price and its implications for further acquisitions.

Perhaps the most difficult and most interesting part of the acquisitive conglomerate question concerns what can be done to improve the performance of acquired companies within this environment: what can be done to achieve operating improvement without operating integration? First, it should be recalled that while we found internal performance continuing at attractive pre-acquisition rates in some cases, there was no evidence of dramatic improvement in performance resulting from operation within the acquisitive conglomerate environment. Still, there were clear indications that within programs of aggressive, diversified acquisition some types of influence will be more feasible and effective than others.

More specifically, in most cases it does not appear reasonable to expect significant, positive influences on the basic character of subsidiary technologies, products, and services or on the basic character of customer groups to which they are sold. The parent corporation cannot expect to meet the demands for expertise specialized to the operations of a large number of subsidiaries in diverse technology-product-market areas. There is some opportunity for improved quality and economy of staff functions shielding the subsidiary from the external environment through performance of these functions on a larger scale and on a more professional basis at the corporate level. This means, among other things, that the larger acquisitive conglomerate can be more effective and efficient in such areas than the smaller one. There is the potential for improved performance through provision of funds where needed and previously unavailable. However, the characteristics of companies preferred by the acquisitive conglomerate imply that funds will have been completely inaccessible only for the exceptional subsidiary. Most significant, there appear to be important opportunities to affect the management process favorably within the smaller acquired subsidiary. In particular, we refer to the process of planning, decision making, reporting, reviewing, and controlling. These and other aspects of the management process represent influences which most easily and understandably flow across the organizational boundaries of diverse operations within the acquisitive conglomerate.

The most desirable acquisition then, in terms of the potential for performance improvement within the acquisitive conglomerate environment, will have the following general characteristics: (1) strength in product technology and market position; (2) weakness in the existing process of planning and controlling operations and in other management and staff functions; and (3) strength in the capability of existing management personnel for further development and increased professionalization. In an era of increasing professionalization of management practices there are rewards for the acquisitive conglomerate which can speed their introduction into new corporate environments.

Bibliography

Alberts, William W., and Joel E. Segall, eds., *The Corporate Merger*. University of Chicago Press, 1966.

Almon, Clopper, Jr., *The American Economy to 1975*. Harper and Row, 1966.

Andelman, M. A., "Acquire the Whole or Any Part of the Stock or Assets of Another Corporation," American Bar Association *Proceedings*, Annual Meeting, 1953.

Arditti, Fred D., "Risk and the Required Return on Equity," *Journal of Finance*, March 1967.

Bain, Joe S., "Industrial Concentration and Government Antitrust Policy," in Harold F. Williamson, ed., *The Growth of the American Economy*. Prentice-Hall, 1964.

Barges, Alexander, *The Effect of Capital Structure on the Cost of Capital*. Prentice-Hall, 1963.

Basset, William R., *Operating Aspects of Industrial Mergers*. Harper, 1930.

Benishay, Haskel, "Variability in Earnings-Price Ratios of Corporate Entities," *American Economic Review*, March 1961.

Biggs, Barton M., "Day of Reckoning? Conglomerates Can't Keep Making Two Plus Two Equal Five Forever," *Barron's*, April 3, 1967.

Bjorksten, Johan, "Merger Lemons," *Mergers and Acquisitions*, Fall 1965. Reprinted in U.S. Senate Hearings, *Economic Concentration*, Part 5.

Blair, John M., "The Conglomerate Merger in Economics and Law," *Georgetown Law Review*, 1958. Reprinted in U.S. Senate Hearings, *Economic Concentration*, Part 3.

————, "Does Large-Scale Enterprise Result in Lower Costs?" *American Economic Review*, May 1948.

————, "The Relation Between Size and Efficiency of Business," *Review of Economics and Statistics*, August 1942.

Briloff, Abraham J., "Dirty Pooling," *Barron's*, July 15, 1968.

Burck, Gilbert, "The Perils of the Multi-Market Corporation," *Fortune*, February 1967.

Butters, J. Keith, "Taxation, Incentives, and Financial Capacity," *American Economic Review*, May 1954.

Butters, J. Keith, John Lintner, and William L. Cary, *Effects of Taxation: Corporate Mergers*. Division of Research, Harvard Business School, 1951.

Caves, Richard, *American Industry: Structure, Conduct, Performance*. Prentice-Hall, 2d ed., 1967.

Chandler, Alfred D., Jr., *Strategy and Structure*. Anchor Books, 1966.

Chenery, Hollis B., "Engineering Production Functions," *Quarterly Journal of Economics*, November 1949.

Collier, W. M., *The Trusts*. Baker Taylor, 1900.

Cossaboom, Roger A., "Segmental Financing of Corporate Conglomerates," unpublished doctoral dissertation, Harvard Business School, 1968.

Crum, William Leonard, *Corporate Size and Earning Power*. Harvard University Press, 1939.

Curtis, Roy E., *The Trusts and Economic Control*. McGraw-Hill, 1931.

Cyert, Richard M., and James G. March, *A Behavioral Theory of the Firm*. Prentice-Hall, 1963.

Dellenbarger, Lynn E., "A Study of Relative Common Equity Values in Fifty Mergers of Industrial Corporations, 1950–1957," *Journal of Finance*, September 1963.

Dewing, Arthur Stone, *Financial Policy of Corporations*. Ronald Press, 5th ed., 1953.

———, "A Statistical Test of the Success of Consolidation," *Quarterly Journal of Economics*, November 1921.

Donaldson, Gordon, *Corporate Debt Capacity*. Division of Research, Harvard Business School, 1961.

Drayton, Clarence I., Jr., ed., *Mergers and Acquisitions: Planning and Action*. Financial Executives Research Foundation, 1963.

Durand, David, "Growth Stocks and the Petersburg Paradox," *Journal of Finance*, September 1957.

Edwards, Corwin E., "Conglomerate Bigness as a Source of Power," in *Business Concentration and Price Policy*. National Bureau of Economic Research, Special Conference Series 5. Princeton University Press, 1955.

Ely, R. T., *Monopolies and Trusts*. Macmillan, 1900.

Epstein, R. H., *Source Book for Industrial Profits*. U.S. Department of Commerce, 1932.

Estes, E. B., "Vertical Integration in the Steel Industry," U.S. Steel Corporation, 1951.

Fisher, Lawrence, and James H. Lorie, "Rates of Return on Investment in Common Stock," *Journal of Business*, January 1964.

Galbraith, John Kenneth, *The Great Crash*. Houghton Mifflin, 1955.

Georgeson & Co., "Trends in Management-Stockholder Relations," No. 177, November 1967.

Gordon, Myron J., *The Investment, Financing and Valuation of the Corporation*. Richard D. Irwin, 1962.

———, "The Savings, Investment and Valuation of a Corporation," *Review of Economics and Statistics*, February 1968.

Gort, Michael, *Diversification and Integration in American Industry*. Princeton University Press, 1962.

———, "Diversification, Mergers, and Profits," in William W. Alberts and Joel E. Segall, eds., *The Corporate Merger*. University of Chicago Press, 1966.

Hale, Rosemary D., and G. E. Hale, "More on Mergers," *Journal of Law and Economics*, October 1962.

Hanna, Richard, "The Concept of Corporate Strategy in Multi-Industry Companies," unpublished doctoral dissertation, Harvard Business School, 1968.

Hennessy, J. H., Jr., *Acquiring and Merging Business*. Prentice-Hall, 1966.

Holmes, Lee M., "Corporate Acquisition Patterns," unpublished master's thesis, Massachusetts Institute of Technology, 1968.

Jenks, J. W., *The Trust Problem*. McClure Phillips, 1900.

"Johnson Shoots for Fortune's 500," *California Business*, July 16, 1967.

Jones, Eliot, *The Trust Problem in the United States*. Macmillan, 1929.

Judelson, David N., "The Role of the Conglomerate Corporation in Today's Economy," *Financial Executive*, September 1968.

Kahlmeier, Louis, "High Court Extends Antitrust Law, Voids Procter & Gamble-Clorox Tie," *Wall Street Journal*, April 12, 1967.

Kamerschen, D. R., "Ownership and Control and Profit Rates," *American Economic Review*, June 1968.

Kelley, Eamon M., *The Profitability of Growth Through Merger*. Center for Research of the College of Business Administration, Pennsylvania State University, 1967.

Kilmer, David C., "Growth by Acquisition, Some Guidelines for Success," *The McKinsey Quarterly*, Spring 1967.

Kitching, John, "Why Do Mergers Miscarry?" *Harvard Business Review*, November-December 1967.

Kottke, Frank J., "Mergers of Large Manufacturing Companies, 1951 to 1959," *Review of Economics and Statistics*, November 1959.

Le Rossignol, J. E., *Monopolies Past and Present*. Crowell, 1901.

Lewellen, Wilbur G., "Executives Lose Out, Even with Options," *Harvard Business Review*, January-February 1968.

Lintner, John, "The Cost of Capital and Optimal Financing of Corporate Growth," *Journal of Finance*, May 1963.

———, "Distribution of Incomes of Corporations Among Dividends, Retained Earnings, and Taxes." *American Economic Review*, May 1956.

———, "Optimal Dividends and Corporate Growth under Uncertainty," *Quarterly Journal of Economics*, February 1964.

——— and Robert R. Glauber, "Higgledy Piggledy Growth in America?" Unpublished paper presented at Seminar on the Analysis of Security Prices, Center for Research in Security Prices, University of Chicago, May 1967.

Little, Royal, "Royal Little Looks at Conglomerates," *Dun's Review*, May 1968.

Livermore, Shaw, "The Success of Industrial Mergers," *Quarterly Journal of Economics*, November 1955.

McCarthy, George D., *Acquisitions and Mergers*. Ronald Press, 1963.

McGuire, J. W., J. S. Y. Chin, and A. O. Elbing, "Executive Incomes, Sales and Profits," *American Economic Review*, September 1962.

Mace, Myles L., and George G. Montgomery, Jr., *Management Problems of Corporate Acquisitions*. Division of Research, Harvard Business School, 1962.

Malkiel, Burton, "Equity Yields, Growth, and the Structure of Share Prices," *American Economic Review*, December 1963.

Manne, Henry G., "Mergers and the Market for Corporate Control," *Journal of Political Economy*, April 1965.

Markham, Jesse W., "Survey of the Evidence and Findings on Mergers," in *Business Concentration and Price Policy*. National Bureau of Economic Research, Special Conference Series 5. Princeton University Press, 1955.

Marris, Robin, *The Economic Theory of Managerial Capitalism*. Free Press, 1964.

May, Marvin M., "The Chain Letter Revisited," *Financial Analysts Journal*, May-June 1968.

Miller, G. William, "Organizing the Conglomerate Company," *The Conference Board Supplement*, January 19–20, 1967.

Miller, Merton H., and Franco Modigliani, "Cost of Capital to the Electric Utility Industry," *American Economic Review*, June 1966.

——— and ———, "Dividend Policy, Growth, and the Valuation of Shares," *Journal of Business*, October 1961.

Modigliani, Franco, and Merton H. Miller, "Corporate Income Taxes and the Cost of Capital: A Correction," *American Economic Review*, June 1963.

——— and ———, "The Cost of Capital, Corporation Finance and the Theory of Investment," *American Economic Review*, June 1958.

Moody, John, *The Truth About the Trusts*. Moody Publishing Company, 1904.

Moore, F. T., "Economies of Scale: Some Statistical Evidence," *Quarterly Journal of Economics*, May 1959.

Myers, Stewart C., "A Time-State-Preference Model of Security Valuation," Working

Paper 265–67, Alfred P. Sloan School of Management, Massachusetts Institute of Technology, June 1967.

Navin, T. R., and M. V. Sears, "The Rise of a Market for Industrial Securities, 1887–1902," *Business History Review*, June 1955.

Nelson, Ralph L., *Merger Movements in American Industry, 1895–1956*. Princeton University Press, 1959.

Nolan, E. J., *Combinations, Trusts and Monopolies*. Broadway Publishing Co., 1904.

O'Hanlon, Thomas, "The Odd News About Conglomerates," *Fortune*, June 15, 1967.

Patton, Arch, "Deterioration in Top Executive Pay," *Harvard Business Review*, November-December 1965.

Penrose, Edith, *The Theory of the Growth of the Firm*. Basil Blackwell, 1959.

Rayner, A. C., and I. M. D. Little, *Higgledy Piggledy Growth Again*. Basil Blackwell, 1966.

Reid, Samuel R., John Bossons, and Kalman H. Cohen, "Mergers for Whom — Managers or Stockholders?" Working Paper No. 14, Workshop of Capital Market Equilibrating Processes, Carnegie Institute of Technology, 1966. Reprinted in U.S. Senate Hearings, *Economic Concentration*, Part 5.

Roberts, D. R., *Executive Compensation*. Free Press, 1959.

Robichek, A. Alexander, and John McDonald, "Financial Management in Transition," Stanford Research Institute, Long-Range Planning Series, Report No. 268, 1966.

——— and Stewart C. Myers, *Optimal Financing Decisions*. Prentice-Hall, 1965.

Scharf, Charles A., *Techniques of Buying, Selling and Merging Business*. Prentice-Hall, 1964.

Seager, H. R., and C. A. Gulick, Jr., *Trust and Corporation Problems*. Harper, 1929.

Siedman, J. S., "Pooling Must Go," *Barron's*, July 1, 1968.

Sloan, Alfred P., Jr., *My Years with General Motors*. Doubleday, 1964.

Smith, Caleb, "Survey of the Empirical Evidence on Economies of Scale," in *Business Concentration and Price Policy*. National Bureau of Economic Research, Special Conference Series 5. Princeton University Press, 1955.

Sommers, H. M., "Estate Taxes and Business Mergers: The Effects of Estate Taxes on Business Structure and Practice in the United States," *Journal of Finance*, May 1958.

Stabler, Charles H., "The Conglomerates, Antitrusters, and Investors Eye Combines Warily, but Firms Still Grow," *Wall Street Journal*, July 25, 1968.

———, "The Conglomerates: Even Accountants Find Some Financial Reports of Combines Baffling," *Wall Street Journal*, August 5, 1968.

Stigler, George J., "The Economies of Scale," *Journal of Law and Economics*, October 1958.

———, "Monopoly and Oligopoly by Merger," *American Economic Review*, May 1950.

———, "The Statistics of Monopoly and Merger," *Journal of Political Economy*, February 1956.

Stocking, George W., and Myron W. Watkins, *Cartels or Competition? The Economics of International Controls by Business and Government*. Twentieth Century Fund, 1948.

Stone, Martin, "Acquisition Technique as a Growth Product," An Address Before the Bond Club of Los Angeles, October 16, 1967.

Temporary National Economic Committee, Monograph No. 13, *Relative Efficiency of Large, Medium-Sized, and Small Businesses*, GPO, 1941.

———, Monograph No. 27, *Structure of Industry*. GPO, 1941.

Thorp, Willard L., "The Merger Movement," in TNEC Monograph No. 27, 1941.

————, "The Persistence of the Merger Movement," *American Economic Review, Supplement*, March 1941.

Tippets, Charles S., and Shaw Livermore, *Business Organization and Public Control*. Van Nostrand, 1932.

U.S. Board of Governors of the Federal Reserve System, *Financing Small Business*, Parts 1 and 2, Report to the Committees on Banking and Currency and the Select Committees on Small Business, U.S. Congress, 1958.

U.S. Federal Trade Commission, *Report of the Federal Trade Commission on the Merger Movement*. GPO, 1948.

U.S. House of Representatives, House Report No. 2337, *Report of the Securities and Exchange Commission on the Public Policy Implications of Investment Company Growth*, 89th Cong., 2d Sess., 1966.

U.S. Senate, Committee on the Judiciary, Hearings before the Subcommittee on Antitrust and Monopoly:

  Dual Distribution, Part 2, Statement of Donald F. Turner, Assistant Attorney General. 89th Cong., 2d Sess., 1966.

  Economic Concentration, Part 2, *Mergers and Other Factors Affecting Industry Concentration*, Statement of Dr. Willard F. Mueller, Director, Bureau of Economics, Federal Trade Commission. 89th Cong., 1st Sess., 1965.

  ————, Part 3, *Concentration, Invention, and Innovation*.

  ————, Part 4, *Concentration and Efficiency*.

  ————, Part 5, *Concentration and Divisional Reporting*. 89th Cong., 2d Sess., 1966.

Turner, Donald G., "Conglomerate Mergers and Section 7 of the Clayton Act," *Harvard Law Review*, May 1965.

Van Horne, James C., *Financial Management and Policy*. Prentice-Hall, 1968.

von Halle, Ernst, *Trusts or Industrial Combinations in the United States*. Macmillan, 1895.

Wall, John, "Want to Get Rich Quick? An Expert Gives Some Friendly Advice on Conglomerates," *Barron's*, February 5, 1968.

Watkins, Myron W., *Industrial Combinations and Public Policy*. Houghton Mifflin, 1927.

Weston, J. Frederick, *The Role of Mergers in the Growth of Large Firms*. University of California Press, 1953.

————, "A Test of the Cost of Capital Propositions," *Southern Economic Journal*, October 1963.

"What *are* Earnings? The Growing Credibility Gap," *Forbes*, May 15, 1967.

Whippern, Ronald F., "Financial Structure and the Value of the Firm," *Journal of Finance*, December 1966.

Williams, John B., *The Theory of Investment Value*. Harvard University Press, 1938.

Wyatt, Arthur R., *A Critical Study of Accounting for Business Combinations*. American Institute of Certified Public Accountants, Accounting Research Study No. 5, 1963.

Court Cases:

  Addyston Pipe and Steel Co. et al. *v*. U.S., 175 U.S. 211 (1899)

  Brown Shoe Co. *v*. U.S., 370 U.S. 294 (1962)

  Northern Securities Company *v*. U.S., 193 U.S. 332 (1904)

  Standard Oil Co. *v*. U.S. 211 U.S. 1 (1911)

  Thatcher Manufacturing Co. *v*. FTC, 272 U.S. 554 (1926)

  U.S. *v*. Aluminum Company of America, 148F 2d 416 (1945)

  U.S. *v*. American Tobacco Company, 211 U.S. 106 (1911)

U.S. *v.* E. I. du Pont de Nemours & Company, 353 U.S. 586 (1957)

U.S. *v.* E. C. Knight Company, 156 U.S. 1 (1895)

U.S. *v.* The Philadelphia National Bank, 374 U.S. 312 (1963)

U.S. *v.* Procter & Gamble Co., 386 U.S. 568 (1967)

U.S. *v.* United Shoe Machinery Co., 247 U.S. 32 (1918)

U.S. *v.* United States Steel Corporation, 251 U.S. 417 (1920)

Index